# Praise for
## *BORN TO RUN*

"Springsteen can write—not just life-imprinting song lyrics but good, solid prose that travels all the way to the right margin. . . . And like a fabled Springsteen concert—always notable for its deck-clearing thoroughness—*Born to Run* achieves the sensation that all the relevant questions have been answered by the time the lights are turned out. He delivers the story of Bruce—in digestibly short chapters— via an informally steadfast Jersey plainspeak that's worked and deftly detailed and intimate with its readers—cleareyed enough to say what it means when it has hard stories to tell, yet supple enough to rise to occasions requiring eloquence—sometimes rather pleasingly subsiding into the syntax and rhythms of a Bruce Springsteen song."
—**Richard Ford,** *The New York Times Book Review*

"*Born to Run* deserves a place on the top shelf besides Dylan's *Chronicles* and Keith Richards's *Life;* it's a performance in which Springsteen offers himself up on the page as authentically, unabashedly and excessively as he does on the stage. He wants to rock the reader's soul and somehow he does. To show brilliance, he realizes, you have to have shadow."
—**John Lahr,** *London Review of Books*

"Anyone who has been to a Bruce Springsteen concert will immediately recognize the tone he brings to his autobiography, *Born to Run*. It's the voice of his onstage storytelling: hearty, comic, forthright, earthy, some- times poetic, and grounded in the everyday yet somehow larger than life."
—**Jon Pareles,** *The New York Review of Books*

"Frank and gripping."
—**David Brooks,** *The Atlantic*

"Intensely satisfying . . . *Born to Run* is, like his finest songs, closely observed from end to end. His story is intimate and personal, but he has an interest in other people and a gift for sizing them up."
—**Dwight Garner,** *The New York Times*

"A virtuoso performance, the 508-page equivalent to one of Springsteen and the E Street Band's famous four-hour concerts: Nothing is left onstage, and diehard fans and first-timers alike depart for home sated and yet somehow already aching for more."
—**NPR**

"*Born to Run* is for us . . . A celebration and an elegy all at once."
—**Rebecca Traister,** *New York*

"Excellent . . . very funny . . . eminently readable and engaging. Springsteen was also born to write. He has an active, energetic style that is part Jack Kerouac and part Instagram post."
—*Asbury Park Press*

"*Born to Run* has a compelling narrative and an organized structure worthy of a Catholic schoolboy of the 1950s. . . . Mr. Springsteen writes fluidly about subjects light, dark and darker. He's funny and solemn, tender and insightful. In *Born to Run,* he risks his mythic stature, but he emerges as more substantial, more admirable. Now Mr. Springsteen isn't merely a star. He is a man— a son, a husband, a father and a friend—willing to share what he's learned."
—*The Wall Street Journal*

"Richly rewarding . . . Bruce Springsteen proves that he has taken on life fully engaged both in living and examining it, and in doing so, he's delivered a story as profoundly inspiring as his best music. . . . It's alternately brutally honest, philosophically deep, stabbingly funny and, perhaps most important, refreshingly humble."
—*Los Angeles Times*

"A master storyteller . . . the language of his memoir often sings and leaps off the page with alliteration and pulse, especially when he's rhapsodizing about rock 'n' roll."
—**Will Hermes,** *All Things Considered,* NPR

"It is undeniably thrilling, breathtaking, heartbreaking, blunt and aspirational. There are passages that echo the likes of Steinbeck and even Faulkner in the beauty of his prose, sections where you'll need to put the book down for a few minutes and soak it all in."
—*Salon*

"Bruce Springsteen is the bard of lost American dreams. . . . The origin of poetry, thought William Wordsworth, was emotion recollected in tranquility. That motto describes both the content of Mr. Springsteen's book and the appeal of his songs, many of which look back on youthful traumas from a mature perspective."
—*The Economist*

"Where Springsteen soars—both as musician and writer—is in his ability to bear witness, not only to his own inner life but to the lives of those left behind in the post-industrial wastelands of this nation. Springsteen made it out of Freehold, but he never turned away from the 'grinding hypnotic power' of the place and its people. *Born to Run* documents the unlikely rise of a rocker hellbent not on escape, but on reckoning with the moral failings of the world he was born into."
—*The Boston Globe*

"The book soars . . . Very few of his peers can articulate the workings of their craft to the degree that Springsteen does here."
—*The National Review*

"Exquisitely detailed and often moving."
—*The Nation*

"*Born To Run* is yet another example of the pact, here in autobiographical book form, that Springsteen has long had with his
audience: If you come to me with a willingness to really listen,
I'll tell you my truths in a way that speaks to your soul. Serious stuff,
but would you expect anything else from the voice of a generation?
Bruce is a rock god cloaked in the humble leather and jeans of a bar band
singer who struggles and yearns just like we all do. Now that his bible
has arrived, you know you'll have to read it chapter and verse."
—*Detroit Free Press*

"A masterpiece . . . Bruce Springsteen could have put out a collection of
recipes in Esperanto, cribbed from Campbell soup cans, and it
would still be an international bestseller. Typically, he went the
distance. And the result is nothing short of magnificent. . . .
I wish I could buy everyone a copy. . . . This isn't just a book for
Bruce fans, but for anyone who loves rock 'n' roll, the Shore
or the last 40 years of Jersey pop-culture history. It's as epic as
his recent four-hour concerts. And just as satisfying."
—Jacqueline Cutler, NJ.com

"The book is an affirmation that, along with his musical brilliance
and matchless performance skills, the man is a terrific storyteller and
writer. . . . Much more than most celebrity autobiographies, this one
has a distinctive voice, and one that bears a wide range of literary
influences. He can remind you of Elmore Leonard, as in this description
of an early manager and longtime friend. At the deathbed of Clemons,
he can sound like Emily Dickinson. But most of all, he sounds like
Bruce Springsteen, and that's reason to raise your hands."
—*The Tampa Bay Times*

"*Born To Run* cements Springsteen's status as one of pop's premiere observationalists, attuned as much to the fine details of American life as the mythic-seeming meanings that hide inside them. . . . It's not only a good, readable, page-turning autobiography, but a Major Work. . . . *Born to Run* is another example of Springsteen's ability to magically transport us from the dreary realities of modern political life, to restore some glimmer of hope in that decaying idea of America Itself; to light a little spark in the blackness, make us forget the world, and keep us dancing in the dark."
—*The Globe and Mail*

"The best business book I've read this year."
—*Fortune*

"The rare memoir that delivers elegant poetry and rafter-shaking exhortations in equal measure."
—*A.V. Club*

"He must be conceded a magic with words: He can spin not only a yarn but often an extended analysis, too. . . . His disclosures here are rich, deep, and useful to help destigmatize mental illness."
—*Slate*

"The book bursts with the same earnest tenacity of his epic concerts. The prose itself thrums electrified, unfiltered need, punctuated by an East Coast staccato."
—*Austin Chronicle*

"As good and rewarding a memoir as anyone could have hoped for
from this author."
—*Public Books*


"A sustained, satisfying, and thoroughly readable self-portrait."
—*American Prospect*


"Springsteen infuses the 510-page book with his music's same lyrical voice,
evocatively weaving together stories of blue-collar America. Yet Springsteen, whose songs are rarely noted for irony, also shows a surprising gift
for humor as he recounts his early days as a struggling artist."
—*The Express Tribune* (Pakistan)

# BORN TO RUN
# BRUCE SPRINGSTEEN

SIMON & SCHUSTER PAPERBACKS

NEW YORK   LONDON   TORONTO   SYDNEY   NEW DELHI

Simon & Schuster Paperbacks
An Imprint of Simon & Schuster, Inc.
1230 Avenue of the Americas
New York, NY 10020

First Simon & Schuster trade paperback edition September 2017

SIMON & SCHUSTER PAPERBACKS and colophon are
registered trademarks of Simon & Schuster, Inc.

For information about special discounts for bulk purchases,
please contact Simon & Schuster Special Sales at
1-866-506-1949 or business@simonandschuster.com.

The Simon & Schuster Speakers Bureau can bring authors to your live event.
For more information or to book an event contact the
Simon & Schuster Speakers Bureau at 1-866-248-3049
or visit our website at www.simonspeakers.com.

*Interior design by Ruth Lee-Mui*
*Photo insert design by Michelle Holme*
*Photo licensing by Crystal Singh-Hawthorne*

Manufactured in the United States of America

10  9  8  7  6  5  4  3  2  1

Library of Congress Cataloging-in-Publication Data is available.

ISBN 978-1-5011-4151-5
ISBN 978-1-5011-4152-2 (pbk)
ISBN 978-1-5011-4153-9 (ebook)

*For Patti, Evan, Jess and Sam*

# CONTENTS

BOOK TWO

# BORN TO RUN

# BOOK THREE
# LIVING PROOF

# FOREWORD

I come from a boardwalk town where almost everything is tinged with a bit of fraud. So am I. By twenty, no race-car-driving rebel, I was a guitar player on the streets of Asbury Park and already a member in good standing amongst those who "lie" in service of the truth . . . artists, with a small "a." But I held four clean aces. I had youth, almost a decade of hard-core bar band experience, a good group of homegrown musicians who were attuned to my performance style and a story to tell.

This book is both a continuation of that story and a search into its origins. I've taken as my parameters the events in my life I believe shaped that story and my performance work. One of the questions I'm asked over and over again by fans on the street is "How do you do it?" In the following pages I will try to shed a little light on how and, more important, why.

## Rock 'n' Roll Survival Kit

DNA, natural ability, study of craft, development of and devotion to an aesthetic philosophy, naked desire for . . . fame? . . . love? . . . admiration? . . . attention? . . . women? . . . sex? . . . and oh, yeah . . . a buck. Then . . . if you want to take it *all* the way out to the end of the night, a furious fire in the hole that just . . . don't . . . quit . . . burning.

These are some of the elements that will come in handy should you come face-to-face with eighty thousand (or eighty) screaming rock 'n' roll fans who are waiting for you to do your magic trick. Waiting for you to pull something out of your hat, out of thin air, out of this world, something that before the faithful were gathered here today was just a song-fueled rumor.

I am here to provide proof of life to that ever elusive, never completely believable "us." That is my magic trick. And like all good magic tricks, it begins with a setup. So . . .

# BOOK ONE
# GROWIN' UP

# ONE
# MY
# STREET

I am ten years old and I know every crack, bone and crevice in the crumbling sidewalk running up and down Randolph Street, my street. Here, on passing afternoons I am Hannibal crossing the Alps, GIs locked in vicious mountain combat and countless cowboy heroes traversing the rocky trails of the Sierra Nevada. With my belly to the stone, alongside the tiny anthills that pop up volcanically where dirt and concrete meet, my world sprawls on into infinity, or at least to Peter McDermott's house on the corner of Lincoln and Randolph, one block up.

On these streets I have been rolled in my baby carriage, learned to walk, been taught by my grandfather to ride a bike, and fought and run from some of my first fights. I learned the depth and comfort of real friendships, felt my early sexual stirrings and, on the evenings before air-conditioning, watched the porches fill with neighbors seeking conversation and respite from the summer heat.

Here, in epic "gutter ball" tournaments, I slammed the first of a hundred Pinky rubber balls into my sidewalk's finely shaped curb. I climbed upon piles of dirty snow, swept high by midnight plows, walking corner to corner, the Edmund Hillary of New Jersey. My sister and I regularly stood like sideshow gawkers peering in through the huge wooden doors of our corner church, witnessing an eternal parade of baptisms, weddings and funerals. I followed my handsome, raggedly elegant grandfather as he tottered precariously around the block, left arm paralyzed against his chest, getting his "exercise" after a debilitating stroke he never came back from.

In our front yard, only feet from our porch, stands the grandest tree in town, a towering copper beech. Its province over our home is such that one bolt of well-placed lightning and we'd all be dead as snails crushed beneath God's little finger. On nights when thunder rolls and lightning turns our family bedroom cobalt blue, I watch its arms move and come to life in the wind and white flashes as I lie awake worrying about my friend the monster outside. On sunny days, its roots are a fort for my soldiers, a corral for my horses and my second home. I hold the honor of being the first on our block to climb into its upper reaches. Here I find my escape from all below. I wander for hours amongst its branches, the sound of my buddies' muted voices drifting up from the sidewalk below as they try to track my progress. Beneath its slumbering arms, on slow summer nights we sit, my pals and I, the cavalry at dusk, waiting for the evening bells of the ice-cream man and bed. I hear my grandmother's voice calling me in, the last sound of the long day. I step up onto our front porch, our windows glowing in the summer twilight; I let the heavy front door open and then close behind me, and for an hour or so in front of the kerosene stove, with my grandfather in his big chair, we watch the small black-and-white television screen light up the room, throwing its specters upon the walls and ceiling. Then, I drift to sleep tucked inside the greatest and saddest sanctuary I have ever known, my grandparents' house.

I live here with my sister, Virginia, one year younger; my parents, Adele and Douglas Springsteen; my grandparents, Fred and Alice; and my dog Saddle. We live, literally, in the bosom of the Catholic Church, with the priest's rectory, the nuns' convent, the St. Rose of Lima Church and grammar school all just a football's toss away across a field of wild grass.

Though he towers above us, here God is surrounded by man—crazy men, to be exact. My family has five houses branching out in an L shape, anchored on the corner by the redbrick church. We are four houses of old-school Irish, the people who have raised me—McNicholases, O'Hagans, Farrells—and across the street, one lonely outpost of Italians, who peppered my upbringing. These are the Sorrentinos and the Zerillis, hailing from Sorrento, Italy, via Brooklyn via Ellis Island. Here dwell my mother's mother, Adelina Rosa Zerilli; my mother's older sister, Dora; Dora's husband, Warren (an Irishman of course); and their daughter, my older cousin Margaret. Margaret and my cousin Frank are championship jitterbug dancers, winning contests and trophies up and down the Jersey Shore.

Though not unfriendly, the clans do not often cross the street to socialize with one another.

The house I live in with my grandparents is owned by my great-grandmother "Nana" McNicholas, my grandmother's mother, alive and kicking just up the street. I've been told our town's first church service and first funeral were held in our living room. We live here beneath the lingering eyes of my father's older sister, my aunt Virginia, dead at five, killed by a truck while riding her tricycle past the corner gas station. Her portrait hovers, breathing a ghostly air into the room and shining her ill-fated destiny over our family gatherings.

Hers is a sepia-toned formal portrait of a little girl in an old-fashioned child's white linen dress. Her seemingly benign gaze, in the light of events, now communicates, "Watch out! The world is a dangerous and unforgiving place that will knock your ass off your tricycle and into the dead black unknown and only these poor, misguided and unfortunate souls will miss you." Her mother, my grandma, heard that message loud and clear. She spent two years in bed after her daughter's death and sent my father, neglected, with rickets, off to the outskirts of town to live with other relatives while she recovered.

Time passed; my father quit school at sixteen, working as a floor boy in the Karagheusian Rug Mill, a clanging factory of looms and deafening machinery that stretched across both sides of Center Street in a part of town called "Texas." At eighteen, he went to war, sailing on the *Queen Mary* out of New York City. He served as a truck driver at the Battle of the Bulge, saw what little of the world he was going to see and returned home. He played pool, very well, for money. He met and fell in love with my mother, promising that if she'd marry him, he'd get a real job (red flag!). He worked with his cousin, David "Dim" Cashion, on the line at the Ford Motor plant in Edison and I came along.

For my grandmother, I was the firstborn child of her only son and the first baby in the house since the death of her daughter. My birth returned to her a life of purpose. She seized on me with a vengeance. Her mission became my ultimate protection from the world within and without. Sadly, her blind single-minded devotion would lead to hard feelings with my father and enormous family confusion. It would drag all of us down.

When it rains, the moisture in the humid air blankets our town with the smell of damp coffee grounds wafting in from the Nescafé factory at the town's eastern edge. I don't like coffee but I like that smell. It's comforting; it unites the town in a common sensory experience; it's good industry, like the roaring rug mill that fills our ears, brings work and signals our town's vitality. There is a place here—you can hear it, smell it—where people make lives, suffer pain, enjoy small pleasures, play baseball, die, make love, have kids, drink themselves drunk on spring nights and do their best to hold off the demons that seek to destroy us, our homes, our families, our town.

Here we live in the shadow of the steeple, where the holy rubber meets the road, all crookedly blessed in God's mercy, in the heart-stopping, pants-dropping, race-riot-creating, oddball-hating, soul-shaking, love-and-fear-making, heartbreaking town of Freehold, New Jersey.

Let the service begin.

# TWO

# MY
# HOUSE

It's Thursday night, trash night. We are fully mobilized and ready to go. We have gathered in my grandfather's 1940s sedan waiting to be deployed to dig through every trash heap overflowing from the curbs of our town. First, we're heading to Brinckerhoff Avenue; that's where the money is and the trash is finest. We have come for your radios, any radios, no matter the condition. We will scavenge them from your junk pile, throw them into the trunk and bring them home to "the shed," my grandfather's six-by-six-foot unheated wooden cubicle in a tiny corner of our house. Here, winter and summer, magic occurs. Here in a "room" filled with electrical wire and filament tubes, I will sit studiously at his side. While he wires, solders and exchanges bad tubes for good, we wait together for the same moment: that instant when the whispering breath, the beautiful low static hum and warm sundown glow of electricity will come surging back into the dead skeletons of radios we have pulled from extinction.

Here at my grandfather's workbench, the resurrection is real. The vacuum silence will be drawn up and filled with the distant, crackling voices of Sunday preachers, blabbering pitchmen, Big Band music, early rock 'n' roll and serial dramas. It is the sound of the world outside straining to reach us, calling down into our little town and deeper, into our hermetically sealed universe here at 87 Randolph Street. Once returned to the living, all items will be sold for five dollars in the migrant camps that, come summer, will dot the farm fields on the edge of our borough. The "radio man" is coming. That's how my grandfather is known amongst the mostly Southern black migrant population that returns by bus every season to harvest the crops of rural Monmouth County. Down the dirt farm roads to the shacks in the rear where dust-bowl thirties conditions live on, my mother drives my stroke-addled grandpa to do his business amongst "the blacks" in their "Mickey Mouse" camps. I went once and was frightened out of my wits, surrounded in the dusk by hard-worn black faces. Race relations, never great in Freehold, will explode ten years later into rioting and shootings, but for now, there is just a steady, uncomfortable quiet. I am simply the young protégé grandson of the "radio man," here amongst his patrons where my family scrambles to make ends meet.

We were pretty near poor, though I never thought about it. We were clothed, fed and bedded. I had white and black friends worse off. My parents had jobs, my mother as a legal-secretary and my father at Ford. Our house was old and soon to be noticeably decrepit. One kerosene stove in the living room was all we had to heat the whole place. Upstairs, where my family slept, you woke on winter mornings with your breath visible. One of my earliest childhood memories is the smell of kerosene and my grandfather standing there filling the spout in the rear of the stove. All of our cooking was done on a coal stove in the kitchen; as a child I'd shoot my water gun at its hot iron surface and watch the steam rise. We'd haul the ashes out the back door to the "ash heap." Daily I'd return from playing in that pile of dust pale from gray coal ash. We had a small box refrigerator and one of the first televisions in town. In an earlier life, before I was born, my granddad had been the proprietor of Springsteen Brothers Electrical Shop. So when TV hit, it arrived at our house first. My mother told me neighbors from up and down the block would stop by to see the new miracle, to watch Milton Berle, Kate Smith and *Your Hit Parade*. To see wrestlers like Bruno Sammartino face off against Haystacks Calhoun. By the time I was six I knew every word to the Kate Smith anthem, "When the Moon Comes Over the Mountain."

In this house, due to order of birth and circumstance, I was lord, king and the messiah all rolled into one. Because I was the first grandchild, my grandmother latched on to me to replace my dead aunt Virginia. Nothing was out of bounds. It was a terrible freedom for a young boy and I embraced it with everything I had. I stayed up until three a.m. and slept until three p.m. at five and six years old. I watched TV until it went off and I was left staring alone at the test pattern. I ate what and when I wanted. My parents and I became distant relatives and my mother, in her confusion and desire to keep the peace, ceded me to my grandmother's total dominion. A timid little tyrant, I soon felt like the rules were for the rest of the world, at least until my dad came home. He would lord sullenly over the kitchen, a monarch dethroned by his own firstborn son at his mother's insistence. Our ruin of a house and my own eccentricities and power at such a young age shamed and embarrassed me. I could see the rest of the world was running on a different clock and I was teased for my habits pretty thoroughly by my neighborhood pals. I loved my entitlement, but I knew it wasn't right.

When I became of school age and had to conform to a time schedule, it sent me into an inner rage that lasted most of my school years. My mother knew we were all way overdue for a reckoning and, to her credit, tried to reclaim me. She moved us out of my grandmother's house to a small, half-shotgun-style house at 39½ Institute Street. No hot water, four tiny rooms, four blocks away from my grandparents. There she tried to set some normal boundaries. It was too late. Those four blocks might as well have been a million miles. I was roaring with anger and loss and every chance I got, I returned to stay with my grandparents. It was my true home and they felt like my real parents. I could and would not leave.

The house by now was functional only in one room, the living room. The rest of the house, abandoned and draped off, was falling down, with one wintry and windblown bathroom, the only place to relieve yourself, and no functioning bath. My grandparents fell into a state of poor hygiene and care that would shock and repel me now. I remember my grandmother's soiled undergarments, just washed, hanging on the backyard line, frightening and embarrassing me, symbols of the inappropriate intimacies, physical and emotional, that made my grandparents' home so confusing and compelling. But I loved them and that house. My grandma slept on a worn spring couch with me tucked in at her side while my grandfather had a small cot across the room. This was it. This was what it had come to, my childhood limitlessness. This was where I needed to be to feel at home, safe, loved.

The grinding hypnotic power of this ruined place and these people would never leave me. I visit it in my dreams today, returning over and over, wanting to go back. It was a place where I felt an ultimate security, full license and a horrible unforgettable boundary-less love. It ruined me and it made me. Ruined, in that for the rest of my life I would struggle to create boundaries for myself that would allow me a life of some normalcy in my relationships. It made me in the sense that it would set me off on a lifelong pursuit of a "singular" place of my own, giving me a raw hunger that drove me, hell-bent, in my music. It was a desperate, lifelong effort to rebuild, on embers of memory and longing, my temple of safety.

For my grandmother's love, I abandoned my parents, my sister and much of the world itself. Then that world came crashing in. My grandparents became ill. The whole family moved in together again, to another half house, at 68 South Street. Soon, my younger sister, Pam, would be born, my grandfather would be dead and my grandmother would be filled with cancer. My house, my backyard, my tree, my dirt, my earth, my sanctuary would be condemned and the land sold, to be made into a parking lot for St. Rose of Lima Catholic church.

# THREE

# THE
# CHURCH

There was a circuit we could ride on our bikes that took us completely around the church and the rectory and back alongside the convent, rolling over the nuns' beautiful, faded blue slate driveway. The slightly raised edges of the slate would send vibrations up through your handlebars, creating tiny pulsing rhythms in your hands, bump—ump—ump—ump . . . concrete, then back around we'd go again. Sleepy afternoons would pass with our winding in and out of the St. Rose compound, being scolded through the convent windows by the sisters to go home and dodging stray cats that wandered in between the church basement and my living room. My grandfather, now with nothing much to do, would spend his time patiently wooing these wild creatures to his side in our backyard. He could get near and pet feral cats that would have nothing to do with another human. Sometimes the price was steep. He came in one evening with a bloody foot-long scratch down his arm from a kitty that was not quite ready for the love.

The cats drifted back and forth from our house to the church just as we drifted to school, to home, to mass, to school again, our lives inextricably linked with the life of the church. At first the priests and nuns were just kind faces peering down into your carriage, all smiles and pleasant mystery, but come school age, I was inducted into the dark halls of communion. There was the incense, the men crucified, the torturously memorized dogma, the Friday Stations of the Cross (the schoolwork!), the black-robed men and women, the curtained confessional, the sliding window, the priest's shadowy face and the recitation of childhood transgression. When I think about the hours I spent devising a list of acceptable sins I could spout on command . . . They had to be bad enough to be believable . . . but not too bad (the best was yet to come!). How much sinning could you actually have done at a second-grade level? Eventually, St. Rose of Lima's Monday-through-Sunday holy reckoning would wear me out and make me want out . . . bad. But out to where? There is no out. I live here! We all do. All of my tribe. We are stranded on this desert island of a corner, bound together in the same boat. A boat that I have been instructed by my catechism teachers is at sea eternally, death and Judgment Day being just a divvying up of passengers as our ship sails through one metaphysical lock to another, adrift in holy confusion.

And so . . . I build my other world. It is a world of childhood resistance, a world of passive refusal from within, my defense against "the system." It is a refusal of a world where I am not recognized, by my grandmother's lights and mine, for who I am, a lost boy king, forcibly exiled daily from his empire of rooms. My grandma's house! To these schmucks, I'm just another spoiled kid who will not conform to what we all ultimately must conform to, the only-circumstantially-theistic kingdom of . . . THE WAY THINGS ARE! The problem is I don't know shit, nor care, about "the way things are." I hail from the exotic land of . . . THINGS THE WAY I LIKE 'EM. It's just up the street. Let's all call it a day and just *go HOME*!

No matter how much I want to, no matter how hard I try, "the way things are" eludes me. I desperately want to fit in but the world I have created with the unwarranted freedom from my grandparents has turned me into an unintentional rebel, an outcast weirdo misfit sissy boy. I am alienating, alienated and socially homeless . . . I am seven years old.

Amongst my male classmates, there are mainly good souls. Some, however, are rude, predatory and unkind. It is here I receive the bullying all aspiring rock stars must undergo and suffer in seething, raw, humiliating silence, the great "leaning up against the chain-link fence as the world spins around you, without you, in rejection of you" playground loneliness that is essential fuel for the coming fire. Soon, all of this will burn and the world will be turned upside down on its ass . . . but not yet.

The girls, on the other hand, shocked to find what appears to be a shy, softhearted dreamer in their midst, move right onto Grandma's turf and begin to take care of me. I build a small harem who tie my shoes, zip my jacket, shower me with attention. This is something all Italian mama's boys know how to do well. Here your rejection by the boys is a badge of sensitivity and can be played like a coveted ace for the perks of young geekdom. Of course, a few years later, when sex rears its head, I'll lose my exalted status and become just another mild-mannered loser.

The priests and nuns themselves are creatures of great authority and unknowable sexual mystery. As both my flesh-and-blood neighbors and our local bridge to the next life, they exert a hard influence over our daily existence. Both everyday and otherworldly, they are the neighborhood gatekeepers of a dark and beatific world I fear and desire entrance to. It's a world where all you have is at risk, a world filled with the unknown bliss of resurrection, eternity and the unending fires of perdition, of exciting, sexually tinged torture, immaculate conceptions and miracles. A world where men turn into gods and gods into devils . . . and I knew it was real. I'd seen gods turn into devils at home. I'd witnessed what I felt was surely the possessive face of Satan. It was my poor old pop tearing up the house in an alcohol-fueled rage in the dead of night, scaring the shit out of all of us. I'd felt this darkness's final force come visit in the shape of my struggling dad . . . physical threat, emotional chaos and the power to *not* love.

In the fifties the nuns at St. Rose could play pretty rough. I'd once been sent down from the eighth grade to first for some transgression. I was stuffed behind a first-grade desk and left there to marinate. I was glad for the afternoon off. Then I noticed someone's cuff link reflecting the sun upon the wall. I dreamily followed its light as it crawled up beyond the window toward the ceiling. I then heard the nun say to a beefy little enforcer in the center first-row desk, "Show our visitor what we do in this class to those who don't pay attention." The young student walked back to me with a blank expression on his face and without a blink let me have it, openhanded but full force, across my face. As the smack rang through the classroom I couldn't believe what had just happened. I was shaken, red-faced and humiliated.

Before my grammar school education was over I'd have my knuckles classically rapped, my tie pulled 'til I choked; be struck in the head, shut into a dark closet and stuffed into a trash can while being told this is where I belonged. All business as usual in Catholic school in the fifties. Still, it left a mean taste in my mouth and estranged me from my religion for good.

Back in school, even if you remained physically untouched, Catholicism seeped into your bones. I was an altar boy waking in the holy black of four a.m. to hustle myself over wintry streets to don my cassock in the dawn silence of the church sacristy and perform ritual on God's personal terra firma, the St. Rose altar, no civilians allowed. There I sucked in incense while assisting our grumpy, eighty-year-old monsignor before a captive audience of relatives, nuns and early-rising sinners. I proved so inept not knowing my positions and not studying my Latin that I inspired our Monsignor to grab me by the shoulder of my cassock at one six a.m. mass and drag me, to the gasping shock of all, facedown on the altar. Later that afternoon in the play yard, my fifth-grade teacher, Sister Charles Marie, who'd been present at the thrashing, handed me a small holy medal. It was a kindness I've never forgotten. Over the years as a St. Rose student I had felt enough of Catholicism's corporal and emotional strain. On my eighth-grade graduation day, I walked away from it all, finished, telling myself, "Never again." I was free, free, free at last . . . and I believed it . . . for quite a while. However, as I grew older, there were certain things about the way I thought, reacted, behaved. I came to ruefully and bemusedly understand that once you're a Catholic, you're always a Catholic. So I stopped kidding myself. I don't often participate in my religion but I know somewhere . . . deep inside . . . I'm still on the team.

This was the world where I found the beginnings of my song. In Catholicism, there existed the poetry, danger and darkness that reflected my imagination and my inner self. I found a land of great and harsh beauty, of fantastic stories, of unimaginable punishment and infinite reward. It was a glorious and pathetic place I was either shaped for or fit right into. It has walked alongside me as a waking dream my whole life. So as a young adult I tried to make sense of it. I tried to meet its challenge for the very reasons that there *are* souls to lose and a kingdom of love to be gained. I laid what I'd absorbed across the hardscrabble lives of my family, friends and neighbors. I turned it into something I could grapple with, understand, something I could even find faith in. As funny as it sounds, I have a "personal" relationship with Jesus. He remains one of my fathers, though as with my own father, I no longer believe in his godly power. I believe deeply in his love, his ability to save . . . but not to damn . . . enough of that.

The way I see it, we ate the apple and Adam, Eve, the rebel Jesus in all his glory and Satan are all part of God's plan to make men and women out of us, to give us the precious gifts of earth, dirt, sweat, blood, sex, sin, goodness, freedom, captivity, love, fear, life and death . . . our humanity and a world of our own.

The church bells ring. My clan pours out of our houses and hustles up the street. Someone is getting married, getting dead or being born. We line the church's front walkway, waiting, my sister and I picking up fallen flowers or thrown rice to be packed away in paper bags for another day to shower upon complete strangers. My mother is thrilled, her face alight. Organ music, and the wooden doors of our church swing open upon a bride and groom exiting their wedding ceremony. I hear my mother sigh, "Oh, the dress . . . the beautiful dress . . ." The bouquet is tossed. The future is told. The bride and her hero are whisked away in their long black limousine, the one that drops you off at the beginning of your life. The other one is just around the corner waiting for another day to bring the tears and take you on that short drive straight out Throckmorton Street to the St. Rose graveyard on the edge of town. There, on spring Sundays, visiting bones, boxes and piles of dirt, my sister and I run, playing happily amongst the headstones. Back at church, the wedding is over and I take my sister's hand. By nine or ten years old, we've seen it all plenty of times. Rice or flowers, coming or going, heaven or hell, here on the corner of Randolph and McLean, it's just all in a day's work.

FOUR
# THE
# ITALIANS

A nuclear surge of energy erupts constantly from the tiny mouths and bodies of Dora Kirby, Eda Urbellis and Adele Springsteen. My mother and her two sisters have screamed, laughed, cried and danced their way through life's best and worst for more than 260 collective years. It never stops. Their Marxian (Brothers) high-voltage insanity constantly borders on a barely controlled state of hysteria. Somehow this has rendered them not only near immortal but triumphant. Falling for the Irish to a woman, they have outlived all their husbands, war, tragedy and near poverty and remained indomitable, undefeated, undeterred and terminally optimistic. They are "THE GREATEST." Three mini Muhammad Alis, rope-a-doping the world.

Here on the Shore the Italians and the Irish meet and mate often. The coastal town of Spring Lake is locally known as the "Irish Riviera." There, on any summer Sunday, the fair-skinned and freckled can be found tossing down beers and turning lobster-red in the frothing surf off the Victorian homes that still bring style and substance to their community. A few miles north lies Long Branch, New Jersey, once home of Anthony "Little Pussy" Russo, my wife Patti Scialfa's next-door neighbor in Deal, and the Central Jersey mob. Its beaches are filled with olive-skinned beauties, belly-busting husbands and the thick Jersey accent of my Italian brothers and sisters wafting through the air on cigar smoke. A *Sopranos* casting call would need to look no further.

My great-grandfather was called "the Dutchman" and I suppose descended from some lost Netherlanders who wandered down from New Amsterdam not knowing what they were getting themselves into. Thus, we wear the name Springsteen, of Dutch origin, but prominently, here's where Irish and Italian blood meet. Why? Previous to the Mexicans and African-Americans who harvested Monmouth County crops, the Italians were in the fields with the Irishmen and working the horse farms alongside them. Recently, I asked my mother how they all ended up with the Irish. She said, "The Italian men were too bossy. We'd had enough of that. We didn't want men bossing us all around." Of course they didn't. If there was bossing to be done, the Zerilli girls would be doing it, although somewhat surreptitiously. My aunt Eda told me, "Daddy wanted three boys but he got three girls instead, so he raised us tough like men." That, I suppose, explains some of it.

As a child, I would return from dinner at my aunt Dora's house exhausted, my ears ringing. Anything more celebratory than dinner and you were taking your life into your hands. You would be fed 'til stuffed, sung and shouted at 'til deaf and danced with 'til dust. Now, as they all move brazenly into their nineties, it continues. Where did it come from? What is the source of their unrelenting energy and optimism? What power has been sucked from the spheres and sent coursing through their tiny little Italian bones? Who set it all in motion?

His name was Anthony Alexander Andrew Zerilli. He came to

America around the turn of the century from Vico Equense, a stone's throw from Naples in southern Italy, at the age of twelve; settled in San Francisco; and found his way east, graduating from City College to become a lawyer at 303 West Forty-Second Street, New York City. He was my grandfather. He served three years in the navy, had three wives, spent three years in Sing Sing prison for embezzlement (supposedly taking the rap for another relative). He ended up on top of a green and gracious hill in Englishtown, New Jersey. He had some money. I have pictures of my mother and her family decked out in impeccable whites in Newport, Rhode Island, in the thirties. He went broke in jail. Their mother, not well, went MIA back in Brooklyn, abandoning my mom and her sisters, then still teenagers, to live alone and make their own way at the farmhouse where they raised themselves.

As a child, this modest farmhouse was a mansion on a hill to me, a citadel of wealth and culture. My grandfather had paintings, good ones. He collected religious art, robes and antique furniture. He had a piano in his living room. He traveled, appeared worldly and just a little dissolute. With gray hair and huge dark circles under big brown Italian eyes, he was a short man with a thunderous baritone, a voice that when cast your way brought with it the fear of God. He often sat, an old Italian prince, on a thronelike chair in his den. His third wife, Fifi, sat knitting just across the room. Tightly dressed, made up and perfumed enough to knock you out, she would plant a huge red lipstick kiss, bringing a warmth to my cheek every time we dropped by. Then from the throne it would come, rolling the "Br" out to infinity, adding and emphasizing an "a," surfing long and low on the "u," then just touching the "ce": "BAAAARRRRUUUUUUUUUUCE . . . Come here!" I knew what was coming next. In one hand, he held a dollar. I received this dollar every Sunday but I had to go get it. I had to deal with what he had in his other hand: the "pinch of death." As you reached for the dollar, he would grab you with the other hand, pinching your cheek between his thumb and the first knuckle of his forefinger. First, the incredibly tight eye-watering pinch, followed by a slow upward twisting motion, abruptly shifting to a downward reverse circular tug. (I'm caterwauling now.) And then the release, a quick flourishing pull, away, out and back, finishing with a snapping of his fingers, accompanied by a hearty laughing, "BAAAARRRRUUUUUUUUUCE . . . WHAT'S THE MATTER?" Then, the dollar.

At Sunday dinner, he held court, yelling, ordering, discussing the events of the day at the top of his voice. It was a show. Some might have thought it overbearing, but to me, this little Italian man was a *giant*! Something made him seem grand, important, not a part of the passive-aggressive, wandering, lost male tribe that populated much of the rest of my life. He was a Neapolitan force of nature! So what if he got into a little trouble? The real world was full of trouble, and if you wanted, if you hungered, you'd better be ready for it. You'd best be ready to stake your claim and not let go because "they" were not going to give it to you for free. You would have to risk . . . and to pay. His love of living, the intensity of his presence, his engagement in the day and his dominion over his family made him a unique male figure in my life. He was exciting, scary, theatrical, self-mythologizing, bragging . . . like a rock star! Otherwise, when you left the house at the top of the hill, as soon as you hit roadside pavement, in my family, WOMEN RULED THE WORLD! They allowed the men the illusion of thinking they were in command, but the most superficial observation would tell you they couldn't keep up. The Irishmen needed MAMA! Anthony, on his hilltop, needed Fifi, HOT MAMA! There was a big difference.

Anthony had separated from Adelina Rosa, his first wife, from an arranged marriage, while they were in their twenties. She had been sent to the United States as a young girl from Sorrento to be an old-world bride. She lived for eighty-plus years in the United States and never spoke a sentence of English. When you walked into her room, you walked into Old Italy. The holy beads, the fragrances, the religious items, the quilts, the dusky sunlight reflecting off another place and time. She, I'm sure, unfortunately, played the "Madonna" role to Anthony's other inamoratas.

My grandmother suffered mightily from the divorce, never remarried and had little to do with the world at large again. She and Anthony were never in the same room with each other for a long, long time. Not at funerals, not at weddings, not at family gatherings. Every Sunday after church when I visited my aunt Dora's, she'd be there in her hairnet and shawls, scented exotically and cooking delicious Italian dishes. She'd greet me, smiling, with hugs and kisses, murmuring Italian blessings. Then one day, on the hill, Fifi died.

Sixty years after their divorce, Anthony and Adelina reunited. Sixty years later! They lived together in their "mansion" for ten years, until Anthony died. After my grandfather's death, in the summers, I would ride my bicycle from Colts Neck to Englishtown and visit. She was usually there alone, and we would sit in the kitchen, conversing in a smattering of broken English and Italian. She claimed she only went with the old man to protect her children's inheritance . . . maybe so. She died peacefully and wit sharp at the age of 101, having seen the invention of the automobile and the plane and men walk on the moon in her lifetime.

Anthony and Adelina's house on the hill remained in a state of suspended animation for twenty-five years. When I walked through it as a fifty-year-old man, it was exactly as it had been when I was eight. To the sisters . . . it was hallowed ground. Finally, my cousin Frank, the jitterbug champ, who taught me my first chords on the guitar and whose son, Frank Jr., played with me in the Sessions Band, moved in with his family and filled the house with children and Italian cooking again.

The power of the "pinch of death" has been handed down to my aunt Dora, who has developed her own version, the "headlock of doom." This little five-foot-two, ninety-year-old Italian lady could rip your neck into permanent whiplash or kick the ass of Randy "Macho Man" Savage should he be foolish enough to bend down for a kiss. While I no longer fear Big Daddy's "pinch of death," still, on many nights, right around eight thirty, Anthony lives . . . as the house lights go dark, the backstage curtain opens and I hear that long, drawn-out . . . "BAAAARRRRU-UUUUUUCE."

Work, faith, family: this is the Italian credo handed down by my mother and her sisters. They live it. They believe it. They believe it even though these very tenets have crushingly let them down. They preach it, though never stridently, and are sure it is all we have between life, love and the void that devours husbands, children, family members and friends. There is a strength, fear and desperate joy in all this hard spirit and soul that naturally found its way into my work. We the Italians push until we can go no further; stand strong until our bones give way; reach and hold until our muscles fatigue; twist, shout and laugh until we can no more, until the end. This is the religion of the Zerilli sisters, handed down by the hard lessons of Papa and the grace of God and for which we are daily thankful.

FIVE
# THE
# IRISH

In my family we had aunts who howled during family gatherings; cousins who left school in the sixth grade, went home and never left the house again; and men who pulled hair from their bodies and heads, leaving great gaping patches of baldness, all within our little half block. During thunderstorms, my grandmother would grab me by the hand and rush me past the church to my aunt Jane's house. There, the gathering of women and their black magic would commence. Prayers were murmured as my aunt Jane threw holy water over all of us from a small bottle. With each flash of lightning, the quiet hysteria would ratchet up a notch, until it seemed like God himself was about to blast us off our little corner. Folktales were told of lightning fatalities. Someone made the mistake of telling me the safest place in a lightning storm was in a car because of the grounding of the rubber tires. After that, at the first sound of thunder, I caterwauled until my parents would take me in the car until the storm subsided. I then proceeded to write about cars for the rest of my life. As a child, all of this was simply mysterious, embarrassing and ordinary. It had to be. These were the people I loved.

We are the afflicted. A lot of trouble came in the blood of my people who hailed from the Emerald Isle. My great-great-grandmother Ann Garrity left Ireland at fourteen in 1852 with two sisters, aged twelve and ten. This was five years after the potato famine devastated much of Ireland, and she settled in Freehold. I don't know where it started, but a serious strain of mental illness drifts through those of us who are here, seeming to randomly pick off a cousin, an aunt, a son, a grandma and, unfortunately, my dad.

I haven't been completely fair to my father in my songs, treating him as an archetype of the neglecting, domineering parent. It was an *East of Eden* recasting of our relationship, a way of "universalizing" my childhood experience. Our story is much more complicated. Not in the details of what happened, but in the "why" of it all.

## My Father

To a child, the bars of Freehold were citadels of mystery, filled with mean magic, uncertainty, and the possibility of violence. Stopped at a red light on Throckmorton Street one evening, my sister and I witnessed two men on the concrete outside of the local taproom beating each other toward what seemed certain death. Shirts were torn; men surrounded, shouting; one man held the other by his hair as he straddled his chest, delivering vicious blows to his face. Blood mixed deeply around the man's mouth as he desperately defended himself, his back to the pavement. My mother said, "Don't look." The light changed and we drove on.

When you walked through barroom doors in my hometown, you entered the mystical realm of men. On the rare night my mother would call my father home, we would slowly drive through town until we drew to a stop outside of a single lit door. She'd point and say, "Go in and get your father." Entering my father's public sanctuary filled me with a thrill and fear. I'd been given license by my mom to do the unthinkable: interrupt my pop while he was in sacred space. I'd push open the door, dodging men who towered over me on their way out. I stood waist-high to them at best, so when I entered the barroom I felt like a Jack who'd climbed some dark beanstalk, ending up in a land of familiar but frightening giants. On the left, lining the wall, lay a row of booths filled with secret assignations, barroom lovers, and husband-and-wife tag-team drinkers. On the right were stools filled by a barricade of broad working-class backs, rolling-thunder murmuring, clinking glasses, unsettling adult laughter and very, very few women. I'd stand there, drinking in the dim smell of beer, booze, blues and aftershave; nothing in the outer world of home smelled remotely like it. Schlitz and Pabst Blue Ribbon ruled, with the blue ribbon stamped on the bartender's pouring spout as the golden elixir was slid expertly into tilted glasses that were then set with a hard knock on the wooden bar. There I stood, a small spirit reminder of what a lot of these men were spending a few moments trying to forget—work, responsibility, the family, the blessings and burdens of an adult life. Looking back, it was a mix of mostly average guys who simply needed to let off a little steam at the end of the week and a few others, moved by harder things, who didn't know where to draw the line.

Finally, someone would notice a small interloper amongst them and bemusedly draw me over to my dad. My view from the floor was bar stool, black shoes, white socks, work trousers, haunches and powerful legs, work belt, then the face, slightly discolored and misshapen by alcohol, peering down through cigarette smoke as I uttered the immortal words "Mom wants you to come home." There would be no introductions to friends, no pat on the head, no soft intonation of voice or tousle of the hair, just "Go outside, I'll be right out." I'd follow my bread crumb trail back out the barroom door into the cool evening air, into my town, which felt somehow so welcoming and hostile. Drifting to the curb, I'd hop into the backseat and inform my mother, "He'll be right out."

I was not my father's favorite citizen. As a boy I figured it was just the way men were, distant, uncommunicative, busy within the currents of the grown-up world. As a child you don't question your parents' choices. You accept them. They are justified by the godlike status of parenthood. If you aren't spoken to, you're not worth the time. If you're not greeted with love and affection, you haven't earned it. If you're ignored, you don't exist. Control over your own behavior is the only card you have to play in the hope of modifying theirs. Maybe you have to be tougher, stronger, more athletic, smarter, in some way better . . . who knows? One evening my father was giving me a few boxing lessons in the living room. I was flattered, excited by his attention and eager to learn. Things were going well. And then he threw a few open-palmed punches to my face that landed just a little too hard. It stung; I wasn't hurt, but a line had been crossed. I knew something was being communicated. We had slipped into the dark nether land beyond father and son. I sensed what was being said: I was an intruder, a stranger, a competitor in our home and a fearful disappointment. My heart broke and I crumpled. He walked away in disgust.

When my dad looked at me, he didn't see what he needed to see. This was my crime. My best friend in the neighborhood was Bobby Duncan. He'd ride with his pop every Saturday night to Wall Stadium for the stock car races. At five o'clock sharp a halt would be called to whatever endeavor we were involved in and at six, right after dinner, he'd come bounding down the front steps of his home two doors down, shirt pressed, hair Brylcreemed, followed by his pop. Into the Ford and off they'd go to Wall Stadium . . . that tire-screeching, high-octane heaven where families bonded over local madmen in garage-built American steel either roaring round and round in insane circles or at field's center smashing the hell out of one another in the weekly demolition derby. For the demo, all you needed was a football helmet, a seat belt and something you were willing to wreck to take your place amongst the chosen . . . Wall Stadium, that smoky, rubber-burning circle of love where families came together in common purpose and things were as God intended them. I stood exiled from my father's love AND hot rod heaven!

Unfortunately, my dad's desire to engage with me almost always came after the nightly religious ritual of the "sacred six-pack." One beer after another in the pitch dark of our kitchen. It was always then that he wanted to see me and it was always the same. A few moments of feigned parental concern for my well-being followed by the real deal: the hostility and raw anger toward his son, the only other man in the house. It was a shame. He loved me but he couldn't stand me. He felt we competed for my mother's affections. We did. He also saw in me too much of *his* real self. My pop was built like a bull, always in work clothes; he was strong and physically formidable. Toward the end of his life, he fought back from death many times. Inside, however, beyond his rage, he harbored a gentleness, timidity, shyness and a dreamy insecurity. These were all the things I wore on the outside and the reflection of these qualities in his boy repelled him. It made him angry. It was "soft." And he hated "soft." Of course, he'd been brought up "soft." A mama's boy, just like me.

One evening at the kitchen table, late in life, when he was not well, he told me a story of being pulled out of a fight he was having in the school yard. My grandmother had walked over from our house and dragged him home. He recounted his humiliation and said, eyes welling . . . "I was winning . . . I was winning." He still didn't understand he could not be risked. He was the one remaining, living child. My grandmother, confused, could not realize her untempered love was destroying the men she was raising. I told him I understood, that we had been raised by the same woman in some of the most formative years of our lives and suffered many of the same humiliations. However, back in the days when our relationship was at its most tempestuous, these things remained mysteries and created a legacy of pain and misunderstanding.

In 1962, my youngest sister, Pam, was born. I was twelve. My mom was thirty-six. That was pretty late to be pregnant in those days. It was wonderful. My mother was a miracle. I loved the maternity clothes. My sister Virginia and I would sit in the living room in the final months of her pregnancy, our hands resting upon her stomach, waiting for our new little sister to kick. The whole house was caught up in the excitement of Pam's birth and our family came together. With my mom in the hospital, my dad stepped up and took care of us, burning breakfast, helping us get dressed for school (sending me there in my mother's blouse, to Virginia's roaring laughter). The house lit up. Children bring with them grace, patience, transcendence, second chances, rebirth and a reawakening of the love that's in your heart and present in your home. They are God giving you another shot. My teenage years with my father were still not great but there was always the light of my little sister Pam, living proof of the love in our family. I was enchanted with her. I was thankful for her. I changed her diapers, rocked her to sleep, ran to her side if she cried, held her in my arms and forged a bond that exists to this day.

My grandmother, now very ill, slept in the room adjoining mine. One night at the age of three, Pam left my parents' room and for the only time in her young life climbed into my grandmother's bed. She slept there all night, lying beside my grandmother as she died. In the morning, my mother checked on my grandma and she was still. When I came home from school that day, my world collapsed. Tears, grief, weren't enough. I wanted death. I needed to join her. Even as a teenager, I could not imagine a world without her. It was a black hole, an Armageddon; nothing meant anything, life was drained. My existence went blank. The world was a fraud, a shadow of itself. The only thing that saved me was my little sis and my new interest in music.

Now things got strange. My father's generally quiet desperation led to paranoid delusion. I had a teenage Russian friend he thought was a "spy." We lived a block away from the Puerto Rican neighborhood. My father was sure my mother was having an affair. As I came in after school one day, he broke down in tears at the kitchen table. He told me he needed someone to talk to. He had no one. At forty-five he was friendless, and due to my pop's insecurities, there was never another man in our home except me. He spilled his heart out to me. It shocked me, made me feel uncomfortable and strangely wonderful. He showed himself to me, mess that he was. It was one of the greatest days of my teenage life. He needed a "man" friend and I was the only game in town. I comforted him the best I could. I was only sixteen and we were both in way over our heads. I told him I was sure he was wrong and that my mother's love and dedication to him was complete. It was, but he had lost his grip on reality and was inconsolable. Later that evening I told my mother and for the first time we had to confront the fact my father was truly ill.

Things were complicated by some strange occurrences around our home. One Saturday night someone shot a bullet through the window of our front door, leaving a perfect slug-size hole in the glass seconds after I'd just walked up to bed. The police were constantly pulling in and out of our driveway and my father said he had been involved with some labor trouble at work. These occurrences fed all of our paranoid fantasies and created an atmosphere of terrible unease throughout our household.

My sister Virginia became pregnant at seventeen, and no one realized it until she was six months along! In her senior year she dropped out of high school, was tutored at home and married her boyfriend and the father of her child, Mickey Shave. Mickey was an arrogant, leather-jacketed, bull-riding, fighting greaser from Lakewood and eventually all-around great guy. He traveled the competitive rodeo circuit from Jersey to Texas in the late sixties. (Unbeknownst to most, Jersey is home to the longest consecutively running rodeo in the United States, Cowtown, and once you hit the southern part of the state, there's more cowboy there than one might think.) My steadfast sister moved south to Lakewood after trouble brought its consequences, had a beautiful son and began to live the working-class life of my parents.

Virginia, who had never boiled water, washed a dish or swept a floor, became the toughest. She had soul, intelligence, humor and beauty. In months, her life changed. She became a hard-core Irish workingwoman.

Mickey worked in construction, suffered through the recession of the late seventies when building ceased in Central Jersey, lost his job and took work as a janitor at the local high school. My sister worked the floor at K–Mart. They raised two lovely young men and a beautiful daughter and now have a slew of grandkids. At that young age and on her own, she found the strength my mother and her sisters have always carried with them. She became a living incarnation of Jersey soul; I wrote "The River" in her and my brother-in-law's honor.

# SIX

# MY MOTHER

I wake in the half-morning light to the sound of weight on the steps leading up to the small landing outside of my bedroom. A door creaks, a turn, a squeak, the running faucet, then the sound of water moving through the pipes in the wall between my room and our bathroom, a turn, then silence, a click, the sound of plastic on porcelain, my mother's makeup case on the sink, time . . . then the last-minute rustling of garments before the mirror. These are the sounds that greet me every morning of my teenage life at 68 South Street. They are the sounds of my mother getting ready for work, preparing to present herself to the world, the outside world, which she respects and where she is confident she has duties to fulfill. To a child these are the sounds of mystery, ritual and reassurance. I can still hear them.

My first bedroom was on the second floor, off the back of our house, over the kitchen. A lazy turn to my right in bed and through my window I had a perfect view of my dad on fifteen-degree mornings down in the yard, back to the frozen ground, cursing and grumbling underneath one of our junkers, that he might get 'er running and make work . . . brrrrrrrr. I had no heat in my room, but there was a small iron grate on the floor I could open or close over the gas jets of the kitchen stove on the east-facing wall. As physics has taught us, heat rises. Hallelujah! For in our first years on South Street those four jets provided me my only warmth and salvation through many a cold New Jersey winter. A voice calling, two half notes, a step up and a rise to the whole note, shouting through the grate, "Bruce, get up." I plead unmusically, "Turn on the stove." Ten minutes later, with the smell of breakfast cooking on the kitchen gas burners, the edge has come off of my icebox and I roll out of bed into the cool and unwelcoming morning. This will change when, with my little sister at her side, my grandmother dies in the room next to mine. At sixteen, I will be visited by a black melancholy I never dreamt existed. But . . . I'll inherit Grandma's room—heat!—and the early-morning symphony of my mother preparing for work.

I get up pretty easy. If I don't, my mom hits me with a glass of cold water, a technique she's refined from dragging my father out of bed to the job. My sister Virginia and I are at the kitchen table, toast, eggs, Sugar Pops; I snow more sugar on, and we all hustle out the door. A kiss and we're off to school, lumbering with our book bags up the street, my mom's high heels clicking lightly in the other direction, toward town.

She goes to work, she does not miss a day, she is never sick, she is never down, she never complains. Work does not appear to be a burden for her but a source of energy and pleasure. Up to Main Street and through the modern glass doors of Lawyers Title Inc. she glides. She walks the long aisle to her desk, farthest in the rear and closest to Mr. Farrell. My mom is a legal secretary. Mr. Farrell is her boss and the head of the agency. She is secretary numero uno!

As a child, I delight in my visits here. Alone, I wheel my way through the door to be greeted by a smile from the receptionist. She makes a call to my mom and I'm given permission to walk the aisle. The perfumes, the crisp white blouses, whispering skirts and stockings of the secretaries coming out of their cubicles to greet me as I stand exactly breast high, feigning innocence while being hugged and kissed upon my crown. I walk this gauntlet of pure pleasure until I end up back at my mother's desk in a perfumed trance. There I'm greeted by "Philly," the beauty queen of Lawyers Title, a knockout and the last stop before my mom. She has me shy and speechless until my mother comes to my rescue, then my mom and I spend a few minutes together as she entertains me with her typing skills. Tick-tack, tick-tack, tick-tack, keys hitting the margin, then the typewriter's decisive bell, slide and bang as her fingers, flying, continue to type out the vital correspondence of Lawyers Title Inc. This is followed by a lesson on copy paper and a crash course on getting rid of unwanted ink smudges as I stand fascinated. This is important stuff! The business of Lawyers Title—and essential business it is to the life of our town—has been momentarily suspended for me!

Occasionally I'll even see "the Man" himself. My mother and I will wander into his wood-paneled office, where Mr. Farrell will sternly tousle my hair, say a few kind words and send me on my privileged way. Some days, come five o'clock, I'll meet my mother at closing time and we will be amongst the last to leave. With the building empty, its fluorescent lights out, its cubicles deserted and the evening sun shining through the glass doors and reflecting off the hard linoleum floor of the entryway, it's as if the building itself is silently resting from its daily efforts in the service of our town. My mother's high heels echo down the empty aisle and we are out onto the street. She strides along statuesque, demanding respect; I am proud, she is proud. It's a wonderful world, a wonderful feeling. We are handsome, responsible members of this one-dog burg pulling our own individual weight, doing what has to be done. We have a place here, a reason to open our eyes at the break of day and breathe in a life that is steady and good.

Truthfulness, consistency, professionalism, kindness, compassion, manners, thoughtfulness, pride in yourself, honor, love, faith in and fidelity to your family, commitment, joy in your work and a never-say-die thirst for life. These are some of the things my mother taught me and that I struggle to live up to. And beyond these . . . she was my protector, stepping literally into the breach between my father and me on the nights his illness got the best of him. She would cajole, yell, plead and command that the raging stop . . . and I protected her. Once, in the middle of the night, my father returning from another lost evening at the tavern, I heard them violently arguing in the kitchen. I lay in bed; I was frightened for her and myself. I was no more than nine or ten but I left my room and came down the stairs with my baseball bat. They were standing in the kitchen, my father's back to me, my mother inches away from his face while he was yelling at the top of his lungs. I shouted at him to stop. Then I let him have it square between his broad shoulders, a sick thud, and everything grew quiet. He turned, his face barroom red; the moment lengthened, then he started laughing. The argument stopped; it became one of his favorite stories and he'd always tell me, "Don't let anybody hurt your mom."

As a young girl of twenty-three, she struggled with the early years of motherhood, ceding far too much control to my grandmother, but by the time I was six or seven, without my mother, there was nothing. No family, no stability, no life. She couldn't heal my dad or leave him, but she did everything else. My mother was a puzzle. Born into a relatively well-off family, used to much of life's good things, she married into a life of near poverty and servitude. My aunts once told me that when she was young, they called her "Queenie" because she was so spoiled. They said she never lifted a finger. Huh? Are we talking about the same woman? If this is so, this was someone I'd never met. My dad's family treated her like the help. My father could be sitting, smoking at the kitchen table, and his parents would call on my mother to go to the store, get the kerosene for the stove, drive them and our relatives where they needed to go—and she did it. She served them. She was the only person my grandmother would allow to bathe her in the last corrosive months of her cancer. She covered for my dad constantly, bringing home the bacon on countless mornings when, depressed, he simply couldn't get himself out of bed. She spent her life doing it. Her whole life. It was never over. There was always one more heartache, one more task. How did she express her frustration? With appreciation for the love and home she had, a gentle kindness to her children and more work. What penance was she doing? What did she get out of it? Her family? Atonement? She was a child of divorce, abandonment, prison; she loved my dad and maybe knowing she had the security of a man who would not, could not, leave her was enough. The price, however, was steep.

At our house, there were no dates, no restaurants or nights out on the town. My father had neither the inclination, the money nor the health for a normal married social life. I never saw the inside of a restaurant until I was well into my twenties and by then, I was intimidated by any high school maître d' at the local diner. Their deep love and attraction and yet the dramatic gulf between my mother and father's personalities was always a mystery to me. My mother would read romance novels and swoon to the latest hits on the radio. My dad would go so far as to explain to me that love songs on the radio were part of a government ploy to get you to marry and pay taxes. My mother and her two sisters have an unending faith in people, are social creatures who will merrily make conversation with a broom handle. My father was a misanthrope who shunned most of humankind. At the tavern, I'd often find him sitting solitarily at the end of the bar. He claimed to believe in a world that was filled with crooks out for a buck. "Nobody's any good, and so what if they are."

My mother showered me with affection. The love I missed from my father she tried to double up on and, perhaps, find the love she missed from my dad. All I know is she always had my back. When I was hauled into the police station for a variety of minor infractions, she was always there to take me back home. She came to my countless baseball games, both when I stunk up the place and the one season lightning struck and I turned into a real fielding, hitting player, with my name in the papers. She got me my first electric guitar, encouraged my music and fawned over my early creative writing. She was a parent, and that's what I needed as my world was about to explode.

# SEVEN

# THE BIG BANG
# (HAVE YOU HEARD
# THE NEWS . . .)

In the beginning there was a great darkness upon the Earth. There was Christmas and your birthday but beyond that all was a black endless authoritarian void. There was nothing to look forward to, nothing to look back upon, no future, no history. It was all a kid could do to make it to summer vacation.

Then, in a moment of light, blinding as a universe birthing a billion new suns, there was hope, sex, rhythm, excitement, possibility, a new way of seeing, of feeling, of thinking, of looking at your body, of combing your hair, of wearing your clothes, of moving and of living. There was a joyous demand made, a challenge, a way out of this dead-to-life world, this small-town grave with all the people I dearly loved and feared buried in it alongside of me.

THE BARRICADES HAVE BEEN STORMED!! A FREE-
DOM SONG HAS BEEN SUNG!! THE BELLS OF LIBERTY HAVE
RUNG!! A HERO HAS COME. THE OLD ORDER HAS BEEN OVER-
THROWN! The teachers, the parents, the fools so sure they knew THE
WAY—THE ONLY WAY—to build a life, to have an impact on things
and to make a man or woman out of yourself, have been challenged. A
HUMAN ATOM HAS JUST SPLIT THE WORLD IN TWO!

The small part of the world I inhabit has stumbled upon an irre-
versible moment. Somewhere in between the mundane variety acts on
a routine Sunday night in the year of our Lord 1956 . . . THE REVO-
LUTION HAS BEEN TELEVISED!! Right underneath the nose of the
guardians of all that "IS," who, if they were aware of the powers they were
about to unleash, would call out the national gestapo to SHUT THIS
SHIT DOWN!! . . . or . . . SIGN IT UP QUICK!! As a matter of fact, the
arbiter of public taste in circa-1950s USA, "MC" ED SULLIVAN, was not
initially going to let this Southern, sexually depraved hick sully the American consciousness and his stage. Once the genie had been let out of the
bottle on national television . . . IT WOULD BE OVER! THE NATION
WOULD FOLD! And we the great unwashed, the powerless, the mar-
ginalized, THE KIDS! . . . would want . . . MORE. More life, more love,
more sex, more faith, more hope, more action, more truth, more power,
more "get down in the gutter, spit on me, Jesus, teach my blind eyes to
SEE" REAL-LIFE RELIGION!! Most of all, we would want more ROCK
'N' ROLL!!

The polite charade, the half-assed circus acts, the anemic singers, the
bloodless (and often highly enjoyable) shit that passed for entertainment
would be revealed for what it was.

In the end, ratings and money did the talking and Ed (actually, on Elvis's first appearance, Charles Laughton, covering for Ed, who'd been way-
laid by a car accident) did the walking, right out to the center of his stage
to cough out, "Ladies and gentlemen . . . Elvis Presley." Seventy million

Americans that night were exposed to this hip-shaking human earthquake. A fearful nation was protected from itself by the CBS cameramen, who were told to shoot "the kid" only from the waist up. No money shots! No shifting, grinding, joyfully thrusting crotch shots. It didn't matter. It was all there in his eyes, his face, the face of a Saturday night jukebox Dionysus, the shimmying eyebrows and rocking band. A riot ensued. Women, young girls and many men, screaming for what the cameras refused to show, for what their very timidity confirmed and promised . . . ANOTHER WORLD . . . the one below your waist and above your heart . . . a world that had been previously and rigorously denied was being PROVEN TO EXIST! It was a world with all of us in it . . . together . . . *all* of us. HE HAD TO BE STOPPED!

And of course, in the end, he was stopped. But not before the money got made and the secret slipped out from between his lips and his hips that this, this life, this "everything" you know is a mere paper construction. You, my TV dinner–sucking, glazed-eyed friends, are living in . . . THE MATRIX . . . and all you have to do to see the *real* world, God and Satan's glorious kingdom on Earth, all you have to do to taste real life is to risk being your true self . . . to dare . . . to watch . . . to listen . . . to all the late-night staticky-voiced deejays playing "race" records blowing in under the radar, shouting their tinny AM radio manifesto, their stations filled with poets, geniuses, rockers, bluesmen, preachers, philosopher kings, speaking to YOU from deep in the heart of your own soul. Their voices sing, "Listen . . . listen to what this world is telling you, for it is calling for your love, your rage, your beauty, your sex, your energy, your rebellion . . . because it needs YOU in order to remake itself. In order to be reborn into something else, something maybe better, more godly, more wonderful, it needs US."

This new world is a world of black and white. A place of freedom where the two most culturally powerful tribes in American society find common ground, pleasure and joy in each other's presence. Where they use a common language to speak with . . . to *BE* with one another.

A "human being" proposed this, helped bring it to pass, a "boy," a nobody, a national disgrace, a joke, a gimmick, a clown, a magician, a guitar man, a prophet, a visionary? Visionaries are a dime a dozen . . . This was a man who didn't *see* it coming . . . he WAS it coming, and without him, white America, you would not look or act or think the way you do.

A precursor of vast cultural change, a new kind of man, of modern human, blurring racial lines and gender lines and having . . . FUN! . . . FUN! . . . the real kind. The life-blessing, wall-destroying, heart-changing, mind-opening bliss of a freer, more liberated existence. FUN . . . it is waiting for you, Mr. and Mrs. Everyday American, and guess what? It is your *birthright*.

A "man" did this. A "man" searching for something new. He willed it into existence. Elvis's great act of love rocked the country and was an early echo of the coming civil rights movement. He was the kind of new American whose "desires" would bring his goals to fruition. He was a singer, a guitar player who loved black musical culture, recognized its artistry, its mastery, its power, and yearned for intimacy with it. He served his nation in the army. He made some bad movies and a few good ones, threw away his talent, found it again, had a great comeback and, in true American fashion, died an untimely and garish death. He was not an "activist," not a John Brown, not a Martin Luther King Jr., not a Malcolm X. He was a showman, an entertainer, an imaginer of worlds, an unbelievable success, an embarrassing failure and a fount of modern action and ideas. Ideas that would soon change the shape and future of the nation. Ideas whose time had come, that challenged us to decide if we would all be attending a funeral of national destruction and decline or dancing while birthing the next part of the American story.

I don't know what his thoughts were on race. I don't know whether he thought about the broader implications of his actions. I do know this is what he did: lived a life he was driven to live and brought forth the truth that was within him and the possibilities within us. How many of us can say that?

That we committed all of ourselves to something? Dismissed as a national joke, he held out a dream of the kind of country this could be, and soon we would go there . . . kicking, screaming, lynching, burning, bombing, saving, preaching, fighting, marching, praying, singing, hating and loving our way forward.

When it was over that night, those few minutes, when the man with the guitar vanished in a shroud of screams, I sat there transfixed in front of the television set, my mind on fire. I had the same two arms, two legs, two eyes; I looked hideous but I'd figure that part out . . . so what was missing? THE GUITAR!! He was hitting it, leaning on it, dancing with it, screaming into it, screwing it, caressing it, swinging it on his hips and, once in a while, even playing it! The master key, the sword in the stone, the sacred talisman, the staff of righteousness, the greatest instrument of seduction the teenage world had ever known, the . . . the . . . "ANSWER" to my alienation and sorrow, it was a reason to live, to try to communicate with the other poor souls stuck in the same position I was. And . . . they sold 'em right downtown at the Western Auto store!

The next day I convinced my mom to take me to Diehl's Music on South Street in Freehold. There, with no money to spend, we rented a guitar. I took it home. Opened its case. Smelled its wood (still one of the sweetest and most promising smells in the world), felt its magic, sensed its hidden power. I held it in my arms, ran my fingers over its strings, held the real tortoiseshell guitar pick in between my teeth, tasted it, took a few weeks of music lessons . . . and quit. It was TOO FUCKIN' HARD! Mike Diehl, guitarist and owner of Diehl's Music, didn't have any idea how to teach whatever Elvis was doing to a young shouter who wanted to sing the elementary school blues. Despite incredible access to these amazing machines, he remained clueless about their real power. Earthbound like everyone else in 1950s America, he was all "Buzzing on the B string," staff paper and hours of stupendously boring technique. I WANTED . . . I NEEDED . . . TO ROCK! NOW! I still can't read music to this day, and back then, my seven-year-old fingers couldn't even get around that big fret board. Frustrated and embarrassed, shortly, I told my mom it was a no-go. There was no sense wasting her hard-earned cash.

The sunny morning I had to return the guitar, I stood in front of six or so of the neighborhood guys and gals in my backyard. I gave my first and last show for quite a while: I held the guitar . . . I shook it . . . I shouted at it . . . I banged on it . . . I sang voodoo nonsense . . . I did everything but *play* it . . . all to their laughter and great amusement. I sucked. It was a joyful and silly-assed pantomime. That afternoon, sad but a little relieved, I dropped the guitar off back at Diehl's Music. It was over for now, but for a moment, just a moment, in front of those kids in my backyard . . . I smelled blood.

# EIGHT

# RADIO DAYS

My mom loved music, Top 40 music; the radio was always on in the car and in the kitchen in the morning. From Elvis on out, my sister and I shuffled out of bed and downstairs to be greeted by the hit records of the day pouring out of the tiny radio that sat on the top of our refrigerator. Slowly, certain songs caught my attention. At first it was the novelty records—the Olympics, "Western Movies"; the Coasters, "Along Came Jones"—the great narrative clowning records where the groups let loose with rock 'n' roll comedy and sounded like they were just having fun. I wore out the jukebox at our local luncheonette pumping it full of my mom's dimes to hear Sheb Wooley's "The Purple People Eater" over and over again ("Mr. Purple People Eater, what's your line? . . . Eatin' purple people and it sure is fine"). I stayed up all one summer night with my tiny Japanese transistor radio tucked under my pillow counting the times they played Lonnie Donegan's "Does Your Chewing Gum Lose Its Flavor (On the Bedpost Overnight)?"

Records that ultimately held my interest were the ones where the singers sounded simultaneously happy and sad. The Drifters, "This Magic Moment," "Saturday Night at the Movies," "Up on the Roof"—records that summoned the joy and heartbreak of everyday life. This music was filled with deep longing, a casually transcendent spirit, mature resignation and . . . hope . . . hope for that girl, that moment, that place, that night when everything changes, life reveals itself to you, and you, in turn, are revealed. Records that longed for some honest place, some place of one's own . . . the movies, downtown, uptown, up on the roof, under the boardwalk, out of the sun, out of sight, somewhere above or below the harsh glare of the adult world. The adult world, that place of dishonesty, deceit, unkindness, where people slaved, were hurt, compromised, beaten, defeated, where they died—thank you, Lord, but for now, I'll take a pass. I'll take the pop world. A world of romance, metaphor; yes, there is tragedy ("Teen Angel"!), but there is also immortality, eternal youth, a seven-day weekend and no adults ("It's Saturday night and I just got paid. I'm a fool about my money, don't try to save"). It's a paradise of teenage sex where school . . . is permanently out. There, even that great tragedian Roy Orbison, a man who had to sing his way out of an apocalypse waiting around every corner, had his "pretty woman" and a home on "Blue Bayou."

Through my mother's spirit, love and affection, she imparted to me an enthusiasm for life's complexities, an insistence on joy and good times, and the perseverance to see the hard times through. Has there ever been a more comforting, sadder song than Sam Cooke's "Good Times"? It's a vocal performance steeped in weary self-knowledge and the ways of the world . . . "Get in the groove and let the good times roll . . . we gonna stay here 'til we soothe our soul . . . if it takes all night long . . ." Slowly the musical sounds of the late fifties and early sixties drew down into my bones.

In those days if you were broke the only family entertainment you had was a "drive." Gas was cheap, thirty cents a gallon, so nightly my grandparents, mother, sister and I cruised the streets to the outer edges of town. It was our treat and ritual. On warm nights, with the windows in our big sedan wide open, first we'd roll down Main Street, then on out to the southwest end of town to the edge of Highway 33, where we'd make our scheduled stop at the Jersey Freeze ice-cream stand. We'd bounce out of the car and up to the sliding window, where you had your choice of two flavors . . . count 'em . . . two . . . vanilla and chocolate. I didn't like either but I loved those wafer cones. The guy behind the counter who owned the place would save me the broken ones and sell them to us for five cents or slip me one for free. My sister and I would sit on the hood of the car in silent ecstasy with the Jersey humidity smothering all sound but for the night crickets humming in the nearby woods. The yellow outdoor lighting would act like a neon flame for hundreds of flitting, circling summer bugs. We'd watch as they buzzed the exterior of the whitewashed ice-cream stand, then we were off and away as the huge plaster Jersey Freeze ice-cream cone, perched precariously on top of the little cinder-block building, slowly disappeared in our rear window. We'd ride the back roads to the north end of town, where scratching the sky in the fields bordering the Monmouth Memorial Home was the town radio tower. It had three bright red lights rising along its gray steel structure. As our radio glowed with the otherworldly sound of late-fifties doo-wop, my mother would explain to me that there in the high grass stood a tall dark giant, invisible against the black night sky. The ascending lights were merely the shining red "buttons" on his jacket. We would always end our journey with a ride past the "buttons." As my eyes grew heavy and we turned toward home, I'd swear I could see the outline of the giant's dark figure.

'Fifty-Nine, '60, '61, '62, '63 . . . the beautiful sounds of American popular music. The calm before the storm of the Kennedy assassination, a quiet America, of lost lovers' laments wafting along the airwaves. On the weekend, sometimes the "ride" would take us all the way to the shore, to the amusements and carnival of Asbury Park or the quieter beaches of Manasquan. We'd park facing the waters of the inlet. Besides the kitchen table, the Manasquan Inlet was my dad's favorite spot in the world. He would sit for hours alone in the car watching the boats come in from the sea. My sister and I would eat hot dogs at Carlson's Corner, changing into our pajamas with a towel wrapped around us on the beach as my mother stood guard. On the way home we'd stop for a double feature at the Shore Drive-In, falling asleep in the backseat, to be carried to our beds by my dad once back in Freehold. As we grew older, we'd step rock by rock out along the dark Manasquan jetty, which jutted east, disappearing into the night sea. There at jetty's end we'd stare out into the pitch-black nothing of the Atlantic, with only the distant sparkling lights of night-charter fishing boats revealing the horizon line. We'd listen to the ocean waves crashing rhythmically on the shore far behind us, the sea lapping against the rocks onto our bare and sandy feet. You could hear a Morse code, a message moving in over that great black expanse of water . . . with the stars burning the night sky bright above us, you could feel it . . . something British this way comes.

# NINE

# THE SECOND COMING

From over the sea, the gods returned, just in time. Rough days at home. My face exploding with acne, that old bastard and now national hero of mine, Ed Sullivan, was doing it for me one more time. Let the battle begin. "Ladies and gentlemen, from England . . . the Beatles!!" Ed said the words "the Beatles" better than anybody else in the world. He'd wind up on the "the," quickly punch and emphasize the "Beat," and then he was outta there on the "les." All rushing by me while jolting my system with ten thousand watts of high-voltage anticipation. I sat there, heart pounding, waiting for the first real look at my new saviors, waiting to hear the first redemptive notes come peeling off the Rickenbacker, Hofner and Gibson guitars in their hands. The Beatles . . . The Beatles . . . The Beatles . . . The Beatles . . . The

Beatles . . . The Beatles . . . an "it ain't no sin to be glad you're alive" mantra and simultaneously the worst and most glorious band name in all of rock 'n' roll history. In 1964, there were no more magical words in the English language (well . . . maybe "Yes, you can touch me there").

The Beatles. I first laid ears on them while driving with my mom up South Street, the radio burning brighter before my eyes as it strained to contain the sound, the harmonies of "I Want to Hold Your Hand." Why did it sound so different? Why was it so good? Why was I this excited? My mom dropped me off at home but I ran straight to the bowling alley on Main Street, where I always spent my first after-school hours hunched over the pool tables sipping a Coke and eating a Reese's Peanut Butter Cup. I slammed myself into the phone booth and called my girlfriend, Jan Seamen. "Have you heard the Beatles?"

"Yeah, they're cool . . ."

My next stop was Newbury's, the five-and-ten-cent store in the center of town. In the front door and an immediate right brought you to the tiny corner record section (there were no record stores in those days in our neck of the woods). There were just a few racks of singles for forty-nine cents a pop. There were no real albums for me, just a few Mantovani records or middle-of-the-road vocal artists, maybe a little jazz on the bottom shelf. They were never looked at. They were for "adults." The teenage world was a world of pure 45s. A small circular piece of wax with a half-dollar hole in the center you had to fill with a plastic adapter. Your record player at home still had three speeds, 78, 45 and 33 RPM. Hence, 45s. The first thing I found was something called *The Beatles with Tony Sheridan and Guests*. It was a rip-off. The Beatles backing some singer I'd never heard of doing "My Bonnie." I bought it. And listened to it. It wasn't great but it was as close as I could get.

I went back on a daily basis until I saw IT. *The* album cover, the greatest album cover of all time (tied with *Highway 61 Revisited*). All it said was *Meet the Beatles*. That was exactly what I wanted to do. Those four half-shadowed faces, rock 'n' roll's Mount Rushmore, and . . . THE HAIR . . . THE HAIR.

What did it mean? It was a surprise, a shock. You couldn't see them on the radio. It is almost impossible to explain today the effect of . . . THE HAIR. The ass whippings, insults, risks, rejections and outsider status you would have to accept to wear it. In recent years, only the punk revolution of the seventies would allow small-town kids the ability to physically declare their "otherness," their rebellion. In 1964, Freehold was redneck ugly and there was no shortage of guys who were willing to make their rejection of your fashion choices a physical affair. I ignored the insults, avoided the physical confrontations as best I could and did what I had to do. Our tribe was small, maybe two or three in all of my high school, but it would grow to be significant and mighty, then meaningless . . . but not for a while . . . and in the meantime each sunrise held the possibility of a showdown. At home all it meant was more fuel for the unpleasant fire burning between my dad and me. His first response was laughter. It was funny. Then, not so funny. Then, he got angry. Then, finally, he popped his burning question: "Bruce, are you queer?" He wasn't kidding. He'd have to get over it. But first, it would get a lot nastier.

At school I made my way. I only got in one real scrap on my walk home from high school. I'd had enough with the jokes and squared off against a kid I was sure I could beat in the driveway of a neighborhood home. We were soon surrounded by a small circle of sensation seekers. Before we started, in the spirit of full disclosure, he told me he knew karate. I thought to myself, "Bullshit. Who knows karate in 1966 New Jersey? . . . NO-FUCKING-BODY!" I threw a few haymakers and he caught me with a perfect karate chop to the Adam's apple . . . aaarrrrrgh. I spit up. I couldn't speak. It was over. Another great victory. We walked the rest of the way home together.

That summer, time moved slowly. Every Wednesday night I sat up in my room charting the weekly top twenty and if the Beatles were not firmly ensconced each week as lords of all radio, it would drive me nuts. When

"Hello Dolly" grabbed the top spot on the charts week after week, I was beside myself. Nothing against "Satchmo," one of the greatest musicians who ever lived, but I was fourteen and on a different planet. I lived for every Beatles record release. I searched the newsstands for every magazine with a photo I hadn't seen and I dreamed . . . dreamed . . . dreamed . . . that it was me. My curly Italian hair miraculously gone straight, my face clear of acne and my body squeezed into one of those shiny silver Nehru suits. I'm standing tall in a pair of Cuban-heeled Beatle boots. It didn't take me long to figure it out: I didn't want to *meet* the Beatles. I wanted to BE the Beatles.

After my father refused to pay a rent hike, we moved to 68 South Street and had . . . hot water! But to get it, we moved next to a Sinclair gas station, into another half house. In the half we didn't occupy lived a Jewish family. My mom and dad, no racists or anti-Semites, still felt the need to caution my sister and me that these were folks who . . . DID NOT BELIEVE IN JESUS! Any theological issues were immediately forgotten when I saw two gorgeous daughters, my new next-door neighbors, who carried with them a fabulous voluptuousness, full mouths, smooth dark skin and weighted breasts—oy! I immediately began imagining warm nights on the front porch, their tan legs pouring out of summer shorts, as we debated the Jesus question. Personally, I would've quickly thrown over our savior of two thousand years for one kiss, one run of an index finger over the coffee colored ankle of either of my new neighbors. Unfortunately, I was shy and they were chaste, still solidly under Yahweh's and Mom and Pop's sway. One evening when I did bring up the Jesus thing, it was like I'd said "fuck." Sweet palms were quickly raised to rose lips, followed by red-faced girl giggling. There would be many restless teenage nights at 68 South Street.

We had black friends, though only rarely did we enter each other's homes. There was a détente in the streets. The white and black adults were cordial but distant. The children played together. There was a lot of easy racism amongst the kids. Insults were exchanged. Arguments were either brushed off, settled by an apology or resolved by a quick beating, depending upon the severity of the offense and mood of the afternoon; then the games would continue. I ran into racist kids, kids who learned it at home a few houses down from mine, but I never ran into kids who wouldn't play with black kids until I bumped into the middle and upper-middle class. On the bottom, we were all lumped in together because of physical proximity and the need for another guy to play the outfield. Fifties racism was so presumed and casual that if a black friend was excluded from a game one afternoon at our "better" friend's house, so be it. Nobody took up the flag. A day later the usual gang, black and white, would all be playing together again and it would be forgotten . . . by us.

I was pals with the Blackwell brothers, Richard and David. David, a lanky, thin black kid, was my age and we hung out quite a bit. We rode bikes, played ball and spent a good amount of time together. We fought to see who was toughest. He'd clock me on the kisser with a couple of good rights and it was over; then we'd go back to playing. His brother Richard was a little older, tall and one of the coolest things I'd ever seen. He'd developed his own walk. It was a piece of art: a step forward with one leg and then a slow drag pulling up the other, a slight bend at the hip, the other arm bent at the elbow, wrist cocked as if smoking a cigarette in a holder; never in a hurry, he'd stride through the streets of Freehold like a jazz musician, his face expressionless and his eyes near half-mast. He spoke long and slow. He'd grace us with a few moments of his time and we'd leave like we'd been blessed by the pope of cool.

Racial tensions at Freehold High exploded into violence. If you entered the wrong restroom, it was lights-out and a beating. I entered the first-floor restroom one afternoon, walked up to the latrine next to a black friend. I went to speak. He just looked at the wall and said, "I can't talk to you right now." I was white and he was black; the lines had been drawn, even amongst neighborhood friends. There would be no communication until it was over, and it wouldn't be over for quite a while. The town erupted in rioting. There were harsh words spoken between two cars at a South Street light and a gun was fired into a car full of black kids. At my corner sub shop there was a demonstration after an elderly black man had been thrown out and had fallen and been injured. I stood on my porch watching just two houses down as the proprietor rushed into a black crowd wielding a meat cleaver. It was taken from him and it was amazing no one was killed. Someone was chased up onto the porch of the house next to mine and pushed through the front window. The times they were a-changing . . . the hard way.

# TEN

# THE SHOW MAN (LORD OF THE DANCE)

My showmanship skills developed early. Seasoned by the Zerilli blood that flowed through my veins, I was born 100 percent grade A ham. So to grab the spotlight before I could play, I DANCED! . . . somewhat. The main thing was I was willing to risk the ridicule of half of the neighborhood's population (the male half ) because I'd found out that the other half found a guy who would dance with them to something other than a bone-grinding slow song enthralling.

Bimonthly on Friday nights, St. Rose of Lima would open up its basement cafeteria and host a heavily chaperoned Catholic Youth Organization (CYO) dance for its wild-hormoned teens. On the dance floor I already had a head start. I'd been pulled out onto the living room rug at family gatherings to Twist with my mom ever since Chubby Checker smashed the hit parade to bits with "The Twist." (My mom even took us to the Atlantic

City Steel Pier to see Chubby "live" as he lip-synched to his hits. Then we went across the boardwalk and caught Anita Bryant on the same sun-filled summer afternoon.) Also I'd been going over to the YMCA Friday night canteen, just fifty steps from the door of my South Street home. This was absolutely forbidden territory by nuns' decree, and you would be racked and tortured in front of the smugly satisfied class of eighth graders on Monday morning if word leaked out that you'd joined the heathen class and their satanic Friday night rituals.

It was here, high in the shadowy bleachers, that I experienced my first kiss (Maria Espinosa!), my first dance floor hard-on (unknown, but could as well have been a wet mop) and the atmosphere of a basketball gym, lights seductively lowered and transformed into a greasy hardwood-floored wonderland. Before I'd stand on these same boards, strapped with my sky blue Epiphone guitar in my first band, the Castiles, I'd dance with anyone who'd have me. Often, still horribly insecure, I'd have to wait for the last few desperate records to get up the guts to cross the no-man's-land between the camps of the boys and girls and pop the question. But on a good night I'd spend the evening dancing with strangers from St. Rose's crosstown rival, the intermediate (gasp, public!) school. Who were these tight-skirted, smoky-eyed young girls, unfettered by the green St. Rose's jumper that tapped down the budding womanhood of my school's female population? Here were girls in their dimly lit, scented glory, gathered in small hushed circles that suddenly erupted into soft giggles as they eyed the guys across the room culling the herd. I was a complete outcast. I didn't really know the guys who were cloistered into their cliques, and there were only a few other eighth-grade Catholic school students who braved the Young Men's Christian Association soirees. I'd been lured to the Y by a secular neighborhood pal for after-school hoops and the pool table in the musty basement. But once I'd gotten the smell of the canteen (some mixture of leftover basketball sweat and dance-floor sex) in my self-consciously Roman nose, there was no going back.

Here I danced for the first time in public and limped those fifty steps back home, blue-balled after some close encounter with a woolen skirt. The chaperones sat up in the bleachers, armed with a flashlight that they flickered on you during the slow dances if things were looking a little hot and tight. Still there was only so much they could do. They were trying to stop a millennia of sexual hunger, and for that job a flashlight just wasn't going to cut it. At the end of the night, by the time Paul and Paula's "Hey Paula" was spun on the decidedly lo-fi gym sound system, every man and woman alike was throwing themselves onto the dance floor just to feel a body, almost any body, up against theirs. There in those death-defying clinches lay the promise of things to come.

By the time I got to the CYO dance at my own alma mater, I had some rudimentary skills. The poor souls who comprised most of my Catholic male colleagues didn't yet realize that GIRLS LOVE TO DANCE! So much so that they'll get on the dance floor with just about any geek who's got a few moves. That geek was ME! I had a ridiculous assortment of gyrations copped and exaggerated from the dances of the day. The Monkey, the Twist, the Swim, the Jerk, the Pony, the Mashed Potato—I mixed them all up into a stew of my own that occasionally got me on the floor with some of the finest women in town. This shocked my classmates, who'd only known me as the poor soul at the rear corner desk in class. I'd hear, "Hey, Springy, where'd you learn that?" Well, I'd practiced and practiced hard. Not just with my mom and at the Y but heavily in front of the full-length mirror tacked up to the back of my door in my bedroom. Way before I played broomstick guitar in front of it, me and that mirror spent hours together in a sweat-soaked frenzy, moving to the latest records of the day. I had a small suitcase stereo with a 45 adapter that held me in good stead, and I'd Frug and Twist and Jerk my way to a soggy T-shirt that wouldn't be rivaled 'til many years later in the midst of a fevered "Devil with a Blue Dress On" in front of a cavernous hall of twenty thousand screaming rock fans.

Then . . . come Friday, I'd slip on my tightest black stovepipe jeans, a red button-down shirt, matching red socks and black winklepicker shoes. I'd previously stolen some of my mother's hairpins, pinned my bangs down tight and slept on them so they'd come out as straight as Brian Jones's. I'd comb them out, then sit under a ten-dollar sunlamp my mother had gotten at the corner drugstore to try and combat some of my fiercest acne. I squeezed a half tube of Clearasil on the rest and stepped out of my bedroom, down the stairs, out the front door and onto the street. Show me the dance floor.

ELEVEN

# WORKINGMAN'S BLUES

My parents had no money for a second shot at the guitar, so there was just one thing to do: get a job. One summer afternoon my mom took me to my aunt Dora's, where for fifty cents an hour I would become the "lawn boy." My uncle Warren came out and showed me the ropes. He demonstrated how the lawn mower worked, how to cut the hedges (not too short, not too long), and I was hired. I went immediately to the Western Auto store, an establishment in the town's center specializing in automotive parts and cheap guitars. There amongst the carburetors, air filters and fan belts hung four acoustic guitars, ranging from the unplayable to the barely playable. They looked like nirvana to me and they were attainable. Well, one was attainable. I saw a price tag hanging off of one funky brown model that read "Eighteen dollars." Eighteen dollars? That was more money than I had ever held in my hand at one time. A lot more.

After a while I noticed my "living expenses" were cutting into my savings from my job at Aunt Dora's, so I was going to have to step up my workload. Across the street from my aunt's house was a lovely, older white-haired lady named Mrs. Ladd. She wanted her house painted and her roof tarred. My grandfather, when his electrician business went south, had become a housepainter, and I'd wielded a brush on the walls of our own home a few times. How hard could it be? I enlisted my pal Mike Patterson to join my workforce and together we'd finish it off in no time. Mrs. Ladd bought the paint, showed us what she wanted, was meticulous: black shutters, white house, period. If she didn't like the way the paint was lying, you did it again. One week I had to miss a day's work. Mike said "no problem," he'd handle it. When I came back, one whole side of the house had been painted yellow! "Mike . . . Did you clean the brushes?" "I thought I did." One more time. We got it done, it didn't look too bad and we went on to the roof. I knew nothing about tarring a roof, so Mike led the way. It was midsummer New Jersey, 90 percent humidity, Fahrenheit ninety-five degrees; the tar was hot, sticky and burning as we slathered it on in the midday sun . . . hell on Earth.

It was done. Me and my twenty dollars went straight downtown. The salesman pulled my ugly brown dream out of the window and snipped off the price tag, and it was mine. I skulked home with it, not wanting my neighbors to know of my vain and unrealistic ambitions. I hauled it up to my bedroom and closed the door like it was some sex tool (it was!). I sat down, held it in my lap and was utterly confused. I had no clue about how to begin. The strings were thick as telephone wires, so I just started making noise, playing by ear. If I accidentally hit on something that sounded like music, I tried to remember it and do it again. I concentrated mainly on the lower-sounding strings, trying to make a "thunk, thunk" sound, a rhythm. It hurt like hell. My soft, pink fingertips were not prepared for the cables strung across this wooden box pretending to be an instrument. I stood up, went to the mirror on the back of my bedroom door, slung the guitar across my hips and stood there. For the next two weeks, until my fingers screamed for mercy, I worked up a whole repertoire of non-tunes to be played on an untuned guitar. I convinced myself I was getting somewhere, then fate and family intervened. My mom, Virginia and I went one Sunday to visit our aunt Eda. Her son, Frank, was an ace accordionist and every time we'd visit, he'd be called on to bust out his box and swing through "Lady of Spain" or some other accordion anthem. (Inspired, I actually took a shot at the accordion one Christmas, ensuring job security for E Street keyboardist and accordionist Danny Federici forever after. It was impossible.)

One Sunday, Frank came into the living room with a guitar instead of his candy-wagon accordion. He proceeded to wail through the folk hits of the moment. The folk boom was full throttle at the time. *Hootenanny* was a prime-time television show and Frank had picked up the guitar and was playing it pretty well. That weekend he sat on the living room floor, guitar in hand, wearing a white T-shirt, black socks, black chinos and white sneakers (I thought this was the coolest thing I'd ever seen up close and I immediately returned home and tried to emulate the look). He was doing a lot better than I was. He took me into his room, showed me how to tune the guitar, taught me how to read chord charts out of an American folk music collection, gave me the book and sent me home. I tuned my guitar as best I could and real- ized immediately I'd have to start from scratch. All of my non-tuned "tunes" were now revealed as the complete crap they were. I opened up the book, went to "Greensleeves," read the opening E-minor chord (only needs two fingers!) and set back to work. It was a beginning. A real beginning. Over the next few months, I learned most of the major and minor chords; scrubbed my way through as many folk standards I could; showed my mother what I was accomplishing, to her encouragement; then put together the C, F and G chords that allowed me to play "Twist and Shout." This was my first rock 'n' roll song. It was good-bye to "lawn boy" and the only real job I would hold my entire life. "Well shake it up, baby!"

# TWELVE

# WHERE THE BANDS ARE

Five months later, I'd beaten my Western Auto special half to death. My fingers were strong and callused. My fingertips were as hard as an armadillo's shell. I was ready to move up. I had to go electric. I explained to my mother that to get in a band, to make a buck, to get anywhere, I needed an electric guitar. Once again, that would cost money we didn't have. Eighteen dollars wasn't going to cut it this time. In my room I had a cheesy pool table I'd gotten the Christmas before when I planned to follow in my father's footsteps as a pool shark. I got pretty decent playing in the basement of the Y on canteen nights, but I never got good enough to challenge my old man. However, it still was good cover to get my girlfriends up into my bedroom. Once I'd romanced them to the bed I'd lean up once in a while and toss the pool balls across the table to keep the old man happy down in the kitchen. But by now the thrill was gone. Christmas was coming. I made a deal with my mom: if I'd sell the pool table, she'd try to come up with the balance for an electric guitar I'd spotted in the window of Caiazzo's Music Store on Center Street. The price was sixty-nine dollars and it came complete with a small amplifier. It was the cheapest they had but it was a start.

I sold my pool table for thirty-five dollars; a guy tied it to the roof of his car and headed out the drive. So there on one slushy Christmas Eve, I stood with my mother staring into Caiazzo's window at a sunburst, one-pickup Kent guitar, made in Japan. It looked beautiful, wondrous and affordable. I had my thirty-five dollars and my mother had thirty-five dollars of finance-company money. She and my father borrowed from season to season, paying off their debt just in time to borrow again. Sixty-nine dollars would be the biggest expenditure of my life and my mother was going out on a limb for me one more time. In we went. Mr. Caiazzo lifted it out of the window and stuck it into a leatherette cardboard case, and we drove home with my first electric guitar. In the living room I plugged in my new amp. Its tiny six-inch speaker "roared" to life. It sounded awful, distorted beyond all recognition. The amp had one control, a volume knob. It was about the size of a large bread box but I was in the game.

My guitar was as cheap as they came but compared to the junker I'd been playing, it was a Cadillac. The strings were smooth wound. Their distance to the fret board was minimal and allowed for easy intonation with the slightest pressure. I got better fast and was soon meeting at a friend's house for jam sessions. I knew a drummer, Donnie Powell. We convened in his living room while his parents were out and made the most god-awful racket you've ever heard. Being able to play a little was one thing; playing "together" was something else . . . uncharted territory.

The one tune every aspiring ax man struggled to master in those days was Bill Doggett's "Honky Tonk." It was unbelievably rudimentary, theoretically within the grasp of the most spastic idiot, and a hit record! "Honky Tonk" was a two-string blues concerto, a low-down dirty stripper's groove, and is still a cool record today. Donnie, the drummer, taught it to me and the two of us hacked at it like ax murderers. Years before the White Stripes, the two of us beat the crap out of the blues . . . except we stunk! Singing? . . . Into what? With what? No one had a microphone or a voice. It was just way below garage-level thrashing, lasting all night long until his parents came home.

We called ourselves the Merchants. A few other neighborhood kids came in, there were a few more exuberant, painful rehearsals, and then the day was done. It was finished and back to my room I went. But . . . there was one kid in the neighborhood who could really play. He'd taken a few years of guitar lessons. His dad was a successful businessman. He had a Gibson guitar—a real instrument—and a real amp. He knew how to read music. I spoke to him and drafted him into a revamped Merchants, now called the Rogues (Freehold version, not to be confused with the later Shore version consisting of actual playing, singing musicians). Suddenly, we sounded close to music. My amp was a joke, so he let me plug into the spare channel of his. We even found a bass player—well, someone who had a bass and, more important, another amp. He joined our combo. He couldn't play but he was a nice, handsome Italian kid and his friendship would literally save my ass from a beating years into the future in a funky little backwoods dive down Route 9 called the IB Club. We plugged on, rehearsing semiregularly, with one radical and rebellious idea: someone would sing.

## Showtime

In small-town Jersey in 1964, no one sang. There were vocal groups with backing bands. There were bands with no vocalists who performed strictly instrumentals, taking the Ventures as their guiding light, but there were no self-contained playing, singing combos. That was one of the revolutions the Beatles brought with them when they came to America. You wrote the songs, you sang the songs, you played the songs. Before that, a typical local band's set list would consist of "Pipeline" by the Chantays; "Sleep Walk" by Santo and Johnny; "Apache," "Out of Limits," "Penetration," "Haunted Castle"—all purely instrumental pieces. In the early sixties at a high school dance, a top hometown band like the Chevelles would play all night, un-miked, without a word being uttered to the audience of frantic dancers. The Chevelles were the instrumental kings of our local scene (challenged up Route 9 by the Victorians). They were real musicians, teachers at Mike Diehl's music school, with good equipment and matching suits.

One day our young combo heard of Sunday matinee shows for teen-agers at the Freehold Elks Club. It cost thirty-five cents to come in and all the bands played for free to a crowd of about seventy-five locals. The show was run by an unusual husband-and-wife team of entertainers, Bingo Bob and Mrs. Bob. They were a circus act and a little on the freaky side but for a few months, until someone stole one of Mrs. Bob's maracas and Bingo launched into a psycho fury, locking us all in the Elks Club until someone pulled a maraca out of their ass, it was a good place for your first baptism by fire. The almost strictly instrumental bands would set up in a circle and square off for a few hours.

With anxiety somewhere around pre–Super Bowl levels, my band-mates and I loaded our gear into our parents' cars, hauled it down to the Elks and set up. Being the newest group, we went on last. We spun through our tunes; panic and cold sweat aside, we weren't bad. Then . . . we released our secret weapon: me . . . *singing* "Twist and Shout." I blared my way through it, putting on the hip-shaking show of my young life, or so I thought. There was a huge, grilled forties-style microphone plugged into the Elks' few hor-rible squawk box speakers, which passed for a sound system. I hid behind the big microphone and screamed my head off . . . "Ahhhh, ahhhh, ahhhh, ahhhhh . . . well shake it up, baby, now . . ." An embarrassing performance but I felt pretty good about it. Some kids even told us we sounded "great." I thought almost everyone else was better than us. They had nicer equipment, more experience, but . . . barely anyone sang.

From there we were booked at a high school dance opening for the

Chevelles. Being booked to play at your high school was the top, top gig in town. It was a risky booking for us. That night we went down to Diehl's and rented an extra Gretsch amplifier with reverb! Reverb, that magic echo chamber that seemed to make you immediately sound like all your favorite records and lent an air of professionalism to what you were doing. Down to the Freehold Regional High School gymnasium we went. We were going to blow the sheet music out of the Chevelles and send them and their fancy music lessons crying back to Mike Diehl's music school. We were the "new wave." No matching suits, no music school, just blues shouting and rock 'n' roll.

Trouble began almost immediately. Our lead guitarist had forgotten his guitar strap, so he had to play the entire set with one knee propped up on his amp supporting his guitar . . . not cool. Also, unfortunately, our bass player remained unable as of yet to play a note, so he stood, knee up (no strap either) on his amp (the one that got him in the band), with his bass turned firmly off for the evening. I brayed into the high school public address system microphone and a nightmare of unintelligible sound poured forth from somewhere in the rafters of the gymnasium. What was even worse, we were so excited about acquiring reverb, my lead guitarist and I plugged into our rented amp, turned the reverb on full and reduced our sound to a quivering, echoing mash, a cheese-ball shitstorm of submerged instrumentation that sounded like it was being puked up from the bottom of some dragon-infested ocean. Our new "effect" reduced whatever we were playing to meandering gibberish. (Full reverb in a high school gymnasium . . . don't try it, young 'uns!) It was humiliating. You could tell as it was going by. I stood there head down, red faced, knowing we sounded awful and without a clue as to what to do about it. The crowd huddled close in front of our band expecting . . . something; we'd been bragging all week. Their faces told the story . . . "What the fu . . . ?" Then the Chevelles came on and smoked. They were professionals. They played real music, as boring and corny as it was. They knew how to control their instruments and perform before a crowd.

We stood there watching, newly humbled, with a few die-hard pals telling us we "weren't so bad."

We went back to the drawing board, except this time, I'd end up there alone. I was informed shortly after our gig by my pal, the guy *I'd* brought into the band, that I'd been voted out. My guitar was "too cheap" and wouldn't stay in tune, and he unnecessarily added that he'd seen the same "piece of junk" in New York City for thirty dollars. Ouch . . . that hurt. I told my mom that day as I walked her home from work that I'd been kicked out of the band but I didn't have the heart to tell her why. She'd anted up everything she had for that "piece of junk" and I was going to make it work.

## In My Room

That night I went home, pulled out the second Rolling Stones album, put it on and taught myself Keith Richards's simple but great guitar solo to "It's All Over Now." It took me all night but by midnight I had a reasonable facsimile of it down. Fuck 'em, I was going to play lead guitar. For the next several months (years!) I woodshedded, spending every available hour cradling my Kent, twisting and torturing the strings 'til they broke or until I fell back on my bed asleep with it in my arms. Weekends I spent at the local CYO, YMCA or high school dances. Dancing was over; I was silent, inscrutable, arms folded, standing in front of the lead guitarist of whatever band was playing, watching every move his fingers made. After the dance, when the other kids were hanging out, heading for pizza at Federici's or trying to make it with the girls, I rushed home to my room and there 'til early in the morning, my guitar unplugged so as not to disturb the house, I tried to remember and play everything I'd seen.

Before long I began to feel the empowerment the instrument and my work were bringing me. I had a secret . . . there was *something* I could do, something I might be good at. I fell asleep at night with dreams of rock 'n' roll glory in my head. Here's how one would go: The Stones have a gig at

Asbury Park's Convention Hall but Mick Jagger gets sick. It's a show they've got to make, they need a replacement, but who can replace Mick? Suddenly, a young hero rises, a local kid, right out of the audience. He can "front": he's got the voice, the look, the moves, no acne, and he plays a hell of a guitar. The band clicks. Keith is smiling and suddenly, the Stones aren't in such a rush to get Mick out of his sickbed. How does it end? Always the same . . . the crowd goes wild.

THIRTEEN
# THE CASTILES

I was sitting in my South Street home one afternoon when a knock came at our front door. It was George Theiss, a local guitarist and singer who'd heard through my sister that I played the guitar. I'd seen George around the Elks. He told me there was a band forming and they were looking for a lead guitarist. While I hesitated to call myself a lead guitarist, I had been hard at it for a while and worked up some very rudimentary "chops." We walked across town to Center Street and into a little half-shotgun house fifty feet up the block from where the metal-on-metal war of the rug mill spilled out open factory windows onto the streets of Texas. In Texas I'd slip on my guitar and join my first real band.

There I met Tex and Marion Vinyard. They were friends of George who had decided to surrender the fifteen square feet of what was called their dining room to local teenage noisemakers. It was a very informal neighborhood, black and white separated somewhat by the rug mill but generally hanging around the streets together, with Tex and Marion's tiny apartment seeming to be the hub of some sort of neighborhood teen club. They were in their thirties and childless, so they took in "strays," kids who either didn't have much of a home life or were just looking to get out of the house to someplace less confining and a little more welcoming. Tex was a temperamental, redheaded, comb-overed, loudmouthed, lascivious, pussy-joke-telling factory worker. Like my pops, he was rarely spotted out of his uniform, khaki work shirt and pants, pocket protector and all. He was also generous, loving, sweet-hearted and one of the most giving adults I'd met up to that time.

Tex and Marion seemed stranded between the teen world and adulthood, so they made a home for themselves and a surrogate parental life somewhere in the middle. They weren't your parents but they weren't your peers either. As we howled away, pushing out the walls of their little home with banging guitars and crashing drums, with the neighbors a mere two inches of drywall away (what tolerance!), they made the rules and set the agenda for what would fly and what would not. Band practice started at three thirty and ended at six, taking place immediately after school. Tex became our manager and Marion the house mother and seamstress to a team of misfit townie rock-'n'-rollers. There was a small collection of teenage girls (bring the guitars and they will come). There was flirting, listening to music, Tex's cackling innuendo followed by Marion's "Teeeeeeexxxxx . . . cut that out!" Some kissing, hand holding, but not much else, not in the house anyway. George, who bore a resemblance to both Elvis and Paul McCartney (the King AND a Beatle, the true double whammy!), was our resident lothario and did pretty well for himself. The rest of us took what we could clumsily find but it was mostly all about the music.

The band consisted of George, myself, drummer Bart Haynes, bass player Frank Marziotti and a revolving set of tambourine-killing hatchet men. The front man position was one for which few locals qualified at the time because you needed to actually have rhythm and sing. We were all little white boys with weak time and voices, but hey, that didn't stop the Stones, and the Stones were our Holy Grail and blueprint of cool. We needed our Mick, a guy out front. First we just took the toughest guy we knew and put him out there. He couldn't sing a note and was visibly uncomfortable as we lessened and lessened his duties until they were reduced to the breathing section in Ian Whitcomb's wheezingly lecherous "You Turn Me On." This was a guy who was now in the band just to breathe! We knew it wasn't working out and drew straws to see which one of us would get a whipping when he brought the bad news. Hey . . . that's what you have a manager for! We let Tex do it. Our "singer" went peacefully with a sigh of relief. After that we picked the best-looking guy we could find, the guy with the coolest hair in school. He looked great onstage and played a pretty good tambourine but, alas, could not sing. George was the best vocalist we had. He had a real voice and charisma and did the job well. I was considered toxic in front of a microphone, my voice the butt of many of Tex's jokes, and years later, after selling millions of records, I would visit Tex and he would take grand pleasure in sneering at me, "You still can't sing. George is the singer."

Tex was my first surrogate father figure. He was loving in his own twisted way. More important, he was accepting. He cherished and encouraged your talents, took you for who you were and put his time, muscle, money and big black Cadillac, hauling equipment, all in service of your dreams. We'd stand together slobbering into the window of Caiazzo's Music over a new Shure microphone. Caiazzo's stood next to Ring's Barber Shop and just twenty feet across the street from the Vineyards' front door. At night as we sat on Tex's tiny stoop, Caiazzo's windows glowed with white pearl drum kits, metal-flake guitars and enough amplifier wattage to wake that dead, shit dump of a town from its stupefying slumber. Tex would sit there, silent, cigarette smoldering, and finally shout, "Fuck it, when I get paid on Friday, we're going to bring that baby home," and he would. Then he'd watch like a proud papa as his "boys" crowed like young roosters into the shiny new microphone and say, "Damn . . . that new Shure, now, that's a sound."

There were adults like Tex and Marion all across the United States, real unsung heroes of rock 'n' roll who made room in their homes and in their lives to cart the equipment; to buy the guitars; to let out their basements, their garages, for practice sessions; who'd found a place of understanding between the two combative worlds of teen life and adulthood. They would support and partake in the lives of their children. Without folks like these, the basements, the garages, the Elks clubs, the VFW halls would've been empty, and skinny, dreaming misfits would've had no place to go to learn how to turn into rock 'n' roll heroes.

## Our First Gig

The Castiles were named after a brand of shampoo George Theiss used. It was a name that fit with the times. There was still a remnant of the fifties doo-wop groups in it but it would also suit to take us toward the Valhalla of the rock and blues skiffle we emulated. Our set list was a mixture of pop hits, R & B, guitar instrumentals, even a version of Glenn Miller's "In the Mood" taught to us by Frank Marziotti so we would have a diverse repertoire. We even tucked an original song or two in here and there.

Our first gig was at the Angle-Inn Trailer Park on Route 33, just west of the Shore Drive-In. It was a summer afternoon cookout social for the residents. We set up in the shade under the overhang of a little garage and stood in front of an audience of maybe fifty souls. Our equipment was at its most primitive. We had Bart's drums, a few amps, and a mike plugged into one of the extra channels of our guitar amplifiers. The opening act was a local country group that featured as its singer a little girl about six or seven who stood on a stool singing Patsy Cline songs into a big radio broadcasting microphone. They were pretty good . . . and competitive. When we started making our noise, they got really pissed off because the crowd was responding. Dancing broke out. Always a good sign. Our lead singer did his breathing in "You Turn Me On," sending George and me into silent hysterics, and we finished up with—you guessed it—"Twist and Shout," as the trailer court went its summer, down-home version of bonkers. It was a huge success, convinced us we could make music and put on a show. And also that our front man must be fired immediately. I still remember the exhilaration . . . we moved people; we brought the energy and an hour or so of good times. We made raw, rudimentary, local but effective magic.

## Wipe Out

Frank Marziotti, our bass player, was a veteran of the local country music scene. He was still in his twenties but had the appearance of a rotund Italian wedding singer. He had wavy black hair combed straight back above an ethnic face and looked like he'd just come off the line working next to my father rather than like he played bass in a blistering, young, soul-rebel rock 'n' roll band. He struck a rather discordant note in our image. He was the only true musician amongst us. He taught me plenty of country-style guitar and played the smoothest bass you ever heard. The only problem was at every gig we'd hear the same question: "Why's your dad in the band?" It didn't bother us but it started to bother him, so he made his graceful exit and blond-haired Curt Fluhr—Brian Jones haircut, Vox amp, Hofner violin bass and all—came in to fill the position.

Bart Haynes, our hell-raising drummer, was impossible to put a leash on. He claimed to be mentally challenged and one of his famous quotes was "I am so fucking dumb." He was a solid timekeeper with one bizarre quirk—he could not play the drumbeat to "Wipe Out." In 1965, the performance of the Surfaris' "Wipe Out" was the yardstick for all aspiring drummers. This simple syncopated beat played on the tom-toms was considered the final sign of your mastery. Listening to it now, you can easily recognize it, great though it was, as a part for slobbering morons. But . . . the bottom line was at some point during the evening, if a drummer wanted to go home with his bona fides intact, he would HAVE to play "Wipe Out." Bart could not. No matter what he did or how hard he tried, his wrists simply refused to tap out that rudimentary rhythm. There was plenty of decent drumming in the blood and bones of Bart Haynes but "Wipe Out" was nowhere to be found. As the nights wore on, the smirking calls would come from com peting drummers in the rear of the crowd: "Play 'Wipe Out.'" At first they would be ignored, then Bart would rejoin with a few fuck-yous under his breath. Then . . . worst of all . . . he would be goaded . . . "Go on . . . Go on . . ." He'd say, "Play that motherfucker." So we would. And the moment of the great drum break would arrive and he would fail, time and time again. His sticks clacking together in his hands, the simple beat somehow going haywire until a stick dropped, his face would run fire-engine red, and the show'd be over. "You fuckers!"

Bart would shortly give up the sticks for good and join the marines. Rushing in one last afternoon, a goofy grin on his face, he told us he was going to Vietnam. He laughed and said he didn't even know where it was. In the days before his ship-out, he'd sit one last time at the drums, in his full dress blues, in Marion and Tex's dining room, taking one final swing at "Wipe Out." He was killed in action by mortar fire in Quang Tri Province. He was the first soldier from Freehold to die in the Vietnam War.

Vinnie "Skeebots" Manniello replaced Bart Haynes and was a swinging jazz-influenced drummer. Young, already married with a child by "Mrs. Bots," he contributed enormously to the professionalism of our band. From there on out it was YMCAs, CYOs, high schools, ice rinks, roller rinks, VFW halls, battles of the bands, Elks clubs, supermarket openings, officers' clubs, drive-in theaters, mental hospitals, beach clubs and any place you could set up a five-piece band that wanted decent local entertainment at a cheap price.

# To the East

Freehold stood dead center between two socially incompatible teen cliques. The "rah-rahs'" turf stretched east to the Shore and the "greasers'" territory ran south down Route 9. The floor at a Freehold Regional High School dance was a no-man's-land of circling cliques, with the rahs in one corner, the greasers in another, the black kids in theirs. There was some communication amongst the upper echelons, in the interest of either stopping or starting a fight, but otherwise it was everyone to their own little world. The rah-rahs danced to pop music, Top 40, beach music; the greasers took the floor to doo-wop, and the black kids to R & B and soul music. Motown was the only force that could bring détente to the dance floor. When Motown was played, everyone danced together. That tenuous brother-and-sisterhood ended with the last beat of the music and everyone slunk back to their UN-designated square of gym floor.

The rahs were the jock, madras-wearing, cheerleading, college-bound, slightly upscale teen contingent who were the homecoming kings and queens and who lorded it over most local high schools. I'm sure they continue to do so today as "preps" or whatever their latest nom de guerre is. You were either in or out. I was way out. The ground zero of rah-rah territory was the Sea Bright/Middletown/Rumson area of the Jersey Shore. There was money there and they did not let you forget it. When we came east to play upon their beaches on hot August afternoons, we were immediately put on notice that we hailed from the wrong side of the tracks. To get to the beach you had to wind your way through the stately homes of Rumson, Central Jersey's most prestigious and exclusive neighborhood. Old-growth trees and palatial estates tucked behind walls of lush green and iron gates let you know "you can look but you better not touch." When you hit the shore at Sea Bright, the beachfront was a long strand of private beach clubs serving the well-heeled. A wall of cabanas and parking lots blocked access to God's own Atlantic Ocean. The sea was there somewhere, but unless you slipped onto the one public beach, you were going to have to pay and pay big to get your toes wet. The teenyboppers, however, needed rabble-rousing entertainment on the weekends to get them off of Mom and Dad's ass while their parents were getting sloshed on martinis at the beach bar. So . . . east meets west . . . With our rep slowly growing, we were imported from the wastelands to do the dirty work.

First we had to lug our equipment onto the sand, where an extension cord had been laid for us to power up our amplifiers. It was sweltering, mid-August, and we were dressed in our full gear: black denim trousers, black Beatle boots, black faux-snakeskin vests purchased at the Englishtown auction, white tuxedo shirts, long hair (still a rarity) and very white "inlander" skin. We were not the Beach Boys. The response was always the same. The parents were amused and bored, the girls flirty and curious, the boys hostile.

As little tanned bikini bodies lined up in front of us, a grumbling from the crew-cut sportsters rose up behind them. We had only one option: to play. Play until they liked it, until they could hear it and, most important, until they DANCED! You had to get the girls dancing! Once the girls started to dance, everybody got happy and suddenly, you were not some threatening alien presence rocket-shipped in from the rings of Greaserville, you were just "in a band." We knew our work and the day usually ended on a good note, with the kids talking to us, wondering about the way we looked, where we came from (the dark interior), and occasionally with a hard-ass trying to start a fight. These were pretty well-supervised events and there was always an older lifeguard or an adult chaperone to keep the lid on. The parking lot was where you had to watch your back. You'd be busting your balls trying to squeeze your equipment back into the car and you'd hear, "What'd you say? What'd you say to me . . . ?" Of course, you hadn't said anything. You were just being set up for a friendly takedown. Time to go home.

# To the South

South of Freehold there were other challenges. The greasers were a teen subcult, leather-jacketed, sharkskin-suit-wearing, see-through-nylon-sock-clinging, beat-your-ass-with-an-Italian-shoe, pompadoured, preening, take-more-time-to-get-ready-for-school-in-the-morning-than-my-auntie-Jane, fight-you-at-the-drop-of-a-hat, Italian-descended, don't-give-a-fuck-about-you inhabitants of their own little terrestrial universe. Many of my better friends were "grease" (so named for their extensive use of hair products and fine, oily Italian skin). They were easier to deal with and understand than the rah-rahs as long as they didn't hold a grievance with you. These were the kids destined to live the decent hardworking lives of their parents and take up their fathers' trades, the future farmers, homemakers and baby makers, if they could scoot through these few years of wild pounding hormones without getting hurt or hurting someone else. If they could keep out of jail for this short stretch, most would go on to be the spine of American society—fixing the cars, working the factories, growing the food and fighting the wars.

Also south, down Route 9, stood Freewood Acres, the first subdivision any of us had ever seen. What distinguished Freewood Acres was not just its "first ever" status as a planned community but the fact that it counted as its inhabitants descendants of Genghis Khan: Mongolians. It was a long ride from the Russian steppes, but due to the grace of Alexandra Tolstoy, daughter of Leo of *War and Peace* fame, they'd arrived locally in the late forties after the war. Alexandra had a foundation that assisted in getting them out of the Soviets' reach, so, persecuted by Stalin and rabidly anti-Communist, they settled in Monmouth County. It was Siberia or New Jersey, a close one, but they were sprung from Stalin's cages and ended up literally on Highway 9. Their children became my classmates at Freehold High.

The Mongolians were physically very big Asians and they went strictly grease. Imagine the biggest Asian you've ever seen in three-quarter-length leather, dress shirt and trousers, winkle-picker shoes and a slick black pompadour that added another inch or two of height on an already-north-of-six-foot frame. These guys had great-great-granddaddies who rode hard and conquered the world, and their New Jersey offspring looked like they could do it again if pressed.

The greasers copped their whole look from the school's black community, which they were friendly with while at the same time virulently racist against. They were in deep pursuit of "uptown" style. The pristineness of the suits; the high-collared pink, lime green and baby blue shirts; the high-water trousers—their grooming was precise and not to be fucked with . . . YOU DO NOT TOUCH MY HAIR . . . YOU TOUCH MY HAIR AND WE FIGHT. A sensitive crew. The greasers were led by someone I'll call "Tony," a godfather before there was *The Godfather*. He walked through the halls of school with the most perfect coal-black pompadour you'd ever seen, attired impeccably in a three-quarter-length black waistcoat, with an Italian sex god's face out of every good little cheerleader's wet dream. He wore it like a king and was the head of the local gang.

Outside of school you'd see Tony regularly in the teen clubs, often wielding a silver-headed cane (occasionally against someone). He'd drift in, a small-town Caesar, mirror-shiny shoes barely touching the ground, surrounded quietly by his minions. Wherever he walked, people made room.

South, into the greaser turf all along Route 9, was where we went next to ply our trade. Route 9 held a chain of nightclubs and pizza parlors that on weekends catered to the teen set. First there was Cavatelli's Pizza near Lakewood. It was just a small highway pizza joint where the owner decided to pick up some extra cash on Friday and Saturday nights by turning out the tables and chairs, hiring a band and holding small dances in front of the pizza counter. The place was ruled by a hard-core contingent of greaser girls with teased bouffant hair, white lipstick, white skin, heavy eye shadow, leather boots, tight skirts, dive-bomber bras— think the Shangri-Las or Ronettes crossed with Amy Winehouse. The most powerful of these ladies was a gal named Kathy. You came in, you set up your stuff, you started to play . . . and nobody moved—nobody. A very uneasy hour would pass, all eyes on Kathy. Then when you hit the right song, she'd get up and start to dance, trance-like, slowly dragging a girlfriend out in front of the band. Moments later, the floor was packed and the evening would take off. This ritual played itself out time and time again. She liked us. We found out her favorite music and played the hell out of it. We became officially sanctioned as one of "Kathy's bands." It was all great, as long as she didn't like you *too* much. That would be very dangerous. Though Cavatelli's Pizza was to my memory mostly a girls' night out, there were always guys around the edges, and a murmur, a rumor, a sign of something more than friendship would not be good for your health. Along Route 9 you tried to cross no one.

Finally, we worked our way up to the IB Club. This was the big show down south. A greaser heaven on Earth. The best groups, real hit doo-wop recording acts, played there. Nicky Addeo was our local doo-wop god, with a falsetto that wet many a pair of cotton panties and could send chills up Satan's spine. He was the real deal and king of the old-school crowd that gathered at the IB. When he sang the Cadillacs' "Gloria," greaser church was in session. The dance floor'd be packed and all you could hear was the rustling of sharkskin hard-ons rubbing against cheap nylon stockings. Doo-wop was still the music of choice amongst the rocker contingent even in 1966, years after the British invasion. I've sung "What's Your Name" and the Five Satins' "In the Still of the Night" many, many times. Along Route 9 in the sixties, a handful of doo-wop numbers was essential to your survival.

For the Castiles this was a big booking. The floor was awash in leather and we'd tailored our set to satisfy. The secret ingredients were doo-wop, soul and Motown. This was the music that made the leather heart skip a beat. It took the dark, bloody romanticism of doo-wop, the true-to-life grit of soul and just that small hint of possible upward social mobility embedded in Motown to define what this crowd's lives were all about. Except for their Top 40 hits, the bohemian poses of the Stones or their other sixties brethren held little relevance to these kids' experience. Who could afford that? You had to fight, struggle, work, protect what was yours, remain true to your crew, your blood, your family, your turf, your greaser brothers and sisters and your country. This was the shit that would get you by when all the rest came tumbling down—when the bullshit was washed away in the next fashion trend and your gal was pregnant, your dad went to jail or lost his job and you had to go to work. When life comes knockin', it's the heartbroken doo-wop singer who understands regret and the price of loving, the hard-living soul man who understands "I take what I want, I'm a bad go-getter, yeah . . ." and the Motown divas, men and women, who know you've got to play a little bit of the white man's/rich man's game. You have to make thoughtful compromises that don't sell out your soul, that let you reach just a little bit higher until your moment comes and then *you* set the rules. This was the credo all along Route 9 and you'd better understand it or else you would die an ugly musical death while risking bodily injury on Saturday night.

## The Reckoning

It was a Saturday night like any other; we were booked into the IB Club and looking forward to a great gig. Though we were now dressing more like a British R & B group (we had outvoted Tex and ditched the uniforms), we'd established a good rapport with the crowd and were popular amongst the locals. It was all cool as long as you stayed away from their girls. We were now on our third lead singer, I'll call him "Benny," a significant improvement. He wasn't great-looking, he was a little older than us and out of high school, but he could sing all right. He was hanging around town, lived alone near me in the neighborhood, had a little bit of an older guy's cool and savvy, so one thing led to another and he ended up shaking his maracas in front of our band.

The club was full, maybe six hundred people, wall-to-wall leather, teased hair, pompadours and enough grease to keep your local garage in business for years. From the stage I saw the Red Sea part as Tony came in with his crew. It was the usual promenade, fun to watch actually. They filtered through the front door, suddenly changing the pace and temperature of the room. The night was now officially on. The Howell Township police visiting the IB Club for fights was not an uncommon occurrence. Public disturbance was many of the IB's patrons' passion and hobby. Hopefully, there were no beefs to be settled and everybody would go home happy and in one piece.

Out of the blue during a band break word filtered to the stage that if Benny did not come down and surrender himself to Tony's crew, they were coming up onstage within minutes to cripple everything and everyone on it. Huh? What happened?

In Middletown, New Jersey, there were two natural, physical phenomena, Gravity Hill and Thrill Hill. It was a common rite of passage to drive out from Freehold in your car and park at the foot of Gravity Hill, and (due to the "lay of the land"? The "mystical magnetic properties of the Earth"? New Jersey hoodoo?) once you shut your car dead off, it would mysteriously appear to slowly roll itself backward up the hill. I'd sat in my '60 'Vette on many occasions impressing some gal on a late-night date with this little blacktop parlor trick.

Thrill Hill was simply a radical and improperly graded rise in the road that when combined with enough speed would lift your car off its wheels, launching you and your passengers into the night for a little "airtime." The catch was that just over the rise of Thrill Hill was an old, low-hanging steel railroad bridge. The "thrill" was cutting that distance between your roof and the bridge. Too much height and you were going to have a really bad night.

As folklore had it, Benny had been on Thrill Hill one night driving a car of four, the sister of one of Tony's friends riding along. They supposedly caught enough of the bottom of the bridge to seriously injure his passengers while escaping with limited injuries himself . . . until now. The brother had petitioned the Godfather for justice, and it was about to be delivered. It would all be settled that night in the next few minutes. Benny offered to surrender himself. I don't think he meant it, and anyway, we wouldn't let that happen. I knew Tony through an old bandmate, which might save me from a beating, but everything else—band, equipment and all—would go. There was only one thing to do. The last shameful respite of any self-respecting Route 9 denizen . . . call the cops. Now! That's what the manager of the place did on our behalf. Benny was escorted off the stage and out of the building by police, walking through a gauntlet of hard stares and leather into the township police car and out of our lives forever. He never played another note with the Castiles, his tambourine permanently retired.

## Work

The Castiles were now a pretty well-honed unit. We played regularly in many different venues for a wide variety of audiences. Firemen's conventions, the Marlboro Psychiatric Hospital (where, yes, the inmates sang along vigorously to the Animals' "We Gotta Get Out of This Place"). One evening we were playing the Surf and Sea Beach Club on the Sea Bright strip, deep in the heart of rah land. We were opening up for a well-known traveling Top 40 cover band. There were a few bands of this type. They didn't have hits of their own but had gotten so good at what they did, they broke their local bonds and were actually able to make a traveling gig out of playing other artists' music. The place was packed with surly, suntanned faces, chinos and madras skirts. We came out and started playing our recent concoction of psychedelic blues, and I felt something wet. We were being spit on, literally, way before it was a punk badge of honor. It was only a few guys, but it was enough. We played our set and left, furious. A year later, the same people would be cheering us at Le Teendezvous, a club in Shrewsbury catering primarily to the rah-rah crowd but the best gig going along the Shore, with their girls hitting on us. We'd come back and victoriously play Surf and Sea many times, but not that night. We took our hundred dollars and headed back inland to our lowly townies.

Though I had a group of good rah friends I'd met along the beach, between the rahs and the greasers, I guess I felt I had more in common with my pompadoured brethren back toward home. They would administer swift justice but would not lord it over you the way our madras-wearing, beer-drinking cousins to the east would. I guess it was just a class thing. I could still feel the shadow of that spit that hit me long ago when I moved to Rumson in 1983, sixteen years later. At thirty-three years old, I still had to take a big gulp of air before walking through the door of my new home.

Carrying on, there were battles of the bands, occasional weddings and our first performance for an entirely black audience as the only white act on the Tri-Soul Revue. The Tri-Soul Revue was held at the Matawan-Keyport Roller Drome and promoted by a young black hipster. He liked what we did and booked us. We also opened for and backed the Exciters. The Exciters, a classic early-sixties vocal group, had a big hit with "Tell Him" and were the first real recording artists we'd ever come in contact with. The night consisted of a record hop with an onstage deejay and live music (us). We were set up down on the dance floor amongst the dancers. The Exciters met us in the roller rink locker room, where the gorgeous girl singers stripped down and got into their slinky gold lamé gowns right in front of us. (Teenage heart attacks and rock 'n' roll heaven!) Then they went out onto the stage, where'd they lip-sync to their records, following it up by performing live versions of the same hits down on the floor, backed by the Castiles. We finished our set filled with soul, soul and more soul. We'd decently won over a black crowd suspicious of the white-boy hippies and backed the Exciters without embarrassing ourselves. We'd been rehearsed that afternoon by Herb Rooney, their singer and group leader. I watched the way he led a bunch of musically illiterate teenagers through their paces 'til they could reasonably back his group. We went home that night adding another notch to our belts for a job decently done, for lessons learned and for entertaining a tough audience that could've gone the other way.

My Kent guitar had long given way to a teal-blue solid-body Epiphone, a real instrument. Epiphone, a subsidiary of Gibson, made good guitars just under the price range of the world-class Gibsons. Mine was a sweet hand-me-down from Ray Cichon, lead guitarist of the Motifs, who were local legends and the first real rock 'n' roll band I'd ever seen.

## The Motifs

Walter and Ray Cichon were two brothers from Howell Township, New Jersey. Ray was so tall he was always hunching forward, either over his guitar, which he wore strapped high up on his chest, or over you, raining down a spray of spit from between the gap in his teeth as he spoke. He wore his hair short and slicked back and dressed grease. When he dug into his guitar he had a lock of hair the pomade simply couldn't hold that would tear loose and come cascading around his ear à la Jerry Lee Lewis when the piano kicking started. He was a big and unusual presence standing at the center of his band. He was uncomfortable with himself in the way of some big guys who are not completely at home with their size. There was never quite enough room for Ray Cichon. Something was always being bumped into, knocked over. He had a tender goofiness and was a fierce and eviscerating guitarist, stunning the local community with his intensity and fluidity.

Ray taught me a lot. We'd seen the Motifs at our local high school dances. They frightened and riveted the crowd with their drama, musical ability and surly stage presence. They wiped the dance floor with the Chevelles, making them seem so painfully old-school they practically hung it up then and there. The Motifs were not high school–aged punks. They were men who made music. When Ray first walked into the Vineyards' home on a request from Tex, we couldn't believe our eyes. A visit by Jimi Hendrix himself couldn't have caused more thunder. Big Ray was there in our neighborhood, in the flesh, gracing our humble dining room practice area (which he barely fit in) with his presence, sharing his great guitar knowledge with undeserving young wannabes like us. Ray had mastered all the riffs the excellent Jimmy McCarty played on Mitch Ryder's great Detroit Wheels hits and he'd lay them out for you note for note. Ray's hands were huge and moved effortlessly over the fret board in configurations physically impossible for me to achieve. He would play, his marble-size knuckles bulging, and the sound that would come out of his Ampeg amp filled me with aspiration. The shocker was that when Ray wasn't inhabiting my local Mount Olympus, shutting down every pretender who thought they knew a hot lick or two, he was a shoe salesman! I visited him once at the shoe store even though the sight, the incongruity, of Big Ray Cichon, my neighborhood guitar god, hunched over trying to squeeze his massive body onto a little shoe stool as he fit some old gal into a size 6 would've been too much for me. There he was, smiling, as sweet and polite as ever, bringing out the shoe boxes, asking when I'd be at Tex's 'cause he'd stop by for a little guitar tutoring.

Ray remains one of my great guitar heroes, not just because of his musicianship but because he was there, reachable, a tangible local icon, a real man with a life who took the time to pass down what he knew to a bunch of not necessarily promising kids. He was no distant guitar genius but a neighborhood guy with all his eccentricities and foibles on view who taught you that with a little help, timely mentoring and the right amount of work, you might be exceptional.

Walter Cichon was another story entirely. The longest hair on man or beast I'd ever seen. The first true star I'd ever been close to. A full-blooded rock 'n' roll animal with the attitude, the sexuality, the toughness, the raw sensuality pouring out of him, scaring and thrilling all of us who came in contact with him. Walter was *not* your everyday guy but something vastly different. With his hooded eyes and olive skin, he was perfect in that very imperfect Brando-esque way. He fronted the Motifs like a lost Asian king.

We were the supplicants at his feet, there to admire the hard, cool indifference with which he stood in front of his microphone mumbling out the lyrics to the Motifs' secret canon of R & B juju. A shaman, a rebel, a Jersey mystic and someone you could not completely believe entered the world through the same human loins you did.

It took all the guts I had to wander up to Walter after a dance one night and stutter . . . "Uh, you were great . . ." Walter packed up his percussion kit, muttered something and wandered off. He was living proof that the real thing could exist right there in Central New Jersey. He lived like he wanted. (Walter took no "longhair" bullshit from anybody. Both brothers' reputations as willing and effective fighters put an end to that.) Walter proved you could stake a rebel's flag right into the heart of the Shore's summer asphalt and make it stand . . . if you carried enough personal weight and magic. If you were powerful enough you could be different, your own man. The nine-to-fivers, the straights, the high-on-Mama's-and-Papa's-money frat boys would just have to eat it. You could be who you were and the rest would just have to stand down and let it be. Once you got beyond this persona, Walter could be as down-to-earth and funny as Ray, though never as easily approachable.

The Motifs were rounded out by Vinnie Roslin, a spirited, charismatic bass player. He lent the Motifs a degree of accessibility. He played a Danelectro Longhorn bass, dangling at knee level, with his shoulder-length hair covering his face 'til in one moment he'd throw it back, revealing a bright smile and the joy he was getting out of playing music. Vinnie would later join me in Steel Mill. Johnny Lewandoski was their slicked-back-blond-haired drummer, as masterful on his instrument as Ray was on his guitar. Johnny set the high bar for drumming, in Dino Danelli's Rascals style, in our area for years to come. It was Walter and Ray, however, who had the greatest impact on me and our group. Simultaneously above and amongst us, they gave us a touchable link to the mystic power and possibilities of rock 'n' roll. No giants from across the sea, they blazed a trail that changed what it meant to be a band at the Shore. More than that, they were righteous figures whose music did not compromise and whose lives were livable, imaginable, within our grasp, but also entirely their own.

Walter and Ray Cichon came to tragic ends. Walter was drafted in the army, where he served as a rifleman in Kontum Province, South Vietnam. There, on March 30, 1968, while attempting to seize a hill, he received a head wound, was examined and was left for dead as his unit was forced to withdraw under enemy fire. However a later body recovery team was unable to locate Walter's body and there were subsequent reports of an American with a head wound, who fit Walter's description, captured in that area on or about that date. At the end of the war, Walter was one of the many thousands of servicemen deemed "missing in action," whose bodies were never recovered.

Years later, Ray, accompanying a friend who had some trouble with some local men, was badly beaten. He came home and died days later from head injuries. No one was charged with his murder. Their deaths anger me to this day; they were our heroes, they were our friends.

In 1967, I would crush my leg and suffer a concussion after being T-boned on my small Yamaha motorcycle by a '63 Caddy on my way home up South Street. The bike crunched and slid under the car's front end. I went sailing (no helmet law, no helmet) twenty feet into the air, landing on the hard-ass blacktop on the corner of Institute and South Street. I was knocked out cold for thirty minutes, all the way from Freehold to the hospital in Neptune. I was hauled into the emergency room and had to have my clothes cut off of me due to the swelling of my leg. While this was going on, I was the butt of jokes amongst a few of the staff about the length of my hair. The next day, as I was laid up in the hospital bed, there were doctors who declined to give me follow-up treatment for my head injury. Back home, as I was unable to move, laid up on the couch, my pops had a barber come in and relieve me of the "offending" locks. That was the last straw. I screamed and swore at him. It was the only time I told my dad I hated—HATED—him. I was hurt and furious, and to make matters worse, I couldn't work with my band for the rest of the summer for fear the volume of the garage assault of the Castiles might create complications from my concussion. Billy Boyle, the soon-to-be mayor of Freehold, who represented me in our legal case, was so disgusted by my appearance, he told me on the way into the courtroom that if he was the judge he'd find me guilty (of what?), then said, "Doug, how do you put up with this? It's disgraceful." My father shook his head and shamefully answered, "Bill, I can't do anything with him." We won.

# FOURTEEN

# ONCE THERE WAS A LITTLE STEVEN

When you weren't doing your own gigs, you were checking out the competition. After the British invasion, teen shows exploded onto prime-time television. *Shindig!* featured the Shindogs, with the great James Burton on guitar; *Hullabaloo* brought your favorite British and American groups into your life on a weekly basis. At home the battle for control of the television set was in full throttle. The fight became ugly and brutish. My father, stretched out on the couch in his white tee and work pants, howled when I switched the channel from his favorite western to see if my latest musical heroes were hitting the stage at the Ed Sullivan Theater.

*Hullabaloo* started a franchise of clubs around the nation, taking over any vacant supermarket or warehouse, fitting it out with never-before-seen black lights (a lighting effect that made anything white, including your teeth, glow phosphorescent), a few big posters and lots of dancing room. They booked the best local bands along with the occasional national act coming through town on tour. In Freehold, in a newly abandoned supermarket, I witnessed the majesty of Britain's Screaming Lord Sutch.

The first Hullabaloo Club we went to was in Asbury Park. I walked in one night with my pal Mike Patterson, and onstage were Sonny and the Starfires, featuring at the drums a pre–"Mad Dog" Vincent Lopez. All Chuck Berry and rockabilly blues, Sonny, a good-looking guy with greased blond hair and black Ray-Ban sunglasses, really knew what he was doing. (He still plays in the area today, as cool as ever.) The next Hullabaloo Club we hit was in Middletown. When I walked in I saw a guy onstage wearing a gargantuan polka-dot tie that stretched from his Adam's apple to the floor. He was the lead singer in a band called the Shadows and they were cruising their way through a version of the Turtles' "Happy Together." Whoever he was, he was funny, and they had a very tight band. They'd picked the records they covered clean; their arrangements and their harmonies were authentically precise.

At the Hullabaloo Club you played fifty-five minutes on and five minutes off, all night long. If there was a fight, you had to go back on immediately and play to distract the crowd in order to keep a full-blown brawl from breaking out. During the Shadows' five-minute break I was introduced to their front man, Steve Van Zandt. The Castiles by now had a significant reputation, so he knew who I was; we talked a little shop, we hit it off and he went back on for his next set. So began one of the longest and greatest friendships of my life.

Over the next years we would visit each other's gigs often. I caught him one summer night in our local battle of the bands at the Arthur Pryor Band Shell on the boardwalk in Asbury Park as the Shadows ran through their Paul Revere and the Raiders routine, playing "Kicks," outfitted in white chinos, white tuxedo shirts and black vests. They captured first place. We formed a mutual admiration society of two. I'd finally met someone who felt about music the way I did, needed it the way I did, respected its power in a way that was a notch above the attitudes of the other musicians I'd come in contact with, somebody I understood and I felt understood me. With Steve and me, from the beginning, it was heart to heart and soul to soul. It was all impassioned, endless arguments over the minutiae of the groups we loved. The deep delving into the smallest details of guitar sounds, style, image; the beautiful obsession of sharing, with someone who was as single-minded and crazy as you were, a passion you simply could not get enough of—these were things you could not fully explain to outsiders . . . because as the Lovin' Spoonful so perfectly put it, "It's like trying to tell a stranger 'bout rock and roll" . . . do you believe in magic?

Steve and I believed big-time and together we created a world of our own, all rock 'n' roll all the time. Steve lived in Middletown, a long hike from Freehold for the wheelless. When Steve formed his new group the Source, I'd visit his gigs at Le Teendezvous. Steve was an early country-rock acolyte, mastering the Byrds' and the Youngbloods' repertoire. When he eventually moved to playing lead guitar he got real good real fast. The Castiles by this time had added an organist, Bobby Alfano, and moved into the psychedelic blues territory of 1967. Steve showed up at many of our gigs and our friendship grew.

## Café Wha?, Greenwich Village

The Castiles had cut a single in a small studio in Bricktown, New Jersey: "That's What You Get for Loving Me" backed by "Baby I," our two self-penned originals. We walked out of the studio that afternoon with a two-track tape and some acetates (little 45-RPM-looking records that were good for only a few clean plays). We already knew we'd hit a wall locally. There was just no place left to go, with either our record or our "career." We were now the big dogs in town. One Saturday afternoon we sat around Tex's and decided that to be discovered we'd have to get out of Jersey. Since Frank Sinatra, no one of import had known the Garden State existed or had come far enough south down the parkway to realize there were people there, much less rock 'n' roll being made. You could play for ten zillion years, wailing your genius into the void, and no one beyond the locals would ever know.

New York City . . . that's where bands found fame and fortune. We had to break in there. Tex made a few calls and somehow got us booked into Café Wha? in Greenwich Village for a Saturday matinee audition. This was major. Few of us had ever been out of New Jersey, and the Village in '68 was something we'd never seen. We set up on the cramped basement stage at the Wha?, faced out into the pewlike rows of black tables filled with Long Island teenyboppers sucking on overpriced, strangely named alcohol-less beverages and cut loose. We got the gig. We didn't get paid. They simply agreed to *let* you play, get your foot into the "big time" of New York and hope somebody stumbled in and decided you were the next big thing.

That didn't happen. Our experience in the Village, however, was critical. None of the bands we saw were well-known but almost all of them were better than we were. There was Circus Maximus, with the young Jerry Jeff Walker singing and playing guitar. There was the Source (New York City version) with future New York congressman John Hall of the band Orleans on vocals and guitarist Teddy Speleos playing Jeff Beck as good as Beck himself. Teddy was an outstanding whiz. Steve and I made the bus trip on many afternoons just to sit there slack-jawed at his sound, technique and nonchalance. He was just a teenager like us but became a huge hero to Steve and me. We were never going to get within fifty feet of Jeff Beck, but this kid, there he was, inches away from our faces, and like the monkeys staring at the monolith in *2001*, we sat there primitively hypnotized by style, substance and flash we could not comprehend. Steve and I rushed home to our guitars, hoping to catch some of the richness of distortion, the molasses thickness of tone Teddy was squeezing out of his Telecaster. Unfortunately we'd end up with a howling, screaming, murdering chain-saw massacre of sound squealing up out of the basement from our Teles. How did he do it? He KNEW how, THAT'S how!

The bus trips became a regular part of our weekends. The arguments on the way up about who was better, Led Zeppelin or the Jeff Beck Group; the immersion in Village life, with the hippies, the gays, the drug dealers, Washington Square Park—we basked in the freedom of it all and it became our true home away from home.

Just a brief year or two after Jimi Hendrix played the Wha?, the Castiles played regularly on Saturday and Sunday next door to the Fugs on MacDougal Street. The Mothers of Invention were around the corner at the Warwick Theater. Steve and I caught Neil Young promoting his first solo album, his signature black Gibson plugged into a tiny Fender amp, blowing out the walls of the Bitter End. Nobody paid us much attention with the exception of a small group of bridge-and-tunnel teenybopper girls who latched on to our band and showed up regularly. This was the big world, the free world; in Greenwich Village in 1968, I could walk with my freak flag held high and nobody was going to bust me. It was a world I could call my own, a little piece of my future beckoning.

I had a friend, a very good New York City guitarist, who was sidelining as a drug dealer. I'd occasionally spend the night in his hotel room with pills of all colors spread out over the night table like spilled Skittles . . . no interest. Back in Jersey drugs were just beginning to become a part of high school life; though I did none myself (too scared), I lived next door to, and was friends with, one of the town's first radical drug experimenters. I was once called into the principal's office and asked a lot of drug-related questions about which I truly knew nothing. Given the times and my appearance, no one believed a word I said. Who cared?

As graduation time drew near, the principal of Freehold High, a basically good guy with whom I had a pretty decent détente for most of my high school years, took it upon himself to suggest at a graduation meeting that to let me attend the ceremony looking like I did would be a discredit and disgrace to the class. He subtly hinted that perhaps someone should do something about it. That was it for me. I would not be the subject/victim of meatheaded vigilante retribution. On my Freehold Regional High School graduation day, I woke up at dawn. That morning, while the house was asleep, I got dressed, went down to the bus terminal and boarded the six a.m. Lincoln Transit Commuter straight to New York City. I disembarked at the Port Authority, grabbed the subway to Eighth Street and walked up the stairs into the early-June sunlight of Greenwich Village feeling free as a bird. My world. I was done. Let them have their little party.

I spent my graduation day wandering around the Village, eating pizza, hanging in Washington Square Park, stopping in at the Wha? and meeting a new girlfriend. My folks finally caught up with me at the Wha? and via phone told me everything would be all right if I would just come home. I caught a bus, bringing my new tagalong gal pal with me. We arrived in the early evening, just hours after the ceremony. My father met me at our front door, the house filled with relatives attending my family graduation festivities, and after he took one look at my gal friend, straight back to the bus depot we went. Once my dad and I were back at home, he ordered me to my room and unscrewed and confiscated my lightbulbs so I'd have to sit in the dark, meditating on what I'd done. I was visited shortly by my aunt Dora, who tried to sweet-talk some sense into me. At that moment, I just didn't care. I'd had it with the school, the family and the whole ten-cent dog and pony show that was fucked-up Freehold, New Jersey. A week later, with summer descending, I walked into the school administration's office and picked up my diploma.

## Summer of Drugs

Two horrible events occurred that summer. The first was a massive heartbreak when my trusty girlfriend dumped me for screwing around with an old ex of mine. Struck with an immediate case of buyer's remorse, I spent the rest of my summer pursuing her through the beach towns of Central Jersey. Filled with angst, I cruised the teen clubs with my prep school road buddies, "Sunrise" Kruger, "Bird" and Jay. We traveled in the "Batmobile," an old black Caddy that belonged to one of the clan. Sunshine was a member of the Pershing Rifles, a corps of semimilitary teens who could do things with a rifle, bayonet attached, that would curl your pubic hairs. They twirled them like batons, and I once watched Sunshine slice his calf performing one of his maneuvers in Bermuda shorts.

These were my boys and that summer they saved my life. We'd cruise the Jersey Shore, top down, soothing my selfishly broken heart 'til they dumped me off in the wee wee hours back in Freehold. My house would be completely locked down, so I'd climb up the latticework by the kitchen onto the side roof, pushing in the fan that was in my bedroom window, to be greeted by my dad in his boxers, Irish skin white as a polar bear's in the dawn, wielding a plunger, ready to beat the hell out of the early-morning cat burglar come to steal his riches. I'd tape the shades down in my room, sleep through the day, and come night, continue my po-faced vigil.

This all culminated with my catching up to my girl one early-fall night as she returned from her summer at the beach. I professed undying love, told her my dream that we would someday visit Disneyland together, and she let me down as easily as she could, but I knew I was screwed. On the first day I was due to attend community college, I pulled another one of my vanishing acts and headed to the Village, spending the afternoon on a bench in Washington Square Park. A fall breeze gently blew over me and it was done. I returned home, reported one day late for my opening semester at Ocean County College and left my high school days and love-struck blues behind me.

Also that summer, the first drug bust in the history of Freehold, New Jersey, occurred. I was standing on the street next to my phone booth outside the corner newsstand. This was the booth I'd spent countless high school hours in, through snow, sleet, rain and sweltering heat. Each night you could find me ensconced there, romancing my current love interest. My father refused to allow a phone in our home. He said, "No phone, no phone bill. No phone and they can't call you for extra duty if somebody else is a no-show at the job." Once planted at the kitchen table, my dad truly did not want the furious flights of his imagination, fueled by Mr. Schaefer, disturbed.

On this night, a sticks and bones local goofball—let's call him Eddie— suddenly came running. Eddie was an early, rabid drug taker. He was a little skinny kid but heavy into the hallucinogens. "I just saw Mrs. Bots in the back of a police car with Baby Bots," he said. Baby Bots was her and Vinnie's child.

"Get ouuuuuuuttttttaaaaaa heeeerrrre," I told Eddie. "You're hallucinating. Nobody gets arrested with their baby!" That night, the Freehold Police Department swept up more than half the Castiles in the town's first drug crackdown. They were all taken, right outta Mama's and Papa's arms in the middle of the night. It was a town scandal, trouble all around and the finale of the Castiles' great three-year run. Our band was fraying anyway. George and I had begun to have some tension between us and the bust gave us all a final out. My epic elementary school of rock was closed forever. The group I'd taken my first baby steps with and strutted my way to small-town guitar-slinging glory with was over. There would be no encore.

FIFTEEN

# EARTH

By 1968 hard-rocking psychedelic blues trios had superseded the beat groups. The era of the guitar god was in full swing. Cream with Clapton and the Jimi Hendrix Experience were having hit records. Long, intense, blues-drenched jams were the order of the day and I was ready. I'd been over to see a friend of Tex's, an ex-marine who said he had a guitar collecting dust in his closet. Upon my visit, he pulled out an unstrung hollow-bodied Gibson with the longest neck I'd ever seen. I brought it home, cleaned it up and strung it. It was a strange piece. My guitar strings barely reached around its distant over-sized tuning pegs. When I plugged it into my Danelectro amp, MAGIC! . . . The thick chunky sound of Eric Clapton's psychedelic painted SG came ripping out at me. The "Sunshine of Your Love" guitar sound flooded my little practice room and I was transported into another league. Nobody—nobody—down there in New Jersey was getting this kind of guitar tone. My Gibson only had one pickup and the frets were awfully far from one another, but the sound . . . the sound said, BRING ON ALL COMERS!

After the Castiles I found a bassist, John Graham, and a drummer, Michael Burke, whom I enjoyed playing with. They were well versed in the techniques it took to play as a three-piece unit. We rehearsed a little and started gigging immediately. From the beginning we wowed the locals. For this new sound we were the only game in town. We had the look, with my Italian Afro and their hair down to their shoulders; the ferocity; and a repertoire of modern blues standards popularized by Clapton, Hendrix, Beck and the like. I took flight as a guitarist; the night was an endless series of long, slashing solos on my miracle Gibson. We were the monster rock kings of our piece of the Shore. We added Bobby Alfano back on organ to give my aching fingers a rest and for a while, we had a pretty nice little band.

The psychedelic era had finally landed at the Shore. The crowd came to sit Buddha-style in front of us for a set and then trance-dance the night into oblivion. One night, some kid who knew his guitars shed some light on the "miracle" in my miracle Gibson. He walked up and congratulated me on the brilliant idea of stringing an old Gibson six-string bass with guitar strings and playing it as a solo instrument. I nodded coolly while thinking, "Holy shit . . . it's a six-string bass!" I'd been soloing like a madman for months on a bass guitar! No wonder its sound was so thick and its fret board so impossible. It worked!

Around this time I was starting to write some acoustic music. I'd bought a twelve-string Ovation acoustic guitar and was penning some prog-style, Donovan-and-Dylan-influenced originals that I'd end up singing in the local coffeehouses when I wasn't thundering through the blues. We had new managers, a couple of college guys, one of whom had just frozen and chopped off the end of his toe to avoid the draft. I figured that was just the kind of commitment we needed, so they started to finance some equipment and book some gigs for us. This occasioned my first trip to Manny's Music in New York City, guitar Valhalla and home of the hit makers. On a three-grand loan from one of our managers' daddies, we walked out of there fully loaded and ready to storm the barricades of the big time. An epic Valentine's

Day gig at the Long Branch Italian-American club was followed by a booking in Manhattan at the Diplomat Hotel (a later venue for the New York Dolls). We charged a fee and bused our fans through the tunnel, straight onto the Diplomat's ballroom floor. It was a great afternoon in the city. As we were packing up I was approached by a Greek guy named George. He introduced himself as a record producer, said he didn't care much for the band but loved what I was doing. He gave me his card and told me to call him. Finally, a connection to the real music business, somebody who'd actually seen the inside of a studio and could make something happen. "Excitement" isn't the word. I felt thrilled, vindicated, validated; my head spun with the possibility of actually making something of all this.

I called immediately and was invited to George's apartment in New York City. I'd never seen anything like it. It had big windows opening out onto the avenue, high molded ceilings and rich wood paneling, all topped off by George's gorgeous blond girlfriend, an afternoon soap opera star. He had a two-track tape deck we recorded some of my music on. Tim Buckley was a great inspiration for me at this time; that's why I had the twelve-string. That's what Tim played, and I did my utmost to ape his vocal timbre and his writing style. That night we went to a session George was producing. I sat in the darkness of a real studio and watched an actual recording session being conducted. I left that night finally feeling a musical future in front of me.

I saw George somewhat regularly. I had some scheduling conflicts because I was still in school. My aunt Dora had pulled some strings and wheedled me a place amongst the Ocean County student body and I didn't want to blow it. Unfortunately, it wasn't a great fit. In the late sixties the counterculture was still a slow train coming in South Jersey. I was once again one of a small handful of freaks in a low-tolerance zone. Just getting to school and back was trouble enough. I could catch a ride there with a pal for gas money but coming home, I often had to improvise. In the winter, I'd stash myself beside a roadside billboard, waiting in the icy Route 9 cold until a bus appeared over the horizon. I'd move out to the road's shoulder, wait for the bus to catch me in its high beams, then wave for passenger pickup. It was fifty-fifty, depending on the attitude of the driver. Many a night I'd be greeted by a shake of a crew-cut head and the big wheels would keep on rolling.

Often I had to rely on my usual ticket to ride: my thumb. It was a long, cold hike in the dark that brought its own dangers. I'd had cars slow down as if to give me a lift, then throw open the passenger-side door to knock me into the ditch. You had to be on your toes. I had a wild booze-fueled ride on the back roads between Toms River and Lakewood with a young black dude roaring and laughing, a bottle of Jack between his legs and the steering wheel, until I was spilled out onto the pavement in front of the Lakewood Greyhound station kissing mother blacktop.

My dad would occasionally come to get me but that made matters even worse. In a rage at the inconvenience, he'd haul ass north on Route 9 toward home, pedal to the metal, using our old junker like it was a death-proof weapon of mass extinction. I couldn't comment. All I could do was ride shotgun on the terror train, waiting for the screeching wail of sheet metal that would signal the end for the both of us. We'd pull in the drive, he'd skid to a stop and, saying nothing, he'd hop out, slamming the door behind him. I'd walk into the house and find him already sitting, smoking, at the kitchen table looking like he'd never seen me before in his life.

It was a transitional moment. My parents wanted me to further my education and I wanted to stay out of the draft. This was 1968, post–Tet Offensive America. The streets were in an uproar, and it wasn't just the hippies but the truckers too. Informed by Walter Cronkite, the influential news anchor at CBS, the country was getting the idea that Vietnam was a losing game. I'd had two close friends, Walter and Bart, killed at war and I had no intention of joining them.

Back in New York George asked me if I wanted to be a full-time musician. I said, "Hell yeah." He asked me if I was committed to school. I said, "Hell no." Then he said I should quit school and dedicate myself to who I was and the music I loved. I said, "Hell yeah, but what about the draft?" I was nineteen and prime cannon fodder. He said, "Guys get out of the draft all the time. You leave it up to me. It's something we can fix." That night, filled with new resolve, I went home, gathered my parents in the kitchen, told them about George and about what I wanted to do. They were hesitant, unsure. I heard the arguments about work that was real and steady, the same arguments I'd give my own kids today about the music business, but I was determined. George had given me confidence and I could feel the early light of the success I longed for. Finally, my parents said it was my life and they reluctantly agreed; they wished me well, and "ring-ring goes the bell," my school days were over for good.

I was never able to get George back on the phone again.

## Draft Dodger Rag

Now a full-time musician, I went about my business, playing gigs and bringing home what money I could. One fall morning, I popped the metal lid of our mailbox and saw a letter addressed to me. I opened it. It read, "Congratulations, you have been chosen to serve your country in the United States Armed Forces." Please report for your physical on such-and-such a date to the draft board in Asbury Park. Here it was—the reckoning. I felt cold in my stomach. Not shocked, but momentarily gut-punched by the real world hitting hard. I was chosen to be a player in history, not of my own accord or desire, but because bodies were needed to stem the perceived Communist menace in Southeast Asia. My first thought was, "Is this real? And what does it possibly have to do with me, my life, my ideas?" The answer to the first question was "You bet your ass." The answer to the second question, I decided, was "Nothing . . . nothing at all." Maybe I was just frightened and didn't want to die. I was not going to have the chance to find out because I decided then and there I was not going to go. Whatever it took—and I did not know then what that might be—to *not* go, I was going to do.

I hid the letter from my parents. There was nothing they could do.

This was just about me. The induction was a month or so off, so there was time for a little research. By 1968 there was plenty of information on the street about how to beat the draft. In my travels I had met and talked to young men who'd fed themselves fat, starved themselves skinny or mutilated extremities. I heard about the wealthy with their doctor notes specially designed for remaining stateside and safe at home. I didn't have recourse to anything so extravagant. The irony was I, Mad Dog Vincent Lopez and Little Vinnie Roslin were all to make our debut at the draft board in Newark on the same morning. So, brothers leery of arms, we put our heads together. We had a friend who'd said he'd covered himself in milk and slept like that for three days, and by the time he reported for his physical the stench was so awful they sent him home immediately . . . sounded pretty good. The one surefire answer that kept coming up time after time with successful local dodgers was "mentally unfit." Mentally unfit . . . hell, that was true. We *were* mentally unfit for Uncle Sam. All we had to do was prove it to them and get that beautiful 1Y mental deferment.

We proceeded as follows:

**STEP 1:** Make a mess out of your forms. Let them know they're trying to corral a drug-addicted, gay, pathologically bed-wetting lunatic who can barely write his name into the US military.

**STEP 2:** Make them believe it. Act the mumbling, bumbling, swishing, don't-give-a-fuck-about-orders freak on STP, LSD and anything else you can get your hands on—a hippie-outcast, destroyer-of-troop-morale, corroder-of-discipline, much-more-trouble-than-you're-worth, get-the-fuck-out-of-here joke of a recruit.

**STEP 3:** Previously, have a bad enough motorcycle accident to truly scramble and concuss your brains, making you a medical risk on the battlefield. Fill in that section of the form truthfully, go home and receive your 4F—physically unfit. (I tried it all, but in the end, that was my classification.)

We drove to Newark that morning on a bus filled with mostly young black kids out of Asbury Park. Almost everybody had a plan. I sat next to a strapping blond rah football player in a quarter-body cast he confided to me was totally bogus. There were draft boards, especially in the South, where this shit would not fly and your ass would be delivered straight to boot camp. But Newark had the reputation of being one of the easiest draft boards in the country. I guess it was. An amazing percentage of the guys on the bus were rejected because they pulled some personalized version of the above-mentioned shtick. At the end of the day, after we'd all driven the US Army around the bend, there was a small table at the end of a long, empty hallway. There sat a bored young soldier looking at you like he was about to give you the worst news of your life. "I am sorry to inform you but you have been judged unfit for military service." Looking back down at his paperwork, he'd add, "You may enter through the next door if you'd like to sign up for some voluntary service." Behind that door was one very empty room. You were then handed a ticket that allowed you a free meal, for being a good sport and taking the ride up, at a restaurant two blocks down the street. We all skipped over there, our feet barely touching the ground. We stepped into a lovely sunlit diner. The smiling host at the door greeted us like we were his long-lost millionaire cousins and escorted us to a set of stairs that led down into a dank basement room. There at one long, musty hardwood table with my fellow yella bellies, I had some of the worst food and one of the best meals of my life.

The bus ride out of the city was pandemonium. There were many fine young black women on the summer streets of Newark and my Asbury Park brothers let them know they were appreciated. Many had been called, few had been chosen. The bus door hissed open in front of the Asbury Park train station, discharging Mad Dog, Little Vinnie and myself, all now free men, intact, with our lives, wherever they might lead, in front of us. As the bus pulled away, the street turned quiet. We'd been up together for three solid days. We looked at each other, exhausted, shook hands and went our own ways. I felt relieved but I also felt like crying. I hitchhiked the fifteen miles back to Freehold. With days of no sleep and little food, wired and weary, I walked up onto the back porch and through the kitchen door of my house to my father. I called my mom in, told my parents where I'd been, that I'd hid it from them so that they might not worry and out of embarrassment that New York George and my big music plans had come to nothing. I told them I failed my draft physical. My dad, who often dismissively uttered the words "I can't wait 'til the army gets ahold of you," sat at the kitchen table, flicked the ash off of his cigarette, took a puff, slowly let the smoke escape from his lips and mumbled, "That's good."

As I grew older, sometimes I wondered who went in my place. Somebody did. What was his fate? Did he live? I'll never know. Later on in life, when I met Ron Kovic, author of *Born on the Fourth of July*, or Bobby Muller, one of the founders of the Vietnam Veterans of America, both men who fought and sacrificed, returning from the war in wheelchairs, men who became strong activists against the war, I felt a duty and a sense of connection. Maybe it was another dose of my survivor's guilt or maybe it was just the common generational experience of living through a war that had touched everyone. It was New Jersey men like them who went and fought in my place. All I know is when I visit the names of my friends on the wall in Washington, DC, I'm glad mine's not up there, or Little Vinnie's or Mad Dog's.

# SIXTEEN

# THE UPSTAGE CLUB

Tom Potter was a fifty-year-old salt-and-pepper-haired, big-gutted, pirate-belt-wearing, sexually preoccupied, goateed boho who opened and ran the strangest music club I'd ever seen. His wife, Margaret, was a pixie-cut-wearing, sexually ambiguous, guitar-playing beautician and bandleader for Margaret and the Distractions. She had a very young, boyish appearance and I didn't initially make Margaret out for a gal until I saw the little round tit popping out from her T-shirt and resting upon the upper body of her Telecaster guitar as she wailed Tommy James's "Mony Mony" in the upstairs room of the Upstage Club. A more fabulously incongruous husband-and-wife team I have yet to come upon.

Dusk 'til dawn, eight p.m. to five a.m.: those were the operating hours of the Upstage Club on Cookman Avenue in Asbury Park. Tom closed the joint for one hour between twelve and one a.m. to sweep out the refuse and get fired up for the night shift. With no booze and theoretically no drugs, the place was a unique all-night haven for Shore street life through the late sixties. The two floors of the club consisted of an upstairs jam floor and downstairs coffeehouse, all dementedly decorated by Tom himself. The interior scheme was mainly a lot of glow-in-the-dark paint and black light, and featured a papier-mâché Day-Glo mermaid who swung swimming from the ceiling. Tom, a self-fashioned beatnik artist, was dictator, top banana and big dog there and he let his impulses run wild. He was a loud, yelling, throw-your-ass-down-the-stairs-and-out-the-front-door, very funny guy if he liked you. If he did not, he was unpleasant to be around.

Asbury Park was not my turf, though I'd visited there throughout the fifties with my parents on holiday weekends. By the late sixties, it had faded from its onetime Victorian splendor into a deteriorating blue-collar resort. The upside of Asbury's decline was it had become a bit of an open city. Gay bars sat next to all-night juke joints, and with the race riots of the near future yet to come, there was a little bit of anything goes. The Castiles had never played there. Ocean Avenue was all bars and beach joints for the over-twenty-one summer drinking set; phony IDs were sold at a premium, and the whole layout felt like a working-class, fading, faux Fort Lauderdale.

When I walked into Upstage, I walked in cold. No one had ever laid eyes on me or seen me play. I'd heard you could jam there. Along with the strange hours, Tom Potter's stroke of genius was that at the end of a long rectangular box of a room, two flights above a shoe store, he had built a small stage. Behind that stage, the wall from one side of the room to the other was honeycombed with ten-inch, twelve-inch and fifteen-inch speakers. An unforgiving, solid and real "wall of sound." The amplifier heads were built into a small cabinet at your feet, so all you had to do was bring your guitar, reach down and plug in. No other equipment was necessary. This innovation and the club's unusual opening and closing times made it a mecca for musicians on the Shore scene. Every band that came into the area to play the Jersey Top 40 clubs ended up at the Upstage playing the music they really loved 'til dawn. In summer at three a.m. there was a line outside the door waiting to get in. It was an incredible clearinghouse for musicians.

The first weekend I was there I saw Dan Federici and Vini Lopez in a group fronted by guitarist Bill Chinnock, the Downtown Tangiers Rock and Roll, Rhythm and Blues Band. The place was a steaming sauna of summer bodies and I knew I'd found my new hang. A few weeks later I returned with my guitar (cue the theme music from *The Good, the Bad and the Ugly*). I waited. The club was not yet full. Someone told me you had to book a jam "slot" with Tom Potter. It was like booking a table at the pool hall. They'd write your name on a list and say from two to two thirty a.m., you had your shot if you could find musicians to sit in with you. My moment arrived and I walked to the stage, the drummer and bass player agreeing to stay on duty for my half hour. I plugged into Tom's mighty wall, stood back and kicked into "Rock Me Baby," cutting loose with everything I had. I fried the paint off the place with all the guitar pyrotechnics and wizardry my eighteen-year-old fingers could muster. I'd had a lot of playing experience by now, but in Asbury I was the Man with No Name, a stranger who was in the process of burning your club down. I watched people sit up, move closer and begin to pay serious attention. I saw two guys pull chairs onto the middle of the dance floor and sit themselves down in them, arms folded across their chest, as if to say, "Bring it on," and I brought it. The insane wall of speakers was vibrating so hard I thought the whole place might just cave onto the shoe-store sales floor below. It all held for thirty scorching minutes of guitar Armageddon, then I walked off.

I made some new friends that night. The two guys on the chairs were Garry Tallent and Southside Johnny; downstairs in Tom Potter's office, I had my first conversation with a freckle-faced Danny Federici. He introduced me to his wife, Flo, also freckle-faced and wearing a blond bouffant wig. Danny hailed from Flemington, New Jersey, and was the same bemused, nonchalant character I would stand next to on his deathbed many adventures and forty years later. I was a hit. There were many very good guitar players in Asbury Park—Billy Ryan was a real blues master; Ricky Disarno had Clapton down. They had great tones and technique but the stagecraft, the singing and the front man skills I'd built up in my apprenticeship with the Castiles moved me ahead of the pack. I would address you, excite you and play guitar like a demon, demanding that you respond.

I shortly ran into Vincent Lopez in the coffee shop on the first floor; head shaved near bald, fresh out of jail, he felt the need to explain his appearance to me (the jail) and then asked if I was interested in joining a version of his group, Speed Limit 25. I was a free agent at the time, and Speed Limit had an Asbury Park rep and was making money. I needed some of that. I liked the Asbury scene and so I said, "Sure, let's see how it goes." A few rehearsals with some of the other Speed Limit members didn't quite click so Vini and I decided to put together something ourselves. Vini knew Danny from Downtown Tangiers, so we all gathered with bass player Little Vinnie Roslin from the Motifs in a cottage on Bay Avenue in Highlands, New Jersey, and started working. This was the band that would initially call itself Child, then morph into Steel Mill, then the Bruce Springsteen Band, and eventually become the core of the original E Street Band.

The accidental presence of a club like the Upstage in Asbury Park was a unique and invaluable resource for the local music scene. I brought Steve Van Zandt there. He wowed them too. Steve and I were the best lead guitarists and front men in the area, and our presence in the club led to the gestation and formation of many bands that became the center of the Asbury Park music scene. With Big Bad Bobby Williams, a three-hundred-pound earthquake of a drummer, and Southside Johnny, Steve started the Sundance Blues Band. Steve and Johnny were deep into the blues and created a powerful unit that played throughout the Shore. Southside Johnny was from Ocean Grove, the Methodist camp town next to Asbury Park. He was our local king of the blues, ergo his sobriquet "Southside." He was a softhearted, crabby closet intellectual, very soulful and slightly unhinged, but he knew everything about the blues and soul artists, their careers and their records. He came from a home with a serious record collection and had immersed himself in the bible of R & B and soul music. We all met down at the club.

## Homesteaders

At home, my father finally decided he'd had enough. The town and his illness had beaten him. He decided he was going to go to California to start a new life. He wanted my mother and all of us to come along but said he'd go alone if he had to. Freehold, New Jersey, would not have Doug Springsteen to kick around anymore. My sister Virginia decided to stay in Lakewood with her new family. I decided to stay in Freehold, where I could make a small living on my already growing reputation as bar band king.

Six months later, in 1969, at nineteen, I stood in our driveway, waving as my parents and little sister Pam pulled away. They had all of their belongings packed on top of their 1960s Rambler. They took $3,000 with them, all the money they had. They slept a night in a motel and two nights in the car and drove three thousand miles, East Coast Okies headed for my father's promised land. With the exception of my dad in the war, none of us had lived outside of Central New Jersey. Our only source of information about the West Coast was a hippie girlfriend of mine who told my parents to go to Sausalito, the artsy tourist trap near San Francisco. When they got there, they realized it was not for them. My mother claimed they pulled into a gas station and asked the attendant, "Where do people like us live?" He answered, "You live on the peninsula," and for the next thirty years, that's what they did. In a little apartment in San Mateo, they tried for a new beginning.

When my father announced his plans to leave for California, my sister Virginia was seventeen, with a new child, couldn't make toast and had a new rough-and-tumble husband. I was living at home on the twenty bucks a week I made from playing. If we chose to stay, we would have to fend for ourselves. It is her greatest regret and the single thing in life she still feels guiltiest about. But off they went with my little sister in tow. My mom and pops were bound by an unknowable thread. They'd made their deal a long time ago; she had her man who wouldn't leave and he had his gal who couldn't leave. Those were the rules and they superseded all others, even motherhood. They were two for the road. They would never part. This was how it began and this was how it would end. Period. My father was able to draw from my mom, a saving and selfless mother, her own ambivalence about family. In this unchartable terrain, strange bedfellows are regularly made. They wanted us with them. They asked us to go. But they could not *stay.*

So we all made do. My sister vanished into "Cowtown"—the South Jersey hinterlands—and I pretended none of it really mattered. You were on your own—now and forever. This sealed it. Plus, a part of me was truly glad for them, for my dad. Get out, Pops! Out of this fucking dump. This place that's so often been no good to any of us. Run if you need to. How much worse off for you can it be? Whatever their motives, sane or insane, runnin' or searchin', it took guts and a last-chance need for a belief in tomorrow. This was just something I could not begrudge my old man. I wanted it for him. Whatever had to be left behind had to be left behind. Even if it was his children, even if it was us! My sister Virginia, in more dire straits with the baby coming at the time, took it harder, a lot harder. Understandably so. In the end, whatever hard feelings I had I just tucked away, and in truth, all I remember is mainly feeling excited to be left on my own. By nineteen, I was gone already. Into that other world. And in that other world, well . . . there were no parents, there was no home, there were just dreams and music, where the clock stuck and was set permanently at "quarter to three." Into the diaspora rode the Freehold, New Jersey, Springsteens, and everything that went with 'em. We were no more.

·    ·    ·

Vini, Danny and I took over the rent in my house on South Street. My first family moved out and my second family moved in. About a week later, we were joined by a very large and lovely woman who went by the name of Fat Pat. She had fallen on hard times, needed a place to stay "for a little while" and became an adjunct of Danny's family. Danny and Flo now had a young son, Jason, on his way. Fat Pat was soon to become nurse and second mom to the first E Street baby. None of us were yet out of our teens. Add a hell-raising, house-trashing, freely shitting mutt named Bingo to the mix and it didn't take long to reach meltdown.

My family home of seven years was instantly transformed into a hippie frat house. My father's sacred kitchen sanctuary was now a hotbed of group meetings, dirty dishes piled to architecturally impossible heights, with half-empty cereal boxes and dishevelment the order of the day. The room where my beloved grandmother had died was turned into the "radio room." Danny, a gadget freak, was addicted to the wonders of CB—citizens band—radio. To the uninitiated this was a system mostly used by long-distance truckers to communicate with one another about the location of "Smoky" (the highway patrol), observe "pregnant roller skates" (VW Bugs) and give a big "10-4" (affirmative) to whoever was in broadcasting range. There were large home units so you could communicate with other nerdily inclined lonesome joes in a wider arc around your area. Danny and Mad Dog would spend hours in the radio room conversing with the mostly rural redneck characters who favored CB communication. These innocents were unaware they were speaking to a house of raving freaks until invisible friendships were made, blind dates arranged, invitations extended, and soon, knocking at our door was the CB-cult population of Monmouth County. They were stunned to walk in and find they had become chummy with a house full of longhairs, leading to bizarre and hilariously uncomfortable evenings of cross-cultural outreach in my mom and pop's old living room (in the end, the bond of CB was usually stronger than cultural estrangement).

To do CB right you needed a big antenna, preferably placed somewhere very high. Vini and Danny's hunger to rope in an even broader swath of the strange and uninitiated led them to scale the roof of my South Street home, kicking out not-to-be-replaced windows along the way, drawing a crowd as they attempted to attach something to our roof that looked like we were trying to communicate with alien life-forms beyond the rings of Saturn. The signal roared, and weirdos came at all hours of the day and night to our door.

During this time Vini's "Mad Dog" persona was in full swing, his temper flaring. He sent a quart of milk exploding off the refrigerator door in an argument with Danny—over what I don't know; broadcasting rights? Airtime? Next a brawl in our South Street driveway between Vini and Shelly, a short-lived tenant, had me rushing into the street to break up the fight in front of my longtime neighbors. Finally, everyone in the neighborhood had had enough and it led to a knock on the door, the landlord explaining he was closing the house for "renovations" and we would have to leave. After I'd spent seven years there with my folks, we lasted exactly one month.

Late one night we packed all our belongings into our manager Carl "Tinker" West's forties flatbed truck, and we threw the living room couch on top. I climbed onto it and we slowly inched our way out of the driveway, our sterling future impeded only by the local police, who explained there was a local ordinance against moving after dark. We shrugged our shoulders and they watched us slip out of town, probably just glad to see us go. It was a beautiful, balmy night and as I lay back on the old couch, the trees and scrolling stars above me, I was seized by a wonderful feeling. I was slipping over the streets of my childhood, no longer a painful player in my or my town's history but a passing and impassive observer. I was struck by the sweet night smell of honeysuckle and remembered the treasure of honeysuckle bushes that lay behind the convent. My gang and I would gather there on dead summer afternoons to suck out the small flowers' sweet juices. I felt filled with the freedom of being young and leaving something, of my new detachment from a place I loved and hated and where I'd found so much comfort and pain. As Tinker's truck glided over streets that still concealed hard mystery upon mystery, I felt a lightness, a momentary untethering from the past. A spark of my future self came up burning brightly inside me. This . . . all of this—my town, my family's legacy—for now was done. I was nineteen; my parents, unreachable, were thousands of miles away, with my beloved little sister. My beautiful older sister, Virginia, had vanished south, down Route 9, into an adult life I would have little understanding of or contact with for a long time.

I would come back and visit these streets many, many times, rolling through them on sunny fall afternoons, on winter nights and in the deserted after-hours of summer evenings, out for a drive in my car. I would roll down Main Street after midnight watching, waiting, for something to change. I would stare into the warmly lit rooms of the homes I passed, wondering which one was mine. Did I have one? I'd drive on past the firehouse, the empty courthouse square; past my mom's now-dark office building; past the abandoned rug mill, down Institute Street to the Nescafé plant and baseball field; past my copper beech tree, still rooted and towering in front of the emptiness that was once my grandparents' house; past the memorial of white crosses for our fallen war heroes at the town's end; past my dead at the St. Rose of Lima Cemetery—my grandmother, grandfather and aunt Virginia—then out onto the pitch-black rural highways of Monmouth County. I would visit there even more often in my dreams, stepping up onto the porch of my grandmother's house, walking into the front hall, the living room, where on some evenings she and my old family would wait, while on others, emptiness, hollow rooms, probing, puzzling, trying to ferret out what had happened and what were its consequences for my current life. I would return and return, in dreams and out, waiting for a new ending to a book that had been written a long time ago. I would drive as if the miles themselves could repair the damage done, write a different story, force these streets to give up their heavily guarded secrets. They couldn't. Only I could do that, and I was a long ways from being ready. I would spend my life on the road logging hundreds of thousands of miles and my story was always the same . . . man comes to town, detonates; man leaves town and drives off into the evening; fade to black. Just the way I like it.

From my perch on the couch atop the truck I watched our wheels cross the town line, turn left on Highway 33, pick up some speed and head for the ocean breezes and new freedoms of the Shore. With the warm night whistling by me, I felt wonderfully and perilously adrift, giddy with exultation. This town, my town, would never leave me, and I could never completely leave it, but I would never live in Freehold again.

# SEVENTEEN

# TINKER (SURFIN' SAFARI)

Carl Virgil "Tinker" West hailed from Southern California, studied to be an engineer and ended up a surf dog working at Challenger Western Surfboards. He came east in the early sixties, where in a squat brick building amid a sandy and deserted industrial park, he opened up Challenger Eastern Surfboards. He was called "Tinker" because there was nothing he couldn't fix. Tinker could redesign anything at all, patch it up, jury-rig or jimmy it back into working order. He could also catch it, skin it and eat it. When Black Friday comes and the Apocalypse rolls back the clock to year zero, you'll want and need only Tinker at your side. I watched him beautifully restore cars and boats from the ground up, build an entire heating system in his garage studio using just an oil barrel and ductwork, and design and build a recording studio and a sound system that kept us on the road for many years. Once under the hood he could make anything run, anywhere, all the while turning out some of the sweetest long boards on the Jersey Shore. A misanthropic genius, Tinker loved and cherished work. It was people he couldn't stand. If you weren't working, he had *no* use for you. While he wore a ponytail, came from the Golden State and smoked the occasional joint, Tinker's tolerance for the hippie, "laid-back" ethos was near zero. Ten years older and in twice as good shape as anyone in the band, he rode herd on the surfboard factory like the big kahuna he was. If you walked in and had personal business that took more than thirty seconds, he shoved a broom into your hand, said, "Make yourself useful," and ordered you to sweep the floor. He wasn't joking. You started sweeping or you left.

Tinker surfed only the biggest days of September and October, hurricane surf, on an original old balsa-wood surfboard that weighed a ton. He'd walk out to the end of the jetty, huge waves crashing all around him; throw in the board at the end of the rocks; dive in after it; and take off on the biggest, darkest thing rolling up out of the East Coast leviathan depths. We'd all be on the beach watching, shaking our heads . . . Tinker. He'd have us preparing for the revolution, shooting bows and arrows, packing and loading cap-and-ball pistols, a vicious streak of fire and light exploding from their barrels as we shot them into the dark of our little teenage wasteland. "Springsteen," he'd say—that's all he ever called me—"Springsteen, you got the goods and you don't fuck around like all these other assholes." I had the goods and nope, I didn't fuck around, no drugs, no booze, girls . . . yeah, but not if they got in the way of "the music," fuck with that and you're out of my life. There would be no wasted days and wasted nights for me. I'd seen that and I wanted no part of it. Tinker and I would get along just fine.

I met Tinker at the Upstage Club. He corralled me after a set, told me he thought I could really play and mentioned he had some connections with the Quicksilver Messenger Service organization in San Francisco. He knew James Cotton, the great bluesman, and said he thought Janis Joplin was looking for a guitarist and I might be a contender for her new band. All of the above was true. He had a spare room in the factory that we could practice in and if there was anything he could do, I should come up and see him. Here was a guy with a business, a few connections, a financial base, a forceful personality, and he was interested in me. I was always in the market for a surrogate and appreciative daddy, so I latched onto Tink. Tinker loved music and knew talent when he saw it. It was the only thing he made allowances for: ability.

Upon leaving Freehold, we initially took up residence a few blocks off the ocean in Bradley Beach. I had an idyllic surf summer and fall, and the first E Street baby, Jason Federici, arrived. We were still teenagers ourselves; he was a child in the care of children. We gathered around him and treated him like the little piece of magic he was. Steel Mill took up artistic residence in the surfboard factory using an extra concrete room Tinker had off the rear of the place as a rehearsal hall. In Bradley, unfortunately, it was always a near-death experience when it came to paying rent. Mad Dog and I would soon make the surfboard factory our primary address (no rent!). We moved in. Vini slept on a mattress in the bathroom, his head inches from the rumbling toilet. I slept in the master suite, a room ten feet away, my mattress in one corner, Tinker's in another that contained a refrigerator and a television set. Over the next several years I would suck in enough fiberglass and resin fumes to deaden the brain cells of a hundred men. Quarters were tight and Tinker and I were forced to romance our ladies in rather close environs. Privacy was at a minimum. Sex was quick and not that pretty at the surfboard factory, performed on concrete floors; up against the brick exterior of the building; in a room a short distance from other sweating, grabby lovers; or—last hope—in the backseat of an abandoned car out in the dusty swales of the industrial park. You could not be too picky. We managed.

Vini Lopez learned to work as a shaper, tapering the fine lines of Tinker's new short boards so they'd skim like lightning through the murky Jersey surf. He'd stand there, covered head to toe in fiberglass dust; take off his surgical mask; and head to the back room for band practice. We called ourselves Child, and we played the bars and nightclubs of the late-sixties Shore. We played original music with some covers, and the simple fact that we were so good was all that kept us working. The Shore, north to south, was still the fiefdom of Top 40 cover bands. You couldn't get arrested unless you played the hits. We played a few but compromised very little. Our ability to excite and entertain, and having our craft down cold, kept us alive.

I was living the life of an aspiring musician. A circumstantial bohemian—and as I've mentioned, I didn't do any drugs or drink. One of my ex-roommates, a fellow guitarist, would end it all with a gunshot to the head after a short life of ingesting too many chemicals and ending up a wasted talent on the skids. I'd seen people mentally ruined, gone and not coming back. I was barely holding on to myself as it was. I couldn't imagine introducing unknown agents into my system. I needed control and those ever-elusive boundaries. I was afraid of myself, what I might do or what might happen to me. I'd already experienced enough personal chaos to not go in search of the unknown. Over all my years in bars an out-of-line drunk in my face was the only thing that could get me fighting mad. I'd seen my dad and that was enough. I wasn't looking for outside stimulants to help me lose or find anything. Music was going to get me as high as I needed to go.

I had friends who were real drug-experimenting radicals and then I had my construction-worker brother-in-law, who, with the exception of bashing a few longhairs like myself, had no "sixties" experience whatsoever. He remained his whole life a man of the fifties (with greatly increased tolerance, however). I was a faux hippie (free love was all right), but the counterculture stood by definition in opposition to the conservative blue-collar experience I'd had. I felt caught between two camps and I didn't really fit in either, or maybe I just fit in both.

# Last of the Bar Bands

The Pandemonium Club, the Shore's newest nightclub, had opened at Sunset Avenue and Route 35. That put it right at the bottom of the hill from the surfboard factory. We could walk there. You played on a small stage right behind the bar, with a small alley of booze bottles, ice, beer and bartenders all that separated you from the patrons sitting at the bar. The bartender's ass (a great one made the night slip on by), the bar, the stool huggers, those standing gathered around the bar, some tables and the dance floor were all spread out in a 180-degree panorama around you.

The Pandemonium did not have to work very hard to live up to its name. It drew an eclectic and often incompatible clientele. Truckers rolling home up Route 35, kids from Monmouth College, summer "bennies" there for the sand and surf of the Shore, hippies who'd come to hear the music and barflies of all shapes and sizes gravitated to the Pandemonium's currentness and pseudo-ritzy décor. Many of these patrons were culturally at odds. You could go to the Pandemonium to listen to music, be congratulated on a recent set *and* get hassled for the length of your hair by some long-haul trucker, preppy football player or polyester-laden Mafia wannabe out of Long Branch. It was usually cool . . . but not always.

When you play a bar inches behind the bartender you witness the unfolding of human events from a unique perspective. The formula was always familiar; the timing was all that changed.

Woman + booze + man + booze + second man + booze = brawl.

I would bemusedly watch this play out night after night until chairs were thrown, punches were landed, blood was spilled, female faux shock was registered and bouncers swarmed. You could read it like a gathering storm. This was how some gals got their kicks. Sometimes you could warn the bouncers and they would cool it off before the first punch was thrown.

But it often hit with the suddenness of a summer squall and was over just as quick. Cut to the last scene: bouncers breathing heavily, their sweaty shirts torn asunder; random small bloodstains; a gawking crowd gathering in the floodlit parking lot; the celebratory red lights of local law enforcement turning faces muted red; the cops hauling the disheveled revelers away. Everybody goes home.

## One Giant Leap for Mankind

July 20, 1969, the night man first walked on the moon, was our first night of a weeklong booking we had at the new club. This was a gold mine for us and we needed to do well. If we could make a steady booking out of the Pandemonium, some of the living hand-to-mouth would be taken out of our lives. We could concentrate on writing, rehearsing and maybe even recording a few of our own tunes. The Pandemonium was managed by "Baldy Hushpuppies." He was so named because he was a hopelessly middle-aged swinger type who was bald and wore Hush Puppies. On this particular evening, Baldy Hushpuppies was out of town and Son of Baldy Hushpuppies, his kid, was running the joint. It just so happened the band was scheduled to start a set exactly as the first manned moon landing was occurring, 10:56. Half the small crowd of thirty or so wanted us to start playing and half wanted us to solemnly observe this epochal moment in human history. We'd start and some would run to the bar shushing us as the landing grew near; we'd stop and some would complain that the band wasn't playing.

Ultimately we decided, "Fuck the moon landing, that's just a trick of 'The Man'; fuck you, Armstrong, Aldrin and Collins, let's rock." Myself, Mad Dog Lopez and Danny were in favor of boogying. The holdout was bass player Little Vinnie Roslin, a bit of a sensitive techie, a man of science, who said we were full-of-shit cretins ignoring history and he would have no part of it. He put his bass down and walked offstage. He was right, but the line was drawn. A small black-and-white television in the corner of the bar was all they had broadcasting the event. It was surrounded by a small group of pro–moon landing clientele, glued to the fuzzy images being sent across two hundred and forty thousand miles of space. The fuck-the-moon-landers were all huddled over their stew at the bar near us.

Finally Mad Dog had had it. He shouted into his microphone, "If somebody doesn't turn that fucking TV off, I'm coming over and putting my foot through it." Upon hearing Vini's throw-down, Son of Baldy Hush-puppies came barreling around the bar and explained to Vini that it was his TV and Vini had better shut the fuck up or we'd all be out on our asses. Mad Dog Lopez did not, and does not, cotton to such talk. Attired typically and eccentrically in a Chinese robe and nothing else that evening, Vini managed to get in a minor scuffle with SOBH. We were fired on the spot. Six nights of a good-paying, close-to-home bar gig vanished into thin air up Vini's Chinese robe. We walked back up the hill, pissed, everybody giving Vini the silent treatment for blowing the gig. We would not be much longer for the Shore bar circuit anyway. The concert business awaited.

# EIGHTEEN

# STEEL
# MILL

We found out another group had registered the name "Child," so, at a late-night brainstorming session at the Inkwell Coffee House in the West End neighborhood of Long Branch, New Jersey, we searched for a new band name. The Inkwell was a longhair-friendly local institution one block in from the Long Branch beachfront. Its proprietor was "Joe Inkwell," a Hitlerian presence who would take the skin off of you for looking at him the wrong way. Nevertheless, he and I got along great and the place was a safe late-night haven for weirdos of all stripes. It was done up inside completely Beat generation. You could grab a cheeseburger, flirt with the blue-jeans-and-black-leotard-clad waitresses and spend a little time in an environment where you felt reasonably secure you would not be under attack, except possibly by the owner. I think it was Mad Dog who volunteered Steel Mill. That was the direction we were going in. It was blue-collar, heavy music, with loud guitars and a Southern-influenced rock sound. If you mixed it up with a little prog and all original songs, you had Steel Mill . . . you know, *STEEL* MILL . . . like *LED* ZEPPELIN . . . elemental-metal-based, bare-chested, primal rock.

We started playing long guitar-crunching concerts under that name and we began to draw and draw big. First hundreds, then thousands came to impromptu appearances in parks, at the local armory, at the Monmouth College great lawn or college gymnasium and any other location that would hold our growing tribe. We became something people wanted to see. We had a raw stage show and songs that were memorable enough for people to want to come back, hear them again, memorize their lyrics and sing their choruses. We began to attract and hold real fans.

Tinker took us down to the University of Richmond in Virginia, where he had a few connections. We played for free in the park, gave the locals a taste of us and then got hired for school events. We became enormously popular in Richmond, drawing up to three thousand people at our Southern concerts, with *no* album to our name. Our voodoo had worked outside of the Garden State! We opened up for Grand Funk Railroad in Bricktown, New Jersey, stole the house and headed south, where we opened for Chicago, Iron Butterfly and finally for Ike and Tina Turner at the Virginia War Memorial. We quickly built ourselves a second home in Richmond. Now we had two cities we could play quarter-annually, charging a buck at the door and coming home with thousands of dollars that would get us through the dry times. The catch was you could not overplay either area and there were only two! Once every four months was a lot. We'd become too big for the bars, too small for the big time, so we became a strange victim of our own local success. We could draw thousands when we played but in order to keep interest and our value up, we had to make ourselves scarce. We scouted around for a few more locations, opening for Roy Orbison at a festival in Nashville, Tennessee, playing in Chapel Hill, North Carolina, but it was our Jersey and Virginia fans who kept us in subs and cheeseburgers. The long weeks in between shows gave us a lot of time to practice, refine our band and settle into the unique position of authentic neighborhood superstars while remaining totally unknown outside of our given areas. So . . . what to do?

## Go West, Young Man

Tinker always regaled us with tales of San Francisco. Hell, it was 1970. Let's get out there and show them what we can do. We'd played with and done well against national bands for a year now. Bring on the big guns, the San Francisco groups. We were cocky as hell and sure we were good enough to make our mark anywhere. We felt we were the best undiscovered thing we'd ever seen, so we begged Tinker to take us to where the hippies ran free. A deal was struck. Tinker said if we each saved one hundred dollars and copyrighted our originals for their protection, he'd lead us to the far coast. Danny and I sat for two hours one evening at our dining room table and only managed to get one song onto staff paper. We figured, "Fuck it, just fill in the rest with a bunch of notes; Tinker will never know." That's what we did. We held one final concert at the surfboard factory for seed money, built a plywood box that would sit tucked inside Tinker's flatbed, covered it with an army tarp to protect the equipment from the rain and set up a separate station wagon (Danny's) with mattresses and water for the drivers' rest and recuperation. With these two vehicles, a hundred dollars each and a prayer, we would make the great crossing in three days. We had a paying New Year's Eve gig at California's Esalen Institute in the mountains of Big Sur. Esalen was one of the first human-potential spas in the United States. At that time, no one had ever heard of such a thing. It was just a gig for us, and we didn't have a clue as to what we were walking into. With the exception of Tinker and our short trips around the Southeast, none of us had ever been out of New Jersey.

The night before we left for California, Mad Dog and I visited our local cinema to see *Easy Rider*. It was not such a good send-off. As we watched the story of Peter Fonda and Dennis Hopper's journey across America, a slow, creeping dread overtook us. When Hopper was blasted off his motorcycle at the end of the film by a Cro-Magnon redneck, it dawned on us it might not be too friendly for folks like us out there. Tinker of course had taken that into consideration; no peace-loving hippies, we were armed. We had our cap-and-ball pistols, all perfectly legal, in the cab of our truck. We'd run into "bad vibes"—an attendant who might not want to gas us up, a tension-filled roadhouse diner—but no trouble. Tinker spoke the common language of automotive mechanics. It's amazing what a cross-cultural barrier breaker a little engine talk can be. We were in a vintage piece of hardware. People were curious about our old Ford truck and what the hell we were up to. Tink could've broken the ice with the grand pooh-bah of the Ku Klux Klan with his laconic command of the mystical ways of the internal combustion engine. Tink had gearhead knowledge accompanied by a strange and mighty confidence that put folks at ease. If those should fail, he seemed like the kind of guy who might shoot you.

The morning came, the truck was loaded, the station wagon prepared; I was twenty-one, and we were going west. West . . . dream time. West . . . California. That's where the music was. The Haight, San Francisco, Jefferson Airplane, the Dead, and Moby Grape, one of Steve's and my all-time favorite groups. West . . . free. Even my folks were there. I'd heard about the deserts, the palm trees, the weather, Seal Rock, the great redwoods of Muir Woods, the Bay, the Golden Gate . . . On our few phone calls, my mom had told me tales of their new life in the West. I hadn't seen my parents and younger sister in almost a year. Back then no one could afford cross-country bus, plane or train travel. I'd never met anyone who'd been on an airplane. So here it was. It would be a combination family reunion and career juggernaut that would set everything straight.

Our caravan of two left at dawn, rolling away from the surfboard factory, out of the industrial park and onto Route 35, over to 33 West, then to the New Jersey Turnpike South. It was winter and we'd take the southern route across the country to avoid as much snow and ice as possible. We were seven: Tinker, myself, Vinnie Roslin, Mad Dog, Danny, a pal headed west who would help drive and Tinker's favorite living thing, J. T. Woofer, his dog. The cabin of Tinker's forties flatbed comfortably held Tinker and me plus J. T. The rest of our travelers rode in Danny's sixties vintage station wagon.

We had three days to get to California. We had no extra money for motels and no camping gear, so we would not be stopping. We would drive in rotating shifts around the clock, pausing roadside only for food and gas. I didn't drive . . . at all. I had no car, no license; at twenty-one my transportation was a bicycle or my thumb. I had hitchhiked everywhere I went since I was fifteen years old and had gotten very comfortable with it. When I say I didn't drive, I mean I DID NOT KNOW HOW. I could not safely operate a motor vehicle. My old man never had the patience to teach me, and after one sprint spinning and jerking my way through the Freehold Raceway parking lot, Tex himself had thrown up his hands and quickly quit too. I was completely incompetent behind the wheel. I was not counted as one of the drivers for this trip. That's why we were glad to have the extra guy. There would be no "racing in the street" for me for a few years.

The trip was going well; then we hit Nashville, Tennessee. Somehow in Nashville, Tink, J. T. and I became separated from the car of drivers with "Phantom" Dan Federici at the wheel. The story later was "We looked around and you were gone." This created an enormous problem. All the drivers were with Danny. To make it to Big Sur, California, three thousand miles in three days from New Jersey, we *had* to drive around the clock. To make it there New Year's Eve for our date, the big wheels had to keep on turning. There were thousands of miles left and Tinker couldn't do it himself; the dog couldn't drive, so that left me. At midnight that evening Tink simply said, "I can't drive anymore, it's your turn." I said, "You know I can't drive." Tinker said, "There's nothing to it. Besides, you have to or we won't make the only job we have on the West Coast." I got behind the steering wheel of the big truck, an ancient behemoth, reminding one of the truck in Clouzot's *The Wages of Fear* that hauled nitroglycerin through the jungles of Central America. What followed was so, so ugly: a massive grinding of fine vintage gears that left us jerking all over the highway, steering that left the huge truck with all of our band equipment and everything of value that we owned in its hatch weaving barely within the lines of our lane. A head-on collision with the unknowing, trusting souls coming our way seemed imminent.

Still, it had to happen. Here's how we did it. Once we realized it was impossible for me to start from a dead stop, Tinker would get the transmission in first gear and get the truck rolling, and then we would switch seats in the tight cab, stepping on J. T. as she howled from the floorboards, and I would take over from second gear through fourth for as long as the highway held. We drove thousands of miles, the rest of the way, employing this method. We never saw or heard from Danny or the other vehicle again. We had no backup plan for someone getting lost. There were no cell phones, no way to communicate. All we had was a common destination, so we headed into the sun. It was not a restful ride for Carl Virgil West. I'd be driving through the desert night during his "sleep" break, weaving all over the highway, and I'd look over to see him with fear flooding his wide-open eyes. I couldn't blame him. My driving sucked. We were lucky I didn't kill us.

The big truck did not get easier to manage. I just drove, no license, no permit, no experience. When we came to a state-line crossing, a toll booth or a weigh station, I'd poke Tinker in the ribs and we'd switch seats again without coming to a stop. We got pretty good at it, but when we hit the mountain passes, terror set in. The truck was an old manual shift without particularly responsive steering. You had to clutch, shift, clutch, shift, clutch, shift, the engine begging for mercy, racing forward and back. I was killing that thing, but by the time we got to California I knew how to drive and Tinker had spent many a sleepless hour sprouting more than a few gray hairs.

# West

The country was beautiful. I felt a great elation at the wheel as we crossed the western desert at dawn, the deep blue and purple shadowed canyons, the pale yellow morning sky with all of its color drawn out, leaving just the black silhouetted mountains behind us. With the eastern sun rising at our backs, the deep reds and browns of the plains and hills came to life. Your palms turned salty white on the wheel from the aridity. Morning woke the Earth into muted color, then came the flat light of the midday sun, and everything stood revealed as pure horizon lowering on two lanes of blacktop and disappearing into . . . nothing—my favorite thing. Then the evening, with the sun burning red into your eyes, dropping gold into the western mountains. It all felt like home and I fell into a lasting love affair with the desert.

On we soldiered, through Texas, New Mexico and Arizona to the California border, then north to the Big Sur mountains. We were almost there but we had one more Halloween horror show of a night. Highway 1 to Big Sur had been washed out in a coastal storm, not an unusual occurrence, so Tinker searched the map for an alternate route. We stopped at an outpost of a filling station for a little local guidance. Tinker pointed at a squiggly thin line on the map and asked, "What about this?" The attendant answered, "It'll get you there but you don't want to take this truck over that road." Tinker and every perverse can-do bone in his body only heard the first part. We took it. For the first few miles, a beautiful freshly paved highway stretched out in front of us, then in one swift mountain bend, the road transformed into sliding dust and gravel. It became a barely passable one-way hell drive with a mountain within reach out the driver's-side window and a guardrail-less sheer cliff and empty grave awaiting outside the passenger's window. Tinker had gone mute at the wheel, eyes burning like a zombie's. He bumped, slid and rolled us for thirty miles and three hours of midnight over this impossible mountain pass. J. T. lay pinned to the floor like mortar fire was threatening her short canine life. She sensed we were hanging by the short ones and after an hour or so, my own stomach couldn't take it anymore. The view from the cab was way too zero sum. I lay down on the seat and closed my eyes. I did not sleep. The truck slipped and swayed, loose mountainside gravel raining on the cab roof like hail. We took one last turn and it was over. The highway opened up before us and we shortly made our way through the gates of the Esalen Institute at Big Sur. The night was pitch-black, without a light source anywhere. I found myself hustling down a small path, searching for our accommodations, on the black side of a mountain in California.

## Gopher's Palace

We would be staying with Gopher, a friend of Tinker's, on the "working" side of a small creek that separated Esalen's wealthy belly-button contemplators from its service staff. It was not easy to find. Gopher lived on the steep side of the mountain in a tree. He had built his "home" around a towering eucalyptus whose roots and trunk sprouted out of his living room floor on up through a sleeping loft and out the roof (hello, Big Sur). There was a fireplace, no facilities and no running water. You climbed the tree in the house to get to the sleeping loft. It was a place fine for a leprechaun but its miniature "rooms" were full with Tink, myself, J. T. and soon, rustling up out of the brush, the lost platoon of Danny and the two Vinnies. They'd followed the sound of my strumming guitar to Gopher's palace and we all had a joyful tall-tale-telling reunion.

At some point during the early evening before our arrival, Gopher had thought he heard a perpetrator amongst the bushes, unloaded his shotgun into the night and knocked out the electrical power for the entire side of the mountain. We sat by firelight, like Neanderthals huddled together in the heart of an unseeable new world. Finally, exhausted, we drifted off to sleep. When we woke at dawn and stepped out of Gopher's front door, we stood speechless before what we saw. Giant old-growth trees, vegetation so lush you'd get lost a few feet in off the walking path, color, winter bloom-ing flowers all set on a verdant mountainside that looked out high over the sun-fired emerald-green Pacific. If you watched for a while, you could see whales spouting in the distance. I'd never stood in the midst of nature like this and you could feel its humbling and intoxicating power. I approached a tree the likes of which I'd never seen before, covered with what appeared to be strange multicolored leaves. As I walked toward its base, thousands of butterflies exploded off its branches and shot into the hard blue sky. This was another world.

We quickly got the lay of the land. We were in the workers' quarters and that was basically where we were supposed to stay. It would be a few years before I would start gazing into my own wealthy belly button, and so across the creek at the institute there were things going on we simply could not comprehend. The first thing Mad Dog and I witnessed was a group of people curled up on a green lawn in white sheets returning to their "amoeba stage." This struck Vini and me as uproariously funny and we quickly came to believe, rightly or not, that the place, while gorgeous, was home to some good old first-rate Jersey carny quackery all dressed up in some new-age doublespeak. They did have great hot springs tucked into the side of a cliff overlooking the sea. There were the springs, a cold bath and everybody naked. This greatly appealed to unworldly Jersey folk such as ourselves and we spent what time we could there charming the rich ladies and bathing in nature's sweet revivifier. A few of the fellows made "friends" with paying guests, leading to midnight creeps around the mountainside. For food, the staff would slip us some breakfast out the back door of the kitchen in the morning and we'd spend the day exploring, watching the dog and pony show at the lodge or practicing in a little shed by the sea for our big New Year's Eve stand.

One afternoon I took a long walk deep into the forest. I stayed on the path so as not to get lost and began to follow the sound of a distant conga drum. About ten minutes in, deep in a wooded clearing I came upon a tall thin black man dressed in a dashiki hunched over a conga drum entertaining the wildlife. He looked up and I found myself face-to-face with Richard Blackwell, my homie from Freehold, whom I'd grown up with. What are the odds! We had a "Dr. Livingstone, I presume" moment, couldn't believe the two of us had ended up there thousands of miles from home at this exact place and time, decided it was destiny, and I asked him if he wanted to sit in with Steel Mill for the rest of our West Coast stretch. First stop, New Year's Eve.

When the night came, it all broke loose West Coast–style. Out of the nearby mountains came tattooed earth mamas, old grizzled mountain men, nubile young hippie girls fueled by acid, talking in tongues and ready to fuck. There were a lot of drugs and the show took off accordingly into the nether lands of California acid culture. Trance-dancing, the locals mixed merrily with the paying guests, and we played the crowd into a frenzy, with Richard Blackwell from the block, joined by Tinker, creating an unending pulse with their conga drums. It went on for a long time, and as a straightedge Jersey boy it was about all the fun I could take. Everybody wanted to give you drugs all the time. I was a stubborn young man and set in my fearful ways. I wasn't going there, so I played and played, and they went, the mountain hippies, their bonfires blazing, ancient faces with eyes rolling back alongside well-off middle Americans trying to find a new light who'd come west and were paying big for what we'd have done for 'em in New Jersey for two bucks.

Finally around dawn it quieted. Folks drifted back up into the hills and we sat exhausted. We'd entertained them and had been thoroughly entertained, but it was different from back home. Here music was a part of some larger tribal "consciousness-raising" event. The musician was more shaman and psychic facilitator. More mystic man than hard rocker or soul entertainer. I had the band and the skills to pull it off but I wasn't sure it was my stock-in-trade.

We stayed on for a few days afterward enjoying the pleasures of Big

Sur. The morning we left I sat on a bench overlooking the Pacific with a very straight middle-aged entrepreneur from Texas. He was lost in freak land and a seeker at the facility. I asked him why he was there. He said simply, "I've made a lot of money and I'm not happy." It'd be years before I'd have to wrestle with that one, but there was something about him that touched me. He wanted something more than the world of commerce that his life had offered him. He'd come all this way, laid down his cold hard cash and opened himself up to try to find it. I wished him well and hoped he was in righteous hands.

A few hours later I sat on a rocky green outcropping on the side of Highway 1. In my lap I held my travel bag; the sun was high and dry as I watched a small army of ants slipping between my boots, carrying bits of dust toward their hillside empire. I searched north up the highway and waited. The smell of eucalyptus bark and high grasses, that uniquely California smell, surrounded me and reminded me I was a young traveler in a strange land. It felt good. A hawk circled above me in the flat blue sky as forty minutes passed, then an hour. A car slowed down and pulled to the side of the road where I was sitting. Through the sun's glare reflecting off the front windshield I saw two big smiles. It was my mom and pop coming to welcome their only son to their promised land.

## Promised Land

My mom and dad's land of hope and dreams was a small two-bedroom apartment up a flight of stairs in a complex in the California suburb of San Mateo. It consisted of a living room/kitchen combo, a bedroom for my folks and a smaller bedroom for my little sis. They were proud of it. They loved California. They had jobs, they had a new life. My dad had taken up watercolor painting by numbers, and he played the home organ, its sour notes squealing beneath those mitts he called hands. He seemed to be all right. Leaving Freehold had done him some good. My mom was once again a respected legal secretary, at a firm in the Hillsdale Shopping Center, and my pop drove a bus at the airport.

I slept on the living room couch, ate some home cooking, shopped at the nearby St. Vincent de Paul or Salvation Army thrift stores and enjoyed being home. I was in the living room watching TV as my eight-year-old sister attempted to make me a homecoming cake. She had a big bowl of batter and an electric mixer set up on the kitchen table. The next thing I heard was a shattering scream, like a squirrel with its tail caught in the family mower. I ran to find batter splattered all over the kitchen walls and my little sis howling with the electric mixer still running and pressed close to her scalp. At first I couldn't figure out what I was seeing. Then I realized the mixer had run straight up a strand of her lovely long brown hair, which had drifted into the mixing bowl, and was now vibrating like a banshee against her little skull. A pull of the plug, a pair of scissors, a few kisses, some laughs and she was okay.

Soon the entire band would be sleeping on my parents' living room floor. It only lasted a few days. We were there to be discovered and that would take work, so we packed up and headed into San Francisco for our first audition. We pulled up to the Family Dog, home of the Quicksilver Messenger Service and a venerable old San Francisco ballroom that was looking for some new bands to open up for their main acts. Tinker had got us a shot. I recollect there were three or four bands auditioning that sunny afternoon. The first two weren't much, so we confidently took the stage and played well. We played about twenty minutes of the stuff that had made us superstars back home and didn't doubt we'd get the gig. After our set, the fourth band played. They were good. They were musically sophisticated, with several good vocalists and some very good songs. They didn't have the show that we did but that didn't seem to concern them. They just played . . . very, very well. They got the gig. We lost out. After the word came down, all the other guys were complaining we'd gotten ripped off. The guy running the joint didn't know what he was doing, blah, blah, blah . . .

That night I went back to my parents' house and lay awake on my couch thinking. They were better than us, and I hadn't seen anybody, certainly anybody who was still unknown, that was better than us—better than *me*—in a long time. The guy doing the booking was right. My confidence was mildly shaken and I had to make room for a rather unpleasant thought. We were not going to be the big dogs we were back in our little hometown. We were going to be one of many very competent, very creative musical groups fighting over a very small bone. Reality check. I was good, very good, but maybe not quite as good or as exceptional as I'd gotten used to people telling me, or as I thought. Right here, in this city, there were guys who in their own right were as good or better. That hadn't happened in a long while and it was going to take some mental realignment.

A few days later we were back at it. We auditioned at a club called the Matrix and this time we got the job. We would open for Boz Scaggs, Elvin Bishop and Charlie Musselwhite and garner one of our first unequivocal raves, in the *San Francisco Examiner* from music critic Philip Elwood. It was titled, due to the San Francisco rain outside, "A Wet Night with Steel Mill" and was everything we could've hoped for. Mr. Elwood wrote, "Never have I been so surprised by completely unknown talent." It gave us the shot in the arm we needed to impress the folks and newspapers back home and allowed us to think there might be a future there for us yet. Our pay at the Matrix was toll money across the Bay Bridge and hot dogs. That was it. We played for free. The experience was great. We got to meet and talk to some real recording artists. We weren't the band people were coming to see, so we had to work hard, and we did. I don't think we scared anybody but we impressed our share of the crowd one show at a time. Our next stop was the San Francisco Valhalla of Bill Graham's Fillmore West.

## In the Hall of the Gods

Everybody had been on this stage—the Band, B. B. King, Aretha, all the great San Francisco groups—and every Tuesday the Fillmore West held audition night. We nailed down a Tuesday slot and, nerves a-jingle-jangle, we headed down to stand on that stage and make our mark. You were one of five or six bands that would play for an hour or so to a paying crowd seated on the floor. Everybody there was good—you had to be to simply get an audition—but I didn't see anybody very exciting. Many simply droned on, playing in that very laid-back San Francisco style. When the workingmen from New Jersey took the stage, all that changed. We rocked hard, performing our physically explosive stage show, which had the crowd on its feet and shouting. We left to a standing ovation and some newfound respect, and were asked back for the following Tuesday. Later in the evening, as I hung around the ballroom talking to the locals and basking in as much West Coast glory as I could, somebody else was lighting up the stage. A band called Grin, its lead guitarist, Nils Lofgren, playing his guitar through a Hammond Leslie speaker, rocked the house 'til its closing. We went home satisfied, counting the days 'til the following Tuesday. We came back one week later and did it one more time to the same tumultuous response, then were offered a demo recording session at Bill Graham's Fillmore studios. Finally, just what we'd come three thousand miles for: our shot at the gold ring.

One crisp California afternoon, Steel Mill pulled up to the first professional recording studio we'd ever seen. It was a classic West Coast wood-paneled, potted-plant-infested rock star hangout, the likes of which I would be spending too much time in over the coming years. We cut three of our best originals, "The Judge Song," "Going Back to Georgia" and "The Train Song," as a demo for Bill Graham's Fillmore Records. When you first hear yourself on professional recording tape, you want to crawl, in a cold sweat, from the room. You always sound better inside your head and in your dreams than you do in the cold light of the playback room. There, the way you truly sound initially lands on you like a five-hundred-pound weight. Inside your head, you're always a little better of a singer, a little better of a guitarist and, of course, as with the layman, a little better-looking. Tape and film have no interest in the carefully protected delusions you've constructed to get through your day. You just have to get used to it. Not being quite as good as I thought was unfortunately becoming a theme I was revisiting throughout our West Coast jaunt.

The demo was as far as we'd get. The deal never happened. We were offered some sort of retainer fee but nothing that showed any real interest. Still, something was happening. We'd been reviewed. We had a semi-steady gig at a big city club, the Matrix. We'd drawn the attention of Bill Graham's Fillmore organization and we were now drawing a small enthusiastic crowd of our own. I saw my folks occasionally, preferring to stay close to the action with the band in a variety of crash pads in Berkeley, Marin County or wherever someone would allow us to take up some floor. I managed to get arrested hitchhiking (my specialty) on the California freeway. I had little money, no ID, no official residence. That seemed to be enough for them to pull me in. Reprising a role she'd played many times in New Jersey, where I'd managed to be hauled into local police stations for hard-core crimes as varied as not purchasing a beach badge, hitchhiking and getting caught in my girlfriend's father's "borrowed" Cadillac, my mother came down, bailed me out and dropped me off at the Matrix for the night's gig. I was still a kid and it was nice having her around to depend on, but soon we had to face the facts. Progress had come to a halt. We had no money, no paying work and no prospects. Unlike in New Jersey, we couldn't do our quarterly concert to make ends meet. Here, we had no viable, financially sound business model. We were as "discovered" as we were going to get. There were simply too many good groups around for someone to pay us to play. I was right when I allowed my parents to leave without me and stayed behind in New Jersey. We could survive as musicians *only* on our little sliver of the East Coast. We had to get back.

Tinker borrowed some fast money for road expenses back home, and feeling not quite like complete failures but not like the successes we'd imagined, we packed immediately. I bade my folks adieu and we hit the road to Richmond, Virginia. Richmond, one of the two places we could make a buck. If we could get there, we could work, make a few dollars and pull back into the Shore area, hopefully resuming our previously underappreciated status as local rock gods.

## Six Days on the Road

Our caravan of two once again headed south. Just a little ways out of San Francisco, Danny, leaning down to fix the radio while driving, managed to swerve off the highway, smash into a "Men at Work" sign, send the road crew scattering into the nearby brush, dent the hell out of our esteemed station wagon and continue happily on, Jersey bound. No problem. The problems would come soon enough. I was riding with J. T., the dog, in the back of the station wagon. We stopped on an Arizona highway for a piss break and got back in, and an hour later I realized there was an awful lot of room in the back of that station wagon now. J. T. had been left somewhere back along the highway. We signaled Tinker to pull over and I gave him the news. His eyes drifting out over the desert, containing his complete disgust, he mumbled, "Go back and get her." Two hours after we left J. T. by the side of the road, we pulled back into what we thought was our original piss location. Nothing . . . just dry silence, so silent you could hear the blood running through your veins in the thin desert air. Emptiness . . . vast, unending emptiness. Then to the west there was just a smudge of movement on the horizon. Something was alive and moving out there. We climbed back into the car and a half mile or so up the road, there was J. T., heading back toward the California border. We threw open our car door and one panting, tail-wagging, happy hound bounded into the rear seat, licking everything in sight. Two hours after we'd left him, we pulled up to Tinker leaning on his truck, standing sentinel by the side of the road. J. T. hopped out and into Tinker's cab, and a stone-faced Tink said, "Let's go."

Two days out of Richmond Danny's station wagon, on its last legs, rolled to a stop. Dead. We didn't have the spare parts and even Tinker's mighty skills couldn't get it running again. Okay, we were booked in Richmond. We had five guys. We had room for three plus the dog in the truck's cab. That left two by the side of the road. Tinker eyed the big plywood box containing our band gear on the back of his flatbed. After thirty minutes of repacking, in between the gear and the end of that box we were able to squeeze out about two feet of crawl space. Two of us were going to have to ride locked in there.

Now, it was midwinter and it was fucking cold; there was little heat in the cab and none in the rear box. I don't remember how we called it but Little Vinnie and I climbed in the back, and winter coats and all, we squiggled down into our sleeping bags. We were locked in, face-to-face, inhabiting a two-by-eight-foot space of freezing blackness. We had some water, a flashlight and each other. With no way to communicate with the cab, we were packed tightly in behind several thousand pounds of rock 'n' roll gear, so if the truck hit a steep incline and the weight shifted . . . problem. We were pressed up against the rear gate on one side and our Marshall amplifiers on the other, our fate entwined with that of Tinker's truck. Anything happens to the truck, we're padlocked in with no way out. We had an empty container for piss and a guarantee from those up front to stop every two hours to check on us. Two days went by. Mad Dog spelled one of us every once in a while. Danny had some "confinement" issues and the tight black box wasn't for him. After a while, you just sat there in the cold dark and let your mind wander.

Whatever its results, the California trip would have a lasting impact on me. I got to see the country. I came up against some real talent and held my own, but the band that took us out at the Family Dog stayed with me. They had something we didn't, a certain level of sophisticated musicality. They were better than us and that didn't sit well with me. It's not that I didn't expect to come up against superior talent; that happens, it's the way God planned it. I was fast, but like the old gunslingers knew, there's always somebody faster, and if you can do it better than me, you earn my respect and admiration and you inspire me to work harder. I wasn't afraid of that. I was concerned with not maximizing my own abilities, not having a broad or intelligent enough vision of what I was capable of. I was all I had. I had only one talent. I was not a natural genius. I would have to use every ounce of what was in me—my cunning, my musical skills, my showmanship, my intellect, my heart, my willingness—night after night, to push myself harder, to work with more intensity than the next guy just to survive untended in the world I lived in. As I sat there in the black, I knew when we got back home, there would have to be some changes made.

NINETEEN

# HOMECOMING

We arrived in Richmond exhausted but glad to be back in familiar territory. We played, they paid us. How sweet it is. We trucked back into Jersey as the conquering heroes and for proof we had . . . our . . . our . . . REVIEW! We had been recognized by a big-time newspaper music critic as Jersey badasses gone to teach those West Coast sissy boys something about THE ROCK! If you didn't believe us, you could read all about it in the *Asbury Park Press*. They covered our return like it was Odysseus's return to Ithaca. We'd put Jersey, the butt of so many hack comedians' one-liners, for a brief moment on the rock 'n' roll map. More would follow, but for now we played a cele- bratory homecoming show and I stashed away some cash in my bank, a sock in the top drawer of my dresser at the surfboard factory. Then I sat down to reconfigure the band.

On our West Coast safari a seam had opened up between Little Vin- nie and the rest of the band. It happens. Only the luckiest bands don't grow apart. There was some disagreement over rehearsal time and effort put in. Everyone moves differently, and no two musicians' commitment is exactly the same. You can fall out of the arc of a group without even noticing it. Vinnie was a good guy, a charismatic bass player and one of my original rock 'n' roll heroes in the Motifs. He hailed from the same greaser neck of the woods I did and had been through the cauldron of our California trip. It wasn't going to be easy letting him go. So I chickened out and let Mad Dog do it. The Dog, being a good deal less sentimental than myself, probably handled it with his usual no-bullshit aplomb. I imagine he just spit it out, made Vinnie feel glad he hadn't been assaulted and went on his way.

It was time to call on my old paisan Steve Van Zandt. Despite our friendship we were both front men and lead guitarists, so we'd never played in the same band together. Steel Mill had built up a substantial enough name that I thought Steve might consider helping me out playing bass for a while. We drove together up north to a music shop, where Steve bought himself a clear Ampeg see-through bass and an amplifier. We headed straight back to the factory, where we immediately began rehearsal, breaking Steve in on our original material. We timed it perfectly to have Steve setting up his equipment just as Little Vinnie came by to pick up his. Nice. Steve stepped into the next room, Vinnie gave us hell, we took it and picked up rehearsal where we'd left off. With Steve on the bass, his playing and our long friendship kicked some new spirit into the band.

## Rock 'n' Roll Riot

We went back to our old circuit, running A to B, Jersey to Richmond, then back again. In the late sixties and early seventies it seemed to be just a part of the cultural lay of the land that you were going to have some police trouble. If you played a few minutes over time, they sent out the local coppers to stop the heathen racket. It became almost routine. The police would gather behind the stage, a debate of sorts would take place between the principals and usually some compromise would be reached. Most of the cops were just interested in getting the concert over, the kids home and themselves back to the doughnut shop, but sometimes you'd run into hard-asses. When Steel Mill played, in conjunction with our audience, we owned the room. We owned it by possession. We didn't have an attitude about it and generally wanted to be cooperative but in those days, culturally opposing forces attracted one another.

At the end of an evening of great fun in the University of Richmond's gym I noticed a heated discussion taking place in the small room containing the gym's power switches. The power room lay only a few feet behind the drum riser. I watched the argument escalate until I saw Billy, our road man, and a local police officer square off against each other in an Abbot and Costello–like wrestling match, each trying to keep the other away from the power switches. The power went on. It went off. It went on. It went off. Vini Lopez, never one to take the interruption of our endeavors sitting down, hopped off his drum kit and joined the melee. The blue-uniformed invaders were literally beaten back and the show continued on with great "fuck the man" drama. Shortly after the show, as we packed our equipment into Tinker's truck we noticed we couldn't find Vini. We searched the hall and the streets around the building and waited for him to show. Nothing. Then a student told us that ten minutes before, he'd seen the police quietly slip up and take a cursing young man away in handcuffs. Vini was transported straight to the county jail, not to be seen again for a tumultuous month.

Without access to enough bail money, we'd have to do what we did best and play a "Free Mad Dog" concert. It was booked at the Clearwater Swim Club in Middletown, New Jersey. Several thousand showed; we'd imported a drummer from Richmond, rehearsed him thoroughly and were ready to gig. The night began uneventfully, but trouble started when the

Middletown police sent a plainclothes narcotics officer to stroll through the crowd and bust those smoking nature's weed. The crowd, sensing strength in numbers, did not stand for this and threw the narc, clothes and all, into the swimming pool at the center of the complex. Tempers began to rise and the situation escalated when the police chief of Middletown sent over a bus full of officers in their newly acquired SWAT gear to make sure this thing got shut down on the button. We'd always play a little longer than usual and in this case it was perceived as provocative criminal intent. The power was cut (déjà vu all over again). Tink, living up to his name, found a bypass to restore electricity to the stage. The crowd cheered. That did it. The cops stormed the place with billy clubs flailing; some of the police came up the front side of the stage and challenged the band members. A little skinny officer was poking at me in the gut and yelling, "C'mon, motherfucker, c'mon." I turned to notice Danny lifting the very expensive Marshall amplifier head off his large stack of cabinets. I saw some officers approaching the stage from the rear, then I saw Danny's speaker stacks "accidentally" go tumbling over upon them. (This would feel roughly equivalent to a box of eight bowling balls rumbling over on your ass.) Some got trapped underneath, crawled out howling and took off. Another officer leapt onstage, immediately grabbed Danny's arm and tried to place him under arrest. Flo, Danny's Jersey-girl-to-the-bone wife, leapt onstage and grabbed her man's other arm. A Keystone Kops tug-of-war ensued, with Danny playing the part of the rope between his wife and the officer as he resisted arrest. A big kid I'd seen at a few shows climbed on the stage, approached the officer to within inches of his face and let loose with the popular invective of the day: "Pig, pig, pig, pig," etc. . . . The officer flipped, let Danny go and leapt off the stage, chasing this kid into the crowd. "Phantom Dan" slipped away into the night.

For a week the local papers were filled with "ROCK 'N' ROLL MELEE!" headlines. Guns and knives were reportedly found under the stage (not true); a police chief was allegedly assaulted with an amplifier (true). The ACLU came down, investigating "police brutality," and everybody was happy. We all hid out, but then a permanent warrant for Danny's arrest was issued for assaulting a police officer. We now had no drummer and no organ player. With the money we made from the catastrophic Middletown swim club fiasco we were able to bail Vini out of jail in Virginia. Now, what were we going to do about Danny? He did not want to surrender. It was understandable; police treatment for longhairs in sixties New Jersey could be rather intemperate. We'd all heard of a dark hole in the Freehold jail where you would reside naked as an ape until you agreed to let the jail barber give you the standard con's haircut. No, compassionate treatment was not a sure thing, so Danny stayed on the run. Problem: we needed to play and we were booked for a big show at Monmouth College in the upcoming weeks. As the date closed in we tried several replacement organists, none quite up to snuff. Finally, the Phantom said he would chance playing. Once we were onstage, we figured, the police wouldn't dare arrest him in front of three thousand screaming hippies. That became our plan.

The night arrived and all we had to do was get Danny in and out of the gym without the cops all over us. We set up; the crowd entered; Danny was hidden in the backseat of a friend's car in the gym parking lot waiting for the high sign. At five minutes before our eight o'clock start time, I slipped out the back door, tapped on Danny's rear window and uttered the password, "Showtime." All I heard was "I'm not coming." Huh . . . ? "I'm not coming. There are cops all over the place. I've seen them on the roof." I stood up, looked around; all I heard was the chirping of the crickets in the nearby trees. I scanned the roof. Nothing. I searched the parking lot. Nothing. Then Danny rolled down his window and the smell of something pungent and sweet wafted into the night air. Danny had smoked himself into a mild state of paranoia. I explained to him in clear language that he would be leaving the vehicle. His safety would be in my hands, and he would be fine.

Following the usual Phantom complaining, begging, cajoling and my step-ping into the tiring shoes of the voice of reason, he got out of the car and, unimpeded, we entered the building.

The minute we were in the door, Danny's friend "Party Petey," another local organ grinder, greeted him with a boisterous shout-out: "Daaaannnnyyyy!" He was coldcocked seconds later by Mad Dog Lopez, and we had to step over Party Petey to get to the stage. We blasted into "The Judge Song," and the concert was rollickingly under way. We danced in our shoes, congratulating ourselves on our brilliance at putting one over on the local PD. Nobody but nobody would bust Danny in front of this crowd. At the end of the evening in a gesture of hippie solidarity I pulled the "brothers and sisters" out of the audience until the stage was an undulating mass of glazed eyes and tie-dye. Danny slipped away from his organ, off the front lip of the stage and out the front door, still free. Power to the people! But at what a fucking exhausting cost. We couldn't continue on like this, so we convinced Danny to turn himself in the following week. We bailed him out, and there was a small trial, my memory being everything ended up a wash. That was it. I'd had enough. Outlaw days over.

Steel Mill with Steve and me continued to be great fun. Besides the enjoyment of having my pal by my side, Steve had an aggressive, bold style as a bassist, and he added some nice vocal harmonies. I'd always doubted myself as a singer. I felt I didn't have enough true tone and range. I didn't give myself credit for being able to immerse myself in what I was singing. Joe Strummer, Mick Jagger and many of the great rock 'n' roll and punk front men did not possess great voices but their blood-and-guts conviction, their ownership of their songs, made up for it and lent them deep personal style. Still, I thought we could improve our band in the area of our lead vo-cals and I was willing to step back as full-time singer to do so. There was a fellow named Robbin Thompson in a great group out of Richmond called Mercy Flight. I thought he had one of the best undiscovered rock voices I'd ever heard. He was a cross between John Fogerty and Rod Stewart and fronted his band with a lot of power and style. Raiding another group for their best guy, particularly a group you know, is not a very neighborly thing to do. I didn't lose too much sleep over it. I wanted the best group I could imagine. I told the rest of the band my idea; they didn't think it was necessary, but they deferred.

Robbin Thompson came north and for a while we were the Sam and Dave of hard rock. It was a good band. Probably not as good as our original four. Robbin was a great vocalist, but there was something in the tightness of the smaller unit and the ownership of my material that ultimately made us better suited to have me singly fronting the band. It was another lesson learned and one I would revisit again thirty years later with the E Street Band.

I had stylistically outgrown Steel Mill's heavy rock, roots 'n' boogie. I was listening to Van Morrison, and Joe Cocker's *Mad Dogs and Englishmen*, and was interested in returning to my soul roots. I talked to Mad Dog and Steve about moving forward with me into something completely different, a ten-piece horns-and-singers-augmented rock and soul band, playing nothing but new original material.

I'd recently been to Upstage and heard a young black keyboardist who floored me. He was sixteen years old and one of the greatest musicians I'd ever heard in Asbury Park. Davey Sancious had pure musical genius and incredible stage presence. He was a star in the making and I wanted him in my band. David had the courage to cross the tracks and enter the primarily white rock world of the Upstage Club in search of musical adventure. In turn he was a completely new presence on the scene and stirred enormous excitement. There was some drifting back and forth across the color line in Asbury in those days, but not a lot. Garry Tallent played with Little Melvin and the Invaders, an all-black soul band with a young Clarence Clemons on sax, in the black clubs surrounding Asbury. I'd wander over to the Orchid Lounge on Springwood Avenue when they brought in my favorite soul acts. As a white man at the Orchid, you were an oddity but never hassled,

We'd all shop at Fisch's clothing store, the premier superfly outlet in the black community. The riots changed all that. They made the two communities more suspicious of each other, burned Fisch's down to the ground and made a trip to Springwood a lot less welcoming, but they also seemed to throw the more musically adventurous into each other's arms. Davey joined my new Bruce Springsteen Band and I left my days of long-haired, guitar-slinging glory behind.

# TWENTY

# ENDLESS SUMMER

At the factory life went on. Mad Dog and I had learned to surf from the kids who came in to have their boards worked on and for a while, we got seriously into it. This led to a lot of sleeping on the beach underneath the pilings at North End Beach in Long Branch. Mad John's Surf Shop was on the pier above us and if it rained you'd find us jammed and crumpled like sardines in our sleeping bags with the other homeless surfers squeezed in amongst the surfboards inside the shop. Come morning we'd stumble out into the mushy Jersey surf for a day of water and waves. We surfed from dawn 'til dusk and I had a couple of the nicest summers of my life. It was all music, girls and waves, just like the song said. I had a secondhand Challenger Eastern long board I really learned how to ride. I loved that board and had the most fun I've ever had in the ocean on it. When the short board revolution hit, I felt pressured to pick up a six-foot rocket ship. Tinker built 'em because it was what the young surfers wanted, but he was stone-cold old-school and never liked 'em. When I first caught a wave on mine, it was so surprisingly fast and maneuverable, it came shooting right out from underneath my feet. Whoa, Silver. I broke my front tooth on it as a landlocked and stunned Steve Van Zandt watched from the shore at Bradley. I walked up on the beach, looked at Steve and said, "Something don't feel right, there's too much air." Stevie, his eyes as big as dinner plates, said, "Your tooth is broken, your front one." For the first time in my life, I visited a dentist (previously, it'd been my old man with one end of a string tied to the doorknob and the other to my loosening tooth). He capped my tooth and straightened my other front one, readying me for the big time.

Later that fall, I nearly drowned in hurricane surf I should never have been out in. Mad Dog and I had sat on the beach all morning debating whether to go out or not. Finally around noon some cowboy bopped along and talked us into going out with him. We were having a blast; then an outside set rose on the horizon. I paddled like a windmill, immediately rediscovering my faith in Catholicism as I prayed like never before: "Lord, please let me slip over the peak of this monster." No dice. I got pounded, thrown toward the rock jetty and dumped on by two more outside crushers; my surfboard was instantly stripped from my hands in the pre-surfboard-leash 1970s. My poor swimming barely saved me as I crawled up onto the sand, like the first creature slipping out of the pre-Jurassic soup, bruised and hurting. I lay there for a long time, breathing in gulps, my heart pounding, thanking the God I did not believe in. Aloha, Hawaii. There would be no fifteen-foot Pipeline for me.

We held auditions for singers for the Bruce Springsteen Band, my new calling card, at the factory. Brave young women answered our ad in the *Asbury Park Press*, driving up into the dark industrial wilderness toward what must have looked like a rapist's paradise just to test their talents. We had

Vegas-style songbirds; opera singers; horrible, hilarious pre-karaoke wannabes who tested our good manners and self-control. I even spoke on the phone to a high school–age Patti Scialfa, dispensing the fatherly advice that this was a traveling gig and it'd be best for a young lady to stay in school. Finally a couple of good black gospel singers from the west side of Asbury, Delores Holmes and Barbara Dinkins, wandered in and perfectly fit the bill. The horns were even harder to find. "Jazzbos" ruled and it was simply tough finding guys willing to play rudimentary R & B parts for no cash. We did it and it was a good band.

I wrote "You Mean So Much to Me Baby," later covered by Southside Johnny and Ronnie Spector on Southside's first album. We played maybe a dozen shows and I found it was impossible to keep a band of that size financially together at our stage of the game. I learned early that people pay for the franchise name. Steel Mill was no longer and neither was my drawing power. The Bruce Springsteen Band, even billed as "formerly Steel Mill," did not attract the same life-sustaining numbers my old band did. I'd declared democracy and band names dead after Steel Mill. I was leading the band, playing, singing and writing everything we did. If I was going to carry the workload and responsibility, I might as well assume the power. I didn't want to get into any more decision-making squabbles or have any confusion about who set the creative direction of my music. I wanted the freedom to follow my "muse" without unnecessary argument. From now on, the buck would stop here, if I could make one.

I look back on this as being one of the smartest decisions of my young life. I've always believed the E Street Band's continued existence—and it's now been forty-plus years since its inception—is partially due to the fact that there was little to no role confusion amongst its members. Everyone knew their job, their boundaries, their blessings and limitations. My bandmates were not always happy with the decisions I made and may have been angered by some of them, but nobody debated my right to make them. Clarity ruled and allowed us to forge a bond based on the principle that we worked together, but it was my band. I crafted a benevolent dictatorship; creative input was welcomed within the structure I prepared but it was my name on the dotted line and on the records. Later, when trouble came knocking, it came my way. So the last word was going to be mine from here on in. Even then, problems arose, but we had in place a reasonably well-defined system to contextualize and deal with them.

The first hit I took for this decision was the loss of most of the audience that was drawn to Steel Mill's heavy power, and the steady money that came with it. Then the Bruce Springsteen Band dwindled from nine to seven when we lost our horn section. We did some work in the South based on our Steel Mill rep and found there were some places, even in 1971, that didn't want us to bring along our black singers. They claimed they didn't want "that sound" and were simply requesting something more like my old band's rock steady. During a Richmond stint, I received a phone call from one of the girls, who'd brought along a troublesome boyfriend. I went to their motel and when she opened the door I found they'd argued and he'd hit her so hard her face was opened to the white bone; the boyfriend was gone. We played that night as a five-piece, limped back home to Jersey, lost our singers and all of our road work.

Around this time, Tinker's misanthropic tendencies had gotten the better of most of the group. Merry insults and abuse were a natural part of Tinker's day. He aimed them at virtually everyone, with the exception of me. The resentments built up, along with quarrels over some of Tinker's managerial decisions. That, and a natural burnout of the relationship, brought an end to Carl West's tenure as manager. Tinker had done a lot for me and he would soon do more. We had a real friendship, and neither Tink nor I had many of those. The Challenger Eastern surfboard factory in Wanamassa was now no more and we had a new clubhouse in a garage in Highlands. Highlands was then a risk-your-ass, redneck fishing town in the lowlands of Central Jersey where the lobsters meet the land. We'd built the interior of this dilapidated space ourselves, banging the nails, raising the walls and insulating our recording studio. The whole thing was a classic off-the-grid, below-the-radar Carl West production. We were ghosts in the machine, a bunch of non-tax-paying, under-the-table-living townies, completely divorced from the straight world.

I went by the garage one fall day to deliver the news. Tinker was out front underneath his truck, his legs hanging out into the street, working on the engine. "Tink . . ." I hear the cool clink of tools being picked up and set down on the pavement but all I can see is his body from the waist down.

"Yeah . . ."

"The guys have decided it's time to go our own way, handle ourselves for a while and see how it goes . . ."

"Whatever you want . . ." Silence. Tools being shifted on the concrete . . . more silence. I walked away.

The new sound I was pursuing, an amalgam of good songwriting mixed with a soul–and–R & B–influenced rock music, would eventually be the basis for the sound of my first two records, *Greetings from Asbury Park* and *The Wild, the Innocent and the E Street Shuffle*. There would be no more guitar histrionics. I now valued ensemble playing at the service of the song. I soon found out that though this was more personally and musically satisfying, in the Garden State, it was simply not as financially fruitful a soil as pounding hard rock, and surviving got harder. I became very dependent upon Tom Potter's $20 a night for jamming at Upstage on the weekends. I could live on thirty or forty bucks a week with no problem. Then Tom decided to close the Upstage Club and head to Florida. I moved into Tom and Margaret's apartment. They'd separated along the way and Tom was now living there alone. It was sad. The place was a freak show specifically built for *two*, two lovely but very strange people. It had a bizarre hard black-and-red color scheme, thousands of bottle caps glued to the kitchen ceiling, constructions of soda cans and bottles everywhere you looked, a refrigerator completely covered in *Playboy*'s Playmate of the Month centerfolds—every piece of junk was used to create something you'd never seen before in Tom's boho-on-acid design style. The whole effect looked like the backseat of Tom Waits's Cadillac. Looking back on it, it was a true piece of outsider art. Living in it was something else, but that's what I and two buddies did.

Tom Potter, crazy, bragging, barrelhouse, fuck-the-world, pirate Tom, was heartbroken. Margaret was gone, her strange attractions with her, and she wasn't coming back. The old hell-raiser's spirit had been beaten out of him. He was quiet, reflective. He'd break into tears and was a sad shadow of the guy who'd ringmastered the Saturday night circus of probably the wildest teen club in the nation. The "shortest miniskirt" contests would be no more. The crawling out of the club at dawn to wander to the boardwalk and crash on the beach was over. Black Tiny, White Tiny, Big Bad Bobby Williams, Southside, Garry, Steve and me, Big Danny, Little Danny, Party Petey, the outlaw motorcycle drifters, the stray teenyboppers, the late-night strippers and the hundreds of Shore musicians who flocked to the place like it was Mecca in summer would have to find a new home. The Upstage, the place I'd formed my most powerful musical friendships, the real birthplace of the E Street Band, was finished.

On the morning Tom left for Florida, we gathered out in front of the club, gave him our thanks for being there when we needed him and for the fabulous mess he'd created. After a few handshakes and hugs, he climbed into his junker and headed south, never to be seen again.

## TWENTY-ONE

# BEATNIK DELUXE

A first-floor drugstore, a second-floor fully equipped abandoned beauty salon complete with two rows of huge beehive hair dryers. This is where Tom and Margaret once worked their day jobs and I wrote the body of *Greetings from Asbury Park*. The third-floor living quarters had a big bay window that looked out upon the Nation of Islam's storefront headquarters. Tom had a gigantic bed he'd set four feet up on stilts that commandeered 80 percent of the room. If it could've talked, Tom would've had to cut its tongue out. I had a back bedroom that led to a small kitchen and a funky roof garden. It was the coolest crib in town, where two friends and I chipped in sixty bucks each for a month's rent. That sixty bucks was about to get a lot harder to come by.

Gigless, shut out of the Shore Top 40 scene by our playlist, our concert days over, we needed a new source of income. Steve and I had an idea.

We'd canvass Asbury on a peak summer-season Saturday night from one end to the other. The club that was doing the lousiest business was where we'd make our pitch to play. We worked north to south and around midnight, we walked into a bar called the Student Prince. It had just been purchased by a bricklayer from Freehold. He was bartending, and with exactly Steve, myself and one other bereft patron haunting a stool down the far end of the bar, we figured this was it. Outside, Asbury was buzzing, but here we had found its black hole. Our pitch was simple. He doesn't pay us a dime. We charge one dollar at the door, play what we want, take the door receipts and go home. He can't lose.

We laid it out; he thought a minute, then said, "What are you gonna play?"

"Whatever we want . . ."

"Uh . . . I don't know."

The place was high-season empty. That is the loneliest feeling a bar owner can have on the Jersey Shore; it sits like a fist in your gut. And still the resistance to original music in our hometown was so great, he "didn't know"?! He gave us the gig. We showed up the next Saturday, the final five of us, Mad Dog, Steve, Dave Sancious, Garry Tallent and myself. We charged our dollar. We played to fifteen people. Five fifty-minute sets, from nine to three a.m. We made fifteen dollars, three dollars apiece, and went home. With Steel Mill, we had made as much as $3,000 a night with no recording contract and $1 admissions. When that money was split, after expenses, band members went home with hundreds of dollars in their pockets. Do you know how long you could live on hundreds of dollars in 1971 or 1972 with no taxes, no dependents and no rent? A long, long, long time. Now I sent my men home with *three* dollars.

The following week, we did it again. We played to thirty music lovers and made $30. Six bucks a man. The next week, we played to eighty, then a hundred, then one twenty-five, then we started playing Fridays and Saturdays, then Wednesdays, Fridays and Saturdays, drawing from one hundred to one hundred fifty people, the club maximum, at a shot. We were making a living. We'd found a small core of fans who gravitated to the only independent music in town. They kept us alive. It was a cool little scene. Friends started to show up and jam. Danny Federici and Flo came down and she busted him with a heavy beer mug for flirting with another girl. Another night a gun was discharged. No one was shot. The club was like a private house party held three times a week for the local street, a pretty hip group of people. The bricklayer was happy. The band was happy. The people were happy.

The Student Prince is where the cultural event of my generation would find me on the weekend of August 15 to 17, 1969, as five hundred thousand people descended on White Lake in Bethel, New York, to flop on Max Yasgur's farm and bring all that had been building to a head. For me, it was a weekend like any other, playing in this little club for a shot and beer audience of locals and friends. From where I stood the whole thing up north looked like too much of a hassle, too much traffic, too many drugs. Even though at the moment, in comparison, it didn't look like much, I was on my own adventure.

## Big Man Walking

I was still interested in my rock and soul sound and still on the hunt for a good sax player. I had immersed myself in the records of Gary U.S. Bonds, King Curtis, Junior Walker, and Dion and I just loved the sound of a ripping rock 'n' roll saxophone. One guy, Cosmo, showed up, jammed with us and was really good. He had a head full of frizzy red hair and a semipsychotic fuse rumored to be shorter than the Mad Dog himself's. Two of those and we'd all have our mug shots on the Asbury Park post office wall.

Garry said he knew a guy named Clarence Clemons. He said he'd played with him in Little Melvin and the Invaders, the local soul band that worked the black clubs in and around Asbury Park. He said Clarence was magic. The problem was nobody could find him. Then by happenstance Clarence was playing the Wonder Bar at the north end of Asbury the same night we were at the Student Prince on the southern end of town. He'd heard about me by now and came with his horn to see what all the fuss was about.

It *was* a dark and stormy night. A nor'easter had blown in and swept the circuit clean. Ocean and Kingsley were a gusty, wet no-man's-land with streetlights rattling in the wind. The town was deserted. We were onstage playing for a few hearty patrons who'd wandered in to warm up, grab a drink and hear some music. As the Big Man approached the front of the Prince, a mighty gale blew down Ocean Avenue, ripping the club door off its hinges and down the street. A good omen. I looked to the back of the room and saw a big black figure standing in the shadows. There he was. King Curtis, Junior Walker and all my rock 'n' roll fantasies rolled into one. He approached the stage and asked if he could sit in. He stepped up onto the bandstand, took his place to my right and let loose with a tone that sounded like a force of nature pouring out of his horn. It was big, fat and raw, like nothing I'd ever heard before. My immediate response was that this . . . this was the sound I'd been looking for. More than that, there was something in the chemistry between the two of us, side by side, that felt like the future being written. The night, however, was just a teaser. C had a steady working gig and I didn't have much to offer yet, so at the end of the evening, we talked, complimented each other and promised to stay in touch. I would meet Clarence again but first I had forty miles of bad road to run.

Some stability had been resumed. One hundred and fifty bucks a night and we all brought home $30 three nights a week. That was $90 a week, depending on the small fluctuations of the crowd. Easy enough to live on and even save a few dollars. During this time, I fell in obsession with a lovely surfer girl, a drug-taking, hell-raising wild child who played by nobody's rules. She was a perfect antidote to the control freak in me and opened up my hunger for every blond perfect thing I never had. She was so alive, funny and broken, I couldn't resist her. She stirred up my Catholic-school-bred messianic complex, then did the bone-and-heart-crushing dance over it that it deserved. She'd been around a little, California and back, knew a few grade-B-level rock stars, brought them down to "discover" my band, then slept with them. I got a handshake and a "you guys are great" T-shirt out of the deal. I stayed with her and her girlfriend in an apartment in Long Branch, New Jersey. While surfer girl played in the dark, the girlfriend let me know what was really going on, comforted my bruised ego, told me I deserved better and you know the rest. She had a small lovely child and I played Daddy for a little while. It was sweet but we were truly a couple of street kids with this beautiful little thing tagging along with us. The one thing I'd saved from my childhood, despite all my moving around, was my first rocking horse. It was made of wood, only about twenty-four inches high, painted a pale cream with light red spots, a playground Appaloosa, and I loved that thing. I gave it to her for her little girl.

Eventually the whole setup threw me for a loop, so in a perfect state of confusion, I decided I'd strike out west once more to try my luck someplace where nothing reminded me of anything. "Sandy, my boardwalk days are through." My surfer girl disappeared and our girlfriend went traveling with the Ringling Bros. and Barnum & Bailey Circus, our paths occasionally crossing on the road. Years later I would occasionally run into mother and daughter at the Stone Pony together, both still beautiful. Before I left Jersey, however, one last significant thing would happen to me on the East Coast.

## Meeting Mike

I was hanging out with a friend of mine, Louie Longo, alongside a trailer park in Highlands, New Jersey. Tinker was living in a small cottage across the street. We kept up our friendship and would see each other rather often. I'd visit him at the new factory we built on Main Street as he designed sound systems and befriended, enraged and insulted the neighbors. Here he lovingly restored his vintage cars and boats, subverted the government, hatched million-dollar schemes and generally went on tinkering. One day he pulled up to Louie's as I sat on the front steps counting blades of grass. "I'm going to New York to see this record producer. You ought to ride with me and play a few songs. Wanna come?" For some reason, that afternoon I was hesitant. Maybe I was worn out from all the phony opportunities I'd run into. By now I'd had quite a few years of meeting folks who coulda/woulda/shoulda got us a foot in the music-biz door and none of it had panned out. But . . . I had recently begun to write some pretty good acoustic music and still felt I was the best undiscovered player I'd ever seen, so I hopped in Tinker's station wagon and up the yellow brick road to the Emerald City we drove.

We pulled up to a building on Fifth Avenue and took an elevator up to Wes Farrell Music. It was after business hours when we stepped out into a darkened office building with a long aisle of writers' cubicles. Standing in front of me was a thirtyish or so short black-haired man who greeted Tinker in a hard New York accent. Tink introduced me and I shook the hand of Mike Appel. We stepped into Mike's office, a small box of a room with a piano, a tape recorder, a guitar and a couple of chairs. It was Brill Building austere, a small space where writers spent their time under contract to a music publisher trying to come up with tomorrow's hits today. In Mike's case that publisher was Wes Farrell, and Mike had had a hand in writing the Partridge Family smash "Doesn't Somebody Want to Be Wanted." Mike spieled me on who he was and what he could do (publish, produce, manage), and I played him a few songs that were the precursors to the songs I'd write for *Greetings from Asbury Park*. Mike expressed some interest and I explained how I was leaving soon for California on my heartbreak '71 tour. I might be back sometime in the future or never. He gave me his number and said if I came back to give him a call.

# TWENTY-TWO

# CALIFORNIA DREAMIN' (TAKE TWO)

In the days before Christmas, Tinker and I prepared to cross the country one more time, via his old Ford station wagon. It would be the same routine, seventy-two hours, three thousand miles, no sleep, straight through. On our way south, we decided to stop in our old stomping grounds of Richmond, Virginia. We ended up in a strip club, where Tinker bonded with a belly dancer. He decided to spend the night with his new pal and I stayed with an old Southern girlfriend. When we met at the station wagon the next morning, there was the belly dancer, her bags packed. She'd decided she'd had enough of the new South and threw her lot in with us to head for the new West. She was a nice gal and a pleasure to have along for the ride. She had some friends on the coast and talked about opening a belly-dancing studio in Northern California, just the sort of area where that kind of thing might take off. The trip was pretty uneventful except for some vicious snowstorms we ran into crossing the western mountains. I still didn't have my license, but as usual, those were the details. We hit areas of the highway where eighteen-wheelers were parked, engines running, drivers asleep in their cabs, backed up for miles, unable in the ice and snow to make it up the steep mountain grades.

One night the road vanished before our eyes; there was so much snow it was impossible to tell the location of the highway's shoulder. We had chains on our tires but we still did plenty of ice-skating over some very treacherous terrain. Our belly-dancing gal pal was getting pretty nervous, so we pulled to a stop. Tinker and I got out on a high mountain pass where there were no other cars visible. There was just a city of snow falling from the sky and gathering around us. It was quiet, dead desert quiet. A truly heavy snowfall can be unnerving. Back east we usually experience the freedom that comes with a good snowstorm. No work, no school, the world shutting its big mouth for a while, the dirty streets covered over in virgin white, like all the missteps you've taken have been erased by nature. You can't run; you can only sit. You open your door on a trackless world, your old path, your history, momentarily covered over by a landscape of forgiveness, a place where something new might happen. It's an illusion but it can stimulate the regenerative parts of your spirit to make good on God and nature's suggestion. A lot of snow, however—I mean a whole lot—is a different thing. That feeling of freeness turns to confinement. The sheer physical weight of the snow becomes existential and the dread of a dark, covered world sets in. I've felt it twice. Once in Idaho, where it snowed circus clowns for seventy-two hours, all power and light gone, eternal night and judgment day upon us. The other was that highway evening on the pass. There was too much quiet, too much weight, too few boundaries and no dimension. The world had been planed down into a snow-blind table you could easily slide off the edges of. It had been simplified into the passable and impassable. The early ocean mapmakers had it right: the world was flat and a wrong move too far to the left or right could bring you to the brink of the abyss, and beyond there be monsters.

We hopped back in the coffin of our car and Tink inched us along the highway, the misanthrope in him elated by the prospect of world's end, until we hit some lower elevations, returned to the land of the living and safer roads. The rest of the trip was truck stops, roadhouses, tales of the erotic life from our passenger and the usual endless highway. We hit the California border and Tinker dropped me off in San Mateo at my folks' front door. My parents met me in their pajamas; I headed inside, threw down my bag and crashed on the couch for twenty-four hours of solid sleep.

I planned on a new life in a new place far away from my lover's blues. I had saved maybe three hundred bucks. That was my "get started" money. The first thing I needed to do was find a paying job playing somewhere. I quickly found out, once again, that while there were places I could play my acoustic music for free—open-mike nights, etc.—none of them would pay. I was a complete unknown again. I'd left my rep as bar band king on the East Coast and was simply another wannabe with a guitar and a pocketful of songs. No luck there, so I set my sights on joining an established club band who needed a singer and guitarist who could rock the house. With that in mind, I went clubbing. One night in San Francisco, I came upon a very good funk and soul band that had the crowd hopping. During a break I struck up a conversation with one of the players, who mentioned they were looking for a guitarist to replace their guy who was leaving. It looked like a perfect fit. Their music was a little jazzier than my style but I figured I could cover it, so we exchanged numbers and set a date for me to come out and jam. One weekday night I pulled up to a warehouse in southern San Fran, walked in, met the guys and plugged in. We played for about forty minutes. Their music pushed me but I thought it had gone well. They took a break, convened in another room; the fellow I had spoken to in the club came out and I was sent jobless on my way. I hadn't felt so completely rejected since my last San Francisco trip. I was starting to get an attitude about the place.

I spent the next three weeks searching high and low for a paying job playing music. Finally, I thought I should just put a band together, audition somewhere, set a club on fire and let nature take its course. I was walking through the Hillsdale mall and I stopped in a one-hour photo shop to develop a few pictures I had taken on the trip. I got talking to a kid who looked in his early twenties behind the counter and he mentioned he played bass. He had a small group looking for a guitarist and asked if I'd like to come out and play with them over the weekend. They were down in San Jose, which was a bit of a drive, but hell, by now I was desperate and running low on cash.

That weekend I borrowed my folks' car, drove the hour south and followed my directions into a middle-class suburb slightly outside of the city. It was straight-up Ozzie and Harriet land: modest ranch houses, side by side, the standard two-car garages and swatches of green front lawn. I came upon my friend's house and there they were, my new band. The garage bay was open, and I could see my pal on bass and what looked to be a couple of fourteen-year-olds on drums and guitar. They were set up in classic formation, facing the street, a few small amps surrounding a kid who looked like Dennis the Menace with long hair on drums. They were kids, real kids, *little* kids, just learning to play. Kids with guitars they probably got for Christmas from Mom and Dad. And here I was.

I hauled my guitar out of the car, set up and put on a show for them all afternoon. I pulled out every trick I knew, and over the afternoon hours, I managed to draw a few folks away from their lawn mowers and barbecue grills. I played like I was at Madison Square Garden. I just needed to. At dusk, I packed up, thanked them for a lovely time and headed north toward home. I felt sad, foolish and happy. I wasn't going to make it. California wasn't going to be mine. From fifteen years old on, I'd made my own money. From the time I picked up a guitar, I'd never taken a dime from my parents, and I wasn't about to start now. They simply didn't have it—not twenty dollars, not ten dollars to spare. My life would be the couch, a pillow, a blanket in my folks' living room and spare change. My teen-beat afternoon clarified everything for me. I had to get back to where I was who I was, a son of New Jersey, gunslinger, bar band king, small-town local hero, big fish in a little pond and breadwinner. Right now, the only place my talents could sustain me was my little fiefdom on the East Coast. Suddenly my girl troubles seemed very small and I started to make plans to go home.

## Mexico (Montezuma's Revenge)

During the remainder of my stay my father asked me to accompany him on a trip to Mexico and said he was planning to stop in Long Beach, where the *Queen Mary* was docked. This was the ocean liner he'd shipped out on for World War II and he wanted to see her one more time. His plan was to go from there down to Tijuana, catch a jai alai game, tourist around a little bit and meet my mom and little sister at Disneyland on the way back. In the spirit of healing old wounds I said yes and off we went. He insisted on bringing the family dog, Smokey, a half sheep dog, half who knows what, who'd just torn the shit out of our Christmas. We'd gone off to midnight mass and on our return, we opened the front door on a scene that looked like Santa's elves had just finished gangbanging Rudolph the Red-Nosed Reindeer in our living room. Tinsel, Christmas balls, water, wrapping paper and ribbon were strewn all over the small apartment. The Christmas tree had been toppled to the floor and every gift had been chewed open. In the middle sat Smokey, panting, waiting to be congratulated.

From the beginning, the joie de vivre in the car wasn't what one might've hoped for. We were doing our best, but we still got under each other's skin. Our stop at Long Beach flopped. I was a punk, grumbling my way through the whole *Queen Mary* tour. My dad's journey on this ship was probably one of the most meaningful of his life and I couldn't respect it. I'd pay anything now to be able to walk that ship with my father again. I would treasure every step, want to know every detail, hear every word and memory he'd share, but back then I was still too young to put the past away, too young to recognize my dad as a man and to honor his story.

We headed south to Mexico, crossed the border at San Diego and holed up in a motel on the outskirts of Tijuana. We locked the dog in the room and headed into town. We caught some jai alai and cruised the tourist district, where my dad bought a watch from a street vendor, bragging to me about the deal he got until it stopped dead exactly twenty minutes later. I had my picture taken on a jackass that had been painted to look like a zebra, my pops smiling in the cart behind me. We wore sombreros; mine read "Pancho" and his "Cisco." When we got back to the motel, Smokey had chewed the hell out of the door, leaving scratches and shavings from the knob down; cursing, the old man had to ante up for the damage. Adios, Mexico.

Back to El Norte. We headed to Disneyland, met my mom and sis, spent an afternoon at the "happiest place on Earth" and headed back by way of some cryptic shortcut of my father's that added three night-filled, spooky hours onto our trip home. Everybody was frazzled.

Shortly after our return, Tinker phoned me up, said he was headed back east, and I told him to count me in. I said good-bye to my folks and little sister, told them I loved them, and then it was seventy-two hours, three thousand miles straight through, 'til we hit Jersey. Through using the same facilities at the apartment, all I left behind for my pops was a case of crabs I picked up somewhere along the way. Good-bye, son, thanks for the memories.

## TWENTY-THREE

# IT'S A BAR, YOU IDIOTS

Immediately on my return I heard Steve, Southside and their Sundance Blues Band were booked at the Captain's Garter in Neptune, New Jersey. I grabbed my guitar and headed straight down to the club to get in on some of the action. The place was packed and we rocked the joint like old times, with the crowd cheering, everyone glued to the stage and the music. It was a great night all around. At the end of the evening, Steve and I headed back to the manager's office to pick up our money and obviously solidify some future bookings. We'd just turned this guy's club inside out and we were expecting some kudos and work.

The manager was a very large, completely white-haired, stolid young man in a red lifeguard's windbreaker. Expressionless, he stood on the far side of his desk and did not offer kudos. We asked what the prospect for future bookings would be and he calmly explained to us that there would be none. He said that yes, the crowd was large and enthusiastic, but no one was drinking. They were too busy listening to the music. He then added, as if we hadn't noticed, "It's a bar, you idiots." They made money by selling liquor. The bartenders made money from tips from selling liquor. No liquor sales meant no money. No money and our little world there on Highway 35 in Neptune stopped spinning. They were not in the concert business and so we, in turn, would not be a part of the bar business at the Captain's Garter. This was my first meeting with bar manager/lifeguard/navy SEAL Terry Magovern, a man who would work with me as my assistant and become my close friend for twenty-three years. He fired us.

## Plan B (Return to the Emerald City)

I still had my room in Tom Potter's beatnik pad in Asbury. I decided my bar band days at the moment were burning out. I needed to travel light and be able to blow somebody away with just my voice, my guitar and my song. Voice . . . guitar . . . song . . . three tools. My voice was never going to win any prizes. My guitar accompaniment on acoustic was rudimentary, so that left the songs. The songs would have to be fireworks. I decided the world was filled with plenty of good guitar players, many of them my match or better, but how many good songwriters were there? Songwriters with their own voice, their own story to tell, who could draw you into a world they created and sustain your interest in the things that obsessed them. Not many, a handful at best.

Dylan was preeminent amongst these types of writers. Bob Dylan is the father of my country. *Highway 61 Revisited* and *Bringing It All Back Home* were not only great records, but they were the first time I can remember being exposed to a truthful vision of the place I lived. The darkness and light were all there, the veil of illusion and deception ripped aside. He put his boot on the stultifying politeness and daily routine that covered corruption and decay. The world he described was all on view, in my little town, and spread out over the television that beamed into our isolated homes, but it went uncommented on and silently tolerated. He inspired me and gave me hope. He asked the questions everyone else was too frightened to ask, especially to a fifteen-year-old: "How does it feel . . . to be on your own?" A seismic gap had opened up between generations and you suddenly felt orphaned, abandoned amid the flow of history, your compass spinning, internally homeless. Bob pointed true north and served as a beacon to assist you in making your way through the new wilderness America had become. He planted a flag, wrote the songs, sang the words that were essential to the times, to the emotional and spiritual survival of so many young Americans at that moment.

I had the opportunity to sing "The Times They Are A-Changin'" for Bob when he received the Kennedy Center Honors. We were alone together for a brief moment walking down a back stairwell when he thanked me for being there and said, "If there's anything I can ever do for you . . ." I thought, "Are you kidding me?" and answered, "It's already been done." As a young musician, that's where I wanted to go. I wanted to be a voice that reflected experience and the world I lived in. So I knew in 1972 that to do this I would need to write very well and more individually than I had ever written before. I'd saved a few dollars playing here and there since I got back and for the first time in my life I stopped playing with a band and concentrated on songwriting. At night in my bedroom with my guitar and on an old Aeolian spinet piano parked in the rear of the beauty salon, I began to write the music that would comprise *Greetings from Asbury Park*.

I called Mike Appel. He remembered me and told me to come on up, so I took Lincoln Transit to New York City, met Mike at Wes Farrell's and played him my new stuff. He said these were songs we could knock down some doors with. He got crazy excited, as only Mike could. The words flew a mile a minute, the hand gestures threatened dismemberment, his face lit up and in thirty seconds he compared me to Dylan, Shakespeare, James Joyce and Bozo the Clown. Mike could raise hard-ons in half a cemetery with his enthusiasm. It was what drew me to him. He could get you excited about yourself. Mike had the carny barker's and tent preacher's 110 percent belief in whatever was flying out of his mouth at any given moment. It's a gift. By the time I left his office, my superstardom had been preordained. All we had to do was get a somebody to listen to a nobody. I kept writing, kept visiting and met Mike's partner, Jimmy Cretecos, a milder, sweeter version of Mike. We started to work together and make some basic tapes. I visited Jimmy's spectacular apartment in Tuxedo Park. He had a gorgeous wife and a ritzy place, so it looked to me like these guys had it made. They'd had some bubblegum hits but Mike said they made most of their money writing jingles. I went with Mike to one of his sessions and ended up playing harmonica on a Beech-Nut Gum commercial demo.

In the meantime, we planned and schemed while only one thing stood in the way. Before Mike would consent to use his many talents on my behalf, he explained, he would have to be protected. That meant contracts. I'd never signed a contract in my life, didn't know shit about them and therefore was extremely suspicious of them. I'd lived off the grid for so long, I was totally ignorant in the ways of the law, musical or any other kind. I knew no lawyers; I'd been paid in only cash my entire life and had never paid a cent of income tax, signed an apartment lease nor filled out any form that might bind me in any way. I had no credit card, no checkbook, just what was jingling in my pocket. I had no college-educated friends. My Asbury Park was an island of misfit, blue-collar provincials. Smart, but not book smart. I'd never gotten to know anyone who'd made an actual record or been signed to a big-time recording contract. I'd never seen a contract of any kind or been in touch with any businessmen. I had no professional resources.

Mike explained each contract, what it would do for me and how we would be protected. Production—that was our recording deal. I was signed to Laurel Canyon Productions, Mike and Jimmy's company, and they would produce my records and sell them to a major label. Publishing—Mike and Jimmy would publish my music under Laurel Canyon Publishing, in theory working to get other artists to cover my songs. I would receive my writer's half of the royalties but none of the publishing revenues. Management—like Elvis and the Colonel, Mike's business model, we would split everything fifty-fifty. The problem would be all the expenses would end up coming out of my half. The whole thing was overreaching and counterproductive on Mike and Jimmy's part, leading to a lot of damage in the end, but who was I to say?

The bottom line was I liked Mike and I knew he understood what I wanted to do musically. We weren't aiming for a few successful records and some modest hits. We were aiming for impact, for influence, for the top rung of what recording artists are capable of achieving. We both knew rock music was now a culture shaper. I wanted to collide with the times and create a voice that had musical, social and cultural impact. Mike understood that this was my goal. I was not modest in the assessment of my abilities. Of course I thought I was a phony—that is the way of the artist—but I also thought I was the realest thing you'd ever seen. I had a huge ego, and I'd built up the talent and craft to pursue my ambitions with years of playing experience and study. I had my doubts and I had a sense of humor about the balls I had and the big bite I was trying to take, but damn, that's where the fun was, and . . . I was a natural. It was in my bones.

In the end, I would've signed Mike's jockey shorts, if he'd presented them to me, to get my foot in the door. I was closer than I'd ever been to the real work I wanted to do. I could feel it. I spent a few nights on my own trying to get through the biz speak, the legalese, of the contracts myself. It was a joke. I sat with Mike's lawyer, Jules Kurz, who mildly explained the basic provisions of the contracts, but in the end, I just said "fuck it"; I had to get in, and if these meaningless papers were the price, so be it. If I'm a bum, then all this stuff adds up to zero, and if I'm champ, then who cares? I'll have gotten there and the rest will be sorted out. I didn't look back until much later, and by then, of course, it was too late. Frightened, slowly, reluctantly, recklessly, contract by contract, I signed, finishing the last one, one evening, on a car hood in a New York City parking lot. Done deal.

# TWENTY-FOUR

# ONWARD
# AND
# UPWARD

Our first audition was at Atlantic Records. All I remember is going up to an office and playing for somebody. No interest. The next thing Mike finagled—and I couldn't believe it—was an audition with John Hammond. John Hammond! The legendary producer who signed Dylan, Aretha, Billie Holiday—a giant in the recording business. I'd just finished reading the Anthony Scaduto Dylan biography and I was going to meet the *man* who made it happen!

The motor mouth of Mike Appel was a fierce and surgical instrument when put to proper use. Mike could've talked Jesus down from the cross, Santa Claus out of Christmas and Pam Anderson out of breast augmentation. He talked us off the street and into the inner sanctum of John Hammond's office. My man was a managerial genius. To give you an idea about how much the music business has changed, John Hammond, a historical figure in the industry, was receiving complete no-names like us off the streets of New York in his office! I'm sure Mike laid down a hell of a spiel, but still . . . John later told me his trusted secretary and gatekeeper, Mikie Harris, after she spoke to Mike, simply said to him, "I think you ought to see this guy." The doors to El Dorado opened and in we strode.

I had no acoustic guitar of my own so I borrowed a cheap one with a cracked neck from Vinnie "Skeebots" Manniello, my old Castiles drummer. He had no case, so I had to haul it *Midnight Cowboy*–style over my shoulder on the bus and through the streets of the city. It's a hokey feeling, as if you're showing off and are about to burst into song at any moment. Bare guitar in my hands, Mike and I walked into John Hammond's office and came face-to-face with the gray crew cut, horn-rimmed glasses, huge smile, gray suit and tie of my music business hero. I would've been in a state of complete panic except on the way up in the elevator I'd performed a little mental ju-jitsu on myself. I thought, "I've got nothing so I've got nothing to lose. I can only gain should this work out. If it don't, I still got what I came in with. I'm a free agent. I make my way through the world as myself and I'll still be that person when I leave no matter the outcome." By the time I got there I almost believed it. I walked in nervous but confident.

Immediately, as the door opened, my representative, Mike Appel, showed a personal tendency for unnecessary confrontation that would weigh on us as time passed. I figure once the door is open you can stop kicking at it. Not Mike; he walked in swinging. Straightaway, with no discernible self-consciousness and before I'd played a note, he told John Hammond of Columbia Records I was perhaps the second coming of Jesus, Muhammad and Buddha and he'd brought me there to see if Hammond's discovery of Dylan was a fluke or if he really had ears. I found this an interesting way of introducing and ingratiating ourselves to the man who held our future in his hands. Mike then sat back on the windowsill, pleased as punch he'd had his "no bullshit" say, and handed the ball off to me, an act we would repeat often in the future. John later told me he was poised and ready to hate us, but he just leaned back, slipped his hands together behind his head and, smiling, said, "Play me something." I sat directly across from him and played "Saint in the City." When I was done I looked up. That smile was still there and I heard him say, "You've got to be on Columbia Records." One song—that's what it took. I felt my heart rise up inside me, mysterious particles dancing underneath my skin and faraway stars lighting up my nerve endings.

He went on, "That was wonderful, play me something else." I played "Growin' Up," then something called "If I Was the Priest." He loved the Catholic imagery, pointed out the lack of clichés and said arrangements needed to be made for me to play for Clive Davis. He told me he'd had his successes and his failures in the acts he'd signed at Columbia and these days, Clive's say was final. He then asked to see me perform live that night. Mike and I said we'd try to find a club that would accommodate us for a few songs; we shook hands and left his office. We got into the elevator and when we slipped out of CBS's big Black Rock building and hit the street, hell broke loose.

We'd climbed to the heavens and spoken to the gods, who told us we were spitting thunder and throwing lightning bolts! It was on. It was all on. After the years of waiting, of struggling toward that something I thought might never happen, it had happened. With Skeebots's junk guitar, the sword we'd just pulled from the stone, now proudly, nakedly slung over my shoulder, we had a celebratory cheeseburger and, floating down the street, jumped into a cab and headed for the Village. I was twenty-two years old.

We started at the Bitter End; no good. The Café au Go Go; nope. My old stomping grounds, Café Wha?; closed. And finally, a basement club on MacDougal Street, the original Gerde's Folk City. Sam Hood was the current manager, a fellow who'd support me greatly in the future when he'd run Max's Kansas City on Union Square. He said they had an open-mike night and between eight o'clock and eight thirty I could go on. John

Hammond breezed in a little before eight and took his place amongst at best six other patrons, and the show was under way. Playing live was something I knew how to do. I'd tell stories, make jokes and dramatize the songs I was singing. "Saint in the City," "Growin' Up," "If I Was the Priest," a song called "Arabian Nights," a few others, and the show was over. John was beaming. I could perform.

Things started to happen . . . slowly. A few weeks after I met John, he ushered me into Clive Davis's office, where I was warmly welcomed. I played Clive a few songs and with gentle fanfare, I was invited to join the Columbia Records family. John took me into their Fifty-Second Street studio and we made a demo he produced. It was the last days of the fifties-style recording studio system. Everybody wore suits and ties and were adults. The engineer, the assistants, all longtime, old-school recording men. I sang a dozen or more songs into a microphone in the middle of a very antiseptic room. I played piano on a few others. It was all very bare bones; that's the way John heard me. Listening to those demos today, I don't know if I'd have chosen that kid to lay all my money down on, but I'm thankful he did.

I was now living on the remainder of my "bureau drawer" savings, a few bucks from Mike and the kindness of strangers. I had a sweet girlfriend who tipped me some eating money once in a while and a gal lightly on the side who owned her own business and drove a fancy sports car. She was fabulously Jewish, a little older than me, and would occasionally sweep me up off the corner of Cookman Avenue to spend a night in her condo apartment high overlooking the beaches of Asbury Park. There we occasionally engaged in what, I'm sure, was some of the worst sex of our lives (if such exists). She held all the aces, which I didn't mind, and we had a nice, screwed-up semirelationship for a while. The periodic evenings in her solidly middle-class digs took the chill out of street-level living in Asbury, and were comforting and most welcome.

My recording advance had not yet clocked in and these were some very thin times, some of the thinnest. For the first time in my life, I actually went completely broke and had to scavenge a little bit for meals. We couldn't even come up with the sixty dollars' rent on Tom's pad. In extremis one night, I called Mike and told him times were desperate, homelessness was at hand, and he said he could give me thirty-five dollars if I could make it into the city. I drained my bureau drawer of its remaining pennies, counted them one by one and figured I had just enough to borrow my gal's Pontiac (with its push-button transmission), pump in a few dollars' gas and have the exact amount for tolls to make it into town. I budgeted myself down to the last cent.

I got the car, threw a few dollars of gas in it and headed for the city. All went well until I hit the Lincoln Tunnel. There in the window of the tollbooth stood the famous "No Pennies" sign. Pennies were all I had. I handed a dollar's worth, my last dollar, to the attendant, who said, "I can't take these." I said, "Ma'am, that's all the money I have and I don't have enough gas to get back home if you force me to turn around." I put myself at her mercy. She said, "Well, you're going to sit here while I count every one." And that's what she made me do. Very meticulously, intentionally slow as molasses, the coins scraping across the hard metal counter in front of her, she counted out one hundred pennies, penny by penny, for the one-dollar Lincoln Tunnel toll. Then, with a poker face, she stuck her hand in the driver's-side window and said, "I can't take this, you'll have to turn around." Pinched in between her thumb and forefinger was one Canadian penny . . . one. I got out of the Pontiac to a cacophony of horns behind me fed up with our little theater and I began to carefully go over every inch of the inside of that car while she raised holy hell. In 1972 there was no self-respecting car in America without a penny trapped somewhere under its seats. After some very long minutes of mining, I found one, in the rear backseat between the cushions. I stood up, handed it to her amid what now sounded to me like a beautiful, profane opera of barking horns and shouting voices from the pissed-off parade that stretched out behind me. All she said was, "Go ahead . . . but don't come back here with these pennies again!" Lesson: In the real world, ninety-nine cents will not get you into New York City. You will need the full dollar.

I met Mike, got my thirty-five dollars and went home. My partners still couldn't make their share of the rent and we would soon be evicted. We snuck out in the middle of the night and I slept on the beach in my sleeping bag with my surfboard and a small kit of all my earthly possessions at my side. A low point. The next day, on my way to Loch Arbour Beach, my favorite local surfing spot, at the north end of Asbury, I passed by an old pal sitting on the roof balcony of a small summer cottage. Big Danny Gallagher's size was Clarence Clemons plus. He was a giant. He had a blinding shock of red hair and when older wore an Old Testament fiery-red beard that made him look like a character out of Irish folklore. In his youth, he cut quite a fearsome figure and occasionally had the temperament to match. As I passed he told me his brother had just died of a drug overdose. He sat in a trance trying to make sense of it. He asked me what was happening and I told him I'd just been tossed from Potter's and was now indigent. He immediately invited me to bunk in with him.

It was a little upstairs apartment, just two rooms. The bedroom held Danny's king-size waterbed, which took up all available space. Then there was a small kitchenette and connected living room, where I took up residence on the floor in my sleeping bag. This is where I lived while I recorded *Greetings from Asbury Park*. I'd bus to the city; work opening for Dave Van Ronk, Biff Rose or Birtha, one of the first female metal bands at Max's Kansas City; get paid a few dollars; and make it to the Port Authority just in time for the last bus to Asbury. Sam Hood had hired me at Max's and I attracted a nice crowd of hipsters: Paul Nelson, the great music writer; Paul Williams, creator of *Crawdaddy* magazine, the first serious word on rock 'n' roll; and David Blue, the folksinger and Village legend. He introduced himself to me after my set one night, then squired me around to meet Jackson Browne at the Bitter End (on tour for his first album) and Odetta, the great folksinger, after her late-night set at a local coffeehouse. Jackson let me sit in during his set on David Blue's word and I played "Wild Billy's Circus Story." I was young, traveling light and excited to be in their company.

## Greetings from Asbury Park

Up in Blauvelt, New York, in Brooks Arthur's 914 Studios, we began to record *Greetings* in an atmosphere of tension. Mike and Jimmy were producing. Mike had his own engineer, Louis Lahav, a former Israeli paratrooper who'd come to America and fallen in with Mike and Jimmy. On the first day of recording my first album, very little recording occurred. Mike was in a running battle with the union engineer from Columbia, who insisted on doing his job and manning the sound board. In several years this would all change and artists would independently choose their producers and engineers of their own volition. Nineteen seventy-three was the dawn of this kind of artistic control, a dawn that had not yet completely broken over the recording industry. The day would devolve into a series of arguments, insults and irate phone calls while I sat around waiting. Mike was his usual ridiculously funny, combative self, putting this poor guy through the wringer. Finally an agreement was reached between the union, record company and Mike and Jimmy's Laurel Canyon Productions. Louis Lahav would engineer, Mike and Jimmy would produce, I would record and the union engineer would show up, get paid a full salary and sit on the couch reading the newspaper. Peace in the valley! Some version of this went on for my first three albums. The studio was located on Route 303 next to a Greek diner. Here we could get a cheap recording rate; carry on as we pleased out of sight of the nosy record company bigwigs, who might be too curious about how their money was being spent; and eat at the Greek diner, where I found for a muse a waitress who had the finest body I'd seen since my aunt Betty. It was all good.

I'd convinced Mike and Jimmy I needed to record with a band. John Hammond, Clive Davis and Columbia had thought they'd signed a folk singer-songwriter. The stock was way up on singer-songwriters in those days. The charts were full of them, with James Taylor leading the pack. I was signed to Columbia, along with Elliott Murphy, John Prine and Loudon Wainwright, "new Dylan"s all, to compete in acoustic battle at the top of the charts with our contemporaries. What I had over my company in the field was that I'd secretly built up years of rock 'n' roll experience out of view of the known world and in front of every conceivable audience. I'd already seen the roughest the road had to offer and was ready for more. These long-honed talents would go a ways in distinguishing me from the pack and help-ing me get my songs heard.

Mike Appel had never seen me play with a full band in front of an au-dience until after we recorded *Greetings*, so my own main man was clueless about what I could do. I tried to tell him, "You don't understand, put me in front of a band and an audience, and I will *bury* the house." When we started to tour in support of *Greetings* I had Mad Dog, Danny Federici, Garry Tal-lent and Clarence Clemons at my side. Mike was no dummy. He saw our first gig and said, "Hey, you know what you're doing." 'Til then, I believe he thought he was just humoring me by letting me use my guys in the studio.

On *Greetings* I managed to bring in my homeboys Vini Lopez, Davey Sancious and Garry Tallent, with a cameo performance by Steve Van Zandt shaking my Danelectro amp's reverb unit at the intro to "Lost in the Flood." Steve was to be on the record but we opted out of electric guitar in my con-cession to the singer/songwriter I was signed to be. We cut the whole record in three weeks. Most of the songs were twisted autobiographies. "Growin' Up," "Does This Bus Stop," "For You," "Lost in the Flood" and "Saint in the City" found their seed in people, places, hangouts and incidents I'd seen and things I'd lived. I wrote impressionistically and changed names to pro-tect the guilty. I worked to find something that was identifiably mine.

We turned it in and Clive Davis handed it back saying there were "no hits," "nothing that could be played on the radio." I went to the beach and wrote "Spirit in the Night," came home, busted out my rhyming dictionary and wrote "Blinded by the Light," two of the best things on the record. I was able to find Clarence, who'd been MIA since that first night in the Prince, and I got his cool saxophone on those last two cuts. It made a big difference. This was the most fully realized version of the sound I had in my head that I would get on my first album. The pre–E Street band did their best to sound studio-worthy while the words flowed like a storm surge, crashing into one another with no regret.

I never wrote completely in that style again. Once the record was released, I heard all the Dylan comparisons, so I steered away from it. But the lyrics and spirit of *Greetings* came from an unself-conscious place. Your early songs emerge from a moment when you're writing with no sure prospect of ever being heard. Up until then, it's been just you and your music. That only happens once.

## TWENTY-FIVE
# LOSING MY RELIGION

I was twenty-two and I'd never had a drink—ever. I played in bars and had been around booze my whole life and never been tempted to even taste the stuff. My experience with my father's drinking had been enough. The terrifying, all-engulfing presence he became when he drank convinced me to never go there. He lost who he was. The goodness and kindness in his heart, of which there was plenty, were erased in a flood of self-pitying rage and a ferocity that turned our home into a minefield of fear and anxiety. You never knew when he was going to go off. As a child, my nervousness became so great I began to blink uncontrollably, hundreds of times a minute. At school, I was called "Blinky." I chewed all of the knuckles on both of my hands night and day into brown rock-hard calluses the size of marbles.

Nope, drinking wasn't for me. But now, as my first album drew to a close, I was nervous about my rock 'n' roll dream finally coming to fruition. Did I make a good record? On a national level, would I cut it? Was I who I thought I was, who I wanted to be? I truly didn't know, but I knew I was about to find out, and that thrilled and frightened me.

I guess it showed. Returning home from his construction job, Big Danny came up to me late one afternoon and said, "You don't look so good. I know what you need, come with me." That evening we drove to the Osprey, a bar in Manasquan, New Jersey, and we walked in. I'd stood outside this bar on countless afternoons listening to the bands inside, concentrating on the music and daydreaming over the brown-skinned college girls as they slipped through the club's swinging doors. All through the summers of '64, '65, '66 and '67 I'd hitchhiked the twenty miles from Freehold to Manasquan and back almost every day. I'd ridden with concerned moms, drunk drivers, truckers, street racers eager to show off what they had under the hood, traveling businessmen, and only one middle-aged salesman who was a little too interested in me. I'd hopped in with guys who had souped-up sound systems with echo chambers connected to their AM radios, "in-car" 45 record players set on springs under the dash near the shifter. Every sort of rube, redneck, responsible citizen and hell-raiser the Jersey Shore had to offer, I rode with 'em. I loved hitchhiking and meeting people. I miss it today.

As a teenager, underneath the sweltering sun I'd stood outside of the Osprey for hundreds of hours listening to the sounds pouring out from within, but I'd never been inside. Back then, I could make out shadows through the club's screen doors. The silhouette of the band who'd set up in the middle of the bar, right inside the entrance. I could hear the beer glasses clinking, the crowd's laughter, boisterous conversation and the high sizzle of the drummer's cymbals cutting through it all and spilling onto the egg-frying mid-August streets of Manasquan. During their breaks, the hip-looking musicians would come out, have a smoke and speak casually to the young kid slouched all afternoon against a car at curbside. They were just bar musicians making their way, but I *wanted* what they had, entrance to that smoke-filled, beer-drenched, Coppertone-scented heaven that lay only a few forbidden feet beyond those swinging screen doors. Their break over, I'd watch them take those coveted steps back inside and rise again as silhouettes behind the bar, above the shouting crowd. As the first few notes of "What'd I Say" or some other frat band classic pealed out from within, I'd resume my sentry position. Class was in session.

So in through the swinging doors we swept and Big Danny bellied us up to the bar only feet from the sidewalk I'd endlessly tutored on. The featured act that night was the Shirelles, who'd had such great hits as "Will You Still Love Me Tomorrow" and "Baby It's You," but first . . . a small shot glass was slammed down onto the bar in front of me and filled with a golden liquid. Danny said, "Don't sip it, don't taste it, just swig it down in one quick gulp." I did. No big deal. We did another. Slowly, something came over me; I was high for the first time. Another round and shortly I was having what felt like the finest evening of my young life. What had I been sweating and worrying about!? All was good, wonderful even. The angels of mescal were circling around and informing my being; all the rest was bullshit. The Shirelles hit the stage. They wore sequined gowns that looked like they were painted on and sounded great. I was singing along. I, the lone ranger, started talking to whoever the hell was around me and at some point during the evening, a miracle occurred. I smelled perfume and sidling up next to me was a very lovely and familiar-looking woman, raven haired, with olive skin. I recognized her as one of the star ex-cheerleaders of my old alma mater, Freehold Regional High School. A conversation started as I kept sucking down a steady flow of my new best friend, Jose Cuervo Gold.

The talk began lighthearted: "How have you been?" Then, as the night and booze set in and we shouted over the band, I heard there'd been a divorce, a separation from a high school sweetheart, tears, it was over. Though I truly couldn't have cared less, I was listening like the secrets of the Dead Sea scrolls were being revealed to me. All I was hearing was her hair, her eyes, her lips, her T-shirt, then, with the dark spirits of tequila slowly working their way down below my belt, it was last call. The house lights were up. The bouncers were herding the crowd toward the door and suddenly I was saying good-bye to . . . Big Danny! I was in a car headed for Freehold, the scene of my childhood sins, and I was ready to add a few more. In the backseat was a pal of mine who'd hooked it up with my gal's girlfriend. The two of us were headed for my hometown.

Somewhere along the highway, just west of a wreck of a theme park called Cowboy City, where you could ride little mules, get held up in a stagecoach and see gunfights of the old West reenacted on any Summer Jersey afternoon, a syrupy lover's lament came on the radio, bringing tears from my cheerleader's slate-blue eyes as she mentioned it was their song and asked if I too was moved. I made the mistake of saying, "Not so" . . . and my buddy and I found ourselves deposited roadside, on Route 33, at four a.m., caught in the emotional confusion of my suddenly self-reproaching high school crush.

We waved good-bye to the taillights and broke into hysterical booze-fueled laughter, rolling in the shoulder-side grass outside the chain-link fence of the Earle Naval Ammunition Depot. We stuck out our thumbs, and it still being the day when midnight drivers would pick up two staggering drunks by the side of the road in the wee hours, we scored a spirited ride with a kindred soul all the way back to Asbury Park. I scuttled in at dawn, having had what I believed to be the greatest night of my life. I believed it all the way to the next morning, when I woke up, head banging, muscles aching, dry mouthed and stupid with my first-ever hangover. Still, it was worth it. I'd shut down my loudmouthed, guilt-infested, self-doubting, flagellating inner voice for an evening. I found, unlike my father, I was generally a merry drinker simply prone to foolish behavior and occasional sexual misadventure, so from then on and for quite a while thereafter the mescal flowed . . . tequila.

*Greetings* was done. I'd gotten the first few dollars of some advance money, which I unfortunately had to use to bail Big Danny out of jail for some unremembered infraction. We went back to our apartment and I played my album for Danny, its first listener. Success! He liked it but he had just one question: "Where's the guitar?" I was the fastest guitar player alive . . . in Monmouth County, and there was no guitar to be found on my record. No one locally had heard this new and very different material I'd been writing. I'd made the conscious decision to double down on my song-writing skills; I felt this was the most distinctive thing I had going. Here in town it would be a few albums before my small legion of fans would under-stand what I was doing, but I'd recorded a real album, one with a real record company, songs and an album cover. It was unheard of.

## I Heard It on the Radio

Things were heating up. A film was sent to every Columbia Records branch in every major city of Clive Davis doing a solo reading of the lyrics to "Blinded by the Light" like it was Shakespeare. Even so, *Greetings* only sold about twenty-three thousand copies; that was a flop by record company standards but a smash by mine. Who were all those strangers buying my music?

I was standing on a street corner before a college gig in Connecticut as a car pulled up to a light and I heard "Spirit in the Night" blasting from the radio, your number one rock 'n' roll dream come true! You never forget the first time you hear your song on the radio. Suddenly, I was a part of the mys-tery train of popular music that had had me in its spell since I'd been driven past the "buttons" of the radio tower in my grandpa's sedan with the smoky sounds of doo-wop caressing my sleepy eyes. The radio had kept me alive and breathing throughout my teens. For my generation, music sounded best coming out of a tiny, tinny radio speaker. Later, when we recorded we had one of those speakers sitting on top of the studio console and we didn't sign off on a mix until the music sounded like it was roaring out of it. Music on the radio is a shared fever dream, a collective hallucination, a secret amongst millions and a whisper in the whole country's ear. When the music is great, a natural subversion of the controlled message broadcast daily by the powers that be, advertising agencies, mainstream media outlets, news organizations and the general mind-numbing, soul-freezing, life-denying keepers of the status quo takes place.

In the 1960s the first version of my country that struck me as truthful and unfiltered was the one I heard in songs by artists like Bob Dylan, the Kingsmen, James Brown and Curtis Mayfield. "Like a Rolling Stone" gave me the faith that a true, unaltered, uncompromised vision could be broadcast to millions, changing minds, enlivening spirits, bringing red blood to the anemic American pop landscape and delivering a warning, a challenge that could become an essential part of the American conversation. This was music that could both stir the heart of your fellow countrymen and awaken the mind of a shy, lost fifteen-year-old in a small New Jersey town. "Like a Rolling Stone" and "Louie Louie" let me know that someone, somewhere, was speaking in tongues and that absurd ecstasy had been snuck into the Constitution's First Amendment and was an American birthright. I heard it on the radio.

As I stood on that corner listening to "Spirit in the Night" through a stranger's car window at a stoplight, I finally felt like a small piece of that glorious train. It was more than a thrill. It was all I wanted to do: find a way to honor those who'd inspired me, make my mark, have my say and hopefully inspire those who'd pick up the flag long after we were gone. Even as young men we took our fun seriously, and forty-three years later I still get the same thrill when I hear new music of mine for the first time coming across the airwaves.

TWENTY-SIX

# ROAD
# WORK

*Greetings from Asbury Park* had been released on January 5, 1973, to many good reviews and a few ripping pans. We then hit the road. Our first official gig was a freebie at a Pennsylvania college opening for Cheech and Chong. Cheech and Chong were at their jokin', dope-smokin' peak and the school auditorium was jammed. Right out of the box we had a rocking little show. The Big Man was there. I strapped on my new guitar, a 1950s mutt with a Telecaster body and an Esquire neck I'd purchased at Phil Petillo's Belmar guitar shop for one hundred and eighty-five dollars. With its wood body worn in like the piece of the cross it was, it became the guitar I'd play for the next forty years. It was the best deal of my life. For our live show we'd recast the songs from *Greetings* into rock and soul music and were having a pretty good time for twenty-five minutes or so, then I felt a tap on my back while I was playing the piano and a guy whispered in my ear to get off the stage.

Somebody decided we were through. We left to a decent ovation and it was one down, one thousand and one to go.

Touring conditions were not the best. All five of us rode in Vini's junker, and everyone but myself took turns driving. I still had no license and my style behind the wheel was considered inept and reckless endangerment by the band. We drove, we slept where we could—cheap motels, promoters' houses, with girlfriends in a variety of cities—we drove, we played, we drove, we played, we drove, we played. We opened for Chuck Berry, Jerry Lee Lewis, Sha Na Na, Brownsville Station, the Persuasions, Jackson Browne, the Chambers Brothers, the Eagles, Mountain, Black Oak Arkansas. We shared bills with NRBQ and Lou Reed and did a thirteen-day arena tour with brass-section hit makers Chicago. We were top billed, with Bob Marley and the Wailers opening (on their first US tour), in the tiny 150-seat Max's Kansas City. On stages across America we were cheered, were occasionally booed, dodged Frisbees from the audience, received rave reviews and were trashed. Mike booked us at car shows and Sing Sing prison. It was all in a day's work and as far as I was concerned, it was the life. There would be no nine-to-five world for me, just a long, often arduous but who's-kidding-who free ride of a seven-day weekend.

Conditions were generally horrible, but compared to what?! The dumpiest motel on the road was a step up from my home digs. I was twenty-three and I was making a living playing music! Friend, there's a reason they don't call it "working," it's called PLAYING! I've left enough sweat on stages around the world to fill at least one of the seven seas; I've driven myself and my band to the limits and over the edge for more than forty years. We continue to do so but it's still "playing." It's a life-giving, joyful, sweat-drenched, muscle-aching, voice-blowing, mind-clearing, exhausting, soul-invigorating, cathartic pleasure and privilege every night. You can sing about your misery, the world's misery, your most devastating experiences, but there is something in the gathering of souls that blows the blues away. Something that lets some sun in, that keeps you breathing, that lifts you in a way that can't be explained, only experienced. It's something to live for, and it was my lifeline to the rest of humanity in the days when those connections were tough for me to make. Can it be hard? . . . Yeah. Is everyone built for it physically and psychologically? . . . No. Are there nights you don't want to go on? . . . Yep. But on those nights, there *will* come a moment when something happens, the band takes flight, a face lights up in the audience, someone, with their eyes closed, singing along to the words, the music you've written, and suddenly you're bound together by the feeling of the things that matter to you most. Or . . . there may be some great-looking women in the crowd—that always works too!

## Show Me the Money

We made thirty-five dollars a week and had our rent and bills paid. That was the deal and it was the only way we could afford to stay on the road. There was an honor system. You stated what your expenses were and you got your money. Each man was different: some had alimony, child support payments, extenuating circumstances; some needed more than others. Everybody played by the rules . . . mostly.

After Steel Mill, I'd decided working with my pal Danny Federici, as lovely a guy as he could be, was just too life shortening. He needed too much caretaking. Everything around Danny was usually all fucked up. However, when it came time to form a touring band, Davey Sancious was unavailable, so I needed a keyboardist and Danny was the best I knew. He played beautifully and was a true folk musician, his style developed from being an accordion player as a child. His right hand had a lyricism, a fluency and spontaneity, I've never heard in another musician. He had the shortest highway between his fingers and his heart I'd ever heard. His left hand did virtually nothing; his self-conscious mind but not his musical intellect was put on hold. The notes came rushing forward, wonderfully chosen and perfectly placed with a freeness that seemed to flow effortlessly out of his soul. He was a real accompanist, humble, always at the service of the song, never overplaying, never stepping on another player's toes, just finding the open space and filling it with the perfect flourish. If I needed to loosen up any piece we'd recorded, I sent Danny into the studio and just let him play. He never missed.

Unfortunately he was also a guy whose nature it was to game any system he came into contact with, so taking a shot with his own homies was as natural to Danny as all those beautiful notes that came floating freely out of his fingers. He was overstating his expenses and skimming off the top. By twenty-three, Danny and I'd already had a long and rocky history. In our previous lives together, we'd been through a shitstorm of trouble. What pissed me off the most was being constantly cast as the unwelcome voice of moderation and reason, the arbiter of professional limits and personal behavior . . . "Daddy." In the end somebody had to set the boundaries, so I did, and then he crossed one. We were broke; he was stealing money from all of us. I drove directly to Dan's apartment, confronted him in a rage, received the usual shrug of the Federici shoulders, put my foot through his expensive stereo speakers and left. I loved Danny but some version of this and worse would be a part of our friendship for the next forty years.

That Christmas we returned triumphant to my hometown of Freehold. What could be a better seasonal surprise than the return of a successful son coming home to his roots, the humility, the generosity, naaah . . . I haven't forgotten you. We did a holiday show for the locals at a Russian social club called Rova Farms on the outskirts of town. It held about five hundred souls and the evening featured the only full-scale truly scary bar brawl of our club lives. All started out well for an hour or so. That we might be able to celebrate the festive spirit of the Christmas season, we'd recently learned the Crystals' "Santa Claus Is Coming to Town." Just as we cracked into it the place exploded into multiple pockets of fistfighting. It may have been gang related, I don't remember. I looked toward the bar and saw the bartender standing on top of the deck impolitely kicking at the faces of his patrons.

There was a second-floor loft with an Old West banister running along it at the back of the joint and as I sang out my yuletide greetings, I saw a man lifted up and tossed over the banister to come crashing down onto the first floor. Richard Blackwell, playing congas that evening, leapt from the stage into the crowd in search of my boyhood pal, his brother David. The concert was raided by the police and brought to a halt. Amazingly no one was killed, though several left on stretchers. An ugly calm returned and we played another half hour or so. Then it was merry Christmas to all and to all a good night. Who said you can't go home?

TWENTY-SEVEN

# THE WILD, THE INNOCENT AND THE E STREET SHUFFLE

In the early days, tours just ran into one another. Nobody was counting. We just played. I was under contract to Columbia for a new album every six months. This schedule was a holdover from the fifties and sixties record business, when singles ruled the charts. Then, artists would put out their hit single with a collection of stomach noises for the rest of the record and call it an album. Then along came *Sgt. Pepper* and the rules changed overnight. The album was now the gold standard for pop recording achievement. Suddenly, if an artist made one every two or three years, it was considered fine and on schedule. Any more, even one a year, and you were thought to be overexposing yourself. Not in 1973.

We made *Greetings from Asbury Park* and *The Wild, the Innocent and the E Street Shuffle* in the same year while continuing to tour. *The Wild, the Innocent* took us three months to record at 914 Studios. By now Mike and Jimmy had seen enough of my performing to know it was time to bring the rock 'n' roll. David Sancious was back on piano to initiate our double keyboard attack; he played beautifully on the album and contributed greatly to our recording and touring team. We drove every day to Blauvelt up from the Shore and back again every night. Richard Blackwell showed and played congas on "New York City Serenade" and "E Street Shuffle." In the end we held marathon sessions around the clock. Clarence and I pitched a tent out back in a small yard and slept there for days while finishing our final overdubs. Toward the end of the mixing process I'd been up for three days with no stimulants. I couldn't stay awake for one complete playback of a song; I kept nodding off a minute or two into each cut until someone would rustle me awake to approve the rest of the mix.

The opening cut of my second record, "The E Street Shuffle," is a reflection of a community that was partly imagined and partly real. It was the early seventies: blues, R & B and soul were still heavily influential and heard often along the Jersey Shore. Musically, I based the song on Major Lance's sixties hit "The Monkey Time," a dance song. The cast of characters came vaguely from Asbury Park at the turn of the decade. I wanted to describe a neighborhood, a way of life, and I wanted to invent a dance with no exact steps. It was just the dance you did every day and every night to get by.

I'd lived in Asbury Park for the past three years. I watched the town suffer some pretty serious race rioting and slowly begin to close down. The Upstage Club, where I met most of the members of the E Street Band, had long ago shut its doors. The boardwalk was still operating, Madam Marie was still there, but the crowds were sparse. Many of the usual summer vacationers were now passing Asbury Park by for less troubled locations farther south along the coast.

After my eviction from Potter's apartment above the beauty salon and my short stay at Big Danny Gallagher's, I moved on and was living with a girlfriend I'd met one sunny fall morning when she was working a concession stand on the north end of the Asbury boardwalk. She was Italian, funny, a beatific tomboy, with just the hint of a lazy eye, and wore a pair of glasses that made me think of the wonders of the library. Our garage apartment was five minutes from Asbury, in Bradley Beach. This is where I wrote "4th of July, Asbury Park (Sandy)," a good-bye to my adopted hometown and the life I'd lived there before I recorded. Sandy was a composite of some of the girls I'd known along the Shore. I used the boardwalk and the closing down of the town as a metaphor for the end of a summer romance and the changes I was experiencing in my own life. "Kitty's Back" was a remnant of some of the jazz-tinged rock I occasionally played with a few of my earlier bands. It was a twisted swing tune, a shuffle, a distorted piece of big band music. In '73 I had to have songs that could capture audiences who had no idea who I was. As an opening act, I didn't have much time to make an impact. I wrote several wild, long pieces—"Thundercrack," "Kitty's Back," "Rosalita"—that were the soul children of the lengthy prog pieces I'd written for Steel Mill and were arranged to leave the band and the audience exhausted and gasping for breath. Just when you thought the song was over, you'd be surprised by another section, taking the music higher. It was, in spirit, what I'd taken from the finales of the great soul revues. I'd tried to match their ferocious fervor and when you left the stage after performing one of these, you'd worked to be remembered.

"Wild Billy's Circus Story" was a black comedy based on my memories of the fairs and the Clyde Beatty-Cole Bros. Circus that visited Freehold every summer when I was a kid. They'd set up a midway and pitch their tents in a field across from the racetrack not far from my house. I was always curious about what was going on in the dim alleys off the midway. As I walked by, my hand safely enclosed in my mother's, I felt the musky underbelly to the shining lights and life I'd just seen in the center ring. It all felt frightening, uneasy and secretly sexual. I was happy with my Kewpie doll and cotton candy but that wasn't what I wanted to see. "Wild Billy" was also a song about the seduction and loneliness of a life outside the margins. At twenty-four, I'd already tasted a good piece of that world and for better or worse, that was the life I wanted to live. "Incident on 57th Street" and "New York City Serenade" were my romantic stories of New York City, a place that had been my getaway from small-town New Jersey since I was sixteen. "Incident" particularly featured a theme I'd return to often in the future: the search for redemption. Over the next twenty years I'd work this one like only a good Catholic boy could.

"Rosalita" was my musical autobiography. It was my "getting out of town" preview for *Born to Run*, with more humor. As a teenager, I'd had a girlfriend whose mother had threatened to get a court injunction against me to keep me away from her daughter due to my low-rent beginnings and defiant (for my little town) appearance. The daughter was a sweet blonde who I believe was the first gal I had successful intercourse with, one fumbling afternoon at chez mama (though, due to the fog of war, I can't be absolutely sure). I wrote "Rosalita" as a kiss-off to everybody who counted you out, put you down or decided you weren't good enough. It was a tall tale from my past that also celebrated my present ("the record company, Rosie, just gave me a big advance") and took a peek into the future ("Someday we'll look back on this and it will all seem funny"). Not that it would all BE funny, but that it would all SEEM funny. Probably one of the most useful lines I've ever written.

At the time of *The Wild, the Innocent*, I had no success, so I had no real concerns about where I was going. I was going up, I hoped, or at least out. With a record contract and a touring band, I felt I was better off than most of my friends, who were locked down in the nine-to-five world of responsibility and bills. I was lucky to be doing what I loved most. With the off-to-the-races opening chords of "Rosie," I geared up my band and hit the road without dread. That would come later.

We put *The Wild, the Innocent and the E Street Shuffle* to bed and we were finished. Half asleep, we drove ourselves back to New Jersey. Mike took the tapes and handed them to the record company and we waited for a hopefully enthusiastic response. This record gave me much greater satisfaction than *Greetings*. I felt it was a true example of what I could do with the recording, playing and arranging of my band. With "Kitty's Back," "Rosalita," "New York City Serenade" and the semiautobio of "Sandy," I was confident we showed the kind of depth, fun and excitement we could stir on records.

## There's Gonna Be a Showdown

John Hammond was gone, retired. Clive Davis was gone. The great record men, my great supporters, the men who brought me into the company, were vanishing. There was a power void and a variety of new people stepped in to fill the gap.

I was called in to see Charles Koppelman, then head of A & R, to review the album. We played a good piece of the first side and I was immediately informed the album was unreleasable. Mr. Koppelman said the musicianship was simply not up to snuff. He asked me to meet him down at a Columbia studio in a few nights and he'd show me what some "real" musicians could do with these songs. I am sure he meant well but I explained I could not do that. I told him this was my band, I was committed to them, I thought the record sounded great, I was proud of it and wanted it released as is. Mr. Koppelman was blunt in his assessment of my prospects. If I insisted on the recording being released as it was it would most likely go in the trash heap, receive little promotion and, along with me, disappear. What could I do? I liked it the way it was, so I fiercely insisted it remain unmeddled with, and what Mr. Koppelman promised was exactly what happened.

When we toured to promote *The Wild, the Innocent*, few even knew it had been released. I hit one Texas radio station where I was told a representative from my record company had visited and, while promoting several new Columbia recordings, literally told them to remove mine from airplay, adding, "The songs are too long." This was a new twist. My own record company trying to get my records *off* the radio. It was only the beginning. A battle royale broke out between rock 'n' roll drill sergeant Mike Appel and the new powers that be at CBS. Mike sent all the executives coal in a stocking for Christmas. Ho, ho, ho.

We played a club, Fat City on Long Island. The top echelon of the record company marched in to see an opening act they were thinking of signing, then marched out en masse just as we came on, insult to injury. Mike stood at the door, pen and pad in hand, writing down the names of the traitors as they left, for his hit list and future retribution.

The basic drift was these guys thought we were just going to go away, return to our day jobs, go back to school, disappear into the swamps of Jersey. They didn't understand they were dealing with men without homes, lives, any practicable skills or talents that could bring a reliable paycheck in the straight world. We had nowhere to go . . . and we loved music! This was going to be it; we had come to "liberate you, confiscate you . . ." and all the rest! There was no going back. We had no money and were receiving no record company support. Our salaries per week had increased to fifty dollars, then seventy-five dollars, but our fortunes at the record company had fallen. Our fathers there were gone. There were other promising artists now and if we were a success, we would be a feather in no one's cap. The men who would've taken the credit had vanished. We'd been orphaned.

## A Deejay Saved My Life

In the fifties, sixties and seventies, the deejay was still a mysterious and ephemeral figure. As the city slept, there he sat alone, accompanied by only shelves and shelves of the greatest music you'd ever heard. He was your friend. He understood you. You shared the secret of the true things that were really important in your life: the music.

He spoke into your ear either as boisterously as your old Cousin Brucie squalling in off the airwaves of WABC-AM, revving you up for what would surely be the greatest Saturday night of your life; or as confident and quiet as a rock 'n' roll séance delivered by Richard Neer or Alison Steele of WNEW-FM. They were human bridges to the world that was unfolding inside your head. They chronicled your changes as records came and went, inspiring you to keep listening for that one song that was going to change your life. I heard that song many times. "Hound Dog," "I Want to Hold Your Hand," "Like a Rolling Stone" all blasting out of the AM dial and encouraging me to tear down the walls of my little town and dream bigger. Or "Astral Weeks," the record that taught me to trust beauty and to believe in the divine, courtesy of my local FM station.

I always remember driving up the New Jersey Turnpike, and shortly before you reached New York, somewhere out in the industrial wasteland, stood a small concrete building. There in the middle of the stink and marshes hung a brightly lit radio call sign. It was just a relay station, I suppose, but as a young tween I'd first imagined it was the real thing. That all my favorite deejays were crowded into this one cramped shack out here in Nowheresville. There, they were bravely pouring out over the airwaves the sounds New Jersey and your life depended upon. Was it possible? Could this abandoned-looking little frontier fort so far from civilization be the center of your heart's world? Here I dreamed in the swamps of Jersey were the mighty men and women you knew only by their names and sounds of their voices.

Back when the members of the E Street Band were struggling club-setters just trying to get their foot into the door of the music industry, I had two distinct radio experiences. I spent one afternoon with the Boston Top 40 promo man driving around town trying to get "Blinded by the Light," my first single, added to Top 40 playlists. It was interesting. The first station we appeared at wouldn't let us in. At the second, we got in to see the deejay and he popped "Blinded" on for exactly twelve seconds, "Madman drummers bummers . . ." Zzzzzrrrriiipppp. The needle scratching across the surface of everything I had and loved as it was removed by lightning reflexes and the question, "When's the new Chicago record coming out?" The rest of the afternoon we drove around, had beers and told dirty jokes. I knew then I was not bound for Top 40. The other experience was as we were playing an empty house gig at the Main Point in Bryn Mawr, Pennsylvania, when in walked David Dye. He was a deejay over at WMMR, Philly's local FM station. He watched us play to thirty people, approached us and said, "I love your band." That night we heard *Greetings from Asbury Park* being spun to music-loving insomniacs as we drove out of town in our tour bus. Eventually I got to know every deejay from every major rock city in America. Ed Sciaky, a great deejay and fan out of Philly whose home I'd occasionally stay at when we played the city of brotherly love. Every Friday night, Kid Leo out of Cleveland marked the end of the workweek with "Born to Run." I'd often call Richard Neer up in the middle of the night while he was on the air just to shoot the bull. There were many others. The relationships were personal. You hung out and knew their cities. They introduced you at your shows. This was all pre-eighties and pre-pay-for-play promo men who bogged the industry down and perhaps presented me with a few hits that I might otherwise not have had. Then came computer programming of stations and nationalized playlists and it was a different business. But back when we were "almost famous," these men and women provided much love and valuable support and a well-needed home for us and our music.

## Adios, Perro Loco

*Madman drummers bummers . . .*

During the tour for *The Wild, the Innocent,* one thing became clear: we needed a steadier hand at the drums. Vini was a beautiful drummer in his own wigged-out way. He was all about his own style. You can hear it clearly on the first two albums. We actually developed out of the jam band tradition of the Upstage Club. We all had grown up playing very busily. On our first two records Vini was all over the place but he knew how to make it work.

His hyperactive drumming was connected to Vini's hyperactive self, and the combination of the thick recorded sound of the kit by Louis Lahav and Vini's playing style made for very eccentric but excitingly unique rhythm tracks.

Vini could be the warmest, most soulful guy in the world one minute, truly kind, and then go completely postal within seconds. As time passed this wore on some of the band members who bore the brunt of the Mad Dog's wrath. Danny had taken his lumps. Steve Appel, Mike's younger brother, who helped out on the road, took a pop in the eye, and so did countless strangers who'd stumbled across the Dog's intemperate side. Going out with Vini was risky business. One night we headed to a second-floor beach bar. As I was climbing the stairs to the entrance I saw a body tumbling by me on its way back to floor one. It was Vini. He was being thrown out before we even managed to get in! The accompaniment of Big Danny stepping in at the right moment and altering someone's attitude occasionally saved us from trouble. Vini showed up at a gig one night all bruised and scratched up. He had his enemies, and someone had found out Vini rode his bike home down the boardwalk to Bradley after the gig every night at three thirty a.m. Some vengeful soul had stretched a thin wire from the railing across the boards right at bicycle tire level. Mad Dog hit it at speed and got launched head over handlebars into an ass full of splinters, cuts and bruises.

Then . . . he took it one step too far. One afternoon he managed to drive Clarence Clemons around the bend. C went off, strangling the hell out of Vini's skinny neck, holding him down on the floor and smashing a heavy stereo speaker inches from his head in an attempt to bring the enlightenment. Vini got up, ran out of the house and made a beeline to my garage apartment in Bradley Beach. He looked like he'd just escaped a hanging but had spent a few moments too long dangling, eyes popping, legs shaking, at the end of the rope. He showed me huge red welts around his neck, screamed that Clarence had tried to murder him and uttered the immortal ultimatum, "Brucie, it's him or me." Not the best way to sum up your grievances on E Street, but it was my band, my town, I was mayor, judge, jury and sheriff, so I calmed him down and told him I'd look into it.

Discussions were held, grievances aired. The fellows had had enough trouble, Mike too. Vini always felt he was let go because he'd been too outspoken about the way our business was being handled. He may have been right about that but everyone had their own reasons for wanting Vini to depart. For me, it all came down to the fact that my music was changing and I needed someone with a more sophisticated palate, with clearer and better time, for the new music I was writing. I loved Vini and still do. He's a great guy, distinctive drummer and singer, and loyal true-blue friend. We'd been through a lot; Vini'd thrown me plenty of hard-core support, he was tough 'n' ready and it was hard separating from someone I'd cared about and had so many adventures with. His drumming graces my first two albums with a beautiful soul and eccentricity that perfectly fit the eclectic spirit of those songs. He was a part of the E Street Band through its toughest times, when it was truly a folk band up from the streets of Asbury Park and filled with musicians whose styles had developed straight out of the musical community we were born into.

# TWENTY-EIGHT

# THE SATELLITE LOUNGE

Telling Vini it was over was rough. I think Mike Appel did it. The week-end Vini was let go we were booked at the Satellite Lounge in Fort Dix. It was a cool club catering to locals and the South Jersey military personnel stationed at the fort. I'd seen Sam and Dave put on some great shows there. It was owned and operated by one of our "friends." We played a few clubs owned by the local boys and always had a great time. The problem was right now, we had no drummer and we would have to cancel. I told Mike and he called me back immediately and simply said, "We *have* to play." There was a problem with the owner at the Satellite Lounge, so Mike had called some of our other "friends" at Uncle Al's Erlton Lounge, a place we always did great and were treated like kings, to intercede on our behalf. That made matters much worse. Mike then gave me the short version of his conversation with the Satellite's owner: "If you don't play, we have your address and will break important digits. If you do play, we will love you." I thought, "Who doesn't want to be loved?" It was an offer I couldn't refuse. So this is the story of how Ernest "Boom" Carter, a drummer I'd barely heard of and only briefly met, ended up playing in the band that weekend, and on the most significant recording the E Street Band ever made and *only* that recording. Boom was Davey's childhood friend. On Davey's call he came to Tinker's factory; rehearsed the entire night 'til dawn, learning our full live set; drove to Fort Dix, where it was not uncustomary to begin a set at one or two a.m.; and played a great gig. Boom Carter, welcome to the E Street Band.

The Satellite's impresario was as good as his word. We *were* loved! This was during the gas crisis, and on tour we'd spent hours rocking in the draft of eighteen-wheelers whizzing by inches from our Econoline van with our tank empty by the side of the road, gasless. We'd resorted to the illegality of the siphoning tube on a few occasions but tonight, as we packed up our gear, our beneficent "friend" escorted us into the parking lot and stood smiling at our side as the police pulled up, fueled our tanks to the brim and wished us well.

Boom turned out to be a great addition. He was a jazzier drummer than I might have initially chosen but once he integrated himself into the band he brought a swing with his rock that was really beautiful. The band was now three black guys and three white guys, and the mixture of musical influences was magic. Davey of course covered all the bases from rock to soul, but he had a deeply rooted jazz and gospel element in his playing that put him out in front of most rock keyboardists. With a mixture now of folk, rock, jazz and soul, we had everything we needed to go wherever we wanted. Career-wise, however, things were still very bleak.

## The Future Is Written

We'd been playing a lot of colleges, then by chance we hit one where Irwin Siegelstein, the new head of Columbia Records, brought over from the TV division, had a son in attendance. We played a great show, but frustrated by our record company's lack of promotion, I slammed Columbia in an interview with the college newspaper. Young Siegelstein had seen the show, read the newspaper and brought it home to his pop. Mr. Siegelstein, who to his credit did not pretend to know more about pop music than he did, listened to his son, and the next thing we knew, we got a call from Columbia Records with an invitation to dine with its new president. Mike, Mr. Siegelstein and I sat down to dinner and Mr. Siegelstein said, "How can we fix this?" He was a straight-up honest broker who realized we were of value to his company and wanted to set things right.

Something else very auspicious occurred around this time. A man in Boston had "seen the future of rock 'n' roll," and it was . . . *me*. We'd played the Harvard Square Theatre opening for Bonnie Raitt (God bless her, she was one of the few acts who'd let us open for her more than once in those days). The writer in attendance for the *Real Paper*, Jon Landau, flipped his critical lid and wrote one of the greatest lifesaving raves of all time.

It was a beautifully written music fan's appreciation of the power and meaning of rock 'n' roll, the sense of place and continuity it brings to our lives, the community it can't help but strengthen and the loneliness it assuages. That night in Boston our band led with our hearts, and that's what Jon did. The famous quote came in reference to Jon's thoughts on the past, present and future of the music he loved, on the power it once held over him and on its ability to renew itself and exert that power in his life once more. As helpful and burdensome (in the long run, more helpful I would say) as the "quote heard round the world" was, it has always been taken somewhat out of context, its lovely subtleties lost . . . But who cares now! And if somebody had to be the future, why not me?

## Light at the End of the Tunnel

After our dinner with Irwin and Mr. Landau's "prophecy," there were ads for *The Wild, the Innocent and the E Street Shuffle* in the newspapers and in major music publications; they all shouted, "I have seen the future . . . ," and there I was, looking good. What a difference a day makes. The record company was back in our corner and record sales picked up for my two albums as we continued to tour, wrecking the house night after night. I was due for a new record. My third and last contractually guaranteed album for Columbia. All our cards were down. The question was, beyond critics, and my small cult following, could I stir interest in that larger audience that lay at the end of the radio dial? Cult artists don't last on Columbia Records. We miss this one, contract's up and in all probability we'll be sent back to the minors deep in the South Jersey pines. I had to make a record that was the embodiment of what I'd been slowly promising I could do. It had to be something epic and extraordinary, something that hadn't quite been heard before. It had already been a long haul but that blood I'd sniffed on that sunny morning in my grandma's backyard so many years ago was once again in the air. For my new album I'd written one song. Its title was "Born to Run."

BOOK TWO

# BORN
# TO RUN

TWENTY-NINE

# BORN
# TO RUN

I wrote "Born to Run" sitting on the edge of my bed in a cottage I'd newly rented at 7½ West End Court in Long Branch, New Jersey. I was in the midst of giving myself a crash tutorial in fifties and sixties rock 'n' roll. I had a small table holding a record player at the side of my cot, so I was just one drowsy roll away from dropping the needle onto my favorite album of the moment. At night, I'd switch off the lights and drift away with Roy Orbison, Phil Spector or Duane Eddy lullabying me to dreamland. These records now spoke to me in a way most late-sixties and early-seventies rock music failed to. Love, work, sex and fun. The darkly romantic visions of both Spector and Orbison felt in tune with my own sense of romance, with love itself as a risky proposition. These were well-crafted, inspired recordings, powered by great songs, great voices, great arrangements and excellent musicianship. They were filled with real studio genius, breathless passion . . . AND . . .

they were hits! There was little self-indulgence in them. They didn't waste your time with sprawling guitar solos or endless monolithic drumming. There was opera and a lush grandness, but there was also restraint. This aesthetic appealed to me as I moved into the early stages of writing for "Born to Run." From Duane Eddy came the guitar sound, "Tramps like us . . . ," then "ba BA . . . BA ba," the twanging guitar lick. From Roy Orbison came the round operatic vocal tone of a young aspirant with limited range attempting to emulate his hero. From Phil Spector came the ambition to make a world-shaking mighty noise. I wanted to craft a record that sounded like the last record on Earth, like the last record you might hear . . . the last one you'd ever NEED to hear. One glorious noise . . . then the apocalypse. From Elvis came the record's physical thrust; Dylan, of course, threaded through the imagery and the idea of not just writing about SOMETHING but writing about EVERYTHING.

I started with the guitar riff. Get yourself a great riff and you're on your way. Then I'd chug along chording randomly while I'd mumble, mumble, mumble . . . then, "Tramps like us, baby we were born to run . . ." That was all I had. The title "Born to Run" I was sure I'd seen somewhere before. It might have been written in silver metal flake on the hood of a car cruising the Asbury circuit, or I may have seen it somewhere in one of the hot-rod B pictures I'd gorged myself on during the early sixties. Maybe it was just out there in the air, floating along on the salt water/carbon monoxide mix of Kingsley and Ocean Avenue on a "circuit" Saturday night. Wherever it came from it held the essential ingredients of a hit record, familiarity and newness, inspiring in the listener surprise and recognition. A smash feels like it was always there and as if you've never heard anything like it before.

It wasn't an easy piece to write. I started my title song that afternoon but I didn't finish it until six months of trial and tribulation later. I wanted to use the classic rock 'n' roll images, the road, the car, the girl . . . what else is there? It was a language enshrined by Chuck Berry, the Beach Boys,

Hank Williams and every lost highwayman going back to the invention of the wheel. But to make these images matter, I would have to shape them into something fresh, something that transcended nostalgia, sentiment and familiarity.

I was a child of Vietnam-era America, of the Kennedy, King and Malcolm X assassinations. The country no longer felt like the innocent place it was said to be in the Eisenhower fifties. Political murder, economic injustice and institutionalized racism were all powerfully and brutally present. These were issues that had previously been relegated to the margins of American life. Dread—the sense that things might not work out, that the moral high ground had been swept out from underneath us, that the dream we had of ourselves had somehow been tainted and the future would forever be uninsured—was in the air. This was the new lay of the land, and if I was going to put my characters out on *that* highway, I was going to have to put all these things in the car with them. That's what was due, what the times demanded.

To move forward, we'd have to willingly wear the weight of our unreconciled past. A day of personal and historical accountability had arrived.

I started out with cliché, cliché, cliché and then I caught a piece of myself and the moment. "In the day we sweat it out on the streets of a runaway American dream . . ." It's a "death trap," a "suicide rap." "I want to guard your dreams and visions . . . I want to know if love is real." This is what is at stake, your dreams, your visions. "Together, Wendy, we can live with the sadness, I'll love you with all the madness in my soul . . . ," because that's what it'll take. "Someday . . . I don't know when, we're gonna get to that place where we really want to go and we'll walk in the sun . . . ," but 'til then all we have is this road, this ever-present *now* that is the fire and marrow of rock 'n' roll . . . "Tramps like us, baby we were born to run . . ."

Over months, I could feel the story I was aching to tell seep into my lyrics. Slowly, I found words I could stand to sing, always my first, last and only criteria to move ahead. Slowly . . . it felt real. Then there it was, my touchstone, my blueprint for my new record all wrapped up in a hot-rod rumble of sound and a low-budget movie setting that brought the trash and undercut the song's pretensions perfectly.

While the lyrics were being written we struggled with the recorded sounds of the instruments, the drum sounds, the guitar sounds. We layered instrument upon instrument, mixing down and down, track to track, combining sections of instruments until we could fit our seventy-two tracks of rock 'n' roll overkill on the sixteen available tracks at 914 Studios. It would be Boom Carter's only recorded E Street appearance on drums. He picked a good one. It would be the last recording I'd do with Davey Sancious. He'd soon be offered his own solo deal on Columbia and together they'd leave the band. Right before the gravy train! It would be the last record we'd make at 914 Studios and the only recording with just Mike and me as a production team. As we sat in the studio at eight a.m., beat from being up all night trying to get a final mix, the next session was pounding on our locked studio door. In those days, there were no automated or computerized mixing boards. It was all hands on deck. Our engineer, Louis Lahav, would have his left hand riding the guitar faders, his right riding the keyboards; Mike might ride the voice, the acoustic guitars in the final verse, while I'd be reaching over their shoulders to nudge the sax solo as it peaked and the guitar riff in the outro. One take, all the way through, no cutting, splicing or editing. As the sound of shouting and knocking on our studio door rose, we took one more pass. We had it, we thought; really, we were way too tired to tell. I brought it home and played it to wake up to every morning with the sun beaming through my bedroom window. It sounded great. I'd returned home with the *exact* record I'd wanted to make. That doesn't happen often.

The record company wanted more vocal. We took it to a New York studio one evening and in a half hour realized the impossibility of our task. We would never corral that sound again; we couldn't even come close to the musical integration, the raging wall of guitars, keys and drums. Out of deference to the bigwigs we listened to other takes from the original session. Some had more voice but they didn't have . . . *the magic*. The singer was *supposed* to sound like he was fighting to be heard over a world that didn't give a damn. No, there was only one that had that 747-engine-in-your-living-room rumble, the universe hanging, for one brief moment, in balance as the cosmic chord goes *twang*. Then the getaway. We had it. We only did it once . . . but once is all you need.

With Boom and Davey gone, we placed an ad in the *Village Voice* for a new drummer and pianist. We played with thirty drummers and thirty keyboard players for thirty minutes each. People came in to audition who just wanted to sit in for a while with the band. Guys brought double bass drum kits and tried to Ginger Baker their way through "Spirit in the Night." An "avant-garde" violinist came in with fingernail-on-the-blackboard atonal voicings and tortured us for half an hour. Whether you were bad or good you got your thirty minutes and a handshake.

In the end, Max Weinberg, a South Orange New Jerseyan, took the drum seat as Roy Bittan, from Rockaway Beach, slipped in behind the keys. They were heads above all the others and would bring a new professionalism to our sound that we would carry into the studio. They were the first guys who weren't from the neighborhood to play with the E Street Band.

With "Born to Run" blasting from FM radio stations (we'd handed it over assuming our LP would soon follow, a brilliant mistake!), we headed back into the studio. After several failed sessions at 914, we could not move the record forward. The most obvious problem was that shit just wasn't working. The piano pedals, recording equipment and sundry other things regularly went on the fritz. We were trying to record "Jungleland"—it had been a staple of our live show for a while and the band had it cold—but with all the technical glitches, you just couldn't build any momentum to get anything done. Something was wrong. After a stretch of bum recording dates, we sat dead in our tracks, my last-chance "masterpiece" going nowhere. We were stuck. We needed help.

# THIRTY
# JON
# LANDAU

It was a winter's night in Cambridge, Massachusetts. I stood on the street in front of our gig, Joe's Place, hopping side to side, trying to stay warm. I was reading a review of our second album; the owner had taped it to the club's front window in hopes of luring in some breathing customers. Then two men walked up on my left. One was writer Dave Marsh, the other was the review's twenty-seven-year-old author, Jon Landau. He sidled over to me and asked, "Whaddaya think?" *Whaddaya think* . . . those were the first and probably most recent of the ten billion words Jon and I have thrown each other's way over a lifetime of ruminating, navel-gazing, philosophizing, analyzing and making music. *Whaddaya think?* Those words have bracketed our friendship for forty years.

The heart of rock will always remain a primal world of action. The music revives itself over and over again in that form, primitive rockabilly, punk, hard soul and early rap. Integrating the world of thought and reflection with the world of primitive action is *not* a necessary skill for making great rock 'n' roll. Many of the music's most glorious moments feel as though they were birthed in an explosion of raw talent and creative instinct (some of them even were!). But . . . if you want to burn bright, hard *and* long, you will need to depend upon more than your initial instincts. You will need to develop some craft and a creative intelligence that will lead you *farther* when things get dicey. That's what'll help you make crucial sense and powerful music as time passes, giving you the skills that may also keep you alive, creatively and physically. The failure of so many of rock's artists to outlive their expiration date of a few years, make more than a few great albums and avoid water treading, or worse, I felt was due to the misfit nature of those drawn to the profession. These were strong, addictive personalities, fired by compulsion, narcissism, license, passion and an inbred entitlement, all slammed over a world of fear, hunger and insecurity. That's a Molotov cocktail of confusion that can leave you unable to make, or resistant to making, the leap of consciousness a life in the field demands. After first contact knocks you on your ass, you'd better have a plan, for some preparedness and personal development will be required if you expect to hang around any longer than your fifteen minutes.

Now, some guys' five minutes are worth other guys' fifty years, and while burning out in one brilliant supernova will send record sales through the roof, leave you living fast, dying young, leaving a beautiful corpse, there *is* something to be said for living. Personally, I like my gods old, grizzled and *here*. I'll take Dylan; the pirate raiding party of the Stones; the hope-I-get-very-old-before-I-die, present live power of the Who; a fat, still-mesmerizing-until-his-death Brando—they all suit me over the alternative. I would've liked to have seen that last Michael Jackson show, a seventy-year-old Elvis reinventing and relishing in his talents, where Jimi Hendrix might've next taken the electric guitar, Keith Moon, Janis Joplin, Kurt Cobain and all the others whose untimely deaths and lost talents stole something from the music I love, living on, enjoying the blessings of their gifts and their audience's regard. Aging is scary but fascinating, and great talent morphs in strange and often enlightening ways. Plus, to those you've received so much from, so much joy, knowledge and inspiration, you wish life, happiness and peace. These aren't easy to come by.

Youth and death have always been an intoxicating combination for the myth makers left amongst the living. And dangerous, even violent, self-loathing has long been an essential ingredient in the fires of transformation. When the "new self" burns to life, the twins of great control *and* reckless-ness are immutably linked. It's what makes life interesting. The high tension between these two forces often makes a performer fascinating and fun to watch, but also a white-cross highway marker. Here, many who've come this way have burned out hard or died. The rock death cult is well loved and chronicled in literature and music, but in practice, there ain't much in it for the singer and his song, except a good life unlived, lovers and children left behind, and a six-foot-deep hole in the ground. The exit in a blaze of glory is bullshit.

Now, if you're not one of the handful of musical revolutionaries—and I was not—you naturally set your sights on something different. In a tran-sient field, I was suited for the long haul. I had years of study behind me; I was physically built to endure and by disposition was not an edge dweller. I was interested in what I might accomplish over a lifetime of music making, so assumption number one is you are going to keep breathing. In my busi-ness, the above case studies prove, no matter who you are, that's not as easy as it sounds.

## Enter the king (Small "k")

Jon Landau was the first person I met who had a language for discussing these ideas and the life of the mind. He had the rabid fan's pure love of music and musicians while retaining his critic's ability to step back and analyze the very thing he loved. In Jon, one impulse did not dampen the other. He was a natural, and together we shared a belief in the bedrock values of musicianship, skill, the joy of hard work and the methodical application of one's talents. These things had resulted in some of our favorite records. Muscle Shoals, Motown and the Beatles' early recordings showed how revolutionary music could flow from a down-home but disciplined studio approach. That was our plan and who we were.

Jon and I related both as conspiratorial music fans and as young men in search of something. Jon would serve me as a friend and mentor, someone who'd been exposed to and held information I felt would augment my creativity and deepen the truth seeking I was trying to make a part of my music. We also had that instant chemical connection that says, "I know you." Jon was better educated than most of my homeboys. I was interested in doing my job better and being great. Not good . . . great. Whatever that took, I was in. Now, if you don't have the raw talent, you can't will yourself there. But if you have the talent, then will, ambition and the determination to expose yourself to new thoughts, counterargument, new influences, will strengthen and fortify your work, driving you closer to home.

In the early days of our relationship, I remember visiting Jon's apartment in New York. We talked music and played records for hours. It was the same kind of intense connection I had with Steve . . . but different. In 1974, I was a young and developing musician. I was interested in forefathers, artist brothers in arms, people who'd thought like this who'd come before me. Jon knew who and where they were, in books, in films and in music. It was all very casual, just friends talking and throwing around ideas about the things that inspired them, moved them, late-night conversations about the things that opened up your world and made you hunger for life. I was moving off my first two records and already developing a new voice. I'd begun to pare down my lyrical style. When we began to work on *Born to Run* together, Jon followed suit with the music. He was a very astute arranger and editor who was particularly excellent at shaping the bottom of the record, the bass and drums. He guarded against overplaying and guided our record toward a more streamlined sound. I was ready to give up some eclecticness and looseness, some of the street party, for a tighter punch to the gut. We simplified the basic tracks so we could stack up dense layers of sound without lapsing into sonic chaos. It made *Born to Run* simultaneously steeped in rock history and modern. We made dense, dramatic rock 'n' roll. *Born to Run* is his greatest production work on one of my greatest records.

Above and beyond production, Jon was the latest in a long line of fans, friends and freaks who subbed as a papa figure. It was a lifetime project, finding someone to pick up the slack for my MIA old man. It was a big and unfair burden to lay on anyone, but that didn't stop me. *Somebody* had to do it. I think Jon needed something himself at that point. He was coming off a debilitating illness, a long hospital stay and a painful divorce. I was a good comrade, perhaps the physical embodiment of some part of his rock 'n' roll dream, and I aided his own development in subtle ways. He'd already produced the MC5's *Back in the USA*; I presented Jon with a venue to continue the hands-on application of his own talents, and those talents in turn made me a more effective and probing songwriter and musician.

My writing was focusing itself around identity issues—who am I, who are we, what and where is home, what constitutes manhood, adulthood, what are your freedoms and your responsibilities. I was interested in what it meant to be an American, one small participant in current history at a time when the future seemed as hazy and shape-shifting as that thin line on the horizon. Can a rock 'n' roll artist help sculpt that line, shade its direction? How much? With influences as varied and seemingly polarized as Woody Guthrie and Elvis, Top 40 radio and Bob Dylan, along with a thousand nights of bar playing behind me, I was curious to press on in search of what I could do and where I belonged.

Alongside my wife Patti, my band and a few close friends, I've shared my mind with Jon more than anyone else. When it's a good match, along the way, your heart ends up thrown in too. There is a love and respect at the center of everything we do together. It's not just business, it's personal. When you came to work with me, I had to be assured you'd bring your heart. Heart sealed the deal. That's why the E Street Band plays steamroller strong and undiminished, forty years in, night after night. We are more than an idea, an aesthetic. We are a philosophy, a collective, with a professional code of honor. It is based on the principle that we bring our best, everything we have, on this night, to remind you of everything *you* have, your best. That it's a privilege to exchange smiles, soul and heart directly with the people in front of you. That it's an honor and great fun to join in concert with those whom you've invested so much of yourself in and they in you, your fans, the stars above, this moment, and apply your trade humbly (or not so!) as a piece of a long, spirited chain you're thankful to be a small link in.

## Up River

In our quest, Jon became the Clark to my Lewis. In the future we would travel together through more than a little wilderness. He had befriended and counseled me when it felt like I was teetering a little too close to the edge of my favorite abyss. Prior to Jon, I knew no one who'd spent three minutes in an analyst's office. I grew up around a lot of very ill people, secretive, susceptive to serious depression, and disturbing, unpredictable behavior. I knew it was a significant piece of my own mental makeup. In New Jersey, in my crowd, the psychiatric profession might as well not have existed. When I looked down and saw bottom, Jon assisted me toward help that would refocus and alter the course of my life. I owe a great debt to my friend for his kindness, generosity and love. He's done a pretty nice job of management too. We're still here after many years. When Jon and I discuss our future course of action, he's always been guided by two things—my well-being and happiness (then the tour gross!). These first two were the answers I was long looking for in the receding mists of Freehold, New Jersey. They are the incredibly complicated and simple answers of parenthood, of friendship. The only ones.

The day naturally came when that changed too. I no longer needed a surrogate dad or a mentor, just a friend and partner. Jon really no longer needed any single embodiment of his rock 'n' roll fantasy and he began to successfully manage a variety of other artists. Adulthood, or something awfully like it, arrived. For a while, in these years of transition, there was tension and some misunderstanding between Jon and me; coded conversations, anxious phone calls, anger lying just beneath the surface, and frustration. It's not easy moving forward together; people get set in their ways, their perceptions cut in stone. Most don't make it. Twenty years after we'd started, I'd changed. So had Jon. That was the idea. For a short while, it seemed we were victims of our own good promise. Then it all eventually came to a head and we sorted through it in our quiet way, sitting one sunny Los Angeles day, talking in my backyard. "Whaddaya think?"

We'd navigated the treacherous part of the river, the part Mike and I couldn't make, where the current changes and the landscape will never be the same. So, breaking into the open I looked behind me in our boat and I still had my Clark. Up front, he still had Lewis. We still had our own musical country to chart, many miles of frontier to travel, and music to make. It's too late to stop now.

# THIRTY-ONE
# THUNDER
# ROAD

As our evening session at 914 ground to a stop, Jon leaned over and whispered, "You're a first-class artist, you should be in a first-class recording studio." That made sense to me. My friendship with Jon had grown slow and steady, so I'd decided to invite him to the studio to observe and perhaps bring some insight into the problems we were having. Back in New York, we went out for a late-night bite. As we sat side by side on two stools at the counter of a small diner, Jon offered, "If you need me to do something, I'd be glad to do it." He seemed to have a clear idea of the steps that needed to be taken to get us out of our midflight stall. I thought about it. I'm insular by nature and I don't let new people in casually. I decided it was necessary and he was the right man. I liked and trusted Jon; our working relationship grew out of our musical friendship. He was not a cold professional but a friend who perhaps had the expertise to help me make a great record. That's what I was here for.

I talked to Mike. I explained this had to happen. He was unsure, but if I felt that strongly about it, he'd agree. A short while later we entered the legendary Record Plant studios on West Forty-Fourth Street in Manhattan. On our first evening there a skinny Italian kid was operating the tape machine. His job was to change the tape reels and turn the player off and on upon the engineer's command. He was a classic New York character, quirky, funny, with attitude to spare. When I came in the next night, he was sitting at the center of the long recording board, replacing Louis Lahav. Jon felt we needed a new engineer and he and Mike decided to take action. I asked Jon if he thought this kid could pull it off. He said, "I think he can." So Jimmy Iovine, brilliant impostor, young studio dog with the fastest learning curve I've ever seen (and soon to be one of the world's biggest music moguls and star of *American Idol*?!), became the engineer on the most important record of my life.

Jon had been to rehearsals in New Jersey and together we'd begun to edit some of our long, winding arrangements. We'd grown out of them. He'd helped me compress the song lengths for maximum impact. He told me longer was not always better; neither necessarily was shorter, but I'd caught the bug and Jon had to stop me before I took an ax to the classic intro and outro of "Backstreets." Jon's opinions were always very measured. What would give us the biggest bang for our buck? The arrangements began to take shape and when we went into the Record Plant to record, suddenly, music got recorded.

I'd loosely imagined the *Born to Run* album as a series of vignettes taking place during one long summer day and night. It opens with the early-morning harmonica of "Thunder Road." You are introduced to the album's central characters and its main proposition: do you want to take a chance? "The screen door slams, Mary's dress sways"—that's a good opening line, you can take it anywhere. "We're pulling out of here to win." That's about as good a closer as you're going to get. It lays out the stakes you're playing for and sets a high bar for the action to come. Then, you're introduced to the soaring, highway-blown-open sound of Clarence's saxophone outro. Ladies and gentlemen, meet the Big Man. "Thunder Road" is followed by "Tenth Avenue Freeze Out," the story of a rock 'n' soul band and our full-on block party. It's Steve Van Zandt's only *Born to Run* appearance, where he spontaneously arranged, badgered and befuddled the jazz players of a prize New York City horn section, amongst whom were the Brecker Brothers and David Sanborn (all of whom must've been thinking, "Who *is* this crazy fucker in the wife-beater tee and straw fedora?"), into honking out some primitive boardwalk soul. Pedal to the metal, we steam into "Night," followed by the stately piano, organ and broken friendships of "Backstreets": "We swore forever friends . . ."

Side two opens with the wide-screen rumble of "Born to Run," sequenced dead in the middle of the record, anchoring all that comes before and after. Then the Bo Diddley beat of "She's the One" (written just so I could hear C blow that sax solo over the top of it) and we cut to the trumpet of Randy Brecker as dusk falls and we head through the tunnel for "Meeting Across the River." From there it's all night, the city and the spiritual battleground of "Jungleland" as the band works its way through musical movement after musical movement. Then, Clarence's greatest recorded moment. That solo. One last musical ebb, and . . . "The poets down here don't write nothing at all, they just stand back and let it all be . . . ," the knife-in-the-back wail of my vocal outro, the last sound you hear, finishes it all in bloody operatic glory.

At record's end, our lovers from "Thunder Road" have had their early hard-won optimism severely tested by the streets of my noir city. They're left in fate's hands, in a land where ambivalence reigns and tomorrow is unknown. In these songs were the beginnings of the characters whose lives I would trace in my work (along with the questions I'd be writing about—"I want to know if love is real") for the next four decades. This was the album where I left behind my adolescent definitions of love and freedom; from here on in, it was going to be a lot more complicated. *Born to Run* was the dividing line.

In a three-day, seventy-two-hour sprint, working in three studios simultaneously, Clarence and I finishing the "Jungleland" sax solo, phrase by phrase, in one, while we mixed "Thunder Road" in another, singing "Backstreets" in a third as the band rehearsed in a spare room upstairs, we managed to finish the record that would put us on the map on the exact day our *Born to Run* tour was starting. That's not supposed to happen. The record should be ready months before you hit the road, released at tour's beginning, but that's how close we cut it. In the early-morning light, after three days of no sleep, we flopped into the waiting cars that would drive us straight to Providence, Rhode Island, and the stage.

Still, I wrestled with *Born to Run* for a few more months, rejecting it, refusing to release it and finally throwing it in a hotel swimming pool in front of a panicked Jimmy Iovine. He'd brought the finished master out on tour but to hear it, the two of us had to go to a downtown stereo store and beg them to let us use one of their record players. I stood in the back of the store, fretting, hemming and hawing as the record played, Jimmy's eyes plastered to every look on my face, begging, "Please just say yes and let's be done." Jimmy, Jon and Mike got crazy but I still just couldn't release it. All I could hear was what I perceived as the record's flaws. The bombastic big rock sound, the Jersey–Pavarotti–via–Roy Orbison singing, the same things that gave it its beauty, power and magic. It was a puzzle; it seemed you couldn't have one without the other. Jon tried to patiently explain to me that "art" often works in mysterious ways. What makes something great may also be one of its weaknesses, just like in people. I let it go.

# THIRTY-TWO

# JACKPOT

On August 25, 1975, all the aces came up, the sevens rolled round and an endless river of noise and silver poured forth from the mouth of the one-armed bandit of rock 'n' roll—JACKPOT! Bingo! Bull's-eye! We had a HIT! I was exhilarated but also extremely wary. A conceptual optimist but personal pessimist, I believed that along with the jackpot would come its terrible twin . . . trouble, as in bad gris-gris, a Gypsy's curse, the *malocchio*, the "evil eye" down on ya. I was right. It was going to be a lot for a twenty-five-year-old to handle.

My first challenge was *Time* and *Newsweek* calling to put me on the cover of their magazines. I hesitated, because, back then, popular entertainers, particularly rock 'n' rollers, were not on the covers of what were considered serious news publications. The media culture of the midseventies was vastly different than that of today. First, nobody called it "media." There was no Internet, no *Entertainment Tonight*, no happy talk news, no E! network, no MTV, no TMZ, no cable, no satellite TV. There were newspapers, and on network television at seven p.m. there were old men in suits reporting the events of the day. That was it. There were tabloids, but they didn't give a damn about rock 'n' roll punks. They wanted to know what kind of adult craziness Elizabeth Taylor and Richard Burton were up to, they were interested in who Frank Sinatra was screwing. *Time* and *Newsweek* were prestigious magazines, but the first taste of future pop culture (and the demise of their influence) was beginning to bubble up. Modern "media" and all its attendant roar, screech and babble were just around the corner.

I had a choice. No interview, no cover. Interview, cover . . . two of 'em. Though I was young, I'd had my season in obscurity. I knew well the near misses, the disappointments, the many miles covered and the small tastes of near discovery that went sour. THIS WAS NO TIME TO BUCKLE! I was reticent and would remain so, but I needed to find out what I had. Forty years later I did not want to be sitting in my rocking chair on a sunny afternoon with the woulda, shoulda, coulda blues. All I could think of was my dad covered in a cloak of cigarette smoke lamenting, "I could've taken that job with the phone company but I would've had to travel . . . ," so instead, it was lights-out, the blues, beer and resenting his own family for what he thought he might've accomplished. Dead meat.

I worried, but in the end my ego, ambition and fear of not taking my shot outweighed my insecurity. I called Mike . . . "Send in the press."

# Hype

When the big noise came down, I was lounging in a deck chair at the Sunset Marquis hotel. The Marquis was an infamous LA crash house for wayward rockers. As the covers hit the stands, we were out west to perform at the Roxy nightclub on the Sunset Strip. These shows were to be the center of our West Coast campaign after the raucous war we'd waged back east at New York's Bottom Line. The Bottom Line was the gig that finally put us on the map as big-time contenders. For five nights, two shows a night, we left everything we had on the tiny stage at 15 West Fourth Street. For us, they were groundbreaking appearances, the band pushing its limits as I cake-walked across the skinny tabletops, leaving that burn in the air of something happening. Yes, we had our naysayers, and if our show couldn't convince you, you were going to remain unconvinced for a while, but inside the band *and* on the street, you could feel the whole thing taking off.

The Bottom Line shows seriously raised the bar. We got born again there. When we left, something new had taken hold of our band. As "Born to Run" had defined us on record, these shows defined us as a live act intent on shaking you by the collar, waking you up, and all-or-nothing performances.

In LA, the first sight I saw was a madly grinning Steve Van Zandt rushing around the pool like he was late on his Middletown, New Jersey, paper route. He was distributing *Time* and *Newsweek* magazines with my mug on 'em to any sin city sun worshipper he could get within tossing distance of. He handed two to me. "Isn't this great!" I looked at them and thought, "Oh my God," and immediately retired to my room. I was *not* comfortable, but what could a poor boy do? As says Hyman Roth in *The Godfather Part II*, "This is the business we've chosen!" Sure, I'd nurtured my ambivalence; it made me happy, gave me plausible deniability and granted me the illusion of staying one step removed from my ravenous ambitions. But . . . this was the course I had striven toward relentlessly . . . STARDOM . . . not a Wednesday, Friday and Saturday gig at the local gin joint, not a musical weekend warrior, not a college kid's down-low secret hero . . . STARDOM! THE IMPACT, THE HITS, THE FAME, THE MONEY, THE WOMEN, THE RECOGNITION, AND THE FREEDOM to live as I pleased, to take it to the limit or wherever all of this was leading me.

I'd fixed it good so I couldn't go back, only forward, so that's where we went. I was just going to have to be good enough, as good as I promised, as good as I thought I was, for all this to make sense. For all the new rumble out in the world, inside of me was where the real show was going on, and it was fireworks. Up, down, inside, out, the mood swings flooded over me as I flew from one pole to the other like a manic-depressive trapeze artist. The only things that kept me from launching into the ozone layer were my band and the shows we played. The shows were *real*, always . . . my friends were *real*, always . . . the audience was *real*, always. I was not alone. I was carrying a lot of weight, but I was not alone. The men I'd chosen to travel with were at my side. Their comfort, their partnership, was invaluable. No matter how weird it got out there, on the bandstand, when I turned around, I saw home. These were people who understood me and knew who I was.

The shows in LA went well. Martin Scorsese and Robert De Niro came down and a few days later Marty screened *Mean Streets* for the band, opening with a short of his, *The Big Shave*. I'd met Jack Nicholson, another Jersey native, brought up in the town adjoining Asbury Park, Neptune City. After the show we hung in a little bar above the Roxy and I asked him how he handled the success. He said by the time it came his way, he was ready for it. I wasn't sure that was me, but I'd soon find out. We were momentarily to leave for overseas and a series of shows that would deeply test just how ready we were.

## London Calling

The Beatles, the Stones, the Animals, the Yardbirds, the Kinks, Jeff Beck, Clapton, Hendrix, the Who—we were heading for the isle of our heroes. The British House of the Second Coming, where the first generation of American blues and rock 'n' roll had shipwrecked on a distant shore, been understood, thoroughly digested and recast as something wondrous. Rock's second generation of Beat groups had pulled off a Herculean task. They'd reinvented some of the greatest music that had ever been made. They'd infused the old forms with youth, pop smarts and hits that soared up the charts. They'd introduced generations of kids like me to the music of some of the most talented Americans who'd ever picked up a harmonica, guitar or pen. I'd heard my first dose of Howlin' Wolf, Jimmy Reed, Muddy Waters and Arthur Alexander through these groups. "House of the Rising Sun," an old folk song, was turned into a growling modern blues of personal destruction by the Animals. The Rolling Stones breathed punk life into Chuck Berry's greatest hits as the Beatles covered early R & B with love and fresh style. I still feel I owe all of these groups, these young Englishmen, an enormous debt of gratitude for valuing and leading me to these artists, who by 1964 were largely unheard in most American households.

In England lived the reasons *we* were here. The cities of London, Liverpool, Manchester, Newcastle rang synonymous with the names of our favorite British Beat heroes. These were mystical destinations, yet here we were, coming in for a landing at Heathrow Airport, new representatives of the musical mother country with a chance to return some small part of the favor . . . if we could.

Upon reaching our hotel, I receive copies of *Melody Maker* and the *New Musical Express*, England's two premier music publications. I'm big on the front page of both, raved about in one and torn to shreds in the other. Let's get it on. We're playing the Hammersmith Odeon, a theater-sized venue in the heart of London. As we pull up to the outside, the brightly lit marquis reads, "FINALLY!! LONDON IS READY FOR BRUCE SPRINGSTEEN." Reflecting, this is not exactly the tone I'd have preferred been struck. It feels, perhaps, a little too . . . presumptuous? Once inside I am greeted by a sea of posters on every available flat surface and in every seat proclaiming me THE NEXT FUCKING BIG THING! The kiss of death! It's usually better to let the audience decide that one. I'm frightened and I'm pissed, really pissed. I am embarrassed for myself and offended for my fans. This is not the way it works. I know how it works. I've done it. Play and shut up. My business is SHOW business and that is the business of SHOWING . . . not TELLING. You don't TELL people anything, you SHOW them, and let them decide. That's how I got here, by SHOWING people.

You try to tell people what to think and you end up a little Madison Avenue mind fascist. Hey, mister *rock star*, get the fuck out of my mind and into my feet, into my heart. That's how the job gets done. That's how you introduce yourself.

I've got to fix it. I tear through the theater, simultaneously reaming out Mike Appel while ripping down every poster and disposing of every flyer I can get my hands on. I need a clean environment to work in. I need to reclaim the theater for my fans, for me and for my band. By showtime, I'm fucked. I'm pathetically wrecked and nervous. At twenty-five, I am still a provincial young man. I have never been overseas in my life. As I've said before, I know I'm good but I'm also a poser. That's artistic balance! In the second half of the twentieth century, "authenticity" would be what you made of it, a hall of mirrors. Put on the work shirt, young man. No big deal. As you get older, it won't concern you. It's just the lay of the land. In your youth, however, you are easy prey for the many tricks of the mind. At this moment, I know my mind is *not* at its most centered. I can tell because I'm afraid, and that's not my style; I don't need to be, but I am. Abject fear is not the state of mind you want to take the stage in, but . . .

It's SHOWtime. We go on. The audience seems reticent, the room feels uneasy. That's my responsibility. You've got to let the audience feel that they're coolly within your hands. That's how you help them feel safe and free enough to let themselves go, to find whatever they've come looking for and be whoever they've come here to be. On this night, my problem is that during the performance I am in and out of myself for a while in a most unpleasant way. Inside, multiple personalities are fighting to take turns at the microphone while I'm struggling to reach the "fuck it" point, that wonderful and necessary place where you set fire to your insecurities, put your head down and just go. Right now, I can feel myself caring too much, thinking too much about . . . what I'm thinking about. My good friend Peter Wolf, the great front man from the J. Geils Band, once said, "The strangest thing you can do onstage is think about what you're doing." He was right, and I am doing the strangest thing you can do onstage RIGHT NOW! It's like one moment, your life feels threatened: your little house of cards, the performance "self" you've built so carefully, so meticulously, your mask, your costume, your disguise, your dream self, is in danger of coming apart, of tumbling down. The next, you're towering, soaring, deeply immersed in your "true" self, riding the music your band is making high above the assembled. These two selves are often only a hair's width apart. That's what makes it interesting. That's why people pay the money and that's why they call it LIVE. Each and every performance for the rest of your life will hold some trace of this arc, along with the potential for catastrophic failure or transcendent success. Most evenings you grab on to the common ground somewhere between the endurable upper and lower regions of this arc . . . but when the graph is excessively steep . . . hold on. It feels like anything can happen, and not in a comforting way.

Everyone knows some version of this in their life, whether on a big or small scale, along with the need to work it out. It's just that most wouldn't prefer to do it in front of thousands, but . . . This is the house of my vocation, the strange place I go to have this conversation with myself. Of course, you have your strategies, so . . . I resort to my will. In performance, when called upon, oh doubting audience member, when you think it's over, when the vultures are circling and our blood is being smelled, tasted, my will, *my band's concerted will*, our insistent commitment to do-or-die, will come back hard to kick your ass and try to resurrect the day. I learned from the best, my mother. She *willed* we would be a family and we were. She *willed* we would not disintegrate and we did not. She *willed* we would walk with respect through the streets of our town, and we did.

We're nearing the end of the set, and now, back on Earth, I feel the heat building in my body, the audience gathering around me and the band stepping up, readying itself to deliver what we came three thousand miles across the Atlantic for. I'm pushing hard, maybe too hard, then it's over. A tough night. I am disappointed in myself for ceding too much to my internal conflicts. After an awkward stop at the record company's "victory" party, I drag myself, alone, back to my hotel room and eat what the British had the balls to refer to as a cheeseburger. On the edge of my bed, underneath a cloud of black crows, I promise myself I will never be joined onstage to such a degree by my infidel again. I tell myself there is always plenty of time to listen to my own voice, to its often sage advice, just not once I've counted my band in. That's no time for reading the wallpaper inside my fabulously fertile and forever doubting mind. On the Shore, mecca to the bar- and show-band elite, rabid disciples of the James Browns, the Sam Moores, the hard-core soul showmen who brought it every time they hit the stage, we come from where "professionalism" is not a dirty word. One . . . two . . . three . . . four . . . Motherfucker! That's the time for action, for living, for manifesting life, for BRINGING IT! . . . NOT for dipping into the black recesses to pick the lint out of your belly button. So I told myself.

You can see all of this on the E Street Band's *Hammersmith Odeon, London '75* film that accompanies the *Born to Run* box set, except you won't. You will not see anything except the band perform a tough but excellent set. You will see us enter the stage armed with a set list I still dare any young band to match and pump out a Jersey stew of rock and punk soul. It was an evening that introduced us to our English fans and began the long and lovely forty-year relationship we've had with them. At the time, I found the evening so disconcerting that I never viewed the concert film until 2004, thirty years later! When I did, I found out it had been filmed quite well and was a great document of the band performing in all its disco-suited, leather-jacketed, knit-hatted midseventies glory. Most of what I'd experienced that night was a movie playing exclusively inside my own head. My body and heart knew what to do and went ahead and did it anyway. I'd trained well. All those unfriendly gigs and rough houses, a decade's worth of firemen's fairs, carnivals, drive-ins, supermarket openings, and hole-in-the-walls where nobody gave a shit about you, came back to lift us up in our hour of darkness. We'd been there many times before—not quite like the Hammersmith, but enough to have prepared ourselves.

That night I lay in bed in a foreign land feeling rather foreign to myself. That sleepless, disconcerting "What just happened?" feeling kept kicking around my head. I lay awake thinking, "Whoa . . . this is a little more than I bargained for." Of course, this was *exactly* what I'd bargained for, I just wasn't savvy enough to know it. Looking back, as ugly, nerve-racking and unpleasant as it was, without the over-the-top hype, and all its attendant noise, around that *one single gig*, it might have taken a good little band from Jersey countless trips overseas to have the same impact or to simply get noticed. All *we* had to do was live up to it . . . and wasn't that on me? Whatever happened, our first night at the Hammersmith Odeon became one of our "legendary" performances, but it was also the moment I learned that unless you are very aggressive, very proactive about what you want, what you've created can be co-opted and taken from you, whatever the results. It's nothing personal. You will simply be stripped bare, for better or worse, at the altar of the great marketing gods, who have a dynamic and an agenda guided by the DNA of commerce.

Way at the top of the music business food chain in that big conference room in the sky (or in my case, somewhere in Japan), at the end of the day they don't ask the man on top, "How many good records have we made this year?" They ask him, "HOW MANY RECORDS HAVE WE *SOLD*?!" His fate and often yours will depend upon his answer. Don't get me wrong; record companies, including big corporate ones, are filled with people who love music, who are fans, who want to be a part of it all and whose talents led them to the business side. They will be your invaluable collaborators and most musicians I know don't have any problem with someone helping sell their records. But if you don't negotiate the terms of an agreed-upon partnership, your talents will be harnessed and guided in the direction others feel is best. No harm intended, though great harm . . . or stardom! . . . or both! . . . may occur. These days the Internet has changed much of the playing field, but not all of it. The dynamic between creativity and commerce remains a convoluted waltz. If you want to fly by your own lights, reach the audience you feel your talents deserve and build a work life on what you've learned, value and can do, be wary. In the early days, my record company harbored no ill intentions. They were a victim of their own jolly business planning and excitement, working at the mercy of the mighty gods of commerce, just doing their job, while I was learning mine . . . real fast.

With London behind us, things calmed down a bit. We went to Sweden, where it was dead winter and permanent midnight. Crushed together on tiny cots in minuscule hotel rooms, we hit the streets, where, in a Stockholm nightclub, we saw a live sex show, stark-naked Scandinavians on a tiny stage bringing their all. We sat, cackling schoolboys in the back row. It was funny, weird and kind of scary. Come morning, sophisticates and international gourmets, we found what I think was the only McDonald's then in Europe, and it was on to Amsterdam, where we played a beautiful opera house and stared, slack-jawed rubes, into the windows of the red-light district ("I ain't going in . . . !"). Then it was back to London for another crack at the Odeon, this time with the boogeymen in my head held at bay. There we played a blaze of a show that left us feeling there might be a place for us there amongst our hallowed young forefathers after all. It was freeing and left a sweet taste in our mouths as we headed back home.

Home . . . for a real cheeseburger. "I'm so glad I'm livin' in the USA." Thank you, Chuck Berry. We left feeling a little less than triumphant and a good deal better than washouts. We were a bit like the wagon train that'd come under assault but had made it through the incomprehensible West, losing only a few scalps along the rutted trail. Still, it shook me. Those four shows were our 1975 European tour. We wouldn't return for five years, until I was sure we'd grown up a little, carried more confidence, had a couple more albums' worth of strong material under our belts and felt ready to conquer the language/cultural barrier and our European brethren once and for all.

*Born to Run* lifted us into another league. We were a new young force to be reckoned with and were removed financially from the red column and placed firmly in the black (hypothetically). We'd landed, a success, for now. It had taken four of the five years of my original Laurel Canyon agreements to get us there. Ironically, just as we hit the big time, I had only one year left in my contractual obligations to Laurel Canyon and Mike Appel. I hadn't even thought about it, but Mike had.

# THIRTY-THREE

# THE
# E STREET
# BAND

With your first success, an image you'll be shadowboxing with for the rest of your life embeds itself in the consciousness of your fans. You've left your fingerprints on your audience's imagination . . . and they stick. That first moment, along with its freedoms and confinements, will remain indelible. That "you," that distinct creative identity you've been searching for? Your audience has just told you you've found it. I suddenly slipped from being "the new Dylan" into being . . . "Bruce Springsteen." And my musicians grew from well-appointed sidemen into the E Street Band.

In the beginning I knew I wanted something more than a solo act and less than a one-man-one-vote democratic band. I'd been there and it didn't fit me. Democracy in rock bands, with very few exceptions, is often a ticking time bomb. The examples are many, beginning and ending with the Beatles. Still, I wanted good musicians, friends and personalities I could bounce off of. I wanted the neighborhood, the block. That's where all the great rock bands came from and there's something about that common blood or even just the image, the dream of it, that stirs emotion and camaraderie amongst your audience. You're not looking for the best players. You're looking for the *right* players who click into something unique. The Beatles, the Stones, the Sex Pistols, the New York Dolls, the Clash and U2 are all groups whose limitations became the seed for spectacular style and musical frontiersmanship.

I wanted the singular creative and decision-making power of a solo artist but I also wanted the live, rambunctious gang feeling only a real rock 'n' roll band can deliver. I felt there was no reason you couldn't have the best of both worlds, so I signed as a solo artist and hired my longtime neighborhood running pack as my band. Not my *backing* band, not *a* band, *my* band. There was a difference. They wouldn't be a group of anonymous sidemen but central characters and personalities in their own right, each a featured performer. James Brown had Maceo and Bo Diddley had his right-hand man, Jerome, accompanied by the Duchess and Lady Bo (two guitar-slinging women!). These musicians gave my heroes a backstory and made them more interesting. (I always imagined these are the folks James and Bo hung with, sang about, who came from the world they came from and were filled with the mystery of the overpowering music I was hearing. Bo had decided that Jerome, shaking the maracas, was more essential to his world, his sound, than a bass player—of which he had NONE. Understand, on 99.9 percent of all the records you've heard for the past fifty years, there's a BASS! But Bo said, "Fuck that, I got all the bass I want here in my right, thunder-makin', guitar-strummin' hand. But what I really need is my man JEROME to shake his maracas!" Ergo: Jerome was important.) That's what I wanted.

I was signed to Columbia Records as a solo artist, so the band performed on Bruce Springsteen records. But live, I wanted the collective identity and living representations of the characters who populated my songs. It was James Brown *and* His Famous Flames, Buddy Holly *and* the Crickets—that "*and*" was really important. It said there was a party going on, a meeting taking place, a congregation being called forth, YOU WERE BRINGING YOUR GANG! So, live we would be Bruce Springsteen *and* the E Street Band. That sounded exciting; that was a world I'd want to see. I always felt the audience should look at the stage and see a reflection of themselves, their town, and their friends. That takes a band.

# E Street

We don't hide our cards. We don't play it cool. We lay ourselves out in clear view. While I love a hidden quality in other performers, as a group we aren't figures unduly shrouded in mystery or mystique. We aspire to be understood and accessible, a little of your local bar band blown up to big-time scale. A real rock 'n' roll band evolves out of a common place and time. It's all about what occurs when musicians of similar background come together in a local gumbo that mixes into something greater than the sum of its parts.

$$1 + 1 = 3$$

The primary math of the real world is one and one equals two. The layman (as, often, do I) swings that every day. He goes to the job, does his work, pays his bills and comes home. One plus one equals two. It keeps the world spinning. But artists, musicians, con men, poets, mystics and such are paid to turn that math on its head, to rub two sticks together and bring forth fire. Everybody performs this alchemy somewhere in their life, but it's hard to hold on to and easy to forget. People don't come to rock shows to learn something. They come to be *reminded* of something they already know and feel deep down in their gut. That when the world is at its best, when we are at our best, when life feels fullest, one and one equals three. It's the essential equation of love, art, rock 'n' roll and rock 'n' roll *bands*. It's the reason the universe will never be fully comprehensible, love will continue to be ecstatic, confounding, and true rock 'n' roll will never die.

It's also the equation you're searching for a trace of while you're putting your band together.

## Roll Call

When the E Street Band initially gathered I had no idea, personally, who my members were. Many of us had just met. It's only after the bandleader utters the incantation "One, two, three, four!" that it begins, the gris-gris is summoned and all is revealed. In Asbury Park our garden wasn't seeded. The bounty of musicians grew wild and you picked 'em where you found 'em. There was no master plan guiding band selection beyond instinct, geography and the power of the music once we began to play. If you're lucky and have chosen well, in the end, that's all it takes.

Max Weinberg, Garry Tallent, Steve Van Zandt, Danny Federici, Roy Bittan, Clarence Clemons. This was the core of the group that over the next forty years would evolve into the hard-rockin', history-makin', earth-shakin', booty-quakin', lovemakin' and, yes, eventually, Viagra-takin' legendary E Street Band.

ON BASS: Garry Tallent, Southern man, rock 'n' roll aficionado. Garry was one of the guys I met my first night at the Upstage Club. He was the club's go-to bass man and a creature of rare stability amongst the woolly outsiders who patronized our Asbury hideaway. His quiet dignity and low-maintenance personality have graced my life and my band from the beginning. Garry's playing shares a little common ground with Bill Wyman, the Stones' original bassist. His playing can seem invisible, transparent, rising up out of your dreams, creating a bed for them to lie on rather than intruding upon them. Then, when you go to the bottom, he's always there. No show pony, he's in the great tradition of silent men drawn to the bass guitar.

**ON ORGAN:** Danny "the Phantom" Federici, another "first nighter" at Upstage. We went through it all. Danny sought trouble and usually found it. For a long while it was drugs, bills, booze and a soft-spoken gentleness covering a heart and soul of confusion. But the playing, the playing made up for a lot. The personal burdens Danny carried disappeared once he was behind the organ. When you listened to Danny play you heard . . . freedom. Most musicians are constrained by what they know. They may play beautifully but somewhere down in their core you hear the shade of what they *know*, *studied*, *learned*, and it just slightly, naggingly, dines on the elegance of what they do. Such is the way for us mortals. Danny didn't *know* what he *knew*. He didn't know your songs, the chord sequences, the arrangement, the key, the lyrics, the what-the-fuck-you-were-ass-in-over-your-head trying to talk about. *He just knew how to play!* If you questioned him about a piece of music before you played it, he often couldn't answer your most basic queries. ("Danny, how does this start?" A shrug.) But once you counted off, he was more than fine. He accessed whatever remote part of his brain he kept the essential information in and lit up. He was free behind that organ . . . but just behind that organ. The real world doesn't cotton much to freedom but the artist's world breathes and bleeds it. This was the world where Danny's beauty flowed forth, where he flew, and like a lot of us he struggled in the other world that waited at the bottom of those stage steps. My departed friend remains to me a barrel of puzzlement and human frailty that was presided over by a mystical, intuitive musicianship like no other.

**ON GUITAR:** Steve "Little Steven" Van Zandt, my Soul Brother No. 1, Mr. All-or-Nothing-at-All, Dr. Ninety-Nine-and-a-Half-Won't-

Do, my absolutist, my comedic foil, my devil's advocate and my A-class rock 'n' roll conspirator. We battled it out together, dueling Telecasters in the teen clubs of the Jersey Shore. Steve's a great bandleader, songwriter and arranger in his own right, and a fierce, slashing guitarist. If I want to raise the rock 'n' roll, I hand Steve his guitar, point him toward the studio and leave. It'll be there when I come back. He's my onstage right-hand man, my great friend, without whom my band and my life would be—and were, in his absence—never the same.

**ON DRUMS:** Max "the Mighty Max" Weinberg. A bundle of drive, neurosis and wily suburban street smarts, and source of great humor, Max found a place where Bernard Purdie, Buddy Rich and Keith Moon intersected and made it his own. The soul of dedication and commitment, each night in the midst of the continuous hurricane our sets are designed to be, the sheer physical pressure of three hours of nonstop, steamrolling rock music lies upon his shoulders more heavily than anyone else's. Onstage, Max goes beyond listening to what I'm saying, signaling; he "hears" what I'm *thinking, feeling*. He anticipates my thoughts as they come rolling full bore toward the drum riser. It's a near telepathy that comes from years of playing and living together. It's a real-world miracle and it's why people love musicians. They show us how deeply we can experience one another's minds and hearts, and how perfectly we can work in congress. With Max at my back, the questions are answered before they're asked.

There are twenty thousand people, all about to take a breath; we're moving in for the kill, the band, all steel wheels on iron track, and that snare shot, the one I'm just thinking about but haven't told or signaled anyone outside of this on-fire little corner of my mind about, the one I want right . . . *and there it is*! Rumble, young man, rumble!

**ON PIANO:** "Professor" Roy Bittan. The *only* member of the E Street Band with a college education! (Actually, now there's one more; Max finished in 1989!) I've long counted on my good friend Roy when I need something very specific, something exactly as I'm hearing it, to bring whatever I'm imagining on the keyboards to life. Roy's ten fingers do the work of thirty. Eighty-eight keys for the Professor are just not enough. His playing forms the signature sound of my greatest records. His piano arpeggios and music box voicings are as identifiably E Street as Clarence's sax. His performance ability spans jazz, classical, rock and all musics known to man! The joke in the band was that if we tracked with piano, bass and drums, we'd be dead in the water because once Roy was on, you were fully orchestrated. Nothing else needed. Roy brought so much music with him, Steve and I would be scratching to find room for our guitars. We had to make him stop that. If Liberace and Jerry Lee Lewis had a baby, and that baby was born in Rockaway Beach, Long Island, its name would be "Professor" Roy Bittan.

This was the group, the powerhouse, I would make my initial mark with. No member, however, captured my audience's imagination, the idealism and deeply felt comradeship associated with our band, more than the big black man playing the saxophone.

# THIRTY-FOUR
# **CLARENCE CLEMONS**

*And the change was made uptown . . .*

Clarence was a figure out of a rock 'n' roll storybook, one perhaps I've partially authored, but you can't *be* the Big Man unless you *are* the Big Man.
If I was some embodiment of Jon's rock 'n' roll dream, Clarence was an
embodiment of mine. I'd searched high and low for years for a true rock 'n'
roll saxophonist. Not a jazzer who'd slum with us, but somebody who felt
the music and the style we played in their bones.

Previous to *Born to Run*, Clarence was just the very large, gifted black
saxophonist in my band. There were only five of us and we had a nice little
R & B–flavored outfit. After the cover of *Born to Run*, he was the Big Man
in the E Street Band. We used that cover, designed by in-house Columbia

art director John Berg, to invent ourselves, our friendship, our partnership on an epic scale. Our adventure began with that double-wide photo, taken by Eric Meola, in the window of every record store in America. That double spread on the front and back of the cover was John Berg's idea. When the cover is closed, the album front is a very charming photo of a young, white, punk rock 'n' roller. But when it opens, a band is born and a tall tale begins. I brought Clarence to the Eric Meola session because I wanted to be photographed with him. Instinctively, I knew there was something about the two of us standing side by side that I wanted to say. It was dramatic, exciting and a little bit more. It captured what I'd felt the first night Clarence stepped on the stage to jam at the Student Prince. That night a real story, one you can't contrive, only discover, was born. It's a story that can be nurtured and brought forth, but first, it has to be there in the dirt, the beer, the bands and the bars that give it birth. When you saw that cover, it was filled with the resonance, the mythology, of rock's past, and a freshness calling toward its future. Eric Meola's image of C and me, like a hit record, was familiar, yet you'd never seen anything exactly like it before. We were unique. There were only two of us.

The cover was filled with the subtle mystery of race and a mischievous sense of fun and power promising to be unleashed. It's a photo that makes you wonder, "Who are these guys, what's the joke they're sharing, what's their story?" That image grew naturally out of the strength and deep feeling between the two of us.

After *Born to Run*, our stage show changed also. Previous to 1975, Clarence often hung at his microphone, playing the gig like a club saxophonist, cool and low. One night I walked up to him and said that would no longer be enough. We could use our musical and *visual* presence to spin a tale, tell a story only hinted at in my songs. We could live it. I think my actual words were something like, "Tomorrow night, let's get off the mikes and get busy," but Clarence instinctively knew what to do. The next night "the Big Man" showed and the crowd lit up when we simply walked toward each other and planted ourselves center stage. The crowd was right. They were big steps then and they continued to be, because we felt they were, carried ourselves as if they were, and then we backed it up.

## The Emperor of E Street

It's hard to imagine that Clarence was once a normal person, a college student, football player and bespectacled counselor at the Jamesburg State Home for Boys. He had a face that would look at home at any point in history. It was the face of an exotic emperor, an island king, a heavyweight boxer, a shaman, a chain-gang convict, a fifties bluesman and a deep soul survivor. It held one million secrets and none at all. C was a creature of a dark-humored cynicism stemming, I suppose, from growing up a big black man in the American South. He also mysteriously contained a near-hopeless optimism and eerie innocence, I guess coming from being a mama's boy like myself. Those two elements when mixed are as potent a combination as raw dynamite, and though C's trigger point softened over the years, you did not want to set those two poles arcing. You would be destined for an unhappy ending, for the middle ground of those two points was a psychic, no-answer no-man's-land.

I watched Clarence barrel through life with a spirited recklessness and humor both admirable and concerning. C's story, like the story of a survivor of a vicious ocean crossing, was best experienced by the warmth of your fireplace, rather than alongside him in the boat. He was married many times, his wives suffering outrageous behavior as he suffered romantic and financial confusion. One thing the layman needs to remember about Clarence is *Clarence* was very important to Clarence. In this he was not so different from most of us, except by fabulous degree. To take care of C, it took a village. He was rich and broke and rich again. Heartbreak and disappointment were often just around the corner, though he would be guaranteed to rise again the next morning, back at it in search of love,

love, love, peace and satisfaction, until he got it right with his beautiful wife, Victoria.

Clarence's racial identity was somewhat clouded by his sheer fantasticalness. He struggled living in the predominantly white world of our band. At that point, the E Street Band was half black and half white; the loss of Davey Sancious and Boom Carter deeply affected him. For a long time he was alone, and no matter how close we were, I was white. We had as deep a relationship as I can imagine, but we lived in the real world, where we'd experienced that nothing, not all the love in God's heaven, obliterates race. It was a part of the given of our relationship. I believe it was also a part of its primal compellingness for the both of us. We were incongruent, missing pieces to an old and unresolved puzzle, two longing halves of an eccentric and potent whole.

If you travel for years in an integrated band, you see racism in action. In the early seventies it was a few schools that didn't want us to bring our black singers. Then on the road with E Street it would—not often, but occasionally—come up out of the murk. Luckily nothing damagingly physical happened, and approaching C in this manner at all showed reckless disregard for self (in our youth I'd watched Clarence stack every weight on each Nautilus machine in the gym to its maximum, make one casual circuit and go home), but still, there were times when it came close.

## Heat of the Night

I've lived around the biggest guys in Central New Jersey. Black-belt bar bouncers who literally drank their beer, then ate the glass to liven up the evening. Every big man uses his size differently: to impress, to control, to intimidate, to protect, to calm. C usually used his to project a quiet, kind, powerful presence that naturally dominated the space around him. It was rarely questioned, but that degree of physical authority always carried with it a warning: "Use only in case of emergency."

It was a summer evening. Clarence and I took a cruise north up Route 9 to check out a club his buddy had opened and maybe do a little jamming to help the place along. As we pulled into the parking lot, it was like entering a dead zone, empty. Inside was the familiar grave of a deserted rock club. A small band was tuning up, getting ready to play to an audience of four walls and a bartender. Depressing, but I've done it plenty of times. You go on because of an old Shore rule . . . "If there ain't music playin', nobody's stayin'."

Suddenly there was noise at the front entrance. Clarence went to check it out, then I heard a bigger rumble. I hustled over to see Clarence tying down two big men in the foyer while the owner grappled with another. Somehow an argument over getting into this black hole had broken out and C had assisted his pal in keeping the peace. Everybody broke apart, some nasty words were exchanged and then as these guys backed off across the parking lot, someone whispered not quite quietly enough, "Nigger." Clarence stood there seething. A few moments passed. I looked around and couldn't find my friend. I nervously scanned the parking lot, fearing the worst. I took a walk.

It was a humid night, the stars above obscured by a veil of slight haze. There was no movement in the air, just an impossible stillness, time hovering to a stop. I've wandered the Shore on many nights like this and they always carry with them a whiff of the end of the world. I found C leaning against the hood of a car at the far end of the parking lot. "I know those guys," he said. "I play football with them every Sunday. Why would they say that?" I should've answered "Because they're subhuman assholes" but I was caught blank, embarrassed by the moment myself, and all I offered up to my friend was a shrug and a mumbled, "I dunno" . . . silence. We didn't play that night, we just drove home, in the quiet of the car with the events of the evening rattling uncomfortably around our heads. A white man and a black man driving on a lifelong trip together on an otherwise meaningless night.

# THIRTY-FIVE

# NEW
# CONTRACTS

By 1975, we'd struck gold. Mike, seriously interested in protecting his investment and our relationship, all through Europe had been carrying around a
new set of agreements. He wanted to meet, explain their benefits and persuade me to sign them. We were both aware our circumstances had profoundly changed. I was no longer the clueless, starving young musician from
the outlands. I held some serious power now . . . and great control. That being
said, I was just looking for a straight-up deal so we could carry on our highly
enjoyable and fruitful partnership. The first money had rolled in, half a million bucks, and it'd been deposited by the record company straight into Mike's
accounts according to the terms of the contracts I'd signed. I received no independent funds or royalties of my own. It all came through Mike, filtered
through those Laurel Canyon production, publishing and management agreements I'd signed so many hazy years ago. They stipulated he paid the artist.

Haltingly, we met briefly overseas. It all proved too confusing and added to the stress of an already difficult trip, so we agreed to wait until we returned to the USA to sort things through. Once at home we met in a restaurant, where Mike extolled the improvements of our new deal. It *was* better than the old deal but now that it was time to tally up, I wanted to know how I'd be treated under our old contracts before I signed anything new. I had simple expectations: conventional management, production and publishing percentages. Let's dole out the cash and move on down the road. We were on top! The hard part was over. The problem was that was *not* what I had signed. Initially, I'd been too intimidated by the idea of the contracts to take them seriously. Now it was reckoning time, and if we were holding to them, I needed to thoroughly understand their terms before I could confidently enter into any new agreements with Mike. It seemed like common sense.

I asked for a lawyer. Mike and his attorney found me one. I figured he was a setup, but I wanted to see what would happen anyway. We met in a New York City restaurant and he focused on the improved terms of the new agreements while steering away from the repercussions of the old one. I knew it was the old ones that would determine the final financial results of Mike's and my past five years of work together so I wanted to know what *they* said. He futzed me. I left knowing I was probing the dark underbelly of Mike's and my relationship. The rules of engagement were very different here than they were in the studio or on the road, where I knew the ropes, knew exactly what was expected of me and it was my world. Here, I'd slipped into the last tent, the one down the end of the midway, where the *business* of music sits at the head of the table. To his right is a bespectacled, green-visored accountant, hunched over, tapping away at his adding machine, each tap a nail in your coffin. To his left, music, with a "Wha . . . happa—?!" look on its face, is bound, gagged and gaffer-taped to a chair. The irony is that I myself had much to do with the pitching and existence of this tent here in the corner of my personal little carnival. Mike shouldn't have been so overreaching, but my young fears, insecurities and refusal to accept responsibility for my own actions also brought much of this into being. Oh well.

I needed advice. Someone independent of Mike's influence. During the making of *Born to Run* my friendship with Jon Landau had grown. I knew Jon was not above the politics of his own emotions or interests. Who is? But Jon had never talked down or diminished Mike's accomplishments. He had never proposed himself in any role other than friend and producer. I knew there was no one else whose intellect and sense of fairness I trusted more, so I gave him a call. Through Jon I was introduced to Michael Mayer, attorney at law. Mike Mayer was a stockily built guy with corkscrew hair and a "kick their ass" confidence. After his review of the agreements, I walked into his office, where he cheerfully informed me that these were the worst contracts he'd seen since Frankie Lymon's. He told me the Lenape Indians (our Jersey tribe) got a better deal when they sold Manhattan for twenty-four dollars than I'd get if I was held to these provisions. I heard . . . slave! . . . rip-off! . . . conflict of interest! . . . I was prepared for that. I thought the contracts were bullshit anyway, a mere formality, and all that really mattered was what Mike was going to say, what he was going to do.

After these unpleasant revelations I had a meeting with Mike over our new contracts in a little bar in New York City. The storytelling went on and on, late into the evening. I wouldn't sign and we both got to laughing so hard; we ordered drink after drink. Mike laid out his sob story, the time we spent, the sacrifices, blah, blah, blah. Mike was always endlessly entertaining, so I enjoyed listening to him yob on, like a Sunday evening used-car salesman who hadn't met his quota, trying to get me to sign. But by now, I was used to his shenanigans and scams. He had bought his partner Jimmy's half of my contract from Jules Kurz (supposedly for a dollar!) after Jules took it as collateral on a loan Jimmy needed. He was expert at dodging creditors left and right and had a small pocketful of nefarious skills he gleefully employed as necessary.

Case in point: When I signed to Columbia, Mike wanted to immediately insure me for one million dollars. He told me he'd made a huge
investment in me, and what would become of him if I died? I said no. At
twenty-two I was not comfortable with someone standing to make a quick
mil off of my demise. As usual, Mike kept hammering at it. He tried to
sweeten the deal by having some of the money go to my parents. "Look,
your poor mother and father will stand to make all this cash and they won't
have to pay me a dime. I'M FOOTING THE BILL!" No. "Don't you think
you owe it to me?" No. Finally, Mike brought in a closer, some insurance
company hotshot who guaranteed Mike he'd seal the deal, and together we
were shut up in a small room at Columbia Records. I listened to this guy
dressed in his suit and tie lay out their pitch for hours as Mike stood waiting
outside. He had nothing new. It was the same old con: Mike's investment,
Mom and Pop, free money, no cost to me . . . I just had to die! I told him I
was superstitious and I didn't want a million-dollar bounty hanging over my
head. After a long afternoon of the hard sell, his jacket off, sleeves rolled, tie
undone, sweat on his brow, he looked me in the eye and said, "Kid, I've got
a wife and family. If I make this sale, it's going to mean a huge commission
for me. How about it?" M-i-i-i-i-i-i-ke!

Mike came in; looked at his hit man, whom he'd just set loose on
me for hours; sussed out where all this was going; realized he'd taken his
swings, struck out, spun on a dime; and said, "Hey, asshole, leave the kid
alone. Get the fuck outta here!" That's my guy.

Here at the bar, Mike was starting over again . . . the accomplishments, John Hammond, *Time*, *Newsweek*, a million-selling record . . . I loved
Mike—I still do—and despite the recent contract revelations, I wanted us
to continue to work together. It'd been crazy but fun and we'd made it to
the top. Toward the end of a very drunken evening, I stopped Mike in the
middle of his po-faced soliloquy. "ENOUGH, GIVE ME THE PEN!" I
downed another shot of Jack Daniel's and with five more years of my life
spread out before me on the table, I moved to sign on the first dotted line.

I wasn't joking. I was going to sign . . . again. Maybe it was just to get the whole fucking business thing, where I was extremely uncomfortable with my ignorance, off my back. I told myself I didn't really give a fuck about the money anyway. I already had what I needed: a band, a roof over my head, food, a car, a guitar, music, a record deal, the beginnings of an audience. Hell, I was alone, only twenty-five, way out of my league in this area, and I was sick of the complicated, confusing adult world of these FUCKING PAPERS! Let's get this shit out of the way and JUST LET ME PLAY!

High on many shots of whiskey, I pressed pen to paper. I felt a hand grab mine. A voice said, "No, not like this." It was Mike. Those papers would never be signed and Mike's and my relationship would soon be in ruins.

## The Last Meet

One final morning Mike and I got together again at my house in Atlantic Highlands. Tension was starting to rise over our unfinished business. As the light from Sandy Hook Bay streamed in through my scenic front window, we sat down to straighten it all out for the last time. It was just him and me. By now I knew the full extent of our early contracts, but what were they compared to us? . . . The music, the audience, what we'd been through, our feelings for each other . . . I started, "Mike, I know the contracts are bad but that's all right. We can fix it, they're just paper. We can tear 'em up and start something new. We have X amount of dollars for five years of work. Let's split it and move on. Just tell me how much is mine and how much is yours." I was looking for a fair and rational answer. Instead, Mike replied, "Well . . . that depends. If you sign with me for five more years, a significant amount of it will be yours. If you don't . . . probably very little." I knew when Mike uttered the words, "that depends," we were in real trouble. Five more years of my life against a fair shake for the five previous years of work was not an equation I'd picked up the guitar, built a life and forged a future, no matter how insignificant, to make. Mike left.

In the following days we negotiated a little further and were almost successful. Many of the new contract's terms would be retroactively applied to the early contracts and the old agreements would be invalid. I was proud, relieved, and thought we'd worked out something reasonable. Shortly thereafter I received a phone call from Mike explaining his father had counseled him that he'd be giving up the candy store (the half mil in the bank) with no guarantee of future success. I tried to explain to Mike that he'd be giving up the Tootsie Roll jar and *keeping* the candy store, but it was a no go. Dad had spoken and it seemed like that was that. I hung up the phone, redialed, and said, "Send in the lawyers."

It later dawned on me that I might have stumbled upon a crack in Mike's faith in me. What timing! It would've gone against everything I'd known and felt about him since the day we met. There was no truer believer than Mike Appel, but we were in a very fickle business where one-hit wonders abound and half a million dollars is the kind of money guys like us may never see again. I knew Mike's mind, and the control of that sum would be a lot for him to give up. *Nothing* is pretty easy to share, but *something* . . . that's tricky, particularly your first and possibly only *something*.

Many nights I lay awake wondering, what did the money and the contracts mean? What did they quantify, symbolize? It seemed, for Mike and me, they meant something bigger than our relationship, all we'd done and might do together. More than our past, present and future. Mike's grasping insecurity and intemperance, perhaps along with my own willful ignorance, my private insistence on the meaninglessness of all those *papers*, had let them come between us. We'd destroyed the joy, affection and promise we'd taken and had felt in each other.

What were the contracts for me? . . . Control? Power? Self-determination? "Sandy, he ain't my boss no more"? An insistence on *business* conforming to my personal worldview? Maybe so. For Mike, was it the same? . . . Power, control, validation in his father's eyes, ownership of our success and personal confirmation of how *he* saw our relationship? Many, if not most, sharp old-school managers had a Machiavellian streak. Mike's idol was El-vis's manager, Colonel Tom Parker. I loved Elvis and it was a fun conceit for the two of us, but I wasn't going to *be* Elvis. Those days were gone. *I* was intentionally trying to *not* be Elvis. I was motivated by powerful, internal forces to determine the arc of my work and the life I was going to lead. I'd let you help me, I'd need your help, but I needed the certainty of being firmly in control. That was the point, beyond the exhilaration, the thrill of feeling my own talents rise up inside of me; that's what all the years of struggle were for and that was the mountain Mike's "that depends" had just pushed up against. On this, I was primally unmovable.

I'd bowed to power in ways significant and trivial throughout my life. We all have. I'd been bullied. It had often shamed me and made me angry, but okay, in any other field, on any other day, I'd eat it, make my peace, do my best and move on. But in music, I'd promised myself that if I could, I'd try to make things a little different. I'd try to lead my life as I chose, and over the past half decade, without parents, much real support or financial reward, I'd done that. I belonged to me. That's the way it was going to be.

Mike's mistake was he fundamentally misunderstood me. He'd voiced what he believed my options to be in the language of *power*. Now, one of negotiation's dance partners is always power, but civility and compromise must have their place on the dance floor also. At that moment, Mike's words went beyond negotiation and became a not-too-thinly-veiled threat. Amongst friends, that's not nice. We would fight, hard.

In the end, it wasn't all about the contracts. During our previous tour, something began to be clear to me. Mike's ability to "represent" me the way I wished, to be my public voice, was rough at best. Mike was a fighter. That was his temperament. It was what he was good at: raw survival, "by any means necessary." We'd reached a point with *Born to Run* where there was no one left to fight. We'd won! Everyone just wanted to play on our team.

What I needed now was a facilitator, someone who could represent my interests confidently, calmly, and then get things done. Offstage, I didn't like drama. Between the madhouse of the early E Street Band and the silent, unyielding intensity of my father's emotional life, I'd had enough. I wanted people around me who would do their best to create the conditions where I could work peacefully and do my best, uninterrupted by countless self-created tempests in a teapot. Meaningless distraction drains you of the energy you should be placing into more serious things or using to simply enjoy the rewards of your labor. Mike knew nothing about the "middle way." Jon had a lighter, more sophisticated touch that brought with it its own quiet authority. It was more in tune with the confidence with which I now saw myself and wanted to project. Jon wasn't a businessman. He'd had no managerial experience and after Mike, I interviewed a variety of the best people in management for the position. They were all perfectly fine professional businessmen, but that was never going to be enough for me. I needed disciples. This would prove an Achilles' heel and in the future, after some costly enmeshments, I'd let it go. But not before it would end several long-time relationships, cost me dearly and come close to weakening our band. 'Til then, I needed to feel the deep emotional hold of sworn travelers to make me feel secure, safe, and prepared to do my job in the pop wilderness. I didn't have normal nine-to-five relationships with the people who worked for me or with my work. A moderate in most other aspects of my life, here I was extreme. At work you were on my time all the time. Jon was already too grown up for a lot of this, but his heart, dedication and love for what I did brought him into the realm. In return all that was expected of me by my apostles was everything I had. I could handle that . . . for a while.

# THIRTY-SIX
# LIVING WITH THE LAW

I wanted to return to the studio and I wanted Jon to produce. Once the deal went down, Mike, of course, wouldn't have it. Standoff. Here come the judge.

We lost many of our early motions. Mike's power, underwritten by the agreements, proved very effective in stopping my career in its tracks. I found out that *agreements* mean you *agreed* to something! Whether you read it, ate it for breakfast or papered the walls of your rumpus room with it . . . you'd AGREED! Then came the depositions.

Discovery, or depositions, is the legal process in which the opposing sides of an argument get together in a little room with a court stenographer and their lawyers and each take turns trying to make spaghetti out of the other guy's story, in search of the answers *you* (or your opponent) need to make your case. It is neither pleasant nor pretty. It is meant to be embarrassing, psychically unsettling and a small wake-up call as to how your ass is going to be filleted once you step into the witness stand and start spouting your bullshit, truth or not. Let us not forget, it is called the *adversarial* system, and anyone who's been deposed for anything from mass financial fraud to running a red light will tell you, it lives up to its name. By now, I'd already blown more than one hundred grand on a losing game plan and we were just getting started. In my first meeting with my new attorneys, Peter Parcher regaled me with the merits of my case: "No upstanding judge or jury in the land will hold up these slave papers . . . greed . . . for fucking Christ, you're signed as an employee! Greed . . . greed . . . ridiculous terms . . . egregious conflict of interest . . . ," yadda, yadda, yadda. I'd heard it all before but it was still music to my ears. After forty minutes or so, I was feeling pretty good, so I excitedly asked, "Well hell then, Mr. Parcher, what kind of a case does Mike have?" He turned on a dime. "Mike? . . . He's got a great case . . . HE'S GOT YOUR NAME ON THE PAPER!" . . . Oh.

Peter Parcher and his colleague Peter Herbert determined that the biggest obstacle to getting Mike to settle the case was Mike's disbelief that our relationship was truly over. It would be my job to convince him of that and it would take getting ugly. I'd been deposed previously with my last attorneys. Mr. Parcher had read the transcripts and told me it had been a pathetic disaster. It was all ambivalence, gray area, indecision, fairness and NO FIGHT! Peter took me in a corner and told me, "*You*, my friend, are not the judge. The judge is the judge. *You* are not the jury; the jury is the jury. You will tell your story to the best of your ability, as he will tell his. The judge and jury will decide who favor shall fall upon. That is not your job."

I'd always had a problem with that. My father spoke so little, I had to provide all the voices, all the points of view of our non-conversations. As well as defending myself, I had to internally argue my old man's case against me. I twisted and turned myself inside out trying to understand what I'd done wrong and what I might do to right it. I didn't know enough to realize the impossibility of what I was wrestling with. Besides, it was the only way I could manage some control over the confounding emotional temper of our home. Consequently, as I moved on in life, this MO often left me with too much empathy for my opponents. No matter how far you took it, I was always trying to understand where you were coming from, see your point of view, walk in your shoes. I later told my children, compassion is a wonderful virtue but don't waste it on those undeserving. If someone has their boot on your neck, kick them in the balls, then discuss. My surfeit of empathy was great for songwriting but often very bad for living or lawsuits.

So, my first day of being deposed under the tutelage of the two Peters, I did not play nice. My answers were profane, part theater, part truly felt anger bordering on the violent. I wasn't mad about the money; it was not owning or controlling any of the music I'd written that infuriated me. That was the fuel I used to set myself on fire. I let it fly and it went on for days, shouting, banging on the table, pushing back my chair and planting my fist into a file cabinet. I worked hard for the Oscar. Finally the depositions were called for misbehavior by Leonard Marx, Mike's attorney. We all had to take the subway downtown to court, where I was politely spanked and ordered by the judge to tone down my act. The deposition transcripts make for fun and fascinating bedtime reading and appear verbatim along with Mike's side of the story in Mike's book *Down Thunder Road*.

Like Dickens said, "It was the best of times, it was the worst of times . . ." Mostly, the worst of times . . . and it went on for years. I was renting a 160-acre farm on Telegraph Hill Road in Holmdel, New Jersey, for $700 a month. I'd hop in my white C10 pickup, which my girl had christened "Super Truck," and head on down to the Stone Pony to sit in, play for the locals, flirt with the waitresses and drown my sorrows in too much blackberry brandy. I had a lot of fun in that C10. I stuffed a half couch, a cooler filled with ice and a small hibachi grill in its bed. I'd take my date and we'd head to the last of the drive-ins. I'd pull in backward, and we'd hop on the couch, drink beer and grill burgers during a late-night double feature. That summer I saw Warren Oates in the fabulous *Born to Kill* at that drive-in, had time on my hands and did a little more than a reasonable amount of drinking and bar-hopping just to relieve the stress. There were some nights when I left my tire tracks on more than a few lawns in Deal on my way home from the Pony.

It all became tiring and depressing, but I took comfort in knowing I could lose all but one thing: myself. No lawsuit, no court decision, no judge, no legal outcome could take what I treasured most. That was the craft and inner life I'd built since I was a teenager, founded on the music I could make with my heart, head and hands. That was mine forever and could not be won from me. I'd think, "If I lose and have nothing when this is over, you can still drop me with my guitar by parachute anywhere in America; I'll walk to the nearest roadhouse, find a pickup band and light up your night. Just because I can."

## Settlement

All good things must come to an end. Slowly, sadly, Mike became convinced it was all over. A settlement was reached, separation papers were drawn up and one quiet night in a dimmed midtown office building, Mike and I finalized our divorce. At the end of a long conference table I sat there, doing what you will do, should you ever be lucky enough to wander into a profession where you have even minor success at your passion. I was doing the very thing that got me into the whole fucking mess in the first place . . . signing more papers I hadn't, and would never, read, in order to get to do the thing I desired most, the thing I needed to do, *make music and play*. The money was gone but the music was primarily mine and I could choose my career path unobstructed.

That done, I walked to the elevator and into a negative image of the ride Mike and I took down from the top floor of Black Rock on the day we were discovered. With my head slowly clearing of the sludge the lawsuit and its troubles had brought, I walked out into the New York night. I would have some dealings with Mike in the future, some good, some cheesy, but once the war was over and time—a good deal of it—passed, the fondness and connection remained. We had been someplace special together, someplace unique, a place where we had to depend upon each other and nothing else, where things that meant something were at stake. We had come to cross purposes—this is the world—but I could never hate Mike; I can only love him. His motor mouth walked me into John Hammond's office. From Asbury Park to New York City and Columbia Records, that's a long walk. When it was toughest, he made it work. He was a hard guy, straight out of the New York/New Jersey mold. It couldn't get tough enough for him. He drew energy from it and reveled in it. He had trouble when it got easier. Some people are just that way; they don't know how to stop fighting.

Along with Jon and Steve, Mike was my musical brother in arms. He knew everything about the great groups, the fabulous hit records, every important nuance of the great singers' voices, the great guitarists' riffs, the heart and soul that were in our favorite music. When we talked, he could finish my sentences. He was a *fan*, with all the beauty and import that word carries for me. Mike was funny, cynical, dreamy and profane, and when you were with him, you were always laughing.

Eventually, for seed money for more kite dreams, Mike sold me back every piece of my music he ever owned. It was another one of his big mistakes, good for me, bad for my pal. Those songs were going to be money in the bank for a long time. Mike, to a fault, was always about . . . now! next! I'm one of the few artists from those days who owns everything he ever created. All my records are mine. All my songs are mine. It's rare and it's a good feeling.

Mike was a cross of Willy Loman and Starbuck. He was a salesman in the classic and most tragic sense. He was a rainmaker. And despite all the hurt and pain of our last years together . . . he'd made it rain.

I thought of my grandfather, Sing Sing alumnus Anthony Zerilli ("You will risk and you will pay"). I risked and I paid, but I won too. I'd tried anonymity and it did not please me. My talents, my ego, my desires were too great. As I walked along, the excited, exhausted chatter of my partners in battle, Jon, Peter and Peter, floated somewhere behind me. I was filled with the light, the exhilaration of being set free, the power of having fought hard for something I felt was rightly mine. I felt a sadness at the decimation of a good friendship, but Mike and I would see each other again. Right now, I felt the shadow of a future, two years postponed, upon me. The time was here to finally turn all this into something.

THIRTY-SEVEN

# DARKNESS ON THE EDGE OF TOWN

Scene one: The grinding, deafening sound of plastic being cut on an open factory floor. I am standing inches behind my dad, holding a brown paper bag containing his night-shift lunch, an egg salad sandwich. I call to him in the din, feel my mouth move, my vocal cords strain, but nothing . . . no sound. He eventually turns, sees me, mouths a few unheard words and takes the bag.

Scene two: I am riding shotgun in my dad's delivery truck. It is one of the great days of my childhood. We are traversing New Jersey on what mission I do not know, but its importance, to me, cannot be debated. We reach our destination, we deliver I don't remember what. All I recollect is the sliding rear door of the truck, rolling up with a metallic roar into its tracks embedded beneath the truck's roof. My father and other men unload large boxes from its enclosed bed, have a smoke, briefly banter amongst themselves, mission accomplished. I remember the bouncing springs of the truck's suspension on the way home, my open window on a beautiful skippin'-school fall day, the black gearshift between my father and me, the smell of 1950s metal and leather in the truck's interior and my heart beating with admiration, accomplishment and the pride of being claimed. I'm riding with the king. My dad has taken me to work. Oh, what a world it could've been.

Taxi driver, assembly line worker, autoworker, jail guard, bus driver, truck driver—these are just a few of the many jobs my pop worked to hold during his life. My sisters and I grew up in blue-collar neighborhoods, somewhat integrated, filled with factory workers, cops, firemen, long-distance truck drivers. I never saw a man leave a house in a jacket and tie unless it was Sunday or he was in trouble. If you came knocking at our door with a suit on, you were immediately under suspicion. You wanted something. There were good neighbors, filled with eccentricity and kindness and basically decent. There were creeps just like anywhere else, and you had your houses where you could tell something bad was going on. From my sixth to twelfth years, we lived at 39½ Institute Street, in the small half of a very small, cold-water-only house. We only bathed a few times a week because the ritual of my mother heating up pots of water on the gas stove, then carrying them up, one by one, to slowly fill the upstairs bath was too much. My sister and I flipped a coin to see who'd get to go in first. Our walls were thin, really thin. The screaming, yelling and worse of our neighbors couldn't be hidden or ignored. I remember my mother in her pink curlers sitting on the steps, her ear pressed to the wall of the half house adjoining ours, listening to the couple next door scrap it out. He was a big burly guy. He beat his wife and you could hear it happening at night. The next day you'd see her bruises. Nobody called the cops, nobody said anything, nobody did anything. One day the husband came home and tied some small glass wind chimes with faux Chinese decoration upon them to the eaves of the porch. This came to disgust me. When the slightest wind would blow they'd make this tinkling sound. These peaceful-sounding wind chimes and the frequent night hell of the house was a grotesque mixture. I can't stomach the sound of wind chimes to this day. They sound like lies.

This was a part of my past that I would draw on for the roots of *Darkness on the Edge of Town*.

By 1977, in true American fashion, I'd escaped the shackles of birth, personal history and, finally, place, but something wasn't right. Rather than exhilaration, I felt unease. I sensed there was a great difference between un-fettered personal license and real freedom. Many of the groups that had come before us, many of my heroes, had mistaken one for the other and it'd ended in poor form. I felt personal license was to freedom as masturbation was to sex. It's not bad, but it's not the real deal. Such were the circum-stances that led the lovers I'd envisioned in "Born to Run," so determined to head out and away, to turn their car around and head back to town. That's where the deal was going down, amongst the brethren. I began to ask myself some new questions. I felt accountable to the people I'd grown up alongside of and I needed to address that feeling.

Along with the class-conscious pop of the Animals, early-sixties Beat groups and the punks, I began to listen seriously to country music and I discovered Hank Williams. I liked that country dealt with adult topics; I didn't believe you had to "age out" of rock music, so I wanted my new songs to resonate as I grew older. Film became a great influence, and my title *Darkness on the Edge of Town* was straight out of American noir. I'd settled on a sound that was leaner and less grand than *Born to Run*, one I felt would better suit the voices I was trying to bring to life. I was on new ground and searching for a tone somewhere between *Born to Run*'s spiritual hopefulness and seventies cynicism. That cynicism was what my characters were battling against. I wanted them to feel older, weathered, wiser but not beaten. The sense of daily struggle increased; hope became a lot harder to come by. That was the feeling I wanted to sustain. I steered away from escapism and placed my people in a community under siege.

*Born to Run* had earned me a Steinway baby grand piano and a 1960 Chevrolet Corvette with Cragar wheels I bought for six grand from a kid behind the counter at the West Long Branch Carvel ice-cream stand. There wouldn't be much else but bills—studio bills, instrument rental bills, bills from all the folks Mike (we?) had stiffed to keep us rolling; there would be lawyers' fees, back taxes and tiresome fighting. Some enterprising young man at the IRS must have seen those *Time* and *Newsweek* covers and said, "Who is this guy?" The answer was, he was a guy who'd never paid a single penny in income taxes his whole life, and neither had most of his friends. Bang! . . . Meet your uncle Sam. We were all so used to living financially off the grid, it never dawned on us that we might qualify as taxpayers. Even after the amount of money coming in would've brought us up to the bar, Mike had said he used it all for our survival. In a flash, I was hit for back taxes for all my "earnings" since in utero and had to pony up for all the band's too, because they were broke. It took a long time. The entire *Darkness* tour I played for someone else *every* night. Lawyers, creditors, Uncle Sam, sound companies, trucking companies—all came out of the woodwork to tap our meager earnings. That, along with piling up astronomical studio bills while we learned our craft, would keep me broke until 1982, ten years and millions of records after I'd signed with CBS. If those records had bombed, I'd have ended up back in Asbury Park, with my only reward a drunken story to tell.

We cut forty, fifty, sixty songs of all genres. Maybe after our two-year shutdown I was just hungry to record, to get all the songs and ideas out of my head, to clear a space for the record I really wanted to make. Very slowly . . . that's what happened. We were so rusty when we returned to the studio, weeks went by before a note of music was played. As with *Born to Run*, our recording process was thwarted by our seeming inability to get the most basic acceptable sounds. Days went by with the only sound emanating from

Studio B at the Record Plant the dull, endless thwack of Max's drumstick on a tom-tom. "Stiiiiiiiiiiiiiiiiiiick!" That was our frustrated mantra, shouted day and night, over and over. It meant rather than the richness and tone of a true snare or tom-tom, one was hearing the unsatisfying slapping sound of slat wood on taut drum skin. We were literally hearing the drum*stick*. No thunder of the gods there. We trudged on, blind men in a black alley.

At bottom, we were amateur producers and simply failed to understand the basic physics of getting sound to tape. Recorded sound is relative. When the drums are forceful but moderate, they leave room for a big guitar sound. When the guitars are powerful but lean, you can have drums the size of a house. But you can't feature *everything*, for in effect you're featuring *nothing*. Phil Spector's records aren't sonically big. The technology wasn't there. They just *sound* bigger than your world. It's a beautiful illusion. I wanted everything, so I was getting nothing. We kept on, exhausting ourselves in the process, but exhaustion has always been my friend and I don't mind going there. Near the bottom of its fathomless pit I usually find results. We failed until we didn't.

I began to find some inspiration in the working-class blues of the Animals, pop hits like the Easybeats' "Friday on My Mind" and the country music I'd so long ignored. Hank Williams, Woody Guthrie: here was music that emotionally described a life I recognized, my life, the life of my family and neighbors. Here was where I wanted to make my stand musically and search for my own questions and answers. I didn't want out. I wanted in. I didn't want to erase, escape, forget or reject. I wanted to understand. What were the social forces that held my parents' lives in check? Why was it so hard? In my search I would blur the lines between the personal and psychological factors that made my father's life so difficult and the political issues that kept a tight clamp on working-class lives across the United States. I had to start somewhere. For my parents' troubled lives I was determined to be the enlightened, compassionate voice of reason and revenge. This first came to fruition in *Darkness on the Edge of Town*. It was after my success, my "freedom," that I began to seriously delve into these issues. I don't know if it was the survivor's guilt of finally being able to escape the confines of my small-town existence or if, as on the battlefield, in America we're not supposed to leave anybody behind. In a country this rich, it isn't right. A dignified decent living is not too much to ask. Where you take it from there is up to you but that much should be a birthright.

Finally, the piece of me that lived in the working-class neighborhoods of my hometown was an essential and permanent part of who I was. No one you have been and no place you have gone ever leaves you. The new parts of you simply jump in the car and go along for the rest of the ride. The success of your journey and your destination all depend on who's driving. I'd seen other great musicians lose their way and watch their music and art become anemic, rootless, displaced when they seemed to lose touch with who they were. My music would be a music of identity, a search for meaning and the future.

## Closing In

Party songs, love songs, Brill Building pop, absolute top ten smashes ("Fire," "Because the Night") all came and went. It was my way. I wasn't sure what I wanted but I smelled something in the air and knew when I didn't have it. As with *Born to Run*, it was the subtle shaping of the times and the work of creating an identity, an immediate "me" I could live with, that kept me moving toward what I hoped was light. I eventually cut the massive block of songs I had down to the ten toughest. I edited out anything that broke the album's mood or tension. The songs I chose wore big titles—"Badlands," "Prove It All Night," "Adam Raised a Cain," "Racing in the Street," "Darkness on the Edge of Town"—and were filled with will, resilience and resistance. "Adam" used biblical images to summon the hard inheritance handed down from father to son. "Darkness on the Edge of Town" proposed that the setting for personal transformation is often found at the end of your rope. In "Racing in the Street" my street racers carried with them the years between the innocent car songs of the sixties and the realities of 1978 America. To make "Racing" and those big titles personal, I had to infuse the music with my own experience, my own hopes and fears.

Out went anything that smacked of frivolity or nostalgia. The punk revolution had hit and there was some hard music coming out of England. The Sex Pistols, the Clash and Elvis Costello all were pushing the envelope on what pop could be in 1977. It was a time of great endings and great beginnings. Elvis had died and his ghost hovered over our sessions. (I'd written "Fire" especially for him.) Across the sea there were raging, young, idealistic musicians looking to reinvent (or destroy) what they'd heard, searching for another way. Somebody somewhere had to start a fire. The "gods" had become too omnipotent and had lost their way. The connection between the fan and the man onstage had grown too abstract. Unspoken promises had been made and broken. It was time for a new order, or maybe . . . no order! Pop needed new provocations and new responses. In '78 I felt a distant kinship to these groups, to the class consciousness, the anger. They hardened my resolve. I would take my own route, but the punks were frightening, inspirational and challenging to American musicians. Their energy and influence can be found buried in the subtext of *Darkness on the Edge of Town*.

*Darkness* was my samurai record, all stripped down for fighting. My protagonists in these songs had to divest themselves of all that was unnecessary to survive. On *Born to Run* a personal battle was engaged, but the collective war continued. On *Darkness*, the political implications of the lives I was writing about began to come to the fore and I searched for a music that could contain them.

I determined that there on the streets of my hometown was the beginning of my purpose, my reason, my passion. Along with Catholicism, in my family's neighborhood experience, I found my other "genesis" piece, the beginning of my song: home, roots, blood, community, responsibility, stay hard, stay hungry, stay alive. Sweetened by cars, girls and fortune, these are the things that guided my musical journey. I would travel far, light-years from home, and enjoy it all, but I would never completely leave. My music began to have more political implications; I tried to find a way to put my work into service. I read and I studied to become a better, more effective writer. I harbored extravagant ambition and belief in the effect of popular song. I wanted my music grounded in my life, in the life of my family and in the blood and lives of the people I'd known.

Most of my writing is emotionally autobiographical. I've learned you've got to pull up the things that mean something to you in order for them to mean anything to your audience. That's where the proof is. That's how they know you're not kidding. With the record's final verse, "Tonight I'll be on that hill . . . ," my characters stand unsure of their fate but dug in and committed. By the end of *Darkness*, I'd found my adult voice.

# THIRTY-EIGHT

# THE
# DROP

After a solid year of endless studio hours, many sleepless nights in my shoe box of a room at the midtown Navarro Hotel and a city in darkness (the great NYC blackout of 1977 found me in Times Square, the world's biggest pinball machine; when the lights exploded back on, whoa!), my first record in three years was complete. It would be Steve Van Zandt's first record as an E Street Band member. It would be the beginning of a long and wonderful relationship with producer Chuck Plotkin and the end of a short but fruitful one with my good friend Jimmy Iovine. It would be the first record on which we recorded our tracks live in studio, as a full band, and my first without Mike. Jon and I were at the production helm and this record continued and deepened our work and friendship. All we needed was an album cover.

I'd gotten to know Patti Smith a little through our work together on

"Because the Night." When I visited her during one of her performances at the Bottom Line, she gave me the name of a South Jersey photographer and said, "You should let this guy take your picture." One winter afternoon I drove south to Haddonfield, New Jersey, and met Frank Stefanko. Frank had photographed Patti at the beginning of her career. He worked a day job at a local meatpacking plant and continued to practice his craft in his spare time. Frank was a rough-edged but easygoing kind of guy. My recollection is he borrowed a camera for the day, called a teenage kid from next door to come over and hold up his one light and started shooting. I stood against some flowery wallpaper in Frank and his wife's bedroom, looked straight into the camera, gave him my best "troubled young man," and he did the rest. One of these photos ended up on the cover of *Darkness on the Edge of Town*.

Frank's photographs were stark. His talent was he managed to strip away your celebrity, your artifice, and get to the raw you. His photos had a purity and a street poetry to them. They were lovely and true, but they weren't slick. Frank looked for your true grit and he naturally intuited the conflicts I was struggling to come to terms with. His pictures captured the people I was writing about in my songs and showed me the part of me that was still one of them. We had other cover options but they didn't have the hungriness of Frank's pictures.

When *Darkness* was released it was not an instant success and few made it out for the fan favorite it would become. Gun-shy to the max from my *Born to Run* experience, I actually started out insisting there be *no* advertising for my new record at all. Jon explained, "No one will know the record exists," and said we needed to at least have the cover photo, album title and release date advertised in the papers. Well, okay. I caught on quick. I wasn't ready to disappear. I'd just recently vanished for three years, had felt barely visible most of my life, and if I could help it, I wasn't going back. Without some promotion, folks wouldn't have a clue as to what the fuck we'd been doing. This music held everything I had, so pronto I started to glad-hand

and make nice with every deejay from the East to the West Coast in hopes of getting what was proving to be a tough record for my fans on the radio. Then we played our ace.

# Touring

With the burden of proving I wasn't a has-been at twenty-eight, I headed out on the road performing long, sweat-drenched rock shows featuring the new album. These were the first shows where the night was split by a brief intermission into two halves. It allowed us to play the favorites we knew our fans wanted to hear and the new music we were haughty enough to believe they needed to hear. We did a variety of radio broadcasts from clubs in Los Angeles, New Jersey, San Francisco and Atlanta. Anything to get heard. Show after show we drove hard, expanding our new songs to their limits until they hit home, until the audience recognized them as their own. Again, the live power, the strength, of the E Street Band proved invaluable and night after night, we sent our listeners away, back to the recorded versions of this music, newly able to hear their beauty and restrained power.

The songs from *Darkness on the Edge of Town* remain at the core of our live performances today and are perhaps the purest distillation of what I wanted my rock 'n' roll music to be about. We remained in North America for the entire tour and finished in Cleveland on New Year's Eve, where an exploding firecracker tossed by an inebriated "fan" opened up a small slash underneath my eye. A little blood'd been drawn, but we were back.

After years of reading "flash in the pan," "Whatever happened to . . ." articles, I began to read reviews in city after city about how we delivered. No, you can't tell people anything, you've got to show 'em.

## THIRTY-NINE
# DOWNTIME

Off the road, life was a puzzle. Without that nightly hit of adrenaline the show provided, I was at loose ends, and whatever it was that was always eating at me rose up and came calling. In the studio and on tour, I was a one-man wrecking crew with a one-track mind. Out of the studio and off the road, I was . . . not. Eventually I had to come to grips with the fact that *at rest, I was not at ease, and to be at ease, I could not rest.* The show centered and calmed me but it could not solve my problems. I had no family, no home, no real life. It's not news; a lot of performers will tell you the same thing. It's a common malady, a profile of sorts, that floods my profession. We're travelers, "runners," not "stayers." But each man or woman runs or stays in their own way. I finally realized one of the reasons my records took so long to make was I had nothing else to do, nothing else I felt comfortable doing. Why not, as Sam Cooke sang, take "all night . . . all night . . . all night"? My recordings were a return to that three-block walk to school I'd try to stretch into an eternity each morning. "Get in the groove and let the good times roll, we gonna stay here 'til we soothe our soul."

*'Til we soothe our soul . . .* that could take a while.

Family was a terrifying and compelling thought for me in 1980. Since I'd been a young man, I was sure it was going to be a suitcase, guitar and tour bus 'til the night drew down. At some point every young musician thinks so. We beat the game; the rest was for "suckers" strapped into the straight life. Yet on *Darkness* I'd begun to write about that life. A part of me truly admired it and felt it was where real manhood lies. I just wasn't any good at it. On my *Darkness* songs, I'd presented that life as a dark, oppressive and sustaining world, a world that took but also provided. "Factory takes his hearing, factory gives him life." That scared me. I only had my father's experience to go by and no intimate knowledge of men who were at ease with family life. I didn't trust myself to bear the burden of, the responsibility for, other lives, for that all-encompassing love.

My experience with relationships and love to that point all told me I wasn't built for it. I grew very uncomfortable, very fast, with domestic life. Worse, it uncovered a deep-seated anger in me I was ashamed of but also embraced. It was the silent, dormant volcano of the old man's nightly kitchen vigil, the stillness covering a red misting rage. All of this sat nicely on top of a sea of fear and depression so vast I hadn't begun to contemplate it, much less consider what I should do about it. Easier to just roll.

I'd had it down. I'd routinely and roughly failed perfectly fine women over and over again. I'd wrapped my arms around that great big "nothing" for a long time and it'd been good. I suppose after my grandmother's death when I was sixteen, my dad's daily emotional bailout, and both parents leaving for California, I figured needing people too much might not provide the best payoff; better off playing defense. But it was getting harder and harder to pretend nothing was amiss. Two years inside of any relationship and it would all simply stop. As soon as I got close to exploring my frailties, I was gone. You were gone. One pull of the pin, it'd be over and I'd be down the road, tucking another sad ending in my pack. It was rarely the women themselves I was trying to get away from. I had many lovely girlfriends I cared for and who really cared for me. It was what they triggered, the emotional exposure, the implications of a life of commitments and family burdens. At work, though I may have occasionally blown it, I could take on all of the responsibility you could load on my shoulders. But in life all I could find was a present I could take no comfort in, a future with harsh limits, a past I was struggling to come to terms with in my writing but also running from, and time . . . tick . . . tick . . . tick . . . time. I had no time for time. Better off in that lovely timeless world inside my head, inside . . . the studio! Or onstage, where I master time, stretching it, shortening it, advancing forward, moving you back, speeding it up, slowing it down, all with the twitch of a shoulder and the drop of a snare beat.

With the end of each affair, I'd feel a sad relief from the suffocating claustrophobia love had brought me. And I'd be free to be . . . *nothing* . . . again. I'd switch partners, hit rewind and take it from the top, telling myself this time it'd be different. Then it'd be all high times and laughs until fate and that unbearable anxiety came knocking and it'd be one more for the road. I "loved" as best as I could, but I hurt some people I really cared about along the way. I didn't have a clue as to how to do anything else.

Now, the less I traveled, the more the truth of what I was doing pressed in on me. It became inescapable. In the past I'd always had one surefire answer: get writing, get recording and get out. The road was my trusty shield against the truth. You can't hit a moving target and you can't catch lightning. Lightning strikes, leaves a scar and then is gone, baby, gone. The road was always a perfect cover; transient detachment was the nature of the game. You play; the evening culminates in merry psychosexual carnage, laughs, ecstasy and sweaty bliss; then it's on to new faces and new towns. That, my friends, is why they call 'em . . . ONE-NIGHT STANDS! The show provided me the illusion of intimacy without risk or consequences. During the show, as good as it is, as real as the emotions called upon are, as physically moving and as hopefully inspirational as I work to make it, it's fiction, theater, a creation; it isn't reality . . . And at the end of the day, life trumps art . . . always.

Robert De Niro once said he loved acting because you got to live other lives without the consequences. I lived a new life every night. Each evening you're a new man in a new town with all of life and all of life's possibilities spread out before you. For much of my life I'd vainly sought to re-create this feeling every . . . single . . . day. Perhaps it's the curse of the imaginative mind. Or perhaps it's just the "running" in you. You simply can't stop imagining other worlds, other loves, other places than the one you are comfortably settled in at any given moment, the one holding all your treasures. Those treasures can seem so easily made gray by the vast, open and barren spaces of the creative mind. Of course, there is but one life. Nobody likes that . . . but there's just one. And we're lucky to have it. God bless us and have mercy on us that we may have the understanding and the abilities to live it . . . and know that "possibility of everything" . . . is just "nothing" dressed up in a monkey suit . . . and I'd had the best monkey suit in town.

FORTY

# *THE*
# *RIVER*

*The River* would be my first album where love, marriage and family would cautiously move to center stage. "Roulette," a portrait of a family man caught in the shadow of the Three Mile Island nuclear accident, was the first song we cut. The MUSE (Musicians United for Safe Energy) concerts at Madison Square Garden had been our entrance into the public political arena and "Roulette" was written and recorded shortly after those shows. Next a road-tested "The Ties That Bind" got the Bob Clearmountain treatment. We were in a new studio, the Power Station, where Studio A had a beautiful high-ceilinged wooden room that was going to let the noise of our band free. Bob was a new part of our team, knew how to capture the room's best, and though we'd soon realize we weren't quite ready for him, he engineered and mixed *The River*'s early incarnation. "Ties" was another rocker focused on "real world" commitments. "You walk cool but darlin' can you walk the line . . ." I held my doubts.

After the tightly controlled recorded sound of *Darkness*, I wanted this record to have the roughness and spontaneity of our live show. I wanted more trash in our sound. This was right in Steve Van Zandt's wheelhouse and he joined me in the production along with Jon and Chuck Plotkin. With Steve's encouragement, I began to steer the record into a rawer direction. This was the album where the E Street Band hit its stride, striking the perfect balance between a garage band and the professionalism required to make good records.

It was 1979 and state-of-the-art production values were still heavily influenced by the late-seventies mainstream sounds of Southern California. Their techniques consisted of an enormous amount of separation between the instruments, an often stultifying attention to detail and very little echo or live room resonance. Most studios, in those days, were completely padded to give the engineer the utmost control over each individual instrument. The Eagles, Linda Ronstadt and many other groups had a lot of success with this sound, and it had its merits, but it just didn't suit our East Coast sensibilities. We wanted open room mikes, smashing drums (the snare sound on Elvis's "Hound Dog" was my Holy Grail), crashing cymbals, instruments bleeding into one another and a voice sounding like it was fighting out from the middle of a brawling house party. We wanted the sound of *less* control. This was how many of our favorite records from the early days of rock 'n' roll had been recorded. You miked the band *and* the room. You *heard* the band and the room. The sonic characteristics of the room were essential in the quality and personality of your recording. The room brought the messiness, the realness, the can't-get-out-of-each-other's-way togetherness of musicians in search of "that sound."

We'd stumbled upon this by accident at the end of *Darkness*. The Record Plant had been tearing apart Studio A to rebuild it. We went in to cut the song "Darkness on the Edge of Town" when the room was still four bare concrete walls. That's it! That resonance, that aggression from the drums, was exactly what we'd been searching for during all our early days of "Stiiiiiiiiiiiick" mania. At the Power Station, we set mikes high above the band to capture as much ambient sound as we could, and we hoped to be able to dial in or out as much of it as we liked. We'd be half successful.

Now, after the unrelenting seriousness of *Darkness*, I wanted more flexibility in the emotional range of the songs I chose. Along with "gravitas," our shows were always filled with fun, and I wanted to make sure, this time around, that didn't get lost. After some time recording, we prepared a single album and handed it in to the record company. It consisted of side one: "The Ties That Bind," "Cindy," "Hungry Heart," "Stolen Car," "Be True." Side two: "The River," "You Can Look (But You Better Not Touch)," "The Price You Pay," "I Wanna Marry You" and "Loose Ends." Everything, in one form or another, with the exception of "Cindy," appeared on the final version of *The River* or later on *Tracks*, our collection of "outtakes" released in November of 1998. That first version of *The River* was completely engineered and mixed by Bob Clearmountain. It sounded beautiful, but as I spent time listening to it, I felt that it just wasn't enough. Our records were infrequent and by now I'd set up my audience to expect more than business as usual. Each record was a statement of purpose. I wanted playfulness, good times, but also an underlying philosophical seriousness, a code of living, fusing it all together and making it more than just a collection of my ten latest songs. (Though, that worked out pretty well for the Beatles.)

I wouldn't suggest this approach for everyone. Needless to say, it has its pretensions, but I was still defining myself and was inspired by artists who created self-aware, self-contained worlds on their albums, and then invited their fans to discover them. Van Morrison, Bob Dylan, the Band, Marvin Gaye, Hank Williams, Frank Sinatra—all made records that had collective power. I wanted a record thematically coherent enough to hold together as a body of work while not so single-minded as to be damned by the term "concept album." I wanted something that could come only from my voice, that was informed by the internal and external geography of my own experience. The single album of *The River* I'd just turned in didn't quite get us there, so, back into the studio we went.

Another year went by as I watched the seasons change from my New York City hotel room overlooking Central Park South. Down in the Wollman Rink I saw people ice-skate, stop, sun themselves on the Great Lawn of Central Park and start ice-skating again. In the studio, not sure of where the record was going, I took out my shotgun again. I'd simply record everything I was writing. When our recording budget ran dry, I took the Francis Ford Coppola route, busting the piggy bank and spending everything I had. The results were I went broke while recording a lot of good music, the two records of *The River* being only a slice (check out disc two of *Tracks*, and there's more still waiting in the vault). Finally, it became obvious I was working on at least a double record. It would be the only way I could reconcile the two worlds I wanted to present to my fans. *The River* got its emotional depth from its ballads—"Point Blank," "Independence Day," "The River" and "Stolen Car" were all narrative-driven story songs—but the album got its energy from its bar band music, songs like "Cadillac Ranch," "Out in the Street" and "Ramrod." Then there was the music that bled across the lines: "Ties That Bind," "Two Hearts" and "Hungry Heart." All of this blended together into a logical extension of the characters I'd studied on *Darkness on the Edge of Town*.

Finally, the commitments of home, blood and marriage ran through the album as I tried to understand where these things might fit in my own life. My records are always the sound of someone trying to understand where to place his mind and heart. I imagine a life, I try it on, then see how it fits. I walk in someone else's shoes, down the sunny and dark roads I'm compelled to follow but may not want to end up living on. It's one foot in the light, one foot in the darkness, in pursuit of the next day.

The song "The River" was a breakthrough for my writing. The influence of country music proved prescient as one night in my hotel room I started singing Hank Williams's "My Bucket's Got a Hole in It," and "Well, I went upon the mountain, I looked down in the sea" somehow led to "I'm going down to the river . . ." I drove home to New Jersey and sat at a small oak table in my bedroom watching the dawn sky draw blue out of black and I imagined my story. It was just a guy in a bar talking to the stranger on the next stool. I based the song on the crash of the construction industry in late-seventies New Jersey, the recession and hard times that fell on my sister Virginia and her family. I watched my brother-in-law lose his good-paying job and work hard to survive without complaint. When my sister first heard it, she came backstage, gave me a hug and said, "That's my life." That's still the best review I ever got. My beautiful sister, tough and unbowed, K-Mart employee, wife and mother of three, holding fast and living the life that I ran away from with everything I had.

*The River* crystallized my concerns and committed me to a style of writing I'd further explore in greater depth and detail on *Nebraska*. The album closes with a title stolen from a Roy Acuff song. In "Wreck on the Highway," my character confronts death and an adult life where time is finite. On a rainy night he witnesses a fatal accident. He drives home, and lying awake next to his lover, he realizes you have a limited number of opportunities to love someone, to do your work, to be a part of something, to parent your children, to do something good.

We finished recording and went to Los Angeles to mix the record at Chuck Plotkin's Clover Studios. We mixed and we mixed and we mixed, and then we mixed some more. We'd wanted to create a sound that was less controlled and we'd had, as ex-president George W. would say, catastrophic success! It was a mess. Bob Clearmountain, with neither the time nor the patience to endure our navel-gazing, had gracefully bowed out . . . years ago. Now everything we'd recorded was bleeding into everything else (those ceiling mikes worked!) and our team, including the steadfast and talented Neil Dorfsman, who'd recorded and engineered everything but "Ties That Bind" and "Drive All Night," didn't quite have a clue about how to rein it all in to achieve a reasonable-sounding mix. As usual, I wanted everything, intelligibility and blazing noise. We spent months mixing the twenty songs we'd chosen and then one night, I invited my old partner Jimmy Iovine, now a successful producer working at A&M Studios, to check it out and give his approval. Jimmy sat expressionless for the eighty minutes of the record. Then, as the final notes of "Wreck on the Highway" drifted out the window onto Santa Monica Boulevard, he looked at me and deadpanned, "When're you going to record the vocals?"

Jimmy was subtly telling me you couldn't hear a fucking thing. The vocals were all but buried beneath what we thought was our masterwork of garage noise and were nearly unintelligible. Sitting there hearing them anew through Jimmy's unbiased ears, I had to admit most of the mixes sucked. I cried . . . really. Mixmaster Chuck Plotkin was doing his mightiest around the clock but once again, WE DID NOT KNOW HOW TO MIX WHAT WE'D RECORDED! Charlie was one of the sickest men I'd ever met when it came to obsessive-compulsive work habits. Some of our mixes remained on the board for three, four days, even a week, as we fussed, mussed and murdered one another in a vain attempt to capture all worlds. We had mixes with three-digit take numbers. We were violently frustrated and puzzled, cursing our brethren, releasing records and touring like normal folk and finally beseeching God himself. Why us, Lord, why? In the end, Charlie's second or third pass through our carousel of twenty tunes brought victory of sorts. We'd done it. Of course, I recollected that Bob Clearmountain had mixed "Hungry Heart," our soon-to-be top five (and only) smash, in thirty seconds, but we could never have worked with Bob. HE WAS TOO FUCKING FAST! We needed to ruminate, contemplate, intellectualize and mentally masturbate ourselves into a paralytic frenzy. We had to punish ourselves until we'd done it . . . OUR WAY! And in those days, on E Street, our way was only one way . . . THE HARD WAY! Like Smith Barney, we made our money the old-fashioned way, we *earned* it, and then we burned it, throwing it away on countless upon countless fruitless hours in a huge, wandering technical circle jerk.

I later realized we weren't making a record, we were on an odyssey, toiling in the vineyards of pop, searching for complicated answers to mystifying questions. Pop may not have been the best place for me to look for those answers, or it may have been perfect. It had long ago become the way I channeled just about any and all information I received from living on planet Earth. Either way, that's how I used my music and my talents from the very beginning. As a salve, a balm, a tool to tease out the clues to the unknowable in my life. It was the fundamental why and wherefore of my picking up the guitar. Yes, the girls. Yes, the success. But answers, or rather those clues, that's what kept waking me in the middle of the night to roll over and disappear into the sound hole of my six-string cipher (kept at the foot of my bed) while the rest of the world slept. I'm glad I've been handsomely paid for my efforts but I truly would've done it for free. Because I had to. It was the only way I found momentary release and the purpose I was looking for. So, for me, there weren't going to be any shortcuts. It's a lot to lay on a piece of wood with six steel strings and a couple of cheap pickups attached, but such was the "sword" of my deliverance.

Bob's near-mystical talents would come in very handy, very shortly, as we lumbered toward *Born in the USA*. But for the time being, I'd need to content myself sunning away my studio tan by the pool at the Sunset Marquis, as other bands recorded, hit the road and came back to record anew. I watched jaws drop when I told my fellow travelers I was still working on the same record as a year previous, no end in sight. Oh, the road, the road. How I longed for anything but another night in the studio. From Clover's small lounge, I'd stare out onto the traffic cruising Santa Monica Boulevard and dream of a life where one might actually live. I wanted to be free, unburdened of my obsession with writing and recording my dreams of people seizing life while refraining from doing so myself.

Finally, I surrendered to the inevitability of doing it the slow way, sort of. The road, its freedoms and life itself would have to wait. I was a studio mole, squinting in the dawn's sunlight after another night's fruitless or fruitful search. It was all right. I realized for now I needed to work like the tortoise, not the hare. Bob's shiny, beautiful glassy spaces and compressed power would've cut off some of the record's amateurish rough edges. *The River* wanted and needed them. It wasn't supposed to sound too good, just ragged and right. Our process was both perversely disciplined and indulgent. It broke me financially and almost spiritually, but in the end, and as I hear it today, we got the right sound for that record.

For an album cover, of course, after many false starts, not-quite-right photo sessions (too slick, too studied, too flattering, too . . . ?) I chose another Frank Stefanko portrait from our *Darkness* shoot, scrawled some B-movie title type on top, and miraculously, we were done . . . just in time. In the last weeks of recording, Jon informed me that almost a decade after being signed to Columbia, several million-selling albums and extensive touring, I had but twenty thousand dollars to my name. The clock had run out. Time to make some money.

## Break Time

And hopefully have some fun. There was a short breather after the record was finished and I hung around in LA for a while trying to relax and come down from what had been another torturous, mind-bending experience. I casually saw a few local women, lightly slipping around on my gal from back home. My pal Jimmy Iovine was living a life surrounded by Playboy Bunnies and would soon marry the wonderful Miss Vicki, lawyer, author, entrepreneur and to this day Patti's and my beloved friend. A few of the girls, all of them quite sweet, invited me to the Playboy Mansion, but I didn't like the trade-off. I had something that I thought meant something and I wanted to protect it. For me, it wasn't the sex, it wasn't the drugs . . . it was the ROCK 'N' ROLL! I'd stayed in New Jersey, I didn't hang out, I wasn't a get-your-picture-taken-coming-out-of-the-hippest-nightclub scenester. That other shit was all the stuff I thought ruined it for my old heroes! It made you feel distant from them. It took you out of it. I didn't really think I was that different from my fans except for some hard work, luck and natural ability at my gig. They didn't get to go to the Playboy Mansion, so why should I? Those I mentioned it to, however, said, "You could've gone to the Playboy Mansion and you didn't? What the fuck is wrong with you?" My attitude was, who cares what's going on at the Playboy Mansion?! That's not where the shit's going down. That's not *real* . . . I deemed it all too frivolous for the stakes I was playing for. And so, I talked myself out of a perfectly good time, as over the long course of my life it has been my wont to do. I had my principles, I wasn't wrong and I knew just what I was doing, but still, a part of me always wished on occasion I hadn't followed them so severely! Oh, the road not taken.

In truth, offstage I never really had the ease or ability to enjoy myself very freely. Don't get me wrong. I had high spirits for days and a happiness, the bright brother of my depression, that was straight out of the Zerilli fountain of youth, but abandon . . . not so much. Sobriety became a religion of sorts to me and I mistrusted those who treated the lack thereof as something to rally around and celebrate. For whatever reason, I carried the short stick up my ass with a certain amount of pride. Maybe I'd worked too hard for stability and needed it more than free license. The dumb and destructive shit I saw done in the name of people trying to "let it all hang out," to be "free," was legion. I remember my pals and me chasing a friend down a mountainside one ten-degree Virginia morning as he ran half naked and screaming underneath the spell of some bad acid he'd taken during our night camping out. I was embarrassed by his exposure. I was much too reserved and secretive to throw it all out there like that. I was never gonna get a first-class ticket to see God the easy way on the Tim Leary clown train.

Still, I have to admit I looked at oblivion with an untrustworthy but longing eye. I half admired what I perceived to be my friend's foolish courage. I was always proud but also embarrassed by being so in control. Somewhere I intuited that if I crossed that line it would bring more pain than relief. This was just the shape of my soul. I never cared for any kind of out-of-control "stonedness" around me. It brought back too many memories of unpredictable and quietly volatile evenings at home. Evenings of never knowing where I stood. I could never be completely at ease, or relaxed, as a young man in my own home. Later I promised myself, never again. As I ventured into the world, if that was going on and it wasn't my scene, I'd leave, and if it was my scene, I was understanding, but beyond a point, you'd leave.

I set boundaries within the band. I didn't get in your business unless I saw it was damaging what we were trying to accomplish or hurting you. I believe those boundaries are one of the reasons that forty-four years later, most of us are alive, standing shoulder to shoulder onstage, content and happy to be there.

Still, my overweening need for control limited the amount of simple pleasure I'd allow myself. It was just an unfortunate part of my DNA. Work? Give me a shovel and I'll dig straight through to China before the sun comes up. That was the upside of being a control freak, a bottomless well of anxious energy that, when channeled correctly, was a mighty force. It served me well. When the crowd files back out of the theater, you, my friend, will be exhausted, hop in your Rolls, drive over to the Playboy "manse" and have a late-night toot and psych session with Dr. Leary, Hef and Misses June, July and August. I'll be digging my hole under a bloody moon. But, come the morning, that fucking hole is DUG! . . . And I'm sleeping like a baby—a troubled baby, but a baby.

This is why drinking was good for me. I never drank for the pleasures of alcohol. As the great singer and my road buddy Bobby King once said to me upon my request for his choice of poison at a tour stop hotel bar, "I don't like none of it, so I'll drink any of it." My feelings exactly, and as a lightweight, four or five shots in me and I'd be the life of the party, groping and flirting with anyone in sight before coming to my senses, filled with the morning's regrets and a guilt I so single-mindedly pursued. Once high, I couldn't do something to embarrass myself quick enough. Still, being able to go there after so many young years of caution meant something to me. It gave me an ass-backward confidence that I could handle it and not turn into my dad. I could be foolish and embarrassing but never intentionally punishing or cruel, and I had a lot of fun. Those who suffered my boorish behavior were usually my close compadres, so I was amongst friends. It unleashed a certain happiness in me: the furniture went out the door, the rug got rolled up, the music was blasted and there was dancing, dancing, dancing.

The one thing I did learn was that we all need a little of our madness. Man cannot live by sobriety alone. We all need help somewhere along the way to relieve us of our daily burdens. It's why intoxicants have been pursued since the beginning of time. Today I'd simply advise you to choose your methods and materials carefully or not at all, depending upon one's tolerance, and watch the body parts!

I used to see my rock heroes enjoying their great fortunes and say, "Damn, I can't wait 'til I get there." Then, when I got there, the shoe only occasionally fit. So much of the raw, dangerous but beautiful hedonism, the exultant materialism, of rock 'n' roll felt naked and without purpose for me. I have since come a long way, live high on the hog, yacht around the Mediterranean (who doesn't?) and private-plane myself between dental appointments. But I've still never regularly quite had the mojo to freely let the "*bon temps rouler*." Except . . . onstage. There, strangely enough, exposed in front of thousands, I've always felt perfectly safe, to just let it all go. That's why at our shows you can't get rid of me. My pal Bonnie Raitt, upon visiting me backstage, used to smilingly shake her head at me and say, "The boy has it in him, and it's got to come out." So there, with you, I'm near free and it's party 'til the lights go out. I don't know why, but I've never gotten anywhere near as far or as high as when I count the band in and feel what seems like all life itself and a small flash of eternity pulsing through me. It's the way I'm built. I've long ago resigned myself to the fact that all of us can't be the Rolling Stones, God bless 'em . . . even if we can.

# FORTY-ONE

# HITSVILLE

We had a hit. A real one. "Hungry Heart" went top ten, doubled our album sales and brought to our live shows . . . women. Thank you, Jesus! Up 'til now, I'd had a hard-core following of young men who made up a high percentage of our live audience, but "Hungry Heart" brought in the girls and proved Top 40 radio's power to transform your audience. Even more than going coed, the *River* tour was most significant for our return to Europe after a five-year absence. We were nervous, with the bitter taste of previous battles still in our mouths, but Frank Barsalona, legendary head of Premier Talent, our touring agency, convinced us there was an audience waiting there if we would go over and win it.

First stop, Hamburg! That's where the Beatles became made men, at the Star-Club! I ran into Pete Townshend a few days before we were to ship out and he added to my pre-tour jitters by telling me the Germans were the worst audience in the world. A few days later we landed in Germany and were lodged in a hotel just blocks away from a midcity carnival that looked straight off the boardwalk. I wandered over to calm myself and steady my legs on foreign soil and follow it up with an evening on the Reeperbahn, training grounds and classroom of the Fab Four. I think the Star-Club was still there, but this part of town was now mainly known as the center of the sex market in Hamburg. Our "virgin" eyes were once again treated to the wide-open sexual bartering taking place, all completely legal. I found myself wandering with my cohorts through an underground garage lit only by black light, where hundreds of women of all shapes, colors, nationalities and sizes stood, waiting to make a fool out of you. I observed patrons make brief "conversation," strike a deal and be led to the rear, where small closetlike rooms were lined up side by side. I found the women provocative but intimidating and at the tender age of thirty (!) I couldn't quite get myself to make believe it was all right. I returned to the hotel for some beer and bratwurst.

Showtime. We were booked in a small, rather antiseptic theater, the Congress Centrum. The audience filed in, we kicked it and as Pete foretold, they sat on their hands the entire first half of the show. As we ended our first set with "Badlands," we must've fumbled upon the magic button, for the crowd rose en masse and rushed the stage. The rest of the show was pandemonium and we were greeted backstage by our German promoter, Fritz Rau, shouting, "What have you done to my Germans?" Europe, this time, would be different.

Next stop, Paris. In the early eighties, for fear of fan safety, we did not play "festival seating" (a standing-room-only, seatless dance floor). I thought they were dangerous. I had many European promoters try to explain to me that this was the way it'd always been done overseas. In Paris, we had them place wooden folding chairs on the auditorium floor. As we played our opening set to a full house, I watched as the French slowly lifted our chairs over their heads and passed them to the side of the venue, depositing them into two bonfire-building piles. By the time we reached the end of our set, the floor was "free space" and the crowd was roiling. Okay . . . *vive la France*! This was the reaction we received north in Norway and south in Spain. Our moment in Europe had come. Spain, only years after Franco's death, was not the country it is today. Even in 1981, the room we played was surrounded by machine-gun-toting police. Outside, equipment from the back of our van disappeared up the street and laundry walked itself out of the hotel into the Barcelona night, never to be seen again. There seemed to be a languid, lovely chaos covering all of Spanish life. But the faces in the crowd were some of the most passionate and beautiful on the planet. We played to just a few thousand, but the hell they stirred shook the band and was unforgettable. We'd be back.

Most of the audiences we played to spoke English, at best, as a second language. It didn't seem to matter. We played to crowd after crowd who let us know they felt about music the way we felt about it, with the same all-consuming, anticipatory rush you knew at sixteen unwrapping your favorite group's latest LP, waiting, waiting a week for a three-minute television appearance or staying up all night, radio on, trolling the dial, trying to catch a single, static-filled play of your favorite record. Maybe it was because we hadn't come across the Atlantic often, were exotic, and therefore inspired a different level of appreciation. All I know is playing for our fans overseas was, and continues to be, one of the greatest experiences of my life. It fully started in 1981, and it's never stopped.

In Berlin, Steve and I ventured through Checkpoint Charlie for an afternoon in the east. Any print you had, newspapers, magazines, was confiscated by the East German border guards. It was a different society; you could feel the boot, the stasis in the streets, and you knew the oppression was real. It changed Steve permanently. After our European trip, the man who had preached that rock 'n' roll and politics should never mix became an activist, his own music turning defiantly political. The power of the wall that split the world in two, its blunt, ugly, mesmerizing realness, couldn't be underestimated. It was an offense to humanity; there was something pornographic about it, and once viewed, it held a scent you couldn't quite get off of you. It truly disturbed some of the band and there was a communal sigh of relief when we moved on to the next town. But we didn't forget; we'd be back in 1988 to play for a horizonless field of Eastern Bloc faces. They came, 160,000-plus strong, with home-stitched American flags, and stretched as far as the eye could see. It was one of the great shows of our lives, and a year later the wall fell.

Europe changed our band, filling us with new commitment and confidence. Even perennially cool Britain glowed with promise. Venturing onto an English stage for the first time since the great self-bamboozlement of '75 was nerve-racking but satisfying. Steadied by two new albums, five years of personal battle and years of hard touring, we were not the naïve beach bums who'd stepped out of a British Airways 747 half a decade back. I knew I had a hell of a band and if we couldn't do the job, show me the men who could. (I did go with Pete Townshend a few nights after our Brighton show to a London club, where a young band with their first album out was playing a powerful set; they had an unusual name, U2 . . . better keep a lookout over my shoulder.) Our 1981 European tour turned us into an international act, ready to take on all comers anywhere on the planet.

## Back in the USA

Back home, driving through the Arizona desert, I pulled over outside of Phoenix to gas up. I stopped in a small drug store, and as I was browsing through a rack of paperback books, I came across *Born on the Fourth of July*, a memoir written by a Vietnam vet, Ron Kovic. The book was a heartbreaking testimony of the experience Ron had as a combat infantryman in Southeast Asia. A week or two later, as I bunked in at the Sunset Marquis, the small-world theory proved itself once again. I'd been seeing a young guy with shoulder-length hair in a wheelchair hanging poolside for a few days. One afternoon, he rolled up to me and said, "Hi, I'm Ron Kovic, I wrote a book called *Born on the Fourth of July*." I answered, "I just read it; it floored me." Ron talked to me about the many returned soldiers who were struggling with a wide variety of serious problems and he offered to take me to the vet center in Venice to meet some of the So Cal vets. I said, "Sure."

A decade of silence greeted the end of the Vietnam War. Popular culture seemed at a loss as to how to contextualize and tell the hard stories of "the only war America had ever lost." There had been very few films, records or books about Vietnam that had made any kind of national impact. All of this rolled through my head as we approached the vet center.

I'm pretty easy with people, but once at the center I didn't know exactly how to respond or what to do. West Coast shadows of the neighborhood faces I'd grown up with stared back into my eyes. Some of the guys were homeless, had drug problems, were dealing with post-traumatic stress or life-changing physical injury. I thought about my friends who'd been killed in the war. I didn't know what to say, so I just listened. I made small talk and answered questions about music and my own comparatively very privileged life. Driving back, Ron and I discussed what might be done to draw some attention to what these still-young men and women were going through.

The tour went on. Backstage in New Jersey I met another vet named Bobby Muller. He'd gone to Vietnam as a lieutenant, been shot and returned to the United States, wheelchair bound, and become active in the antiwar demonstrations alongside John Kerry and other returning veterans in Washington, DC. Due to generational differences and the nature of the war, many returning vets did not feel at home in their World War II– and Korean War–vet–populated local VFW. He felt the Vietnam vets should have their own service organization that would administer specifically to their own medical and political needs, an organization that might also serve as a conscience for the country, that we might never make the same mistakes or suffer the same consequences again. In 1978, he'd started the Vietnam Veterans of America but he said that most businessmen and politicians had turned their backs on the organization. To establish the VVA as a viable concern, they'd need publicity and financing. Those were two things I knew I could deliver.

The concert for the Vietnam Veterans of America was held at the Los Angeles Memorial Sports Arena on August 20, 1981. The bandstand was flanked with risers holding vets from the local vet centers and the Los Angeles VA hospital, including some of the guys I met on my first trip to Venice with Ron Kovic. Ron, who'd set all of this in motion, was there. Bobby Muller gave a short speech from center stage on ending the silence surrounding Vietnam, then rousingly introduced the band. Fronted by Jersey draft dodger number one, we opened with Creedence Clearwater Revival's "Who'll Stop the Rain" and played hard and well. It was the beginning of lifelong friendships with Ron and Bobby and the start of putting some piece of what I did to pragmatic political use. I was never going to be Woody Guthrie—I liked the pink Cadillac too much—but there was work to be done.

## The River Flows, It Flows to the Sea

Three weeks later we brought the tour to a close in Cincinnati. Satisfactorily altered by a potent drink mix of Clarence's dubbed "Kahuna Punch," we held one final bash at the hotel, and I awoke the next morning with a new friend and a pounding punch headache. We headed home.

A wide variety of influences and forces had shaped the *River* tour. First, our return to Europe and the political perspectives that awakened. Then, our work with the MUSE concerts and Vietnam veterans show proved a practical social use for our talents was waiting. Finally, a sense of history opened by reading Henry Steele Commager's *A Pocket History of the United States*, Howard Zinn's *A People's History of the United States* and Joe Klein's *Woody Guthrie: A Life* all provided me with a new view of myself as an actor in this moment in time. What happened here was, in some infinitesimally small way, my responsibility. This was my place, my moment, my opportunity for my voice, no matter how faint, to be heard. If I passed it by, I'd have to answer to those children I was beginning to imagine.

History was a subject that had bored me in middle and high school, but I devoured it now. It seemed to hold some of the essential pieces to the identity questions I was asking. How could I know who I was if I didn't have a clue as to where I'd personally and collectively come from? What it *does* mean to be an American is all caught up in what *did* it mean to be one. Only some combination of those answers could lead you to what it *might* mean to be an American.

## Woody

How serious was I about all this? I couldn't tell you. I didn't know. All I knew is I was pushed forward by a wide variety of personal and work motivations to address the issues that had begun to unfold on *Darkness on the Edge of Town* and *The River*.

I searched in new places. Country music, gospel music and the blues were all forms that gave voice to adult lives under stress and seeking transcendence, but I would have to go farther back than Hank Williams to find music that dealt with the social forces at work on those lives. Joe Klein's biography of Woody Guthrie opened my eyes and ears to Dylan's immediate predecessor at just the moment I was ready to hear the news. I was aware of Woody's name, and of course, "This Land Is Your Land," but as a pure student of hit radio, I was mostly unaware of the details of his life and his music. I immersed myself and found the subtle writing, raw honesty, humor and empathy that's made his music eternal. In his stories of depression-era Okies and migrant workers, he revealed the folks trapped on the fringes of American life. His writing wasn't soapbox rambling but finely wrought personal portraits of American lives, told with toughness, wit and common wisdom. In concert we began to cover "This Land Is Your Land" nightly and we worked to give voice to stories that in Reagan's 1980s America rock 'n' roll wasn't often telling.

The turn in my writing in "Factory," "Promised Land," "The River" and "Point Blank," and the direction of our shows, provided me a way of honoring my parents' and my sisters' lives, and of not losing complete contact with that part of myself. Even with the relatively modest success and financial security I'd graduated to, my life was now very different from the lives of those I'd chosen to write about. This worried me. Despite devoutly pursuing it, I viewed the world of success with great skepticism. I wondered, who were that world's inhabitants and what did they have to do with me? I was practically the only one of them I knew! Regardless of being "born to run," I didn't want to change that part of my life. I remained, from some combination of provincial fear and/or devotion, a mere ten minutes from my hometown, secure on my turf. There would be no New York, London, Los Angeles or Paris for me for a long while. I'd stay home, where I felt like I belonged and told the stories I still felt were mine to tell.

The distractions and seductions of fame and success as I'd seen them displayed felt dangerous to me and looked like fool's gold. The newspapers and rock rags were constantly filled with tales of good lives that had lost focus and were stumblingly lived, all to keep the gods (and the people!) entertained and laughing. I yearned for something more elegant, more graceful and seemingly simpler. Of course in the end, nobody gets away clean, and I'd eventually take my own enjoyment (and provide my share of laughs) in fame's distractions and seductions, but not until I was sure I could handle them. Then they just become the good life, and if you've worked hard for them, they're there at your pleasure. But for the time being my indulgences were modest, and I worked to make myself aware of fortune's distorting powers and to temper its hold over me.

It wasn't that hard. On the Irish side of my immediate family, saying no was in our DNA. No doctors, no cities, no strangers, no travel, "the world is out there and it's a monster, waiting to eat you alive. You'll see." It's yes that doesn't come very easy to us. But I was also extremely protective of my music and what I'd begun to create. I valued it, seriously, almost to a fault, above most other things . . . maybe everything. Still, caution and sobriety have their blessings and their purposes, and for the time being, they had their moment. That wariness, that slight outsider's perspective, would help me retain the vitality and currency of my own work and keep me in the trenches and close to my audience.

In my writing I was increasingly interested in the place where "This Land Is Your Land" and "The River" intersected, where the political and personal came together to spill clear water into the muddy river of history. By the end of the *River* tour, I thought perhaps mapping that territory, the distance between the American dream and American reality, might be my service, one I could provide that would accompany the entertainment and the good times I brought my fans. I hoped it might give roots and mission to our band.

Beyond this, I personally needed to know where my family—my grandparents, my mom, dad and sisters—fell in the arc of American experience and what that meant for me, the fortunate son.

# FORTY-TWO

# HELLO WALLS

I returned to New Jersey after the *River* tour. While on the road, I'd been tossed from my farmhouse and transplanted to a ranch house in Colts Neck, rented sight unseen. The place sat nicely on a reservoir, just a spit from the rope swing my surfing pals and I would visit with our girlfriends on the days the Atlantic lay flat upon the shore. The tour had made sure I finally had my creditors paid and what felt to me like a small fortune in the bank. I'd have to find some new things to worry about. I'd driven strictly vintage automobiles my whole life. My two-thousand-dollar '57 Chevy morphed into my six-thousand-dollar 'Vette, backed by my 1970 Ford pickup as a daily driver. In the winter I'd load my truck bed with tree trunks for rear-wheel traction and run the icy roads of Monmouth County. Debts paid, career established, all should have been pretty free and easy, but I'm not free and easy. So, I sat around and anguished over whether I should spend ten thousand dollars on a *new* car. I was thirty-one and I'd never owned a new car in my life. For that matter, outside of studio expenses, I'd never spent ten thousand dollars on myself. I didn't know anyone who was making more than they could live on, so the money I'd made left me feeling uncomfortably different and somewhat embarrassed. Still, I bit the bullet, rode down to the dealer and drove away in a 1982 Chevy Z28 Camaro. I felt as conspicuous as if I were driving a solid-gold Rolls-Royce.

## A House Is Not a Home

My ranch house was wall-to-wall orange shag carpet. I know, it was Frank Sinatra's favorite color, but I could feel a serial killing comin' on. I decided I needed a permanent home. I found a real estate agent, several real estate agents, and started looking. I scoured the state and looked at everything from the humble to the high and mighty. Every available crib in Central and Western New Jersey was cleared of its inhabitants, invaded and scrutinized. Nothing. They were all either too big, too small, too old, too new, too cheap, too expensive, too far or too close. At first, I felt like, "Well, I just didn't see anything I liked." It took a while and some mental probing, but I came to see that NO HOME BUILT BY MAN! was going to hold/ satisfy the Jersey Devil. As was my way, I turned the minutest of decisions into full-blown identity issues: What car? What shirt? What house? What girl? I had not mastered the simple principle that to live shy of insanity, to paraphrase Freud, sometimes a cigar *needs* to be just a cigar.

At the end of the day, I was simply a guy who was rarely comfortable in his own skin, whatever skin that might be. The idea of home itself, like much else, filled me with distrust and a bucket load of grief. I'd long convinced myself . . . almost . . . that homes were for everybody else. But now, something was fucking with my movie. (That movie would be the one where I play an itinerant musician, unlucky at love but fabulously and unrewardingly talented; a charismatic man whose happy-go-lucky exterior covers a bruised but noble soul. As I drift from town to town, two things regularly occur. One, a beautiful woman always falls helplessly in love with me, a love that I cannot reciprocate due to the fact that my "heart" belongs to the highway. And two, I transform the life of everyone I meet to such a degree that they welcome me into their homes, feed me, lay upon my brow laurels, give me their girlfriends and will "always remember" me. I nod my head in humble acknowledgment, then travel on, whistling, suitcase in hand, along the dusty back roads of America, lonely but free, to seek out my next adventure. I lived that masterpiece for a long time.)

A winter morning sun shines on a roadkill doe, its fur covered in a pink frost, as I drive toward my "Rosebud"—Freehold, New Jersey. I still spent many hours a four-wheeled phantom on the edges of my birth city. Mine was a pathetic and quasi-religious compulsion. On my visits to my hometown, I would never leave the confines of my car. That would've ruined it. My car was my sealed time capsule from whose bucket seats I could experience the little town that had its crushing boot on my neck in whatever mental time, space or moment I chose. Come evening I rolled through its streets, listening for the voices of my father, my mother, me as a child. I'd pass by the old stores and Victorian homes of Freehold and daydream . . . of purchasing a house, moving back, away from all the noise I'd created, bringing it all full circle, fixing things, receiving the blessings of these streets, finding a love, one that would last, marrying and walking through town, my children in my arms, my woman at my side. It was a pleasant fantasy and I suppose I took comfort in the illusion that I could go back. But I'd been around long enough to know history is sealed and unchangeable. You can move on, with a heart stronger in the places it's been broken, create new love. You can hammer pain and trauma into a righteous sword and use it in defense of life, love, human grace and God's blessings. But *nobody* gets a do-over. Nobody gets to go back and there's only one road out. Ahead, into the dark.

# FORTY-THREE

# *NEBRASKA*

Houseless and clueless about where to turn next, I decided to lose myself in the marginally more controllable terrain of my musical life. With the spiderweb of my past gumming up my works, I turned to a world I'd walked through as a child, remained on familiar terms with and heard calling to me now.

*Nebraska* began as an unknowing meditation on my childhood and its mysteries. I had no conscious political agenda or social theme. I was after a feeling, a tone that felt like the world I'd known and still carried inside me. The remnants of that world were still only ten minutes and ten miles from where I was living. The ghosts of *Nebraska* were drawn from my many sojourns into the small-town streets I'd grown up on. My family, Dylan, Woody, Hank, the American gothic short stories of Flannery O'Connor, the noir novels of James M. Cain, the quiet violence of the films of Terrence Malick and the decayed fable of director Charles Laughton's *The Night of the Hunter* all guided my imagination. That and the flat, dead voice that drifted through my town on the nights I couldn't sleep. The voice I heard when I'd wander in a three a.m. trance out onto the front porch of my home to feel the sticky heat and listen to streets silent but for the occasional grinding gears of tractor-trailers groaning like dinosaurs beneath the dust cloud, pulling up South Street to Route 33 and out of town. Then . . . quiet.

The songs of *Nebraska* were written quickly, all rising from the same ground. Each song took maybe three or four takes to record. I was only making "demos." "Highway Patrolman" and "State Trooper" were recorded only once each. "Mansion on the Hill" was first, "My Father's House" last, with the song "Nebraska" serving as the record's heart. I tapped into white gospel, early Appalachian music and the blues. The writing was in the details; the twisting of a ring, the twirling of a baton, was where these songs found their character. As in *The Night of the Hunter*, I often wrote from a child's point of view. "Mansion on the Hill," "Used Cars" and "My Father's House" were all stories that came out of my experience with my family.

I wanted black bedtime stories. I thought of the records of John Lee Hooker and Robert Johnson, music that sounded so good with the lights out. I wanted the listener to hear my characters think, to feel their thoughts, their choices. These songs were the opposite of the rock music I'd been writing. They were restrained, still on the surface, with a world of moral ambiguity and unease below. The tension running through the music's core was the thin line between stability and that moment when the things that connect you to your world, your job, your family, your friends, the love and grace in your heart, fail you. I wanted the music to feel like a waking dream and to move like poetry. I wanted the blood in these songs to feel destined and fateful.

Frustrated at blowing all my money on studio time, I sent my guitar tech out to get a recorder, a little less lo-fi than the cassette recorder I usually used to lay down my new song ideas. I needed a better and less expensive way to tell if my new material was record-worthy. He came back with a four-track Japanese Tascam 144 cassette recorder. We set it up in my bedroom; I'd sing, play, and with the two tracks left, I could add a backing vocal, an extra guitar or a tambourine. On four tracks, that's all you could do. I mixed it through a guitar Echoplex unit onto a beat box like the kind you'd take to the beach, total cost for the project: about a grand. After that, I went into the studio, brought in the band, re-recorded and remixed everything. On listening, I realized I'd succeeded in doing nothing but damaging what I'd created. We got it to sound cleaner, more hi-fi, but not nearly as atmospheric, as authentic.

All popular artists get caught between making records and making music. If you're lucky, sometimes it's the same thing. When you learn to craft your music into recordings, there's always something gained and something lost. The ease of an unself-conscious voice gives way to the formality of presentation. On certain records, that trade-off may destroy the essential nature of what you've done. At the end of the day, satisfied I'd explored the music's possibilities and every blind alley, I pulled out the original cassette I'd been carrying around in my jeans pocket and said, "This is it."

FORTY-FOUR

# DELIVER ME
# FROM NOWHERE

*Nebraska* and the first half of *Born in the USA* were recorded at the same time. I thought I was working on one record but *Nebraska*'s intransigence to integration soon awakened me to the situation at hand. We toyed with the idea of a double record, the acoustic *Nebraska* and the electric *Born in the USA* in one package, but the tonality of the music was just too different, too oppositional. *Nebraska* had been so funkily recorded, it would not go onto an LP. It would distort, feed back and declare revolution on the common materials of recording. We discussed releasing it on cassette only, then Chuck Plotkin managed to find an old mastering lathe at Atlantic Studios and my lo-fi latest surrendered itself to vinyl. *Nebraska* entered respectably on the charts, got some pretty nice reviews and received little to no airplay. For the first time, I didn't tour on a release. It felt too soon after *The River*, and *Nebraska*'s quiet stillness would take me a while longer to bring to the stage. Life went on.

I drifted away from my very lovely twenty-year-old girlfriend and packed for a cross-country road trip. I'd recently purchased a small cottage in the Hollywood Hills and figured I'd winter out west in the California sunshine. This was the trip where the ambivalence, trouble and toxic confusion I'd had volcanically bubbling for thirty-two years would finally reach critical mass.

## The Trip

It was a '69 Ford XL with a white ragtop, sea green and Cadillac long. I'd bought it for a few grand and my friend and road buddy Matt Delia, along with his brothers Tony and Ed, fitted it out for the ride. In the midseventies, up in Bergen County, Matt, Tony and Ed owned the last Triumph motorcycle dealership in New Jersey. Introduced to me through Max Weinberg, Matt had set me up with a late-sixties Triumph Trophy, something clicked, and Matt, Tony and Ed became the brothers I never had.

Matt was now a Goodyear dealer, and the morning of our departure, we hung at the shop, putting the finishing touches on the XL, taking farewell photos and doctoring the all-important sound system. It'd be just Matt and me making the crossing. It was fall; our plan was to run south, pick up some warm weather, drop the top and head west.

I'm driving. Matt's suffered a recent breakup with his girl and has fallen on some blue times. He spends most of our first day riding shotgun, arms locked around a huge teddy bear. Matt's built like a block, with thick arms and forearms, and the sight of those ropes wrapped around a five-year-old's toy bear emanates bad voodoo for our trip. I try to explain to him the teddy is throwing a kink into our Kerouac *On the Road* cool, but Matt's committed to his blues and his bear, so we drive on.

## Matt

My lifelong friend Matt Delia hails from smack-dab in the middle of a family of fourteen children. A mother prone to the arts and a father in the salvage business have left Matt with the talents and physique of a mechanic and the soul of a poet. For a living, he wrenches day and night on motorcycles and cars and is completely at home both dealing with the gearheads, dirt trackers and random motorcycle gang members who routinely show up at the shop's front counter in search of his services and discussing music, politics and culture with the likes of me. Car-hoppin' image aside, I, like many others confronting vehicular trouble, will reach not for the toolbox but for God's gift to man, the cell phone. But I like to be on wheels, and in the ancient days about which I will soon regale you children, THERE WERE NO CELL PHONES! So, Matt is my partner and hands-on pipeline to the world of automotive freedom. It's all Route 66, two guys in a convertible, magic as long as one of us can fix this fucker when it unromantically breaks down on the outskirts of nowheresville. Back in the day, when wheels got flat, radiators blew steam, fan belts shredded, carburetors clogged, engine blocks spewed oil and the automobile was a less trustworthy traveling companion, the Delia brothers, sturdy as tree trunks and many times more reliable, provided company and solace on several of the biggest road trips of my life. Matt, the eldest of the three, in his youth, bore a fleeting resemblance to *In Cold Blood*-era Robert Blake, and in our thirty-five years of friendship, we've driven the country together more than a few times. He is my Dean Moriarty.

## Driving

We travel through South Jersey, across the Delaware Memorial Bridge, through Washington, heading all points south toward the first stop in our pilgrimage: "long-distance information, give me Memphis, Tennessee." It's the birthplace of rock 'n' roll, it's Elvis, the blues and Beale Street. We make a quick stop at the shuttered Sun Studio, take a few photos out front and travel on. We get nailed in Southern backcountry by a vicious late-summer thunderstorm and head to New Orleans. I've made cassette mixes featuring music from every part of the country we've planned to pass through. I drive as Matt drifts, and the sound of Memphis rockabilly gives way to Mississippi country blues. Then, before we know it, Professor Longhair's piano is rolling us into Louisiana and the Big Easy. We spend a day and night in New Orleans, listening to sidewalk musicians and wandering in and out of the bars on Bourbon Street.

We wake early the next morning and head west.

This is where the country opens up and things get a little weird. I let off some steam at Matt for being momentarily worthless, wrestling away the teddy bear and depositing it in the trunk. Now Matt's behind the wheel and driving, where he belongs. I'm feeling noticeably unsettled and that's disconcerting. For years, music and travel have been my faithful companions and surefire medication. As Sisyphus can count on the rock, *I* can always count on the road, the music and the miles for whatever ails me.

As we cross the Mississippi River and venture into the wide-open of Texas, it's beginning to feel a little . . . wide open . . . out here. Our map's a patchwork of the many towns we visit along the way. Matt, my usually silent partner (the exemplar of a friend you "don't always have to talk to"), is on an endless, meandering ramble fed by his lovesick blues. He's diseased, and it could be viral, so I threaten divorce and a return to Jersey. He stops. Together, we move on in silence. Then one evening . . . there is a town.

## The Last Town

In the blue light of dusk, there is a river. By the river, there is a fair. At the fair, there is music, a small stage, filled by a local band playing for their neighbors on a balmy night. I watch men and women lazily dancing in each other's arms, and I scan the crowd for the pretty local girls. I'm anonymous and then . . . I'm gone. From nowhere, a despair overcomes me; I feel an envy of these men and women and their late-summer ritual, the small plea-sures that bind them and this town together. Now, for all I know, these folks may hate this one-dog dump and each other's guts and be screwing one another's husbands and wives like rabbits. Why wouldn't they? But right now, all I can think of is that I want to be amongst them, of them, and I know I can't. I can only watch. That's what I do. I watch . . . and I record. I do not engage, and if and when I do, my terms are so stringent, they suck the lifeblood and possibility out of any good thing, any real thing, I might have. It's here, in this little river town, that my life as an observer, an actor staying cautiously and safely out of the emotional fray, away from the con-sequences, the normal messiness of living and loving, reveals its cost to me. At thirty-two, in the middle of the USA, on this night, I've just exceeded the once-surefire soul-and-mind-numbing power of my rock 'n' roll meds.

We leave town. The flat night highway rises up and it's all headlights and white lines . . . white lines . . . white lines. I've just pulled a perfect swan dive into my abyss; my stomach is on rinse cycle and I'm going down, down, down. Finally, an hour out, still internally reeling, I ask Matt to go back, back to that last town. "Now, please." Matt, God bless him, does not ask me to explain. Car wheels slide on roadside gravel, a perfect K turn is executed and we're on our way back. We travel with the western sky black and press-ing in around us, then I see lights. I need this town. Right now, it's the most important town in America, in my life, in God's firmament. Why, I don't know, I just feel a need to get rooted *somewhere*, before I drift into ether. We reach the outskirts, but it's now early morning, pitch-black, and no one's in sight. We slow and park on a side street. I want to cry, but the tears won't come. Worse, I want to go in the trunk and get the fucking teddy bear. Matt is silent, quietly staring out of the windshield onto a dusty little block that appears bused in from another dimension. I feel a deeper anxiety than I've ever known. Why here? Why tonight? Thirty-four years later, I still don't know.

All I do know is as we age the weight of our unsorted baggage becomes heavier . . . much heavier. With each passing year, the price of our refusal to do that sorting rises higher and higher. Maybe I'd cut myself loose one too many times, depended on my unfailing magic act once too often, drifted that little bit too far from the smoke and mirrors holding me together. Or . . . I just got old . . . old enough to know better. Whatever the reason, I'd found myself, once again, stranded in the middle of . . . "*nowhere*," but this time the euphoria and delusions that kept me oiled and running had ground to a halt.

Beyond the hood of the Ford lie what looks like a million miles of uncharted space. There are several street lamps creating pools of light on a desert that passes for curb and front lawn on the street of my epiphany. I study them. A sandy-colored, hungry-looking dog wanders slowly through these small circles of eternity and then, its beige coat turning gray, slips into inky blackness. Matt and I sit . . . my cold sweat slowly drying, my despair subsiding, and looking down into the chasm beneath the dashboard, at the black rubber mat swallowing my boots like quicksand, I mumble, "Let's go."

Two lonely cosmonauts circling the sun-scorched and abandoned Earth, we fire our engines and leave orbit. Our home destroyed, we now have to take our chances in the void. The rest of the trip is uneventful. The road, the free sky, the infinite chain of towns, Matt running the XL, top down, ninety miles per hour, through a cleansing rainstorm, its waters skimming over the windshield and misting down upon my face in the slipstream . . . none of it cures my blues or removes the specter of my evening at the fair. Long ago, the defenses I built to withstand the stress of my childhood, to save what I had of myself, outlived their usefulness, and I've become an abuser of their once lifesaving powers. I relied on them to wrongly isolate myself, seal my alienation, cut me off from life, control others and contain my emotions to a damaging degree. Now the bill collector is knocking, and his payment'll be in tears.

The night and highway suck us up, the rain clears; I roll down my window and look at ash-gray stars, pop in my "Texas" cassette, and Bobby Fuller's "I Fought the Law" murmurs at low volume through the XL's interior.

# FORTY-FIVE

# CALIFORNIA

Matt and I crawl through near-impenetrable smog, gridlocked traffic, onto an exit ramp off the LA freeway and head east. At Laurel Canyon, we wind our way through the Hollywood Hills to my small cottage. Ten days out of Jersey we step out of the dusty XL and stand amid butterflies and bougainvillea at the wooden door of the first home I've ever owned. It might as well be Hearst Castle. My modest new digs, previously home to Charlie Chan's Sidney Toler, induce torrents of self-loathing in Doug Springsteen's "number one son" and I want out . . . *now*. Once inside, I immediately start thinking about leaving. Where am I going? Anywhere, as long as it's away from this lovely little home that seems to be asking me for something I find so primally disturbing I cannot submit or surrender to it. It wants me to *stay* . . . and I don't stay, for this little house or for anyone. That's for everyone else. I *go*. The only thing that stops me is I know if I get in the car and make that long trip back east, once my toes tickle the Atlantic, I'll be driven to turn around and return here, in a never-ending cycle of wheel-spinning madness. With nowhere to go I am locked down inside my own miniature West Coast death row. I flop onto the couch I've recently purchased (along with every other stick of furniture in this joint in a two-hour spending spree at the local mall), existentially spent, my emotional well of tricks dry. There is no tour to hide behind, no music to "save" me. I'm face up against the wall I've been inching toward for a long time.

Matt is privy to none of this. My road lieutenant is in the next room, clankily lifting my home weights, awaiting orders that ain't coming. I return to my bedroom overlooking the foggy LA basin, stare out the window, and I phone Mr. Landau.

I've broached these subjects in several long semianalytical conversations with Jon in the past. He gets the drift. It's dark and getting darker. My well of emotion is no longer being channeled and safely pipelined to the surface. There's been an "event," and my depression is spewing like an oil spill all over the beautiful turquoise-green gulf of my carefully planned and controlled existence. Its black sludge is threatening to smother every last living part of me. Jon advises, "You need professional help." At my request he makes a call, I get a number and two days later I drive fifteen minutes west to a residential home/office in a suburb of Los Angeles. I walk in; look into the eyes of a kindly, white-haired, mustached complete stranger; sit down; and burst into tears.

## Now, We Begin

I started talking, and it helped. Immediately, over the next few weeks, I regained some equilibrium; I felt myself steadying, righting myself. I'd danced and driven my way, all on my own (sans drugs or alcohol), to the brink of my big black sea, but I hadn't jumped in. By the grace of God and the light of friends, I wouldn't live and die there . . . I hoped.

So began thirty years of one of the biggest adventures of my life, canvassing the squirrely terrain inside my own head for signs of life. *Life*—not a song, not a performance, not a story, but a *life*. I worked hard, dedicatedly, and I began to learn things. I began to map a previously unknown internal world. A world that, when it showed its weight and mass, its ability to hide in plain sight and its sway over my behavior, stunned me. There was a lot of sadness, at what had happened, at what had been done and what I'd done to myself. But there was good news also: how resilient I'd been, how I'd turned so much of it into music, love and smiles. I'd mostly beaten the hell out of myself and my loved ones, the usual victims. However, I understood what had recently drawn me so far down had also rallied to my defense as a child, had covered my heart and provided shelter when I needed it. For that, I was thankful, but now, those wayward blessings were standing squarely between me and a home and life I needed. The question was, could I tolerate those things? I needed to find out.

## Three Dreams

*I am standing on a rise behind my old farmhouse, the farmhouse where I wrote* Darkness on the Edge of Town *and lived during the late seventies. If you were standing there today, the ruddy soil would seem to have ceased growing its feed corn and soy and spontaneously sprouted McMansions. But in my dream, I look out over blue skies, green trees and falling farm fields to a distant black stand of woods. A child, perhaps six or seven, is standing at forest's edge. It's me. He doesn't move. He waits, just showing himself. There's a pause, then my boy raises his head, finds his thirty-two-year-old self in the distance, watches, then smiles. It's a smile I know from the many faded black-and-white Polaroids in our family album.*

*In my dream, I am young and unburdened by the original sins of my tribe. I am not my father's, not my mother's, nor my grandmother's or grandfather's. I am simply me; I am my own. It's a sad dream. I have often brought the weight down, hard, on this little boy. I've taken over my father's cruelest work and often done it too well. To do it well, you must mistake and distort your child, your most beloved treasure, into being something he is not, a competitor in the household. Then, when his eyes gaze up, past the garrison belt, beyond the buttons on the olive work shirt, up, until they meet the eyes that hold the answer to "Who am I?," that answer comes clear and devastatingly hard, and is silently packed away and carried, until its weight overwhelms.*

*From my bluff at the rear of my farmhouse, I receive a small wave from my younger self and a smile that signals, "It's okay . . ." The smile is followed by a soft turn and an unfearful walk back into the trees. I wake. The dream repeats itself many years later, but this time, the boy who steps forward from the trees is in his late teens or early twenties; the wave and the smile are the same. "I'm okay . . ." Then years after, the dream comes again, but this time, I'm greeted by my forty-year-old adult self, staring from that distance back into my eyes. These images of my youth came to me in my dreams, having passed through my crucible, returning to say, "We're okay. We lived, now it's your turn" . . . to live.*

*We're all honorary citizens of that primal forest, and our burdens and weaknesses always remain. They are an ineradicable part of ourselves, they are our humanity. But when we bring light, the day becomes ours and their power to determine our future is diminished. This is the way it works. The trick is, you can only brighten the forest from beneath the canopy of its trees . . . from within. To bring the light, you must first make your way through the bramble-filled darkness. Safe travels.*

## What's Up, Doc?

In this way, I slowly acquired the skills that would eventually lead to a life of my own. That was still many tears, mistakes, heartbreaks away and often remains a struggle to this day. The price I paid for the time lost was just that. Time lost. You can blow your fortune, should you be lucky enough to obtain one, and make it back, damage your reputation and, with effort and dedication, often restore it. But time . . . time lost is gone for good.

I had my winter in California, then returned to New Jersey. I was referred to a Dr. Wayne Myers, an avuncular, soft-spoken man with an easy smile, in New York City. And over many meetings and long-distance phone calls during the next twenty-five years Doc Myers and I would fight many demons together until his passing in 2008. When I was in town, we would sit face-to-face, with me staring into his understanding eyes patiently, painstakingly putting together a pretty good string of wins, along with some nagging defeats. We successfully slowed down that treadmill I'd been running on while never getting it to completely stop. In Doc Myers's office, I got a head start on my new odyssey; his knowledge, along with his compassionate heart, guided me to the strength and freedom I needed to love things and be loved.

In all psychological wars, it's never over, there's just this day, this time, and a hesitant belief in your own ability to change. It is *not* an arena where the unsure should go looking for absolutes and there are no permanent victories. It is about a *living* change, filled with the insecurities, the chaos, of our own personalities, and is always one step up, two steps back. The results of my work with Dr. Myers and my debt to him are at the heart of this book.

# FORTY-SIX

# *BORN IN THE USA*

Some books, a few scattered guitar picks, and a harmonica rack jostled with the crumbs of the afternoon's lunch, crowding my notebook for space. I shifted my weight and sat my stockinged feet up on the carved lion's-claw base of the oak table I've written at for twenty-five years. An antique lamp laid dim light on the only other object on the tabletop, a film script. It'd been sent to me by screenwriter and director Paul Schrader. Paul had written *Taxi Driver*, and had written and directed *Blue Collar*, two of my favorite films from the seventies. I strummed a few chords on my sunburst Gibson J200, paged through my notebook, stopped and murmured a verse of a song I had under way about returning Vietnam vets. I glanced over at the unread script's cover page and sang out its title; I was "born in the USA."

I copped "Born in the USA" straight off the title page of that Paul Schrader script. The script was a story of the trials and tribulations of a local bar band in Cleveland, Ohio. The film would later be released as *Light of Day*, featuring my song of the same name, my polite attempt at paying Paul back for my fortuitous and career-boosting theft.

The Power Station. I counted off; I had lyrics, a great title, two chords, a synth riff, but no real arrangement. It was our second take. A marshall wash of sound poured into my headphones. I started singing. The band watched me closely for an on-the-fly arrangement and Max Weinberg gave his greatest recorded drum performance. Four minutes and thirty-nine seconds later "Born in the USA" was in the can. We set down our instruments, walked into the control room and listened to lightning in a bottle.

More than ten years after the end of the Vietnam War, inspired by Bobby Muller and Ron Kovic, I wrote and recorded my soldier's story. It was a protest song, and when I heard it thundering back at me through the Power Station's gargantuan studio speakers, I knew it was one of the best things I'd ever done. It was a GI blues, the verses an accounting, the choruses a declaration of the one sure thing that could not be denied . . . birthplace. Birthplace, and the right to all of the blood, confusion, blessings and grace that come with it. Having paid body and soul, you have earned, many times over, the right to claim and shape your piece of home ground.

"Born in the USA" remains one of my greatest and most misunderstood pieces of music. The combination of its "down" blues verses and its "up" declarative choruses, its demand for the right of a "critical" patriotic voice along with pride of birth, was too seemingly conflicting (or just a bother!) for some of its more carefree, less discerning listeners. (This, my friend, is the way the pop political ball can often bounce.) Records are often auditory Rorschach tests; we hear what we want to hear.

For years after the release of my biggest-selling album, come Halloween, I had little kids in red bandanas knocking at my door with their trick-or-treat bags singing, "I was born in the USA." I guess the same fate awaited Woody Guthrie's "This Land Is Your Land" around the campfire, but that didn't make me feel any better. (When Pete Seeger and I sang "This Land

Is Your Land" at President Barack Obama's inauguration, one of Pete's requests was that we sing *all* of Woody's controversial verses. He wanted to reclaim the song's radical text.) In 1984, add to this an election year, a Republican Party intent on co-opting a cow's ass if it has the Stars and Stripes tattooed on it, sitting president Ronald Reagan cynically offering thanks for "the message of hope in songs of . . . New Jersey's own Bruce Springsteen" on a campaign swing through the state and, well . . . you know the rest. Conversely, the first guy I played the finished version of "Born in the USA" for was Bobby Muller, then president of the Vietnam Veterans of America. He entered the studio and sat at the front of the console, and I turned up the volume. He listened for a few moments and a big smile crossed his face.

A songwriter writes to be understood. Is presentation politics? Is the sound and form your song takes its content? Coming off *Nebraska*, I'd just done it both ways. I learned a hard lesson about how pop and pop image were perceived, but I still wouldn't have made either of those records differently. Over the years, I've had an opportunity to reinterpret "Born in the USA," particularly in acoustic versions that could not be misconstrued, but those interpretations always stood in relief against the original and gained some of their new power from the audience's previous experience with the album version. On the album, "Born in the USA" was in its most powerful presentation. If I'd tried to undercut or change the music, I believe I would've had a record that would've been more easily understood but not as satisfying.

Like my previous albums, *Born in the USA* took time. For the follow-up to *Nebraska*, which contained some of my strongest songs, I wanted to take its same themes and electrify them. The framework of that idea, along with many of *Nebraska*'s subtexts, can be found beneath the surface of "Working on the Highway" and "Downbound Train." These songs both began their lives acoustically on that Japanese Tascam demo recorder.

Much of *Born in the USA* was recorded live with the full band in three weeks. Then I took a break, recorded *Nebraska* and didn't return to my rock album 'til later. "Born in the USA," "Working on the Highway," "Down-bound Train," "Darlington County," "Glory Days," "I'm on Fire" and "Cover Me" were all basically completed in the very early stages of the record. Then brain freeze settled in. I was uncomfortable with the pop aspect of my finished material and wanted something deeper, heavier and more serious. I waited, I wrote, I recorded, then I waited some more. Months passed in writer's block, with me holed up in a little cottage I'd bought by the Navesink River, the songs coming like the last drops of water being pumped out of a temporarily dry well. Slowly, "Bobby Jean," "No Surrender" and "Dancing in the Dark" joined my earlier work. The rains had eventually come. By that time, I'd recorded a lot of music (see disc three of *Tracks*), but in the end, I circled back to my original group of songs. There I found a naturalism and aliveness that couldn't be argued with. They weren't exactly what I'd been looking for, but they were what I had.

The wait was worth it. Those last songs were important pieces of my record's final picture. "Bobby Jean" and "No Surrender" were great tributes to the bonding power of rock and my friendship with Steve. "My Hometown" would be an important bookend to "Born in the USA," capturing the racial tension of late-sixties small-town New Jersey and the post-industrialization of the coming decade. Then, very late to the party came "Dancing in the Dark." One of my most well-crafted and heartfelt pop songs, "Dancing" was "inspired" one afternoon when Jon Landau stopped by my New York hotel room. He told me he'd been listening to the album and felt we didn't have a single, that one song that was going to throw gasoline on the fire. That meant more work for me, and for once, more work was the last thing I was interested in. We argued, gently, and I suggested that if he felt we needed something else, he write it.

That evening I wrote "Dancing in the Dark," my song about my own alienation, fatigue and desire to get out from inside the studio, my room, my record, my head and . . . *live*. This was the record and song that'd take me my farthest into the pop mainstream. I was always of two minds about big records and the chance involved in engaging a mass audience. You should be. There's risk. Was the effort of seeking that audience worth the exposure, the discomfort of the spotlight and the amount of life that'd be handed over? What was the danger of dilution of your core message, your purpose, the reduction of your best intentions to empty symbolism or worse? On "Born in the USA," I experienced all these things, but that audience can also let you know how powerful and durable your music might be, and its potential impact upon your fans' lives and the culture. So you take those steps tenderly, until you reach the chasm, and then you jump, for there is no steadily inclining path to the *big* big time. There is always that engulfing abyss where each traveler measures his next move, questions his motives. So, move with spirit, but be aware that along with the thrill and satisfaction of exploiting your full talents, you may find the clear bounds of your music's limitations, as well as your own.

My *Born in the USA* songs were direct and fun and stealthily carried the undercurrents of *Nebraska*. With my record greatly enhanced by the explosiveness of Bob Clearmountain's mixes, I was ready for my close-up. Onstage, this music swept over my audience with joyous abandon. We had hit after hit and in 1985, along with Madonna, Prince, Michael Jackson and the stars of disco, I was a bona fide mainstream radio "superstar."

Sometimes records dictate their own personalities and you just have to let them be. That was *Born in the USA*. I finally stopped doing my hesitation shuffle, took the best of what I had and signed off on what would be the biggest album of my career. *Born in the USA* changed my life, gave me my largest audience, forced me to think harder about the way I presented my music and set me briefly at the center of the pop world.

# FORTY-SEVEN

# BUONA FORTUNA, FRATELLO MIO

Halfway through recording the biggest record of my life, Steve Van Zandt left the band. I've always felt a combination of personal frustration, internal politics and unhappiness with some of my decisions led to Steve's departure. That along with my closeness to Jon Landau left my friend feeling distant from his pal and the direction my work'd taken me. Though I would have never gotten where I am without the E Street Band, it is ultimately my stage. By thirty-two, Steve needed to take his own long-deserved shot at the title, fronting his group and playing and singing his own songs. Steve is one of the best songwriters, guitarists and bandleaders I've ever known and the timing must've felt to him like now or never. Looking back, I think Steve would agree it didn't have to be that way. We could've done it all, but we weren't the same people then that we are today. I was still very protective over my right to self-determination and proprietary over my career. I would listen, but I didn't consider what we were engaged in a "partnership," and Steve, back then, was an everything-or-nothing kind of guy. That's always been my pal's blessing and his curse . . . mostly his curse. The night he left, he visited me in my New York City hotel room. A very difficult discussion about our friendship, his position in the band, past grievances and our future together was had. There were certain things we could not agree upon We were still pretty young and without the perspective time can bring to smooth out the rough spots. We had no overview to help us see the beauty and full value of our long friendship. What we did have was a lot of passion, transferred emotion and misunderstanding.

That evening Steve asked for a fuller role in our creative relationship, but I'd intentionally set limits on people's roles within the group. The E Street Band is so filled with talent, no one gets to use but a small percentage of their abilities at any one time, so naturally, there was some frustration felt by everyone, Jon included. But this was how I shaped my work, kept my hands on the reins and my ship tight. I was an easygoing guy but I had hard boundaries dictated by both my creative instincts and my psychological strengths and frailties. Steve's frustrations were intensified by his sizable ego (join the club!), his underutilized talents and our lengthy friendship. He was extremely dedicated to me and our band, and probably felt some guilt and confusion from his own ambition and desire to move to the front.

In the teen clubs of our youth, we'd been not only friends but friendly competitors. It was good. But as we began to work together, this was probably something that neither of us was completely comfortable with or up front about. Steve had given himself completely to his role at my side and had long been an ambivalent front man. One night at the Inkwell, when Southside Johnny was originally signed to a record deal (before Steve joined the E Street Band), I questioned Steve about why *he* simply didn't perform and record the great songs he'd written for Southside, himself. (Don't worry, Southside, you did good.) Since we were young, I'd watched Steve masterfully front his own bands. That evening, he said it just wasn't completely "him," and a big and wonderful part of Steve's personality (and my good fortune) was his vision of himself in a premier but supportive role as my musical lieutenant.

But now, Steve's move to the center mike would be complicated further by those very years he'd spent at my side in the E Street Band. It's hard for an audience to accept you in a new role, to hear you without the veil of the established popular image that comes with being a part of a successful group. I understood Steve's position. He wanted more influence in our work. But I'd gently played him and Jon off each other for a purpose. It was why they were *both* there. I wanted the tension of two complementarily conflicting points of view. It bred a little intended professional friction in the studio and perhaps some unintended *personal* friction outside of it, but that was the way I needed it. We were all big boys, very dedicated, and I figured everyone could handle it. They did. But this, along with the intentional gray area I kept the band in, created a purgatory *I* was happy with but, perhaps, confused and unsettled some of my bandmates. Each band member and every fan probably has their own definition of who and what we are (and for most, we're probably just Bruce Springsteen . . . *and* the E Street Band), but at the end of the day, I get, and got, to *officially* decide. From the day I walked alone (and very aware of what I was doing) into John Hammond's office, that'd been the setup.

These questions, along with the maelstrom of emotions they brought forth, were at the heart of Steve's and my estrangement and his absence from the band during the eighties and nineties. I loved and deeply love Steve. As we parted that night, he paused for a moment at the door. Filled with concern over the loss of my friend and right-hand man, I said that despite where we were headed, I was still the best friend he had, we were still *each other's* great friends, and I hoped we would not let that go. We didn't.

FORTY-EIGHT

# THE BIG
# BIG TIME

*Born in the USA* went nuclear. I knew I had a real runner in the title cut but I didn't expect the massive wave of response we received. Was it timing? The music? The muscles? I dunno, it's always a bit of a mystery when something breaks that big. At thirty-four, I decided to ride it out and enjoy it. I'd grown strong and knew how to withstand the spotlight, but over the next few years, I'd be rigorously tested.

Nils Lofgren came aboard and filled a difficult position perfectly. Our paths had first crossed in 1970 at the Fillmore West auditions, then again at the Bottom Line in 1975, where Nils was booked following our stand. One afternoon in the early eighties we'd run into each other at the Sunset Marquis. With an empty afternoon in front of us, we took a drive north along the California coastline and stopped roadside off Highway 1. We climbed to the top of a sand dune looking out over the sparkling Pacific, sat and talked.

He'd had a run of misfortune with his record companies; solo work was a tough grind and he imagined someday he wouldn't mind moonlighting in a great band. (I think he mentioned Bad Company.) This was long before the position in our band came open, but I'd always remembered our afternoon conversation. Nils had been poised for stardom just as we began recording *Born to Run*, and Jon and I had referenced Nils's first solo album for our sessions. We strove for its sharpness, cleanness and great drum sound. It became a part of our blueprint for *Born to Run*. Nils's early career caught some bad breaks and he never reached the broader audience his talents merited. He was a voracious student, one of the world's great rock guitarists, with a voice like a rebel choirboy, and his wonderful stage presence took some of the sting out of Steve's absence and was a perfect addition to the 1985 revamp of the E Street Band.

## Bar-Hoppin' Mama

One crowded evening I stood in front of the stage at the Stone Pony as a young redhead joined the house band, took the mike, then smoked and sassed her way through the Exciters' "Tell Him." She had a voice filled with the blues, jazz, country and the great girl groups of the sixties. Patti Scialfa had it all. We met, flirted, had a drink and became bar pals. I'd drop by the Pony, where we'd have a cocktail and a dance. The night would end up with her riding shotgun on my lap as Matt drove us for an after-hours cheeseburger and chat at the Inkwell. Around three a.m. Matt and I dropped her off at her mom's; a few smiles, a kiss on the cheek, a "See you at the club," and the night would come to a close.

After Steve left, I decided we needed to raise the bar on our harmony singing. I listened to a few local voices and invited Patti to an "audition" at my home (along with Richie "La Bamba" Rosenberg; oh, the choices one must make). That was followed by an audition rehearsal, while we were preparing for our tour, on the Clair Brothers soundstage in Lititz, Pennsylvania. The band holed up at the local motel, rehearsed in the afternoon and hung out in the evening. I drove around in my 1963 convertible Impala, "Dedication," a gift from Gary US Bonds for writing and helping produce, with Steve, his comeback hit, "This Little Girl." The night before we headed home, after a dinner, I had the whole band in the car, the convertible top down and Garry Tallent at the wheel. As we crested a hill Patti and I, sitting in the rear, heads leaning back, drinking in the night sky, heard a collective "oooh" rise from the guys as the blue trail of a shooting star cut the Pennsylvania sky in half. A good omen, all the way around.

Three days before we hit the road, Patti Scialfa joined the E Street Band. As the first woman in the band, she sent shock waves through the troops, broke the boys' club, and everybody had to adjust, some more than others. Make no mistake, a rock band is a tight-knit, rigid little society with very specific rituals and unspoken rules. It is *designed* to ward off the world outside, and particularly *adult* life. The E Street Band carried its own muted misogyny (including my own), a very prevalent quality amongst rock groups of our generation. By 1984, we were a much tempered version of our earlier incarnations, but scratch the surface and the "way of the road" with all its pleasures, prejudices and punishments would slither into view. Patti handled all of this exceedingly gracefully. She neither displaced nor ceded her place to my dedicated and long-standing bandmates.

Through Patti's addition, I wanted to accomplish two things. One, I wanted to improve our musicality. I wanted dependable, well-sung harmony vocals. Two, I wanted my band to reflect my evolving audience, an audience that was becoming increasingly grown-up and whose lives were about men *and* women. It was a tricky course to chart, for at the end of the day, a big part of rock music continues to be its value as escapist entertainment. It's a house of dreams, of illusions, delusions, of role-playing and artist–audience transference. In my line of work, you serve at the behest of your audience's imagination. That's a very personal place. Once you've left your fingerprints there, crossing that imagination can have grave consequences (disillusionment, or worse . . . loss of record and ticket sales!). But in 1984, I wanted, on my stage, that world of men *and* women; so, I hoped, would my audience.

## Opening Night

June 29, 1984, the Civic Center, St. Paul, Minnesota. We'd spent the afternoon filming "Dancing in the Dark," our first formal music video. We'd released one video previously, for "Atlantic City," a beautiful black-and-white short, directed by Arnold Levine, but neither I nor the group appeared in it. I'd always been a little superstitious about filming the band. I believed the magician should not observe his trick too closely; he might forget where his magic lay. But MTV had arrived, was potent, pragmatic and demanded tribute. Suddenly we were in the short-film business and new skills would be needed. Videos happen fast: an afternoon, a day, then it's in the hands of the director and editor and there's no going back. It's a medium that's more dependent on collaboration than record making, and *a lot* of money can be burned in a short time. The finished product can only be indirectly controlled by the recording artist. To do it well, you need a team of directors, editors, art directors, stylists, who get what you're about and can help you translate that to the screen. It had taken me fifteen years to put together a record production team that could do that for me; now I'd have to raise a complete film team in fifteen minutes. Still, the times and ambition demanded it. This collection of songs, accompanied by Bob Clearmountain's mixes and Annie Leibovitz's images and cover photo, reached farther for a mass audience than I'd ever done before.

You never completely control the arc of your career. Events, historical and cultural, create an opportunity; a special song falls into your lap and a window for impact, communication, success, the expansion of your musical vision, opens. It may close as quickly, never to return. You don't get to completely decide *when* it's your time. You may have worked unwaveringly, honestly, all the while—consciously or unconsciously—positioning your-self, but you never really *know* if your "big" moment will come. Then, for the few, *it's there*.

The night I counted the band into "Born in the USA," we kicked one of those windows wide open, a big one. A breeze rife with possibility, danger, success, humiliation, failure, lightly drifts in and rustles your hair. You look at that open window. Should you step closer? Should you look through? Should you lift yourself up and take the measure of the world being revealed? Should you climb through and drop down, feet on un-known terrain? Should you step forward? Those are big choices for the best musicians, and I know great ones who turned them down, tempered them, took another route, made highly influential music and had important ca-reers. The big road isn't the only road. It's just the *big* road.

So here I am, on the big road, and standing in front of me is Brian De Palma, a friend of Jon's. The director of *The Untouchables*, *Scarface* and many other great films, is here to give us a leg up on "Dancing in the Dark." We had a false start a week or two previous with another director, so Brian's come to make sure justice is done to what will turn out to be my greatest hit. He introduces me to a pixie-ish, dazzlingly blue-eyed young girl in a freshly minted *Born in the USA* shirt, deposits her at the front of the stage and says, "At the end of the song, pull her up onstage and dance with her." He's the director. So a baby-child Courteney Cox takes her cue, while I white-man boogaloo and daddy-shuffle my way to the number two spot on the *Billboard* charts. Until Brian told me later he'd chosen her from a casting call in New York City, I thought she was a fan! (A star was born . . . make that two!)

We were held out of the number one spot only by Prince's "When Doves Cry." We would make many videos in the future—I'd even come to enjoy them—but none would ever elicit the same knee-slapping guffaws and righteous, rolling laughter from my kids as me doing my Jersey James Brown in "Dancing in the Dark." ("*Dad . . . you look ridiculous!*")

Ridiculous or not, we were soon, once again, to be the biggest thing since the last big thing. Our video complete, it was now time for the easy work. Three hours of fire-breathing rock 'n' roll. Opening night for her first appearance as an E Streeter, Patti was, to say the least, "lightly rehearsed." We just hadn't had the time. A mere few hours before the show, a small monitor and a microphone were positioned for her somewhere between Roy and Max. It was a jig rig. Wardrobe? The *Born in the USA* tour was notable for the sartorial horror sweeping E Street nation. The band has never looked and dressed so bad. I'd grown weary of being a wardrobe Nazi, coordinating the men into what was supposed to look like an effortless, unified front. In '84, I abandoned everyone to their worst instincts and they came through glowingly. The eighties ruled! C's Gap Band box cut, Nils's bandana and satin jockey jacket, Max's perm, Roy's Cosby sweaters, and my soon-to-be-iconic bandana and pumped muscles. Looking back on these photos now, I look simply . . . gay. I probably would have fit right in down on Christopher Street in any one of the leather bars. We were all certainly united—united to strike fear into the heart of the nearest hipper-than-thou stylist. It varied from night to night, and some evenings approached tolerable, but all in all, "fashion" mayhem reigned. Most bands are at their most visually iconic when they are sitting on the borderline of caricature (or slightly over it). By 1984, we were working those fields, and I still see teenagers and young men, who couldn't have even been a glint in Mom and Pop's eyes in '84, at my shows in headbands and sleeveless shirts today. They're cute.

With five minutes to go to St. Paul showtime, Patti knocks on my dressing room door. She enters wearing a pair of jeans and a simple white peasant blouse. "How's this?" she asks with a smile. I pause; I've never had to do this before, critique a woman's stage gear. I'm a little nervous . . . "Uhhhh," I'm thinking to myself, "she looks kind of . . . *girly*. I want a woman in the band, but I don't want her to *look* like one!" I notice at my feet my small Samsonite suitcase stuffed with my T-shirts. I kick it open and, smiling, say, "Just pick one of these!"

The show starts and Nils immediately fucks up his first solo. It's

Patti's and his debut with the band, there are twenty thousand screaming Minnesotans and despite all his experience, he's caught briefly, a deer in the headlights. He goes red, we laugh it off, he settles in and aces the rest of the evening. It's a great night. Patti looks terrific (in my T-shirt!) and does beautifully under difficult conditions. Our new edition is battle ready and prepared for what lies ahead.

## Pittsburgh, Pennsylvania

On the evening of our show in Pittsburgh, I declined the compliment paid me earlier in the day by President Reagan. His attention elicited from me two responses. The first was . . . "Fucker!" The second was, "The president said my name!" Or maybe it was the other way around. The important thing that happened that night was I met Ron Weisen, ex-steelworker and radical union organizer, who'd just opened a food bank for steelworkers laid off by the closing of the mills in the Monongahela Valley. I didn't grow up in a political household. Beyond asking my mother our party affiliation ("We're Demo-crats, they're for the working people") I don't remember a political discussion ever being held. I did grow up a child of the sixties, so social conscience and political interest were bred into my cultural DNA. But it was really the iden-tity questions that became prominent after my success that spurred me to be a voice on the forces that'd impacted my parents', my sisters' and my neighbors' lives. If you're thirsty, you go where the water is, and by now I knew some of the answers and questions I'd been looking for lay in the political arena.

Dylan had deftly melded the political and personal in a way that added resonance and power to both. I agreed the political *is* personal and vice versa. My music had been developing in that direction for quite a while, and the confluence of the Reagan presidency with my history, musical direction and meeting people whose boots were on the ground stimulated my interest in integrating all these elements into a cohesive whole. That night in Pitts-burgh, I met and talked with Ron, and he filled me in on the tough times people were suffering in the valley. As with the Vietnam vets, we were able to provide some publicity and financial support. Before he left, he mentioned a counterpart in central LA. Once in Los Angeles, I reached George Cole and met poet Luis Rodriguez, both ex-steelworkers in south-central Los Angeles, a little-known major steelmaking corner in Southern California. George and his organization had a food bank and a traveling political theater company. With the help of my assistant manager, Barbara Carr, we slowly began to network with organizations in other towns.

The national food bank system was just getting under way and over the coming years and tours, they'd allow us to bring to our audience local sources and workable solutions for battling poverty and hunger and harnessing political action in the places we passed through. These were modest and simple efforts but we were in prime position to accomplish them.

I never had the frontline courage of many of my more committed musical brethren. If anything, over the years, too much has been made of whatever service we've provided. But I did look to develop a consistent approach. Something I could follow year in and year out, and find a way to assist the folks who'd been hit hardest by systematic neglect and injustice. These were the families who'd built America and yet whose dreams and children were, generation after generation, considered expendable. Our travels and position would allow us to support, at the grassroots level, activists who dealt, day to day, with the citizens who'd been shuffled to the margins of American life.

# White Man's Paradise
# (Little Steven vs. Mickey Mouse)

Our first stop in Los Angeles for the *USA* tour was marked by the visitation of Little Steven Van Zandt and the two of us with our "entourage" being unceremoniously thrown out of Disneyland for refusing to remove our bandanas. It went like this: Steve is the biggest kid I know. For days we'd planned on a trip together to the Magic Kingdom. As we neared it, Steve's excitement rose to light hysteria (not too great a leap from his daily demeanor). Space Mountain! The Haunted House! The Pirates of the Caribbean! We were going to do it all. I was accompanied by "first fan" Obie Dziedzic, who'd followed us since we were sixteen back on the Shore. Today, her reward would be bestowed upon her. A trip with Steve, Maureen (Steve's wife) and myself, to, as the sign says, "THE HAPPIEST PLACE ON EARTH."

We buy our tickets. Steve, giggling excitedly, can't wait and enters through the turnstiles first. He proceeds approximately thirty feet inside, where he is stopped, asked to step aside and told that in order to remain in the park, he will need to remove his bandana. This, say the powers that be, is so he will not be misidentified as a gang member, Blood or Crip, and fall victim to a drive-by while hurling his cookies on Space Mountain. Steve's bandana is neither red nor blue but an indeterminate hue, chosen carefully and precisely to complement the rest of his "look" by the man who invented the male babushka. So the removal of such . . . I wish to enlighten Mickey's storm troopers . . . is . . . NOT FUCKIN' GONNA HAPPEN! In solidarity, I, sporting my *Born in the USA* do-rag, also refuse to remove my head scarf. The main honcho of the several security guards now gathering around us then tells us that he will "overlook" the way the rest of our crowd looks (Steve's wife! and number one fan Obie!) but *we* simply cannot be allowed to stay wearing our current headgear.

"WE'RE OUTTA HERE! SCREW YOU, FASCIST MOUSE! WE'RE GOING TO KNOTT'S BERRY FARM!" And we do.

On the way over, I ask Steve how he feels having just been thrown out of "THE HAPPIEST PLACE ON EARTH" and I draw his notice to the fact that we, obviously, do not deserve that degree of happiness! Steve is now a shouting one-man thesaurus of every conceivable four-letter word and guttural obscenity, all directed at Mickey's right-wing sartorial hit squad and the cabal that's keeping an eye on Mr. Disney's white man's paradise. Upon reaching Knott's Berry Farm, *before* we buy our tickets, we are enlightened by our ticket taker that our bandana-laden skulls are not going to get in here either! FUCK YOU! and all of sunny Southern California.

Silently, morosely, we drive back to Los Angeles and for two solid hours, Steve pours it on. The Constitution! The Bill of Rights! Fucking dress codes! Nazis! "I'm going with this on NATIONAL TELEVISION!" . . . blah, blah, blah. We decide to catch a late dinner at Mirabelle, a lovely restaurant on Sunset Boulevard. As we stand at the bar, the owner, a friend, dressed in a suit, comes up for some convivial chatting. Steve, still going, says, "You don't have a dress code in here, do you?" He looks at us and answers, "Of course I do. Do you think I'd let you guys in here if I didn't know you?"

## Little Girl, I Want to Marry You

A while earlier: I was thirty-four, far enough out of Catholic school to have shimmied off some of the carnal shame and guilt that came with my Italian/ Irish Catholic upbringing. I figured now was the time to take advantage of the sexual perks of superstardom. Generally a serial monogamist, I never looked too hard for company on the road. First, I wasn't out there to party. I was there to *work*, and too much fun would get in the way of the hair shirt I insisted on wearing. Secular penance was my joy and raison d'être. Still, all work and no play, etc., etc., etc. Wilt Chamberlain would not have to start looking over his shoulder any time soon but at the beginning of the *USA* tour I decided to . . . *see*. So . . . I *saw*. I generally adhered to a "don't fuck with the civilians" code when I did, but I had no time for the "professional groupies" either. I did not want to be a notch on someone's belt. That diminished the field quite a bit. Still, where there's a will . . . I make no claims on sainthood, a thrill's a thrill, and I've occasionally taken mine where I found them, but . . . I didn't last long, it just wasn't worth it! So, with the occasional exceptional evening and *company* excluded, after each show I returned to my late-night bacchanal of fried chicken, french fries, TV, a book

(choosing not Frank's but Dino's way), then bed. Let the good times . . .
zzzzzzzzzzzzzzz . . .

After my short shot at being Casanova, my psychological/biological clock must have been ticking. I wanted something serious. I wanted to get married. By now, I knew my model came with a sexual catch-22, not quite right for the confines of monogamy but no libertine either. I operated best within a semi-monogamous (is there such a thing?) system, generally holding firm and steady, but occasionally deploying the United States military's "don't ask, don't tell" policy. That's a hard sell.

In Los Angeles I met Julianne Phillips, an actress out of the Pacific Northwest. She was twenty-four, tall, blond, educated, talented, a beautiful and charming young woman. We hit it off and began seeing each other regularly. Six months into our dating, I proposed on my cottage balcony in Laurel Canyon. We were married in Lake Oswego, Oregon, where a scene straight out of a Preston Sturges film unfolded. Our pending betrothal had leaked and the little town exploded. At Julianne's house, the ten-year-old kid next door climbed on his garage roof with a cardboard box camera and junior-paparazzi'd our wedding party munching hot dogs in the backyard. He sold it to the newspapers for skateboard money and overnight became a local celebrity. Once we took out our marriage license, the press feeding frenzy was on. The local priest got a special dispensation from his bishop to let us marry without the required time to kick the tires. He asked us twenty questions, and we were signed, sealed and delivered to the Catholic church (Al Pacino, *The Godfather Part III*: "Just when I thought I was out, they pull me back in").

We got married at midnight, hoodwinking the sea of press. The next day, whirlybirds, jammed with tabloid photographers, filled the sky over our reception brunch. My dad sat smoking at a picnic table, looking as if he'd been lifted by a crane out of his California kitchen and set down unruffled in a field in Lake Oswego. I kept constant company with Mr. Jack Daniel's and my old man was my only relief, for short of a planet-demolishing apocalypse nothing could ever change his kitchen-table demeanor. As the choppers buzzed overhead, I walked over and took a seat across from him at the brown plank table. He sat, his suit straining his girth, like it'd been sewn on over a rhinoceros; took a long drag on his Camel cigarette; and deadpanned, "Bruce . . . look what you've done now."

Julie and I honeymooned in Hawaii and set up house in my Los Angeles cottage. Things were good; she pursued her career, I pursued my music and we pursued our life together. The only thing eating at me was I knew I'd never made it past a two-or-three-year period in any of my other relationships. Usually, that was when the image of myself, physically and emotionally, would be punctured, and my flaws revealed. I was broken and so sadly punctual, my mom would rag me about it ("Bruce, it's been two years!"). So now, in the dead of night, my contented sleep would occasionally be disturbed by the dreaded ticking, emanating as from the belly of Hook's alligator, of my "clock."

I suppose I should've advertised myself as damaged goods but I decided I couldn't let that knowledge or my fears dictate my actions or negate my feelings. I had to go on faith that I could love someone, *this* one, and find the resources to make it work. Following our wedding I was struck by a series of severe anxiety attacks I fought my way through with my doctor's help. I tried to hide them as best I could and that was a mistake. I also had (shades of my pop) paranoid delusions that scared me.

One evening, while I sat across from my beautiful wife in an upscale Los Angeles eatery, a conversation formed silently inside my head. There, as we politely chatted by candlelight, hand in hand, a part of me tried to convince myself that she was simply using me to further her career or to get . . . something. Nothing could've been farther from the truth. Julianne loved me and didn't have an exploitive or malicious bone in her body. Inside, I knew that, but I was out where the buses don't run and couldn't center myself around the truth.

I was sliding back toward the chasm where rage, fear, distrust, insecurity and a family-patented misogyny made war with my better angels. Once again, it was the fear of *having* something, allowing someone into my life, someone loving, that was setting off a myriad of bells and whistles and a fierce reaction. Who'd care for me, love me? The real me. The me I knew who resided inside my easygoing façade. I became hypersexual, then non-sexual, suffered multiple anxiety attacks and swung from one side of the graph of funky human behavior to the other, all the while trying to keep a lid on it. I was scared, but I did *not* want to scare the wits out of my young bride. It was the wrong way to handle it and created a psychological distance at just the moment I was trying to let someone into my life.

Julie was already sleeping one evening as I came to bed. There, in the darkness, the bedside lamp caught a glint of my wedding ring. I'd never taken it off; something inside of me told me I never would, never should. I sat on the edge of the bed, gave it a light tug and watched as it slid off my finger. An ocean of despair swept over me and I felt faint. My pulse leapt and I could feel my heart threatening to push through my chest. I got up, made my way to the bathroom, ran cold water over my face and neck, then, gathering myself, beneath the bathroom's fluorescent light, I slipped my ring back on. I walked back into the shadows of our bedroom, a room containing all my mysteries and fears, where my lovely wife lay in bed, her body just an outline, a dark, gentle ridge of tousled covers. I placed my hand upon her shoulders, moved my palm over her cheek, breathed in, felt the air return to my lungs, pulled back the sheets, climbed in and went to sleep.

## Europe

June 1, 1985, Slane Castle, Dublin, Ireland, our first stadium show, *ever*. Precariously perched in a field fifty miles outside of Dublin were ninety-five thousand people. The largest crowd I'd ever seen. They completely filled a grassy bowl bounded by the Boyne River at our stage's rear and Slane Castle, perched in front on a high green knoll, in the distance. The crowd closest to the stage, an immediate couple of thousand, were deeply into their Guinness and dangerously swaying from left to right. They were opening up gaping holes amongst themselves as audience members by the dozens fell to the muddy ground, vanishing for unbearable seconds 'til righted once again by their neighbors. Then, once standing, they'd slosh back the other way and the whole interminable, nerve-grinding exercise would be repeated again, ad infinitum. It was a sight way too hairy for my tender eyes. I thought somebody was going to get killed and it'd be my fault.

At stage right, Pete Townshend and a variety of rock luminaries bemusedly watched me break into the big time. At stage left stood my wife; this was our first trip together as a married couple and I felt like I was going to come apart before her eyes. I was singing, I was playing, I was *thinking* . . . "I can't stand up here and sing these songs, not *these* songs, while putting people in a situation where they could be grievously injured." I kept singing, I kept playing, but I was in a pure rage and simmering panic. Okay, Mr. Big Time . . . how'd you get here?

We broke for intermission. I was seething. Mr. Landau joined me in my trailer during intermission and there, in the middle of the biggest concert of my life, we had a highly charged debate about canceling the entire tour. I could not face what was happening in front of the stage at Slane on a nightly basis. It was irresponsible and violated the protective instinct for my audience I prided myself on. Fans were pouring, red faced, soaked in booze and heat exhaustion, over the front barriers to be taken to the medical tent or to flank the crowd, throw themselves back in and take another crack at it. Our insistence on having seats at our concerts had begun in the early seventies, after I stood, hidden, at the side of the bleachers in a college gymnasium one evening and witnessed the cattle rush to the front of the stage. I didn't like the way it looked. I'd made my compromises with European local customs over the years, but this was something else.

Keep in mind this was the first and only stadium show I'd ever performed *or* attended. I had nothing but this night to judge my decisions upon. Jon wisely counseled we postpone our decision until we had at least a few more concerts to judge by. (We'd already committed to, and sold out, the entire tour.) He was frightened also, and said if it was a recurring situation, he'd honor my feelings; we'd cancel and take the heat. It never happened again. The crowd settled during the second half of the Slane show and I observed there was a sketchy but ritual orderliness to what appeared from the stage to be pure chaos. The crowd protected one another. If you fell, the nearest person to your left or right reached down, grabbed an arm and pulled you upright. It wasn't pretty (or, to my eye, safe), but it worked. The other ninety-three thousand gatherers were clueless about the soul-searching minidrama being played out right before their eyes. To them, it was just a beautiful day with a rocking band. In the end, Slane joined a rising number of our other performances to attain "legendary" status and, despite my distraction, turned out to be a solid show. On the streets of Dublin, it is often mentioned to me. If you were there, you were *there*. I was certainly there.

## Newcastle, England

At our *second* stadium show, it was all sunshine and smiles. The band, already growing more confident in the bigger venues, played spiritedly, and a safe, festive atmosphere prevailed. Question dismissed. We *could* play stadiums, but I never forgot my experience at Slane. Short note: When a crowd of that size gathers, particularly a young crowd, danger is always in the air. It's simply a matter of the math. An unexpected mishap, a little hysteria, and the day can shift hard and very quickly. Over the years, we've been careful and lucky at our stadium concerts. Some very well-intentioned and serious-hearted musicians, who carry a deep commitment to their fans, haven't been as fortunate. Today's stadium concerts are thoroughly organized but still, in those numbers, the potential for danger always lurks.

## Headaches and Headlines

We traveled on. The tour became complicated by several issues. Since my marriage, I'd suddenly become tabloid news fodder. In a Scandinavian newspaper, the day after we checked out of our local digs, I was shown a picture of Julie's and my bed. We weren't in it. It was just a picture of a freshly made bed. It was new, unsettling and a pain in the ass. Photographers were everywhere.

In Gothenburg, Sweden, things got broke. We were either confined in our hotel or followed by a pack of paparazzi wherever we went. This was *not* what I'd signed up for. I was a private person and not comfortable with my personal life in the spotlight. What I wanted most, when I didn't have a hundred thousand eyes *on* me, was all eyes *off* me. In the second half of the twentieth century, in the public arena, this was not a deal you could cut. Fuggeddaboutit! So you took your blessings and accepted the fact that this nuisance was the price you'd paid for . . . *getting everything you ever wanted*! In '84, beneath the white-hot spotlight, during the whitest-hot moment of my career, this sanity-inducing knowledge was not yet in my possession . . . so.

A shiny, new, black Takamine acoustic guitar was whizzing within inches of the thinning hair on my trusted amigo Jon Landau's pate. As it skimmed over his few remaining hairs, he startled but remained impressively calm. Then the atonal twang of rock 'n' roll bells ringing, the splintering crack of dead midnight in the house of a thousand guitars, filled the backstage halls as my Takamine burst into a million pieces on the wall of my Gothenburg dressing room. Unless you're Pete Townshend, I do not generally counsel or condone the demolishing of perfectly good musical instruments. I would go so far as to say wrecking the righteous tools of Mr. Gibson, Mr. Fender or any other craftsman of fine guitars is near sacrilege. But when a healthy insanity calls, you do what you must. I'd had it just about up to here with the whole merry-go-round I'd just jumped on. Plus, I had no way of knowing if this was going to be my life, my *whole* life, everywhere I'd go, day after day, country after country, bed after bed, in a *Groundhog Day* of stultifying, inane attention, brought on by my own sacred ambitions crossed by the normal human longing for life and love. Would there eventually be one thousand pictures of freshly made beds my wife and I had slept in, printed, published and preyed on? There would not. But at that moment, on that day, who could guess?

Mr. Landau, who'd simply been trying to bring a little perspective to my predicament, quietly moved back from his friend, the guitar smasher, and out into the hall. There he joined many others, who at that moment were glad they did not have his job.

After my guitar Armageddon, we went out and proceeded to literally destroy the Ullevi stadium. The jumping up and down and synchronized twisting of so many gonzo Swedes during "Twist and Shout" cracked its concrete foundation. That'll teach 'em.

# FORTY-NINE

# GOING HOME

The European leg of our tour spun on without a hitch, the seats full, the crowds rapturous. We'd grown comfortable in the expanded environs of the stadiums that had become our workplace. Our anthems were built to fill and *communicate* in places of this size, so from Timbuktu to New Jersey, crowds dropped one by one to the powerhouse show we'd started developing overseas. Some cities stood out: three shows, centered around the Fourth of July, drew seventy thousand fans a night (with Steve dropping by to sit in) to London's Wembley Stadium. Our debut in Italy, the motherland, brought us to Milan's eighty-thousand-seat stadium. We walked down its damp, dim, gladiatorial tunnels with the distant ear-shredding sound of eighty thousand Italians rising, louder and louder, until we broke onto the sunlit field. A cheer rose that sounded like we'd just returned from the

Crusades with our vanquished enemies' heads held high on the necks of our guitars (or perhaps we were just about to be fed to the lions).

Walking amid the thunder toward the ramp leading to stage front, I noticed an entire section of empty seats. Our promoter at my side, I said, "I thought the show was sold out." He answered, "It is. Those seats are for the people who are going to break in!" Got it. And so they did. We hung huge video screens on the outside of the stadium to satisfy those unable to attend, but that only held them for a little while. Gates were rushed, security was breached and soon all "seats" were full, and then some. I stood in front of the mind-bending hysteria I'd come to realize passes for a normal reaction from an Italian audience as women blew kisses and cried, men cried and blew kisses, and all pledged undying love and beat their hearts with their fists. Some grew faint. We hadn't even started playing yet! When the band crashed into "Born in the USA," world's end seemed near; the stadium shook and swayed as we played for our lives. *Marone!*

Back in the USA, our show at Pittsburgh's Three Rivers Stadium proved unique. A crowd of sixty thousand Steelers fans got to watch me count off "Born in the USA" while several key members of the E Street Band, Roy and Nils, were cluelessly locked in deadly battle on our backstage Ping-Pong table! My testosterone-drenched "One, two, three, four" and the sound of Max's crushing snare were met not by Roy's massive synth riff but by Danny Federici's tinkling glockenspiel! New records were set in the quarter mile by Nils and Roy as they listened to the most heart-sinking syllables of their lives, the distant stadium-echoing, "Your ass is in a sling and I'm going to burn that fucking Ping-Pong table DOWN!," incredulous "One, two, three, four" of their front man. I watched sixty thousand faces go from awe to aw-shit as I stood, not too happy, pants metaphorically around my ankles, experiencing one of the greatest weenie-shrinkers of all time. Ping-Pong tables were banned for years. Heads rolled.

Giants Stadium: six sold-out shows to three hundred thousand of our

New Jersey faithful brought the tour's size and significance home. My people. Never the hottest audience on our tours (it's hard to beat those Europeans!), but damn, they show up *and* they are my life-giving, loving homies.

In Texas, an infestation of locusts the size of your thumb swooped like World War II dogfighters around and over our heads during the show. On a cool night, they'd been drawn to the warmth of the stage lights and gathered in congregation on every available inch of our bandstand. Nils (a bug-o-phobe) ran skittering to Danny's organ riser. One went eye-to-eye with me perched on my microphone stand, popped to my hair and, during "My Hometown," slowly crawled down the neck of my shirt to sit in the center of my back. Thousands littered the stage, to be swept away by long brooms at intermission time. It was biblical.

A short while later we were greeted by snow and thirty-degree temperatures at our show in Denver, Colorado's Mile High Stadium. The audience, in ski jackets, carrying blankets, came dressed for a winter football game. We cut off the fingers of our gloves to play our guitars through, did what we could to stay warm and froze our asses off. Steam rose in plumes from our shoulders as hot sweat met freezing air. About three-quarters of the way through our three hours, you could feel the cold coming in for the kill, settling in your bones. Once I put my guitar down, my fingers went numb and couldn't be revived; every syllable I sang left a cloud of visible breath streaming from my lungs. On to sunny, warm Los Angeles!

September 27, 1985, the Los Angeles Memorial Coliseum, site of the 1984 Olympics. Our finale was a four-night wrap party. Hard blue skies and balmy temperatures greeted the band and eighty thousand Los Angelenos. The band peaked amid an atmosphere of end-of-the-road celebration. We were now one of the biggest, if not *the* biggest, rock attractions in the world and to get there we hadn't lost sight of what we were about. There were some close shaves, and in the future I'd have to be doubly vigilant about the way my music was used and interpreted, but all in all, we'd come through intact, united and ready to press on.

## Where Do We Go from Here?

Julianne and I returned home to our cottage in LA and I felt great . . . for two whole days. On day three, I crashed. What do I do now? Jon visited and mentioned the tour had been very successful . . . *economically* successful, so successful, in fact, I would need to meet my accountant. My accountant? I'd never met him (or her) . . . ever! Fourteen years into my professional recording career, I'd never met those whose job it was to count my money . . . and watch it. Soon I would shake the hand of a Mr. Gerald Breslauer, who would tell me I had earned a figure that at the time sounded so outrageous I had to ban it from thought. Not that I wasn't happy; I was—giddy, in fact. But I couldn't contextualize it in any meaningful way. So I didn't. My first luxury as a successful rock icon would be the luxury to not think about, to downright ignore, my luxuries (some of them). Worked for me!

The aftermath of the *Born in the USA* tour was a strange time. It was the peak of something. I would never be here, this high, in the mainstream pop firmament again. It was the end of something. For all intents and purposes, my work with the E Street Band was done (for now). We would tour together once more on my solo record *Tunnel of Love*, but I would intentionally use the band in such a way as to cloud its former identity. I didn't know it then but soon we'd be finished for a long while. The tour also was the beginning of something, a final surge to try to determine my life as an adult, a family man, and to escape the road's seductions and confinements. I longed to finally settle in, in a real home, with a real love. I wanted to lift upon my shoulders the weight and bounty of maturity, then try to carry it with some grace and humility. I'd worked to get married; now, would I have the skills, the ability . . . to be married?

# FIFTY

# *REGRESAR A MÉXICO*

Right before the *Born in the USA* tour, I bought a home in the Republican stronghold of Rumson, New Jersey, only minutes from the plot of sand that once held the old Surf and Sea Beach Club, where we "townies" had been spit on by the children of my new neighbors. The house was a rambling old Georgian-style "mansion" on the corner of Bellevue Avenue and Ridge Road. I went through my usual buyer's remorse, but I held out, promising myself I'd fill the big old house with what I'd been searching for: family and a life. One morning I received a phone call from my father. This was unprecedented. The man who banned telephones from our home for nineteen years, if alive today, would never be in any danger of maxing out his minutes. I'd never received a phone call directly from my dad so I was apprehensive. I called California.

An unusual buoyancy was in his voice. "Hi, Bruce!" He wanted to go to Mexico on a fishing trip. My pop, who hadn't had a line in the water for the past twenty-five years, dating back to the two of us moping (fishing, *not* catching) at the end of the Manasquan jetty, now wanted to Ernest Hemingway it and go marlin fishing. The only marlin the old man had ever been close to would've been the one hanging over the bar at his favorite watering hole, but with the exception of our previous Mexican run to Tijuana, my dad had never asked me to go anywhere. Amused by his enthusiasm, flattered and curious, I listened to his pitch. Somewhere inside still lingered my hunger for that second (third? fourth? fifth?) chance with the old man where all would go right. I said, "Sure." I asked him if he needed me to make any arrangements and he proudly said he and his neighbor Tom (my pop's only male friend of the past fifteen years) had "taken care of it all." "This one's on me," he jauntily responded. What could I say?

A few weeks later, I flew to San Francisco and drove to Burlingame, California. There on a windy hill, bordering Silicon Valley, the Oakland Bay in the distance, was my folks' new residence and answer to their "gold rush" of '69. It was a modest place they'd breathlessly picked out, my mother informing me of its every architectural detail as I listened on the phone back in Jersey. I spent the night. Then Tom, my dad and I hopped on Aeroméxico to Cabo San Lucas. The flight down was raucous, filled with other fishermen and vacationers, high and excited to be going south of the border. My dad, now a huge man, struck up a friendship with some girls on the plane. (Something, considering his general immutability, he never failed to be able to do.) Once on the ground we all jammed, girls included, into a Ford Econoline van long past its warranty. We passed scenes of abject poverty, roadside shacks with rooftop TV antennas, a blue glow emanating from within, as our driver, dodging local livestock, recklessly drove us off the road 'til we settled in screams and a cloud of dust amid the roadside brush. Upon reaching our resort, I had to admit, Pops hadn't done bad. No TVs, no telephones, but pretty cushy. Cabo at the time seemed caught between going upscale and a donkey-ramblin' twilight zone. A phone at the local post office, placed on a lonely stool, presided over by an olive-skinned beauty, was our only connection to folks stateside.

The following morning, we rose in darkness, hopped into a cab, and were deposited at dawn on a remote beach several miles from our hotel. It was there in the morning's blue twilight that something just didn't feel copacetic. Long minutes passed, my father silent, Tom shuffling, until puffs of white smoke could be seen rising from behind the nearest rock outcropping. These were followed by the blub-blub-blub sound of an ancient overworked diesel. Slowly coming into view was a bright orange wooden crate of a boat that had to have Bluto (Popeye's nemesis) himself at the wheel. Shit. My regrets on not having commandeered our arrangements were coming fast and hard. I was loaded! We could have been going out on Ted Turner's *Courageous* if we wanted to! But instead, we were about to risk our lives in this rust bucket.

A small tender with a straw-hatted, parchment-skinned old man on the oars rowed toward us. There was no English to be had, so upon reaching shore, incoherent greetings were mumbled by both parties and he motioned for us to get in the boat. My father was outfitted for his encounter with Moby-Dick in his usual street attire: heavy, laced, brown brogan shoes; white socks; dress pants; a crumpled dress shirt; suspenders; and thinning, still-coal-black hair, slicked back. He looked great for a Polish picnic in Queens but was *not* prepared for the Mexican sea. Parkinson's, body fluid buildup, diabetes, psoriasis and an array of ailments too numerous to mention, along with a life of nightly smokes and six-pack séances, had left him severely limited physically. We shuffled him over to the boat and with waves lapping on the sand, one leg at a time, we guided him in.

With a wood-on-wood ka-thunk, we bumped up against the side of our *Titanic*. There was no boarding ladder, so the three of us, without the benefit of a common dialect, had to lift 230 pounds of nickels in Sears slacks onto a rocking tugboat. Jesus Christ. The fulcrum reached its apex, weight shifted and with a resounding thud, the source of my presence on Earth rolled into the death trap he'd rented us. It was six thirty a.m. and I was already soaked in sweat. Our expressionless captain turned his "lady" around and headed silently out to sea. Not far beyond the cove, away from the sheltered waters of the coast, there were some serious seas stirring. We were a bobbing rubber duck in a five-year-old's bathtub. When we were down in the trough of a wave, the following wave crested at wheelhouse height. Within fifteen minutes, Tom was blowing his all-you-can-eat buffet breakfast over the port side. My dad was in lockdown mode, gripping the armrests of the fishing chair with his usual couldn't-give-a-shit calm.

I tried to communicate with our skipper using some of my high school Spanish, but "*¿Cómo se llama?*" got no response. I found if I kept my eyes on the horizon and rode it out, I might spare myself a retching over the stern. Our engine, in a wood box set square above deck in the boat's center, was belching diesel fumes and adding to the vicious mix of elements that attacked our normally landlocked digestive systems. An hour passed, the sun burned, land receded and there was nothing but an endless chromatic panorama where sea and sky melded that was making me terrifically claustrophobic. Death at sea felt imminent. After a second hour had passed I commanded Tom to go on top and find out EXACTLY how much farther we had to go. Our skipper raised one finger, then turned back to his wheel. Good, one more mile . . . no . . . no . . . turns out, ONE MORE HOUR! About a half hour back, we'd come upon a Boston Whaler with two locals inside, miles out at sea. They were obviously sinking, for the boat was low in the sea, filled with water up to their shins. I motioned to the captain for us to go to their rescue. Then, as we moved closer, I saw . . . fish, many fish, swimming in circles inside the boat around their legs. They reached barehanded, caught one and, smiling, lifted it up for our approval . . . bait . . . they were selling bait.

Finally, on the horizon a small circle of boats appeared . . . fishing grounds. In ten minutes the lines were readied and there was a quick tug; I passed the pole into my dad's hands and he did his best to reel in . . . something. It was about half the size of my arm and went straight into the ice chest. Then, hours of nothing. There would be no epic, man-versus-nature, Darwinian battle. No Doug Springsteen versus my father's favorite foe—*everything*—showdown. We sat, an infinitesimal cork bobbing on the bouncing sea, then, late afternoon, we headed back, *three more hours* of back. I laid myself out on a wooden bench in the stern, gobbled the paper-bag lunch the hotel had provided, sucked diesel fumes and slept. I'd had enough. After the ritual we started the morning with was reversed (my dad lowered, like a sack of United Nations grain, into the tender), we were deposited, grateful survivors, back on the beach. We donated our catch to our crew and watched them smoke and blub their way into the sunset (no doubt, bored with another pack of clueless gringos and headed for a drink and a laugh at our expense at the local cantina). The beach was empty and silent but for the small surf lapping upon the sand. My dad, in an alternate universe for the past several hours, suddenly looked over at me, as the sun dropped into the sea, and said—seriously—"I've got the boat for tomorrow too!"

We did not use the boat tomorrow, or ever again. Instead I took the old man to a little beach bar, looking out over white sand and blue Pacific. I bought a round of beers and we spent a civil afternoon watching the girls on the beach and having some good belly laughs about our adventure. On our way through the marina, back to our car, we were offered several day trips by fishing rock 'n' roll fans on glistening white, state-of-the-art yachts (the perks of rock stardom followed us even this far south). We were headed back in the morning so we politely declined—"Next time"—and went back to our hotel, slept and flew home the next day.

On our flight back, looking over at my bemused pops, I reminded myself my father was not "normal" or very well. I'd been around him for so long in his condition, I'd gotten used to it and I could forget. I'd grown up on the Shore, knew plenty of real open-sea fishermen; I could've arranged for him to have a shot at catching that marlin, had it stuffed and nailed up over his beloved kitchen table with a Marlboro in its mouth, if he'd liked, but maybe that was never the real point. Maybe he just wanted to give *me* something, something for the gifts I'd given him and my mom once success hit, something that came wrapped in his seafaring fantasy. He did.

# FIFTY-ONE

# TUNNEL
# OF LOVE

After *Born in the USA*, I'd had enough of the big time for a while and looked forward to something less. Assisted by my engineer Toby Scott, I'd slowly invested in home recording equipment. Four tracks grew to eight to sixteen to twenty-four, and I soon had a decent demo studio set up in the garage apartment of my Rumson home. I'd recently begun writing some new material that, for the first time, wasn't centered around the man on the "road" but the questions and concerns of the man in the "house." *Tunnel of Love* captured the ambivalence, love and fear brought on by my new life. Recorded in approximately a three-week period, cut with just myself on acoustic guitar to a rhythm track, like *Nebraska*, it was another "homemade" record where I played most of the instruments myself. After *USA* I wasn't ready for producers, a big band or *any* band. The music was too personal, so in the studio, it would just be Toby and me.

My first full record about men and women in love would be a pretty rough affair. Filled with inner turmoil, I wrote to make sense of my feelings. The beginnings of this new music went back to "Stolen Car" from *The River*. That song's character, drifting through the night, is the first to face the angels and devils that will drive him toward his love and keep him from ever reaching her. This was the voice that embodied my own conflicts. I was no longer a kid and now neither were the people who populated my new songs. If they didn't find a way to ground themselves, the things they needed—life, love and a home—could and would pass them by, rushing out the windows of all those cars I'd placed them in. The highway had revealed its secrets and as compelling as they were, I found its freedom and open spaces could become as overpoweringly claustrophobic as my most clichéd ideas of domesticity. All those roads, after all those years, when they converged, met down the end of the same dead-end street. I knew, I'd seen it (it's in Texas!).

I had a left-field hit with "Brilliant Disguise," the song that sits thematically at the record's center. Trust is a fragile thing. It requires allowing others to see as much of ourselves as we have the courage to reveal. But "Brilliant Disguise" postulates that when you drop one mask, you find another behind it until you begin to doubt your own feelings about who you are. The twin issues of love and identity form the core of *Tunnel of Love*, but *time* is *Tunnel*'s unofficial subtext. In this life (and there is only one), you make your choices, you take your stand and you awaken from the youthful spell of "immortality" and its eternal present. You walk away from the nether land of adolescence. You name the things beyond your work that will give your life its context, meaning . . . and the clock starts. You walk, now, not just at your partner's side, but alongside your own *mortal* self. You fight to hold on to your newfound blessings while confronting your nihilism, your destructive desire to leave it all in ruins. This struggle to uncover who I was and to reach an uneasy peace with time and death itself is at the heart of *Tunnel of Love*.

Bob Clearmountain cleaned up my playing so I sounded like I knew what I was doing; I brought Nils, Roy and Patti in to sweeten a track or two;

then Bob did the mixes, adding the sharp spiritual space the music resides in. *Tunnel of Love* was released on October 9, 1987, and went to number one on the *Billboard* album chart. I hadn't planned to do any touring but sitting at home while a record containing what I felt was some of my best and freshest writing went untended didn't seem right. I was asking my audience to follow me from highway's end, out of the car, into the house and through marriage, commitment and the mysteries of the heart (is that rock 'n' roll?). A lot of them by now were living these issues every day. Would they want to hear and be entertained by them too? I was rolling the dice that they would, and I wanted to give my music a chance to find its audience. For me, that always meant playing, and so, a tour was soon planned.

*Tunnel* was a solo album, so I wanted to distance the tour from being compared to our *USA* run. I shifted our stage layout, moving band members out of their long-held positions as a subtle way to signal to the audience that they should expect something different. I added a horn section, brought Patti to the front of the stage and left of center, and designed a carnivalesque proscenium to frame the action and play off my main metaphor of love as a scary amusement park thrill ride. In keeping with Annie Leibovitz's cover photo, we "dressed up." The blue jeans and bandana were gone—I wore a suit for the first time in quite a while—and the band left their casual wear at home. My good friend and assistant Terry Magovern donned a bowler hat and tux to perform the role of "ticket taker" and emcee. It was a nice show, with Patti providing a sexy female foil I could play off of, comically and seriously, to underscore the album's themes. We covered Gino Washington's "Gino Is a Coward" and the Sonics' "Have Love Will Travel," and performed my own unreleased song "Part Man, Part Monkey" to flesh out the tour's plotline. After *Born in the USA*, it was an intentional left turn and the band was probably somewhat disoriented by it, along with my growing relationship with Patti.

Patti was a musician, was close to my age, had seen me on the road in all of my many guises and viewed me with a knowing eye. She knew I was no white knight (perhaps a dark gray knight at best), and I never felt the need to pretend around her. Julie had never asked me to either; I just did. When Julie was filming on location, I'd be at home in New Jersey, slowly slipping back to my old ways, the bars, the late nights—nothing serious, just my usual drifting—but it wasn't the married life. It was during one of these periods Patti and I got together under my ostensible excuse of working on our "duets." It was a September night, the moon a slim fingernail in the western sky over the silhouetted wood that bordered the backyard. We hung out, sat in my little bar, talked and pretty soon, I could feel something was on. After seventeen years of sporadically bumping into each other, then two of working side by side, somewhat flirtatiously, there came a moment when I looked at Patti and saw something different, something new, something I'd missed and hadn't experienced before. I was always busy, as Patti would later say, "looking in other fields." Patti is a wise, tough, powerful woman, but she is also the soul of fragility, and there was something in that combination that opened up new possibilities in my heart. In my life, Patti is a singularity. So, it started.

At first, I told myself it was just "a thing." It wasn't. It was *the* thing. The surreptitiousness didn't last long and I came clean to Julie as soon as I knew how serious Patti and I were, but there was no decent or graceful way out of it. I was going to hurt someone I loved . . . period. Soon I'd be separated and photographed in my tighty-whities with Patti on a balcony in Rome. I dealt with Julie's and my separation abysmally, insisting it remain a private affair, so we released no press statement, causing furor, pain and "scandal" when the news leaked out. It made a tough thing more heart-breaking than necessary. I deeply cared for Julianne and her family and my poor handling of this is something I regret to this day.

Julianne was young, just getting her career started, while at thirty-five, I could seem accomplished, reasonably mature and in control, but, inside, I was still emotionally stunted and secretly unavailable. She's a woman of great discretion and decency and always dealt with me and our problems honestly and in good faith, but in the end, we didn't really know. I placed her in a terribly difficult position for a young girl and I failed her as a husband and partner. We handled the details as civilly and as graciously as possible, divorced and went on about our lives.

After our divorce was final, I took a few days and visited my parents, gave them the news and listened to my mom hector me with "Bruce, three years, your limit! . . . Whaaaaa!" They loved Julianne, but I was their son. I stayed awhile, having my wounds treated with home cooking and sympathy, then headed back to New Jersey. My dad drove me to the airport. Ten minutes out he turned to me and said, "Bruce, maybe you should move back home for a while." I was tempted to mention that I was a nearly forty-year-old self-made multimillionaire and the prospect of moving back into an eight-by-twelve-foot room in my parents' house, still holding my stuffed Mickey Mouse, was . . . not impossible, but not likely. Nevertheless, when I looked over at my pop, his suspendered girth squished between the wheel and the driver's seat, all I could say was, "Thanks, Dad, I'll think about it." The old man finally wanted me around the house.

## '88

Seven years after Steve and I first walked through Checkpoint Charlie, I brought my band back to East Berlin. Steve wasn't there, but 160,000-plus East Germans showed up. The wall still stood, but the first cracks were definitely appearing in its once impregnable façade. Conditions were *not* what they had been a decade ago. There in an open field stood the largest single crowd I'd ever seen or played to, and from center stage, I couldn't see its end. Home-stitched American flags flew in the East German wind. The tickets claimed we were being presented by the Young Communist League and were playing a "concert for the Sandinistas"?! It was news to me! The entire show was broadcast on state television (another surprise!) with the exception of my short speech about the wall, which somehow was conveniently deleted. I went from being a complete nobody sashaying unmolested down the streets of East Berlin, on the day *before* our show, to a national superstar in twenty-four hours. When I poked my head out of our hotel the day after our gig, I was surrounded by hipsters, grannies and everything in between vying for an autograph. "*Ich bin ein Berliner!*"

We partied at the East German consulate and then headed back to West Berlin and a show for seventeen thousand that, despite our good West German fans, felt a lot less dramatic than what we'd just experienced. (Rock 'n' roll is a music of stakes. The higher they're pushed, the deeper and more thrilling the moment becomes. In East Germany in 1988, the center of the table was loaded down with a winner-take-all bounty that would explode into the liberating destruction of the Berlin Wall by the people of Germany.)

## Around the World in Forty-Two Days

Heading back home, we had the option to continue our *Tunnel of Love* tour or go to work for Amnesty International, the highly regarded human rights organization. Amnesty was making a concerted push to enlist and engage young people around the globe in the fight for civil liberties and figured what better way to prick up the ears of the youngsters than rock 'n' roll. Guided by Peter Gabriel, we were enlisted by Amnesty's then executive director, Jack Healey, and our *Tunnel of Love* tour morphed directly into Amnesty International's "Human Rights Now!" tour. We shortly found ourselves on a 747 with Peter; Youssou N'Dour, the sensational Senegalese singer; Tracy Chapman; and Sting, international rock stars all, hopping around the world, dropping for a moment from the clouds to tell you how to run your show. I'd always felt rock music was a music of both personal and political liberation and I thought the tour would give us an opportunity to practice some of what we preached. It did, but in the process, I got mugged by SCHOOL-WORK! Nobody told me I was going to have to STUDY! We had to do a full press conference in *every* country and we needed to know in detail the human rights issues in each. Trying not to look like the dilettante I was, I studied like I hadn't since Sister Theresa Mary stood over me, ruler in hand, at St. Rose grammar school.

The audiences were spectacular. The concerts lasted for eight hours and featured local opening acts. In Zimbabwe, the great Oliver Mtukudzi tore the house down with African soul. A little over a year from now, Nelson Mandela would be released from prison and the slow dismantling of the apartheid system would begin to occur, but at this moment in 1988, the battle was raging. The simple mix of a white and black crowd of this size, something that was forbidden and illegal a mere three hundred miles south, brought an urgency to our appearance.

In the former French colony of Côte d'Ivoire, I was greeted, for the first and only time since the 1966 Tri-Soul Revue at the Matawan-Keyport Roller Drome, by an audience, a *stadium* audience, of completely black faces! I finally knew how Clarence felt. We were *one* black man and seven white folk from New Jersey. Was this gonna work? Was the wooden-legged, four-four beat of Jersey Shore punk 'n' soul going to communicate to an audience used to the swaying and supple rhythms of Afrobeat? Headlining, we were last to go on. A cool sweat slowly formed on the uppermost layer of my skin beneath my black vest and shirt. We went for the nuclear option, kicking straight into "Born in the USA." Time . . . crept to a standstill . . . then . . . BOOM! The place exploded into a frenzy, the crowd moving en masse as if they'd been wired together and had suddenly decided this was okay! It was the most joyful mutual celebration of discovery I've ever experienced. We were the wrong color, singing in the wrong language, to the wrong beat, and still, the crowd shed upon us their generosity, openness and national hospitality. It was the first audience the E Street Band had had to truly *win*, cold, in a long, long time. Women leapt onstage and danced, the crowd rocked in ecstasy and the band walked off feeling exhilarated and validated. (It works! All the way over here! It works!) We felt the closeness of old hands being challenged and, in league with this unexpected and willing audience, becoming victorious. The mysteries of music's communicative power to cross great divides proved themselves once more and we knew we'd just experienced something special.

Somewhere along the way we played a few dates in the United States, where our usually politicized press conferences were peppered by celebrity questions and a vacuousness that sometimes made me embarrassed for the locals. We also stopped in Japan, Budapest, Hungary, Canada, Brazil and India and finished up in Argentina, a country of stunning landscapes and a gorgeous, sensual citizenry that made me want to learn Spanish immediately! In South America were countries that had recently experienced the full brunt of dictatorship and the daily trampling of simple human freedoms. Thousands of sons and husbands were disappeared off the streets during the reign of brutal regimes in Argentina and Pinochet's Chile. Here, Amnesty's job was immediate, critical and personal. There was something hard to push up against and to feel pushing back. With Pinochet still in power, we played on the border of Chile in Mendoza, Argentina. There the "mothers of the disappeared," whose loved ones had vanished from their homes and the streets in the years of Pinochet's dictatorial rule, stood holding placard photos of lost loved ones along the roadside as we drove toward the venue. Their faces were filled with the remnants of terrible things we simply had no clue about or ability to understand back in the USA *and* proof of the ongoing human will, desire and primal need for justice.

The Amnesty International tour made me thankful to have been born in the USA, in my little, repressed, redneck, reactionary, one-fire-hydrant crap heap of a hometown that I loved, where despite the social pressure of the ignorant and intolerant, you could walk and speak freely without fear for life and limb (mostly).

Six weeks after we'd started we'd had our say, boosted Amnesty and its international agenda, played our rock 'n' roll and stood, for a moment, thumbs out, political-cultural hitchhikers at the crossroads of history.

# Home Again

Patti and I said our good-byes to Peter, Sting, Youssou, Tracy and Amnesty's mighty road crew (whose human rights were consistently violated with long working hours and untenable conditions during the tour), and we returned to New York City. We'd rented an apartment on the East Side and I gave my one and only try at becoming a city boy. It was a no-go. The East Side wasn't for me, its only redeeming feature being I was just a walk away from Doc Myers's office, which helped because I was not at my best. I came home torn by the confusion of my divorce, and with no recourse to roads 'n' wheels, the city days were long indeed. In New York City, I was "the magic rat" in his maze. I couldn't get sky, couldn't see sun and couldn't run. Yeah, the museums, the restaurants, the shops, but I was still SMALL-TOWN! I couldn't change, so Patti (a nineteen-year New York City resident, in Chelsea) capitulated and we packed up our bags and headed back to Jersey, where she, I and my ice-cold feet spent a lost summer, with me up to some of my old ways and thoughtless behavior. Patti was patient . . . to a point.

# Adjustment

Back at home, Patti and I fought a lot, which was a good thing. I'd never argued much in most of my other relationships and it had proved detrimental. Too many issues simmering, unresolved, beneath the surface always proved poisonous. Like my father, I was a passively hostile actor. Denial and intimidation, not direct confrontation, was my style. My dad had controlled our home by quietly sitting there . . . smoking. He was all passive anger until he'd break and rage, then return to his beer and monklike silence. He was our own one-man minefield, filling our home with the deadly quiet of a war zone as we walked on point, waiting . . . waiting . . . for the detonation we knew was coming. We just never knew when.

All of this had seeped into my bones and ruined so much. I didn't "lose it" often, but I could, silently and just enough to put the fear of God into my loved ones. I'd learned it at the feet of the master. Worse, I'd picked up his bad habits behind the wheel and I could be very dangerous. I would use speed and recklessness to communicate my own rage and anger, with the sole purpose of terrorizing my rider. It was gross, bullying, violent and humiliating behavior that filled me with shame afterward. I was always full of a thousand apologies, but of course, it was too little, too late, and I suppose I'd learned that too. These incidents occurred only with people I cared about, loved. That was the point. I wanted to kill what loved me because I couldn't stand being loved. It infuriated and outraged me, someone having the temerity to love me—*nobody does that* . . . and I'll show you why. It was ugly and a red flag for the poison I had running through my veins, my genes. Part of me was rebelliously proud of my emotionally violent behavior, always cowardly and aimed at the women in my life. There was assertion, there was action, there was *no impotence*. The passivity of the men I grew up surrounded by frightened and enraged me. My own passivity embarrassed me, so I went in search of my "truth." This . . . this is how I feel about myself, about you, how I feel, how you make me feel in my darkest of dark hearts, where I truly reside.

Over the years I had to come to the realization that there was a part of me, a significant part, that was capable of great carelessness and emotional cruelty, that sought to reap damage and harvest shame, that wanted to wound and hurt and *make sure* those who loved me paid for it. It was all straight out of the old man's playbook. My father led us to believe he despised us for loving him, would punish us for it . . . and he did. It seemed like he could be driven crazy by it . . . and so could I. When I tasted this part of myself, it made me scared and sick, but still I held it in reserve, like a malignant power source I could draw on when psychically threatened, when someone tried to go someplace I simply couldn't tolerate . . . closer.

# FIFTY-TWO

# GOIN' CALI

New York, burned. New Jersey, burned. All we had left was my Golden State, "Little San Simeon" in the Hollywood Hills. As soon as we hit California, things got better. The light, the weather, the sea, the mountains, the desert, all colluded and brought with them a clearer state of mind. We rented a beach house in Trancas and a peace of sorts settled over me. It took a while and one massive end-all blowout of an argument where Patti, finally fed up with my bullshit, threw down the gauntlet and laid it out. Stay or go. This is what I'd pushed her toward and with one foot out the door (someplace, at my worst, I always twistedly thought I wanted to be), I stopped for a moment and the weak but clear-thinking part of me asked, "Where the hell do you think you're going? The road? The bar?" I still enjoyed them, but it wasn't a life. I'd been there, thousands of times, seen all they had to offer. What was conceivably going to be different? Was I going to get back on that hamster's wheel of indecision, of lying to myself that it would all never grow old (it already had), and throw away the best thing, the best woman, I'd ever known? I stayed. It was the sanest decision of my life.

To take the edge off my heebie-jeebies, in the day, I rode through the Santa Monica and San Gabriel mountains, some of the nicest motorcycle routes in the West. In the San Gabriels, the Mojave lies to your left and below, spread out and vanishing into a hazy infinity as you carve your way from the desert floor six thousand feet up, to the little ski town of Wrightwood. Here, in the midst of the tall pines and high desert scrub of the Angeles National Forest, my troubles would slowly melt away. The air was dry, thin, it pierced you, and as it rushed over me, on the slim black ribbon of the Angeles Crest Highway, I could feel its clarity sharpening my thoughts and fine-tuning my emotions. Nature can be sanity inducing, and here, you were in one of the upper rooms of California and could feel the state's great natural spirits and God's bountiful hand visiting upon you. On the Angeles Crest Highway you're just thirty minutes out of Los Angeles, but make no mistake, it's wilderness, and people get lost up there in the heat *and* the snow every year. There are coyotes, rattlesnakes and mountain lions only slightly above and mere miles away from the smog-filled perdition of the City of Angels. From Wrightwood, and sixty-degree temperatures, I'd drop straight down into the foothills of the San Gabriels and the one-hundred-degree Mojave high desert, where long straight highways were filled with the "desert culture" of trailer parks, mom-and-pop snack stands and curio shops. There, the long black wires of steel electrical towers dissected the crushing blue sky into a geometric puzzle, pierced only by the white vapor trails of fighter jets out of Edwards Air Force Base.

It was a three-hundred-mile day trip, just enough to bake and momentarily silence the ongoing racket inside of me. I'd make my way down to the Pearblossom Highway, then slowly back around to the beach, where, in the twilight, Patti and I would watch the red evening sun slip into the Pacific. Together, we settled into a reassuring quiet, not trying to push each other too hard or make too much of things. Patti cooked, I ate. We gave each other a lot of room and something happened. It was a sweet surrender and I've always felt that it was there, at that time, in the gentle days and nights we spent at the sea, that Patti and I "emotionally" married. I loved her. I was lucky she loved me. The rest was paperwork.

## Southwest '89

That fall, I turned thirty-nine. Patti and I invited some friends from the East, a few close relatives and my road buddies the Delia brothers for a birthday party at our beach shack. We spent a few days in the sea and the sun, then prepared for a motorcycle trip through the Southwest we'd long dreamt of taking. It was only ten days, but it would be a great ride, one of the great rides, and would begin on the cusp of earthquakelike changes that would be as profound and life altering as the day I first picked up the guitar.

My birthday dispatched, Matt, Tony, Ed and I departed for our two-thousand-mile Southwestern motorcycle excursion. We rode through California, Arizona, Nevada, Utah, up through the Navajo and Hopi reservations, to the Four Corners area and Monument Valley. Off the interstates, it was beautiful but hard country, and the Indian reservations were poverty stricken. Old dark-skinned grandmas huddled beneath rickety wooden highway stands, shawls protecting them from the harsh rays of the desert sun. Desert heat, *real* heat, is a creature all its own. Unlike our Jersey Shore's sweltering August humidity, which makes you want to strip down, drop the top and make a run for the ocean, desert heat and sun make you want to cover up completely.

As we rode through the low desert of Arizona, at 105 degrees, the highway turned into a shimmering mirage, and a simple dip in the road would bring a rise in temperature from the heat wafting up out of the baked blacktop. To protect ourselves from the sun's rays, we had blue-jean shirtsleeves rolled down, sunglasses, gloves, boots, and jeans, and bandanas soaked in water completely covering our heads and faces. Ride in these conditions, eight to ten hours a day, and soon no sun on your skin can be tolerated. There were roadside showers where for a few coins you could get the dust off. You'd soak yourself from head to toe, but with the desert gusts acting like nature's coin-operated dryer, fifteen minutes later, rolling in one-hundred-plus temps, you'd be dry as a bone.

We stayed on the state roads. In the Southwest, off the interstates, remnants of 1940s and '50s America still remain. Filling stations, motor courts, roadside attractions and fewer corporate franchises bring the taste of the country that was (and, despite the Internet, for many, still is) back into your mouth. On one stretch of deserted highway crossing the Navajo reservation, we came upon a handmade sign reading "Dinosaur Tracks, 100 yards." We pulled down a dirt lane where a twelve- or thirteen-year-old Navajo boy skittered out from the shade of a crudely built wooden lean-to and, with a smile, greeted us and asked us if we wanted to see the dinosaur tracks. I asked him, "How much?" And he replied, "Whatever it's worth to you . . ." Okay. We followed him a few hundred yards into the desert, and while I'm no paleontologist, I'd have to say, there they were, large tracks, fossilized in the stone, followed by smaller ones, mama and baby. He then asked if we'd like him to guess our weight and ages. We were in for a penny, so . . . okay. He looked at me, said, "One hundred eighty pounds" (right on the button), then looked me in the face and said, "Twenty . . . twenty . . . twenty . . . take off your sunglasses! Thirty-eight!" (He was good, and ready for the Jersey boardwalk.)

We moved on to the Hopi Reservation. The Hopi live at the edge of three plateaus. Here are some of the oldest permanently inhabited villages in North America. We drove down another dusty lane following a sign pointing to *the* oldest village and came upon stone huts perched high and on the extreme edge of a plateau overlooking the dried seabed of the Arizona desert. The village appeared deserted but for one small store at its center. We shuffled in and were greeted by a teenage Hopi boy, baseball hat on backward, decked out in a Judas Priest T-shirt, and started to make small talk. We were informed the village was currently riven between inhabitants who wanted to move into trailers closer to the road in order to obtain electricity and those who wanted to remain in the primitive stone structures they had lived in for years. Our narrator was preparing for a Hopi ritual he called Running Around the World. He told us young men would race, circumnavigating their mesa in a coming-of-age ritual, for the honor of their family. He also told me of the metal concerts he'd seen in Phoenix and that most of the young folks up on the mesa eventually moved away, off the res. He didn't know what he would do. Here was a kid torn between two worlds. As we said our good-byes, he wanted his picture taken with us but told us it was forbidden in the community. Standing outside of his shop, he looked around and whispered, "They're watching me right now." The village seemed empty, completely still and silent. We couldn't see a soul. He then said, "Fuck 'em," busted out his point-and-shoot box camera, snapped a quick one and we were off. As we fired the engines on our bikes, he shouted, "Look for me in Phoenix. I'll be in the front row . . . stoned!"

We made our way to Monument Valley, the location for some of my favorite John Ford films, and camped for the night in Mexican Hat, Utah. We woke up the next morning and fought sixty-mile-per-hour side winds as we drove south to Canyon de Chelly. The desert was flat, without windbreaks, and forced us to put our bikes into a deep lean to counteract the gusts. The heavy haze of a dust storm sandblasted any exposed skin 'til we made it to the canyon, and we spent the night in a motel of rigged-up box trailers, bikes heavily chained together out front. We eventually made our way back around to Prescott, where I laid down an afternoon jam with some locals in a little western bar, then moved on to Salome ("Where She Danced"), a four-corner desert town in western Arizona. There, at midnight, with the after-burn of the day's heat comfortably smothering you, you could sit outside your little motel room, beatbox at a low hum, drinking beer, exhausted well beyond the reach of your anxieties, finally and blessedly present.

Ten days later, we returned to Los Angeles, burned, bushed and grizzled. There at sundown, washing dust off chrome, Patti watching from the hood of Gary Bonds's "Dedication," we toasted our trip with tequila shots. The Delia brothers returned to their nuts, bolts and contrary engines; I had a sweet reunion with Patti, slept for three days, then went north to visit my folks. Upon my return, I walked into our bedroom, morning light streaming through our window. Patti was sitting upright in bed. Her face gone soft, hair falling over her shoulder, she looked at me and said, "I'm pregnant." I stood, gathering in what I'd just heard, then sat heavily on the edge of our bed. I turned from Patti and looked into the mirror on our closet door, and felt *different*. This, this was what I'd feared and longed for, for so long. I felt the frightened part of me make its bid to steal the moment . . . but no . . . not now. Then a lifting light entered me, something that felt so good, I tried to hide it. My back was turned, my face hidden, all was still. Then my mouth, subtly, almost imperceptibly and beyond my control . . . as I caught a splash of red hair over my shoulder in the mirror, a smile slipped out. There, for that eternal moment, with Patti leaning over me, her hair cascading alongside my cheek, her arms around my chest, her belly full against the center of my back . . . we sat . . . the *three* of us. Our family. Patti whispered, "I saw you smile."

BOOK THREE

# LIVING PROOF

## FIFTY-THREE
# LIVING
# PROOF

It's a boy! On July 25, 1990, at eleven thirty p.m. on the fifth floor of Cedars-Sinai Medical Center in Los Angeles, Evan James Springsteen is born. All protective veils slip, all defenses are down, defeated, all emotional "conditions" are suspended, all negotiations are ceased. The room is filled with the light of blood spirits past, present and future. The truth of your partner's love sings brightly before you. Your love, the love you've worked so hard to show, to hide, has been ripped from you and its presence shames your lack of faith while raining light upon the good you've created. All of your excuses for staying "protected," in isolation, all of the reasons for your "secrets," your hiddenness, are blown away. This small hospital room would be the great house of your contrition, of a life's happy penance, except there is no time for your bullshit here. You dwell in your lover's body, in her bloody pinks and reds, in the creams and whites of transcendence. The spirit is made physical. You are not *safe*; love and risk are everywhere and you feel a flesh-and-blood link in your tribe's chain, a trace of the dust in God's hand as it passes over the Earth. Patti's face is the weary, grace-filled face of my grammar school saints, her green eyes drifting upward, locked on something beyond me. It is final; this is my gal, bringing the rumble of life.

CITIZENS OF LOS ANGELES: EVAN JAMES SPRINGSTEEN IS BORN. A SON OF NEW JERSEY, BORN IN EXILE, HERE IN BABYLON!

The raging river of my ambivalence, my lifelong low ambient hum of discontent, is silent. Dismissed by rapture. The doctor hands me scissors; a snip, and my boy's on his own. I lay him upon his mama's belly and this vision of my son and wife takes me far into my own highest room. We are huddled together with seven pounds and eleven ounces of living proof. We are one short breath of night and day, then dirt and stars, but we're holding the new morning.

Making life fills you with humility, balls, arrogance, a mighty manliness, confidence, terror, joy, dread, love, a sense of calm and reckless adventure. Isn't anything possible now? If we can populate the world, can't we create and shape it? Then reality and diapers and formula and sleepless nights and child seats and yellow custard shit and cream cheese vomit set in. But . . . oh, these are the blessed needs and fluids of my boy and at the end of each headachy, tiring new world of a day, we are exhausted but exalted by new identities, Mom and Pop!

At home, I take the midnight shift, walking my boy lost miles across our tiny bedroom floor 'til his eyes go from full to half-mast to . . . sleep. Lying there with our son upon my chest, I watch him rise and fall with each breath I take, I listen and count each and every exhalation of his lungs, his breaths still so few as to remain countable, a prayer to the gods I've doubted. I inhale his baby smells, secure him gently in my hands, synchronize our breathing, and I drift to sleep in peace.

The endorphin high of birth will fade, but its trace remains with you

forever, its fingerprints indelible proof of love's presence and daily gran-
deur. You have offered up your prayer. You have vowed service to a new
world and laid a bedrock of earthly faith. You have chosen your sword, your
shield, and where you will fall. Whatever the morrow brings, these things,
these people, will be with you always. The power of choice, of a life, a lover,
a place to stand, will be there to be called upon and make fresh sense of your
tangled history. More important, it will also be there when you waver, when
you're lost, providing you with the elements of a new compass, encased
within your heart.

From here on, the hard gravitational pull of the past will have a formidable challenger: your current life. Together, Patti and I'd made one and
one equal three. That's rock 'n' roll.

This new life revealed that I was more than a song, a story, a night,
an idea, a pose, a truth, a shadow, a lie, a moment, a question, an answer, a
restless figment of my own and others' imagination . . . Work is work . . . but
life . . . is life . . . and life trumps art . . . always.

# FIFTY-FOUR

# REDHEADED REVOLUTION

She is a one-woman, red-haired revolution: flaming beauty, Queen of my heart, waitress, street busker, child of some privilege, hard-time Jersey girl, great songwriter, nineteen-year New Yorker, one of the loveliest voices I've ever heard, smart, tough and fragile. When I look at her, I see and feel my best self. Vivienne Patricia Scialfa grew up in Deal, New Jersey, sister of Michael and Sean, daughter of Coast Guard Lieutenant Commander Joe and great local beauty Pat Scialfa. A freckle-faced Raggedy Ann of a little girl, her smile beams, openly, expectantly, from childhood pictures. If we love those in whose company is reflected the best of us, that's the light she shines on me. For a couple of loners and musicians, we've made it pretty far.

She grew up next door to New Jersey mob boss Anthony "Little Pussy" Russo. Mr. "Pussy" wanted a Sicilian next door, so he sold the adjacent beachfront house to Patti's pop, Joe. Joe was not connected, but he was classic Sicilian stock. A crazy handsome man's-man Italian mama's boy spoiled by three sisters, Joe was a self-made multimillionaire via his local real estate speculations and as a proprietor of Scialfa TV, a talented, manic, brutally tough act for a dad and a wild card for a father-in-law. Patti's mom, Pat, was hardworking Scots-Irish, a sixties dream of a showpiece, determined, tough and every bit Joe's match. She worked side by side with Joe at the TV store, day in, day out, while a young Patti slipped down in between the Motorolas and the Zeniths, doing her homework. From Long Branch, Jersey's Italian paradise by the sea, to Spring Lake's Irish Riviera, Patti and I carried on the Irish-Italian mating ritual that seems to have swept our section of the central coast for the last century.

I first spoke to Patti when she was seventeen and I was twenty-one. She'd answered an ad I placed in the Asbury Park Press for background singers for my ten-piece rock 'n' soul Bruce Springsteen Band. We spoke for a while on the phone. She was very young and I told her we were a traveling gig and she should stay in high school. We met for the first time in 1974. Enthralled by the girl groups of the sixties, I was entertaining the idea of a girl singer in the band. She answered an ad in the *Village Voice* and auditioned a cappella for Mike Appel in his midtown office. Mike, feet up on his desk, arms locked behind his head, would utter the command, "Sing!" A prospective E Streeter would then, completely unaccompanied, have to start belting out the Crystals' "Da Doo Ron Ron." If you passed muster, you were sent down to a little industrial park in Neptune, New Jersey, where you'd find the pre–*Born to Run* band, preparing for their breakout release. I was twenty-five, she was twenty-one, she sang some Ronnie Spector with the band, then we sat at the piano together and she played me one of her songs. She was lovely and very good but we ended up going with our regular lineup, not quite ready to break up the "lost boys" yet.

Ten years later, in 1984, one night as I hung out at the Stone Pony, a redheaded gal showed up and sat in with the Sunday night house band, singing the Exciters' "Tell Him." She was good, had something I hadn't seen in the area before, and she'd mastered that sixties quality in her voice along with something else that was distinctly hers. At the time I was a pretty big fish in a small pond and where I walked, ripples occurred. We found ourselves standing in a buzzing crowd at the back bar as I introduced myself to her and the rest was a long, winding semi-courtship.

Patti told me I was always looking in "other fields" for companionship. I'd always had a lot of ideas about the who, what, when, where and why of my romantic choices that would prove in the long run irrelevant. When I opened up and stopped looking in those "other fields" . . . Patti was there before me. She'd eyed me up and waited 'til I was ready, then I was. It's an unusual story of two people who'd circled around each other, cautiously and tangentially touching for eighteen years, before connecting.

We toured as bandmates through the *Born in the USA* tour. She had plenty of admirers and was a tough dance card if you tried to tame her New York independence. She lived alone and like a musician, like me. She was *not* domestic. She did *not* live to make you feel safe. I liked all of this. I'd tried the other and it hadn't worked. I knew something very, very different and perhaps difficult was called for and Patti was it. We settled into domesticity, slowly and very carefully. Her psychological intuition was very high and I felt the risk of a formidable partner. When I started seeing Patti, she was deeply pleasurable, intelligent and exciting, but she scared me. I was putting my trust in her and despite her interest, I wasn't so sure she really wanted it. Patti had a part of her that carried a charged sexuality; she could seduce and she could stir you to jealousy. There was a lot of emotional dueling, the occasional flying beauty product and plenty of arguing. We tested our ability to withstand each other's insecurities, hard. It was good. We could fight, surprise, disappoint, raise up, bring down, withhold, surrender, hurt, heal, fight again, love, refit, then go at it one more time. We were both broken in a lot of ways but we hoped, with work, our broken pieces might fit together in a way that would create something workable, wonderful. They did. We created a life and a love fit for a couple of emotional outlaws. That similarity bound and binds us very close.

My wife is a private person, not known through whatever her "public persona" may be, and not nearly as fond of the limelight as I. Her talents have only been hinted at in her work. She has great elegance and dignity and we've built a lot together out of those broken pieces. We found once those pieces were set in place, they weighed in as hard stone, each piece pressuring and holding the pieces above and beneath it for twenty-five years (in a dog's life and musical companionships, that's somewhere around 175 years!). Two loners, we weren't necessarily destined for the gold ring(s), but we stole them . . . and locked them away.

The night I fell in love with Patti's voice at the Stone Pony, the first line she sang was "I know something about love . . ." She does.

# FIFTY-FIVE

# CHANGES

I spent some money. Quite a bit, actually. We bought a house on a canyon road near Sunset Boulevard. It was luxurious and extravagant and I was ready for some of that. I had a family now; I still drew a good deal of press attention and we needed to ensure we'd have some security and privacy. Our new digs, situated off a couple of private drives, delivered that. I bought some nice guitars. I'd never collected before. I'd always considered my instrument a tool, like a hammer: one good one and maybe a spare or two were all you really needed. Now I wanted a beautiful guitar in each room. I wanted music throughout the house.

A lot had changed. The late eighties and early nineties had proved tumultuous, upending my life. I was working on new music in a new land with a new love. At the moment I had no driving theme or sure creative point of view thundering through my head, and after the *Born in the USA*, *Tunnel of Love* and Amnesty tours, I felt a little burned out. I was unsure of where to take the band next and in '89, I'd essentially placed them on hiatus.

Over time, like all the guys, I'd developed my own set of underlying grievances. Some of the fellas making me a little too crazy, some feeling of a lack
of appreciation coupled with the burden of having life issues and baggage
constantly dumped at my doorstep with a little too much frequency and too
many expectations that I should make it all better. All of this, along with my
creative uncertainty and artistic curiosity, finally turned me around the corner. We'd all lived on E Street for a long while. During that time, many good
habits were formed, things that in the long run would keep us together, but
there were also some bad habits that had taken hold. I felt I'd become not
just a friend and employer for some, but also banker and daddy.

As usual, I'd created a good deal of our state of affairs myself by not
providing clear boundaries and by creating an emotional structure where in
exchange for the band's undying loyalty and exclusivity, I gave an unspoken and uncontracted promise to cover everyone's back in whatever befell
them. *Everyone*, without concrete, written clarification, will define the terms
of your relationship in accordance with their own financial, emotional and
psychological needs and desires, some realistic, some not. A lawsuit with
some trusted employees that had turned into a rather long and nasty divorce case made me realize the importance of clarifying your, and your band
members', commitments in as reasonably undisputable a fashion as possible. That meant contracts (previously anathema to me). The *Tunnel of Love*
tour was the first time I insisted on written contracts with the band. After
all this time, to some, I suppose, it suggested mistrust, but those contracts
and their future counterparts protected *our* future together. They clarified
beyond debate our past and present relationships with one another, and in
clarity lie stability, longevity, respect, understanding and confidence. Everyone knew where everyone else stood, what was given and what was asked.
Once signed, those contracts left us free to just *play*.

On the day I called each band member to explain that after years with
the same lineup, I wanted to experiment with other musicians, I'm sure it
hurt, especially Clarence, but I was met to a man by the same response. The

E Street Band is old-school; we are filled with gentlemen, raucous, rousing, sometimes reckless rock 'n' roll gentlemen, but gentlemen all. Everyone was generous, gracious—yes, disappointed, but open to what I was saying. They wished me well and I did them the same.

It was painful, but in truth, we all needed a break. After sixteen years, a reconsidering was in order. I left in search of my own life and some new creative directions. Many of the guys did that as well, finding second lives and second careers as musicians, record producers, TV stars and actors. We retained our friendships and stayed in touch. When we would come back together I would find a more adult, settled, powerful group of people. Our time away from one another gave us all a new respect for the man or woman standing next to us. It opened our eyes to what we had, what we'd accomplished and might still accomplish together.

# FIFTY-SIX

# LA
# BURNING

In 1992 the Los Angeles riots were sparked by the acquittal of four Los Angeles Police Department officers accused in the vicious beating of motorist Rodney King after a high-speed police chase. Widespread arson, looting and assault fanned out across the LA basin. The broadcast of a home movie videotape of the assault welcomed the LAPD into the information age and set Los Angeles on fire.

As I rehearsed with my new band in an East Hollywood studio, someone came running in and shouted there was "trouble" in the streets. Two blocks from where we were working, he'd just barely escaped assault. We turned on the TV, realized we were uncomfortably close to the center of the disturbance and decided to call it for the day. I hopped in my Ford Explorer and headed west. Sunset Boulevard was jammed, with "panic in year zero" dread coursing through the veins of fleeing motorists, all trying to get out of the center and eastern parts of town. I had to get to Benedict Canyon and then on to the coast, where we'd rented a cottage that seemed safely removed from the events of the day. I'd ridden many of LA's back roads, so I literally headed for the hills, threading my way along the curves of Mulholland Drive. I stopped for a moment near the Hollywood Bowl, where my windshield was filled with city-wide fury. It was a fiery, smoking panorama from a bad Hollywood disaster picture. Large smoldering black clouds rose from fires all across the LA grid to mix with chiseled azure skies like billowing ink on blue tile. I moved on to Benedict Canyon, where I picked up Patti and the kids.

Unlike the Watts riots of 1965, the fire this time looked as if it might spread out beyond the ghetto of those afflicted. Fear, and plenty of it, was in the air. The lapping waves of California's surf paradise, the well-entrenched, well-paid-for silence of Trancas, Malibu and Broad Beach, was broken by the thukka-thukka-thukka rotors of National Guard helicopters running low above the sea. Beach deck TV screens were filled with the flames of boredom, despair and protest, just a few perhaps-not-so-well-guarded miles east.

Fifty-three citizens died, thousands were injured, businesses were destroyed, lives were ruined.

This is America. The prescriptions for many of our ills are in hand—child day care, jobs, education, health care—but it would take a societal effort on the scale of the Marshall Plan to break the generations-long chain of institutionalized destruction our social policies have wreaked. If we can spend trillions on Iraq and Afghanistan in nation building, if we can bail out Wall Street with billions of taxpayer dollars, why not here? Why not now?

# FIFTY-SEVEN
# GOING TO
# THE CHAPEL

Patti and I courted in Chelsea. Near her New York apartment there was a lovely little bench on the edge of a small park directly across from the Empire Diner. We'd meet there, spending spring days drinking beer from cans covered in a paper bag and talking. It became a very special place for us. One afternoon after a lunch at the Empire, on the way out, I grabbed a twig from a small bush by the side of the diner. I twisted it into a makeshift ring, and by the time she got to the bench I was down on one knee. I popped the question, was proud when Patti said yes, and we were on our way. My next step was to get a proper engagement ring.

My dad never showed off my mom. As a matter of fact, due to his paranoia, he practically hid her most of our lives. This had seeped into my bones. I was always a little embarrassed of love, of showing my need for something or someone, of showing my open heart, sometimes of simply being with a woman. My dad had sent a subtle message that a woman, a family, weakens you, makes you feel exposed and vulnerable. This was a horrible thing to live with. Patti changed much of that. By her intelligence and love she showed me that our family was a sign of strength, that we were formidable and could take on and enjoy much more of the world.

There was one thing I was sure of: it was going to be Patti and me for life, until the wheels came off. Now it was time to make it public. Jesus, we'd been together for three years, survived a burst of scandal, and already had a child and another one on the way. But I hated making anything public. Perhaps it was a result of being in the limelight for so long, or perhaps it was just the stubborn side of me wanting to keep Patti, our family and our love all to ourselves. By now I mistrusted those feelings and knew they weren't healthy.

There are plenty of folks in great relationships without the marriage certificate, but we felt there was something meaningful and important in the declaration of our feelings, something that for us was essential. That's why there is a statement of vows, a public promise, a blessing of your union, a celebration. When you do this in front of your friends, your family, your world, it's a coming out of sorts, an announcement to everyone that this is how we're going to officially roll from here on in, together, two for the road.

# Wedding Day

June 8, 1991. Patti's and my wedding day dawned bright and sunny in Southern California. I spent the morning trying to fit my dad onto one of my choppers down in the courtyard while Patti was squeezing into her wedding dress in our bedroom. She'd neglected to tell the seamstress she was carrying a little three-months-along Jessie Springsteen grumbling in her belly, so there were a few alterations due. This was a big day. I'd let Patti know me like I'd never done with anyone else. This frightened me. I believed a lot of me wasn't so nice to know. My self-centeredness, my narcissism, my isolation. Still, Patti tended to be a loner herself and this gave her a pretty good heads-up on how to handle me, but would she still love me if she really knew me? She was strong and had proven she could stand against my less-than-constructive behavior. She was confident in us and that gave me confidence that we would be all right. Patti had changed my life in a way that no one else ever had. She inspired me to be a better man, turned the dial way down on my running while still leaving me room to move. She gave me my motorcycle-canyon-running Sundays when I needed them and always honored who I was. She took care of me perhaps more than I deserved.

We decided to be married on our own property in a beautiful little grotto over by our studio house. You walked through a natural growth of eucalyptus until you came to a gray slate courtyard that held at its head a beautiful gray stone fireplace. Here, garlanded in flowers, we'd say our vows. We'd invited about ninety-five people, mostly friends and immediate family. The band brought their acoustic instruments—Soozie her fiddle, Danny his accordion, a few guitars, and we learned a piece of music I'd written specifically for this day. Evan James was done up in a white suit, looking very handsome and calling "Dada, Dada" during the ceremony from his front-row seat next to his grandmas, Pat and Adele.

My buddies the Delia brothers were in attendance along with my great friends Jon, Steve and many of the important people who work for us. We were still somewhat tabloid news fodder and our security caught one reporter trying to sneak in with a catering truck. The LAPD who worked security at our home had promised that when the moment came they'd send up a chopper and give us one shot to chase intruders out of the sky above our property, insuring our privacy. Such were the conditions for our wedding in the nineties.

It was a great day. All the band, family and visitors at the house made the warm afternoon roll slowly and sweetly with so many familiar faces around. I was a little nervous; when you've blown a marriage you can be a little gun shy, but it was a day of encouragement and support from our closest friends, and it added to the certainty Patti and I felt about our love. Come late afternoon, the LAPD kept their promise, and beneath clear skies we gathered in a small procession, instruments playing to accompany us over to the courtyard for our ceremony. There, a Unitarian minister we'd been introduced to by friends did a lovely job with the service. I had a chance to tell our guests about my love for Patti and then we adjourned for an easy dinner by candlelight and a night of partying. Patti's dad, Joe, always the joker and the apple in a crate of oranges, noted the fence around our property and asked me how I was going to get away. I explained to him that I'd been there and that with his daughter I was finally where I wanted to be.

## The Honeymooners

We honeymooned fifties-style in a little log cabin Abe Lincoln himself could have been born in, in Yosemite Park. It was fun, but we also suffered a week of simultaneous and funny anxiety attacks when we looked at each other as husband and wife. Somewhere inside we were still two loners trying something new. We traveled, staying in little roadside motels, listening to our favorite music, as I drank Jack Daniel's and we played 500 Rummy on the motel lawns as the sun set on the desert across the highway. We did miss our Evan, so five days later we pulled back into our LA digs just as an anonymous sky writer etched a huge heart in the flat blue sky over our home. What timing! We found Evan on a blanket in the grass inside a small courtyard, playing with his grandma Pat. We spent the rest of the afternoon there with our family. At one point I leaned over and, with Evan between us, I kissed Patti. From here on in I wouldn't be alone.

## Pony Girl

On December 30, 1991, Jessica Rae Springsteen was born. A red-faced, coal-black-haired baby girl, she popped out with her furrowed brow and fretting hands belying the beautiful young woman and self-confident athlete she'd become. Stubborn to the bone, then and now, while still in her high chair, she would scream and fume if you unbuckled her little safety belt for her. She couldn't speak! But still, she would sit there, her complexion turning Bazooka-bubblegum pink as her stubby little digits, pulling and tugging, struggled with the buckle and she exerted her tiny, mighty little will to DO IT HERSELF! . . . And she usually would. That's never changed.

Patti and I are sitting in our Rumson living room directly beneath Jessica's bedroom. We hear a thud. I go up and see she's climbed the wooden bars of her crib and thrown herself out. I place her back in and return downstairs. Five minutes later, thud. I climb the stairs, I place her back in. Five minutes . . . thud . . . I watch as she toddles herself to a single bed on the far side of the room and, struggling, climbs in. The crib is done, for good. That's the way she rolls.

When Jess is four years old, Patti and I, searching for some land, visit a local farm on Middletown's Navesink River Road. A horse is quietly grazing in its small meadow. Jess asks, "Can I go see?" With the owner's acquiescence, we climb over the fence and walk through calf-high grass, and as we reach the horse, Jess closes her eyes and places her tiny palms flat upon its flanks. She stands there in meditation, offering up . . . a wish? A prayer? Then, "Can I get on?" . . . a nod from the owner . . . okay. I lift her and set her on bareback. She sits quietly, then, after twenty years of five-thirty a.m. mornings, countless barns, hundreds of hooves picked and manes and coats brushed, and thousands of miles traveled throughout the Northeast and Europe, she is an excellent and lifelong horsewoman, an internationally recognized equestrian, defying gravity, taking fifteen-hundred-pound animals five feet into the air . . . a natural. She has no memory of never having ridden.

*Patti and I drive Jess one Saturday morning when she is five years old to the Meadowlands, scene of many E Street triumphs. There is a horse show, her first. I tell her,*

*"Jess, when we get there, if you don't want to do this . . ." We arrive; she slips quickly into her riding gear, then walks, a small elegant figure, down the concrete ramp leading to the arena's underbelly, where, over the years, we've unloaded tons of rock 'n' roll gear on many a victorious night. In the staging area, she's lifted onto her pony; the lights in the complex are on full. The floor, usually the province of screaming fans, is covered in eight-inch-deep dirt footing, front to back. Dad moves close and says, "Now, Jess . . ." I receive no acknowledgment whatsoever and I witness for the first time the game face she wears to this day. Patti and I move into the stands and the name Springsteen, Jessica Springsteen, echoes around the cavernous spaces of our hometown stomping grounds. Patti and I sit, arm in arm, dumbstruck. Jess competes in the very beginning of the equestrian competition, the day's lead-line class. She captures a green ribbon and places sixth. The ride home is quiet as she sits in her riding gear, mysteriously humming. We tell her how well she did, how proud we are. She says nothing. Then, from the musical quiet in the backseat come two questions: "What was the name of the girl who won?" and "What did she do to win?"*

## New Band/New Day

Six months earlier, from our LA auditions, I'd put together an excellent touring band filled with great musicians from a variety of backgrounds. The auditions were a lot of fun and I got a chance to play with the best the city had to offer. Great drummers, bass players and singers filed in, one after another. Afternoons of music stretched on and on and I really learned a lot about what an individual player can and cannot bring. With drummers I found a fascinating rule of law. There were those who could groove and keep time like you wouldn't believe but when asked to open up in a rock vein, à la Keith Moon (or Max Weinberg), they subtly dropped the ball. Then you had guys who could really rock and hit hard but were slightly time challenged. I found it fascinating that more of these, the very best guys, couldn't cover both territories, but modern records at the time had moved away from drum fills; click tracks (electronic timekeepers) were in vogue in recording, so most of these players were probably rarely asked for unassisted Al Jackson time threaded with a Hal Blaine–like perfect storm of record-ending drum thunder. Finally, Zach Alford, a young kid with both hard rock and funk experience, came in and perfectly fit the bill.

The rest of the group consisted of Shane Fontayne on guitar; Tommy Sims on bass; Crystal Taliefero on guitar, vocals and percussion; and Bobby King, Carol Dennis, Cleopatra Kennedy, Gia Ciambotti and Angel Rogers on background vocals. Nice folks, excellent musicians and great singers all.

We hit the road on June 15, 1992. I enjoyed touring with them and benefiting from their musical experience. We'd sit on the bus and pass the beatbox around, and everyone would take a turn playing their favorite music. Tommy Sims was all Ohio Players, Parliament Funkadelic and seventies funk, music I wasn't that familiar with; he also brought deep knowledge of the slick Philly soul epitomized by the Chi-Lites, the Delfonics and Harold Melvin and the Blue Notes, heirs to the Motown hit machine. Tommy gave me a new appreciation for those records.

Cleopatra Kennedy and Carol Dennis would bring the high gospel. Bobby King was straight, hard soul music. He was a stocky, gospel-trained weight lifter and we spent a good deal of time in a variety of hole-in-the-wall gyms together. He was also one of the funniest people I've ever met, a great raconteur, a street philosopher, with a lot of life experience to back it up. We became great friends, still speak on the phone regularly, and I've tried many times to persuade him to come back to tour and sing with me. Sometime after the *Human Touch* tour, Bobby quit singing secular music, recommitted himself to his Lord, his street mission and his family. He works in construction and still lives down in Louisiana, visiting prisons while bringing gospel music and God's word to those in need. God bless you, Bobby.

It was a lot of good shows, good company and good times. I felt momentarily free of the baggage I'd collected with my good friends on E Street. Then one day, while playing in Germany to a crowd of sixty thousand, I wandered off to the far side of the stage's runway. The sound of my new band, projected by tons of stage-front sound equipment, drifted far off into the late afternoon, and the setting sun was turning everything and everyone in the large crowd golden, but there on a green hill, high at the edge of the amphitheater, stood a lone fan, holding aloft a sign that simply read, "E Street." He was a true-blue loyalist. I waved and smiled. There would be other times and places.

# FIFTY-EIGHT

# EARTHQUAKE SAM

Our life in Los Angeles had settled into a comfortable rhythm when on January 5, 1994, Sam Ryan Springsteen was born. Long seconds passed as I watched him slide into the doctor's hands, umbilical cord wrapped around his neck, trailing his fleshy tether behind him.

Sam came forth a little hard-faced character with a moon-round kisser, Irish to the bone. As he grew, with his hair slicked back off his forehead, he looked like a Joycean urchin off the streets of Dublin. Twelve days after Sam clocked in at seven pounds, fifteen ounces, the 6.7-magnitude Northridge earthquake shook Southern California. Northridge was just over the hill from our California home. At 4:31 a.m., I woke to hear what I thought was our two dogs in a hell of a fight directly under our bed. The night had been broken by their "early alarm" howling and the mattress beneath us quaking like somewhere under there, two pit bulls were fucking a porcupine. I swung my head over the side of the bed, peered under and saw . . . nothing, empty floor. Then seconds later, the freight train rumble and room-shattering shake of the biggest quake I'd ever experienced hit us.

I'd been in earthquakes plenty of times: in a high-rise hotel in Japan, in the studio in LA, at my Hollywood Hills house, in the early morning after filming Roy Orbison's *Black and White Night*. On that occasion, right around dawn, the house started rocking and I was greeted by the vision of a hysterical Matt Delia at the foot of my bed, naked but for one pillow over his privates and one over his ass. He wanted to run into the street but the quake ceased before Matt's gnarly physique had a chance to damage the psyches of my LA neighbors. Despite these experiences, the Northridge quake was something else. It seemed to last a long time, long enough for me to make my way to the kids' room, where three-year-old Evan was up in the middle of the floor, arms outstretched, balancing himself like he was surfing a wave. He didn't appear frightened, just in wonder, mystified. I snatched him up, then grabbed Jessie, who was standing, awake and crying, in her crib as Patti held Sam, who so far had been managing to sleep through the whole thing. Then we did it all wrong, running down the shaking stairs out of the house and into the yard before it ceased. There, for most of the morning, we camped, as one aftershock after another rolled through, rattling our nerves every twenty minutes or so. Over the next few days, there were hundreds, big and small, and we kept Sam in the kitchen, in a basket, below a solid oak coffee table, near the yard.

We were visited by friends, some of whom were truly in shock. We heard horror stories from those we knew at the beach, where the sand beneath their homes liquefied to jelly, turning large pieces of furniture into deadly projectiles tumbling and shooting around the room. Our chimney cracked straight through the center of the house and took months to repair. The aftershocks continued night and day. At first we had no television service and so little information we had to phone friends back east to get news about what was going on where we lived. Finally, after three days of shake, rattle and roll, Patti, recuperating from her pregnancy, barely two weeks out of the hospital, mother of a newborn child and two more still in diapers, looked at me and said, "Get us out of here." I said, "Aw, honey, we can tough it out." She said, "You tough it out, I've got three children to consider."

The city was on edge; there had been reports that the Northridge quake could be just a preliminary to something bigger to come! That thought was disconcerting. I did not want my new family to end up the first citizens of the new Atlantis. I pulled the emergency cord. I called Mr. Tommy Mottola, then president of Sony Records, and three hours later, a Sony jet pulled up in Burbank to pick up a valuable rock star and his brood. Patti and I, fortunate and responsible parents, headed back to the Garden State. Adios, Estado Dorado. New Jersey may have the Mafia, street gangs, insane property taxes, belching industrial areas and crazy, crooked politicians galore, but the land beneath all this insanity is relatively stable. That can make up for a wide variety of shortcomings, so with the newly christened "Earthquake Sam" riding the jet stream Nile like the baby Moses in his basket, we flew back to the land of his blood brethren and relief.

I'd ridden out plenty of earthquakes before with no noticeable aftereffects, but once we were ensconced again in our Rumson home, I noticed a strange trace from our experience. If Patti's leg moved in the bed at night, if the furnace in the basement turned on with a low house-shaking rumble, my heart rate would spike, and I'd jolt to consciousness, veins filled with adrenaline in a fight-or-flight response to the slightest stimulus. Soon I realized I'd contracted a very mild form of post-traumatic stress. It took me the better part of six months to completely calm.

Sam developed into a pug-faced little bruiser. Upon becoming frustrated with his older brother's systematic tortures, he could build up enough steam to let a gut punch go into his intimidating sibling's solar plexus. Evan, ever the sophisticated sadist, played the affronted gentleman perfectly. Rather than whomping on his overmatched little bro's head, he would drolly report, "Dad, Sam's hitting me," and leave it to the authorities. He could be emotionally rough, but physically he cut his little brother quite a bit of slack. Sam is a good, intelligent soul and as a young child he impressed upon me a great lesson. Initially, Sam was the only child I could not get to respect me or my requests. When it came time to give dad his "props," he resisted. This angered and frustrated the old-school part of me terribly. Children should respect their parents! It seemed he would not give me my tribute. He would ignore me, disobey me and generally look upon me as a bossy, annoying stranger who held little influence over his young developing soul. Patti interceded. I was *behind* with Sam, and that's what he was telling me. He was schooling me on what it would take to be his dad. I wasn't showing my respect for him and so he was reciprocating. To children, respect is shown through love and caring over the smallest elements in their lives. That's how they feel honored. I wasn't honoring my son so he wasn't honoring me. This worried me deeply.

Long ago, I'd promised myself that I would never lose my children in the way my father had lost me. It would've been a devastating personal failure, one for which I would have had no excuse, and I would not have been able to forgive myself. We began having our children late—I was forty, Patti thirty-six—and that was a wise decision. I knew enough about myself to understand that I was neither mature nor stable enough to parent well at any earlier point in my life. Once they were here, Patti and I knew our children would be our first priority. All of our tours would be booked around school schedules, children's events, birthdays, and because of Patti's insistence, planning and dedication, we made it work. I worked hard not to be an absentee dad, but in my business, that's not always possible and Patti picked up the slack. She also guided me when she thought I was falling short. For years, I'd kept musician's hours, a midnight rambler; I'd rarely get to bed before four a.m. and often sleep to noon or beyond. In the early days, when the children were up at night, I found it easy to do my part in taking care of them. After dawn, Patti was on duty. Once they got older, the night shift became unnecessary and the burden tilted unfairly toward the morning hours.

Finally, one day she came to me as I lay in bed around noon and simply said, "You're gonna miss it."

I answered, "Miss what?"

She said, "The kids, the morning, it's the best time, it's when they need you the most. They're different in the morning than at any other time of the day and if you don't get up to see it, well then . . . you're gonna miss it."

The next morning, mumbling, grumbling, stolid faced, I rolled out of bed at seven a.m. and found my way downstairs. "What do I do?"

She looked at me and said, "Make the pancakes."

Make the pancakes? I'd never made anything but music my entire life. I . . . I . . . I . . . don't know how!

"Learn."

That evening, I queried the gentleman who was cooking for us at the time for his recipe for pancakes and I posted it on the side of the refrigerator. After some early cementlike results, I dialed it in, expanded my menu and am now proud to say that should the whole music thing go south, I will be able to hold down a job between the hours of five and eleven a.m. at any diner in America. Feeding your children is an act of great intimacy and I received my rewards, the sounds of forks clattering on breakfast plates, toast popping out of the toaster, and the silent approval of morning ritual. If I hadn't gotten up, I would've missed it.

Rule: when you're on tour, you're king, and when you're home, you're *not*. This takes some adjustment or your "royalness" will ruin everything. The longer I was gone, the more I returned home a drifter and the harder it would be to move myself into the family upon my return. It is my nature to "dissemble" (a.k.a. fuck up), then bring roses, blow kisses and do backward somersaults in a manic frenzy trying to charm my way out of the hole I've dug. That's no good with kids (or a wife either). Patti had counseled me to "do one consistent thing a day with Sam." I knew he had a habit of waking in the night, wanting a bottle and then coming into our bed, so I started to make these nightly forays with him. Down into the kitchen we'd go, getting the milk, then it was back to *his* bedroom, where I'd tell him a story and he'd slip peacefully back off to sleep. The whole thing would take about forty-five minutes, but in less than a week, he began to respond, looking for me in the late hour, depending on me. My commitment had been all he was really looking for. Luckily for parents, children have great resilience and a generous ability to forgive. My wife guided me in this and my son taught me.

With my eldest son our relationship held its own complications. Over the years, I'd subtly sent signals of my unavailability, of my internal resistance to incursions upon my time by family members. As a young child he astutely picked these up and to "release" me he learned to say, "Thanks, Dad, but I'm busy right now, maybe later, tomorrow." I'd often breathe a sigh of relief and run back to my fortress of solitude, where as usual I felt at home, safe, until, like a bear in need of blood and meat, I'd wake from my hibernation and travel through the house for my drink from the cup of human love and companionship. But I always felt I needed to be able to shut it all off like a spigot. Patti saw all this and called me on it. For a long time I'd felt the greatest sin a family member could commit was interrupting me while I was working on a song. I felt music was fleeting and once you let it slip through your hands, it was gone. Through Patti, I learned that their requests came first and how to stop what I was doing and listen to them. I came to understand that music, a song, will always be there for me. But your children are here and gone.

While I may never lay claim to the title "father of the year," I worked hard to get straight with those who depended on my nearness to nurture and guide them. Patti made sure I had good strong relationships with our kids, free of much of the turmoil I experienced as a child.

# Cool Rockin' Daddy

I was always afraid my kids might steer away from music due to the fact that it was the family business. So I was pleased one day when I poked my head into Evan's room and saw him entranced in front of his computer, ears locked on some vicious-sounding punk music. He invited me in and played me some Against Me! The band sounded hard and soulful. He said they'd soon be coming to a local club, the Starland Ballroom, and asked if I would like to attend the show with him. I accepted immediately. The night came and we drove up Route 9 to Sayreville and the Starland. We were going to hear his heroes.

We parked in the lot and headed in to find the floor in front of the bandstand awash with teenagers. Evan and a pal headed into the swirl of bodies as I took my place at the side bar with a scattering of parents.

Two fine bands opened the show, Fake Problems and the Riverboat Gamblers. Then during the break a young man with a yellow Mohawk who was standing to my left said, "The bass player in Against Me! is a big fan of yours." I said, "Really?" I was shortly introduced to Andrew Seward, a sturdily built, bearded, auburn-haired young man who warmly greeted me and invited us backstage after the show to meet the band. Home run!

Against Me! took the stage and played a ferocious set, turning the crowd into a sweating soup of flailing bodies. Every word of every song was shouted back to the band at full volume. After an hour and with the roof firmly raised, Evan and his friend returned from the mosh pit soaked and spent. Would they like to meet the band?

"Yes!"

We made our way up some back stairs into the kind of cramped club dressing room I'd spent a good part of my young life in and we said hello to four wrung-out young musicians. Some small talk was made, photos were taken, and as we were about to leave the bass player stepped forward to my son, rolled up his sleeve and showed Evan a verse of "Badlands" he had tattooed on his forearm. Pointing to it, he said, "Look, it's your dad." Evan just stared. When our kids were young, we never pushed our music at home. With the exception of some guitars and a piano, our house was free of gold albums, Grammys or any other musical mementos. My kids didn't know "Badlands" from matzoh ball soup. When they were children, when I was approached on the street for autographs, I'd explain to them that in my job I was Barney (the then-famous purple dinosaur) for adults.

That night, moments before we left, the bass player rolled up another sleeve to show us a tat of myself stretching from shoulder to elbow. For one brief moment I took a silent pride in seeing my influence passed on and feeling like the coolest dad in the room.

After I promptly promised E Street tickets to all in sight for life, we said our good-byes and left. On the way home, Ev said, "Dad, that guy has you tattooed on his arm."

I said, "Yeah, what do you think?"

"It's funny."

Toward the end of that week I stopped in his bedroom and probed a little more. "Did you have fun the other night?" Without turning away from his computer or even looking at me, he responded, "Greatest night of my life."

With my son Sam, it was classic rock: Dylan, Bob Marley and Creedence Clearwater, whom he picked up from his "Battlefield Vietnam" video game. He wandered into our bedroom one night and saw Dylan at Newport on our TV. "Who's that guy?" He was interested, so I bought him some of the early Dylan folk albums. Sam was in middle school and probably only ten or eleven when I entered his bedroom to hear "Chimes of Freedom" from Dylan's *Another Side of Bob Dylan* album playing on vinyl in a dimly lit distant corner. As he lay in bed, he reminded me of the many nights I lay in darkness with Spector, Orbison and Dylan playing at my bedside. I sat on the edge of his bed and I asked him what he thought of the young Bob. Out of the dark, his voice still containing the rising sweetness of a child . . .

"Epic."

Jessie is the keeper of the keys to all things Top 40, blasting out hip-hop and pop at full volume, taking me to see Taylor Swift and Justin Timberlake and singing at the top of her lungs in the car with her girlfriends. She is my guide to and interpreter of *what's happening now* over the airwaves. In the past I have spent many a holiday evening at Z100's Jingle Ball, meeting Shakira, Rihanna, Fall Out Boy and Paramore, along with many other hit makers. In Madison Square Garden, at peace, I'd sit surrounded by squealing teens and stout-hearted parents. I once sat next to a lovely woman who pointed to Jess and asked, "Is that your daughter?" I said, "Yes." She then pointed to the stage, where an on-the-cusp-of-fame Lady Gaga, dressed in a white tutu, was singing her first hit and said, "That's mine."

When my kids first came to our shows, they were small. And after some early shock and awe, they usually fell promptly asleep or drifted back to their video games, happy to leave Mom and Pop to do their work and come home. At the end of the day, as parents, you are *their* audience. They are not meant to be yours. I always figured young kids wouldn't mind seeing fifty thousand people boo their parents, but what kid wants to see fifty thousand people cheer their folks? None.

When they got older, things changed somewhat and the knowledge of Mom and Dad's work life slowly seeped into our home. I enjoy hearing my kids critique my records and seeing them have fun at our shows. But I'm happy in the knowledge they were baptized in the holy river of rock and pop by their own heroes, in their own way, at their own time.

# FIFTY-NINE

# "STREETS OF PHILADELPHIA"

In 1994, I received a phone call from Jonathan Demme asking if I'd consider writing a song for a film he was directing called *Philadelphia*. The film was about a gay man's battle with AIDS and his fight to retain his position with a prestigious Philadelphia law firm. I had my studio set up at home in Rumson and for a few afternoons, I went in with some lyrics I had partially written dealing with the death of a close friend. Jonathan requested a rock song to open the film. I spent a day or so trying to accommodate, but the lyrics I had seemed to resist being put to rock music. I began to fiddle with the synthesizer, playing over a light hip-hop beat I programmed on the drum machine. As soon as I slowed the rhythm down over some basic minor chords, the lyrics fell into place and the voice I was looking for came forward. I finished the song in a few hours and sent the tape off to Jonathan, feeling like I hadn't gotten it. He phoned me in a few days saying he loved it and placed it over the images of Philadelphia at the top of the film.

"Streets of Philadelphia" was a top ten hit because of the film and because it addressed something the country was attempting to come to grips with at that moment. How do we treat our sons and daughters confronting AIDS? Jonathan's film came at an important moment and did its work. It was good to be a small part of it. Oh . . . and I won an Oscar. When I traveled north from LA to show it to my folks, it showed up on the airport x-ray and I had to drag it out of my bag. Upon reaching San Mateo, I walked into the kitchen, where my father was still sitting and smoking like a blue-collar Buddha, and plopped it down on the table in front of him. He looked at it, looked at me and said, "I'll never tell anybody what to do ever again."

After "Streets of Philadelphia" I spent the better part of the year in Los Angeles trying to come up with an album in that vein. It was an album centering on men and women and it was dark. I'd just made three of those records, varying in tone, in a row. The last two had been met with not indifference, but something like it. I was feeling a faint disconnect with my audience.

One evening as Roy and I took a drive, he suggested that perhaps it was the lyrical content that was distancing some of our fans. You can get away with a one-off of anything—*Tunnel of Love* and *Nebraska* are excellent examples—but it has to be finely crafted and fully realized. I'd made my meat and potatoes writing about the broader lives of people, often working people particularly, and while at the time I told Roy he didn't know what he was talking about, I think he actually was onto something. I don't write strictly for my audience's desires but we are, at this point, engaged in a lifelong dialogue, so I take into consideration their voices. You need to be adventurous, to listen to your heart and write what it's telling you, but your creative instinct isn't infallible. The need to look for direction, input and some guidance, outside of yourself, can be healthy and fruitful. This would've been my fourth record in a row about relationships. If I could've felt its fullness, I wouldn't have hesitated to put it out. But a not-fully-realized record around the same topic felt like one too many. I had to come to terms with the fact that after my year of work writing, recording, mixing, it was going on the shelf. That's where she sits.

## Greatest Hits

I was again at loose ends. Where am I going? Who am I now? What do I have to give to my audience? If these questions were in my head, I knew they were in my audience's as well, so, when in doubt . . . retreat! It was 1995, seven years since the E Street Band had played together. That's a generation in rock 'n' roll. We'd never made a greatest hits record and we decided it was time to remind people a little of what we'd done.

It'd been ten years since the band had stood side by side in a recording studio together but I picked up the phone, called the guys, explained what I wanted to do and that it was a one-shot. On January 12, 1995, we gathered in Studio A at the Power Station, scene of many of our *USA* sessions; exchanged hugs and warm greetings; then set to work. After a session or two, I received a phone call from Steve, who said he'd heard we were recording. I was a little gun-shy. It had been fifteen years but a few nights later Steve sat on a stool in the studio with the same Groucho Marx–like, big-eyed, soft grin I'd loved and missed, plucking the mandolin for "This Hard Land."

Later we filmed a short promo set of the band playing live at Sony Studios. I showed the film to Jimmy Iovine in my LA den one night and as we slipped into "Thunder Road," he said, "You should jump on this now. Time is funny and this just feels right." I heard what he was saying but I wasn't ready to go there. *Greatest Hits* did nicely, gave my midnineties drift a little focus and a kick, then we once again went our separate ways.

I had one song left over from the project. It was a rock song I'd been writing for the band but couldn't complete. "Streets of Philadelphia" and

Jonathan Demme had gotten me thinking about writing on social issues again. This was something I'd steered away from for the past decade. As my success increased, there was something about that "rich man in a poor man's shirt" that left an uneasy taste in my mouth surrounding this type of writing. But drawing on my own young history and what I'd seen, I'd written about these things very well and over the years I'd refined a voice that was identifiably mine on these subjects. It was a story, a part of my story that I had to tell. You lay claim to your stories; you honor, with your hard work and the best of your talent, their inspirations, and you fight to tell them well from a sense of indebtedness and thankfulness. The ambiguities, the contradictions, the complexities of your choices are always with you in your writing as they are in your life. You learn to live with them. You trust your need to have a dialogue about what you deem important. After twenty-five years of writing, the song that helped me crystallize these issues and their currency for the second half of my work life was "The Ghost of Tom Joad."

# SIXTY

# THE GHOST OF TOM JOAD

We were now bicoastal, spending July to December in New Jersey and January to June in California. It was during our California stay that I began to think about my new record. Working once again on my home equipment in our guesthouse, I began to record a variety of acoustic and country rock songs I had recently written. *The Ghost of Tom Joad* was the result of a decade-long inner debate I'd been having with myself after the success of *Born in the USA*. That debate centered on a single question: Where does a rich man belong? If it was true that it's "easier for a camel to go through the eye of a needle than for a rich man to enter the kingdom of God," I wouldn't be walking through those pearly gates any time soon, but that was okay;

there was still plenty of work to be done down here on Earth. That was the premise of *The Ghost of Tom Joad*. What is the work for us to do in our short time here?

I began recording with just myself, my acoustic guitar and the remnant of "Tom Joad" I'd tried to write for the band. Once I cut that song in the version that appears on the album, I had a feeling for the record that I wanted to make. I'd pick up where I'd left off with *Nebraska*, set the stories in the midnineties and in the land of my current residence, California. The music was minimal, the melodies uncomplicated; the austere rhythms and arrangements defined who these people were and how they expressed themselves. They traveled light; they were lean, direct in their expression, yet with most of what they had to say left in the silence between words. They were transient and led hard, complicated lives, half of which had been left behind in another world, in another country.

The precision of the storytelling in these types of songs is very important. The correct detail can speak volumes about who your character is, while the wrong one can shred the credibility of your story. When you get the music and lyrics right, your voice disappears into the voices you've chosen to write about. Basically, with these songs, I find the characters and listen to them. That always leads to a series of questions about their behavior. What would they do? What would they never do? You need to locate the rhythm of their speech and the nature of their expression. But all the telling detail in the world doesn't matter if the song lacks an emotional center. That's something you have to pull out of yourself from the commonality you feel with the man or woman you're writing about. By pulling these elements together as well as you can, you shed light on their lives and honor their experiences.

I'd been through the Central Valley of California many times on the way to visiting my parents. I'd often stop and spend some time in the small farm towns off the interstate. But it still took a good amount of research to get the details of the region correct. I traced the stories out slowly and carefully. I thought hard about who these people were and the choices they were presented with. In California, there was a sense of a new country being formed on the edge of the old. You could feel the America of the next century taking shape in the deserts, fields, towns and cities there first. That vision has come to fruition and all you need to do is take a walk down the main street of my own three-thousand-mile-away Northeastern hometown, Freehold, on any summer evening to see the influx of Hispanic life, the face of the nation changing as it's changed so many times before, along with the hard greeting most of those who bring that change face upon arrival.

The old stories of race and exclusion continue to be played out. I tried to catch a small piece of this on the songs I wrote for *Tom Joad*. "Sinaloa Cowboys," "The Line," "Balboa Park" and "Across the Border" were songs that traced the lineage of my earlier characters to the Mexican migrant experience in the new West. These songs completed the circle, bringing me back to 1978 and the inspiration I'd taken from John Ford's film adaptation of Steinbeck's *The Grapes of Wrath*. Their skin was darker and their language had changed, but these were people trapped by the same brutal circumstances.

"Youngstown" and "The New Timer" were two songs inspired by a book called *Journey to Nowhere* by my friends Dale Maharidge and Michael Williamson. Both songs chronicled the effects of post-industrialization in the United States and the weight of lost jobs, outsourced labor and the disappearance of our manufacturing base on the citizens whose hard work built America. I'd seen it firsthand when the Karagheusian Rug Mill, based in Freehold, rather than settle a labor dispute with its workers, closed up shop and shipped south for cheaper, nonunionized labor. The jobs were gone. My dad had worked on the floor there when I was a kid; my musical life and the Castiles had been born not fifty yards from its belching smokestacks and clacking looms. (It closed in 1964 after sixty years of operation.)

By the end of *Tom Joad* I'd written about the death and destruction that accompany the lives of many of the people who inspired these songs. I was working on "Galveston Bay," a song that originally had a more violent ending, but it began to feel false. If I was going to find some small window of light, I had to do it with this man in this song. I'd already written "Across the Border," a song that was like a prayer or a dream you have the night before you're going to take a dangerous journey. The singer seeks a home where his love will be rewarded, his faith restored, where a tenuous peace and hope may exist. With "Galveston Bay" I had to make these ideas feel attainable. The song asks the question: Is the most political act an individual one, something that happens in the dark, in the quiet, when someone makes a particular decision that affects his immediate world? I wanted a character who is driven to do the wrong thing but does not. He instinctively refuses to add to the violence in the world around him. With great difficulty and against his own grain, he transcends his circumstances. He finds the strength and grace to save himself and the part of the world he touches.

*The Ghost of Tom Joad* chronicled the effects of the increasing economic division of the eighties and nineties, the hard times and consequences that befell many of the people whose work and sacrifice created America and whose labor is essential to our everyday lives. We are a nation of immigrants and no one knows who's coming across our borders today, whose story might add a significant page to our American story. Here in the early years of our new century, as at the turn of the last, we are once again at war with our "new Americans." As in the last, people will come, will suffer hardship and prejudice, will do battle with the most reactionary forces and hardest hearts of their adopted home and will prove resilient and victorious.

I knew that *The Ghost of Tom Joad* wouldn't attract my largest audience.

But I was sure the songs on it added up to a reaffirmation of the best of what I do. The record was something new, but it was also a reference point to the things I tried to stand for and still wanted to be about as a songwriter.

On November 21, 1995, I stepped onto the stage at the State Theatre in New Brunswick, New Jersey, for my first full solo acoustic concert since the early seventies at Max's Kansas City. I was going to have to hold this audience for two and a half hours . . . without a band.

The nakedness and tightrope drama of solo performance is a nervous revelation. It's one man, one guitar and "you," the audience. What's drawn forth is the emotional nucleus of your song. What's revealed is the naked bones of your relationship to one another and the music. If your song was written well, it will stand in its skeleton form. "Born in the USA" exploded into a Delta slide blues, its full meaning laid bare; "Darkness" hovered in its aloneness. In the house, my sound engineer John Kerns used the power of our audio system to turn my one acoustic guitar into a percussive orchestra or a barely heard ambient scratching accompanying my voice. I found new subtleties in my vocals, developed a high falsetto and learned to use my guitar for everything from a drum to a feedback-screeching canvas of sound. By the end of that first night, I felt I'd discovered something not as physical but as powerful as what I did with the E Street Band that spoke to my audience in a new tongue.

I devised a new repertoire of guitar tunings and voicings, refreshed my fingerpicking techniques and used the full power of my voice throughout its range. This allowed for a variety of musical settings that kept two hours of a guy and a guitar from feeling claustrophobic. The fans had to bring the quiet, and they did. Many of my characters were isolated men and you needed to feel the weight of the space and emptiness around and inside of them. You needed to *hear* their thoughts to bring the starkness of their land-scape to life. The magic of this music was in its dynamic range, from guitar crescendo to whispering silence.

These concerts revived me. They inspired me to dig deeper into the core of my songwriting, sending me back to my hotel room each night to spend the early hours of the morning with my song book, working the new vein I'd found.

I ended the tour recommitted to my "topical" songwriting, something I'd abandoned during the last several records. I finally felt comfortable again in my own skin. There were new songs to write.

# SIXTY-ONE

# WESTERN MAN

In California, my dad worked very hard, stayed employed as a bus driver, went to work each day, lost weight, played tennis, coached Pam's athletic teams and had a modest but loving renaissance. When I visited, he was easier, more mellow, physically healthier. It seemed like some of the pressure had been taken off. It didn't last. When his sickness returned, it came back with a vengeance.

When I'd visit my parents on tour, if I brought along any of my male friends, my father would suffer severe paranoia. He would burst out of his bedroom late at night, shouting angry nonsense, imagining we were making sexual advances toward my mother. I began to have to warn my pals or just keep them away. We began to get him help. He was diagnosed as a paranoid schizophrenic. Finally it was all beginning to make sense. He needed professional help and though he was resistant, he began to be treated.

Things would be all right for a while and then he would crash. As he got older he exhibited a very strong manic side. My dad was always heavy. He had a football player's build and would tend to put on weight easily. I was shocked when I visited my folks one year to find him thinner than me. He'd taken up walking and had manically walked himself skinny. He looked like a stranger, but the worst of it was I could tell his mind wasn't working right. There was an unnatural tightness in his face, a distant rigidity in his features he couldn't control. He would answer the most mundane questions cryptically.

"Hey, Pop, looks like a pretty nice day out there."

In between cigarette puffs he'd answer, "Oh yeah, that's what you think."

He was drifting between reality and delusion. He wouldn't be able to stop moving and then it would switch off, and he'd gain weight, be depressed and not budge from the kitchen table for months. Once he drove all the way to New Jersey, nonstop from California; left a note on my door saying, "Sorry I missed you"; drove over to my mom's relatives (in my pop's mind, always a disapproving hotbed of insurrection) and cursed them out; then turned around and drove, nonstop, back to the West Coast. He zipped around the country like a madman with my mom riding shotgun, supposedly enjoying their retirement, but my mother knew there was more at hand. By that point, he had been diagnosed and received treatment, but he often refused to take his medicine. They drove, drove, drove and drove. He was going to kill himself, my mother, or somebody else if he kept going.

At one point he disappeared for three days. My mother called; I flew to California and found he'd been arrested somewhere in the desert outside of LA. It was over an automobile violation of some kind but according to his story, he'd stood before the judge and refused to pay a small fine and so they put him in jail. Then, days later, he was bused to another jail in Los Angeles and released. Finally, a phone call came. I found him at six a.m. on the streets of Chinatown in a little "old man's" bar with a good-hearted bartender watching over him. We stopped on the way back for an early-morning breakfast at McDonald's. There my dad almost got us into a tremendous argument with the guy at the next table. Out of the blue my pop had started shouting profanity-laced non sequiturs and the guy thought he was talking to him. I apologized, explained as best I could, and we hustled out with our Egg McMuffins. It was sad. My dad was hearing the voices in his head and he was answering them.

Back at home in San Mateo, he remained rebellious. He would NOT stop. He would NOT take his medicine. He told me he was frightened it would all go away: the energy; the purpose, even if it was aimless; the egocentric strength; the high of his manic state—everything but the long, drawn-out depressions. I understood. I'd been there, though not to his extremes. Manic depression, the bipolar personality. It's the prize in the Cracker Jack box in our family. I told him I understood but that ultimately he would hurt someone, my mother or himself, and that I could not live without them. I could not live without *him*. Our family loved and needed him. I loved and needed him. He was essential to our strength. He was our center, our heart, so would he please allow me to help him care for himself? It wasn't an easy sell. There was shouting and crying, but in the end he walked out the door with us to the hospital.

He remained there for three days. He was observed, tested and put on some medication that returned him to Earth and to us. It would not all be easy sailing from here on, but modern pharmacological medicine gave my father ten extra years of life and a peace he might never have had. He and my mother got to celebrate their fiftieth wedding anniversary. He got to know his grandchildren and we became much closer. He became easier to reach, to know and love. I'd always heard my father in his youth described as "full of the devil," "rakish," "full of fun," as someone who loved to dance. I had never seen it. I only saw the lonely brooding man, always on edge, disappointed, never at home or at rest. But in the last years of his life, his softness came to the fore.

He wasn't always well and we'd have drives where he'd spout the most hair-raising stream of consciousness as if it were all events that had happened yesterday in our driveway. My father, who'd uttered fewer than one thousand words throughout most of my childhood, in the grips of his illness, opened the door a crack on the temple of dreams and devils he'd been dueling with in the dark of the kitchen for forty years. On a casual drive up Sunset Boulevard, I'd hear fantasized on-the-road adventures strangely and innocently told. I would hear, of all things . . . philosophizing!? The meaning of life (good), love (very important), money (not so important). Money? Not so important? Coming from my old man, who used to say he'd strangle somebody for a buck? So much of it had been a big fucking synapses-misfiring illusion. The state of the world and a wide variety of previously verboten subjects were now all grist for the mill for Doug Springsteen. The Sphinx spoke! My dad showed himself, or some part of himself, though under tenuous conditions. So, rather than revelation, his pronouncements brought only more mystery and a longing to understand what was ultimately unfathomable. Still, over the last ten years of his life, much of the time, he seemed calmer and more settled than ever before, with his manic side in check. You just had to make your peace with the rest. The past was done. There was no further purpose or any practical mechanics for its plumbing. The future was in the palm of the next day and so the present needed to hold its charms. We were left with a quiet, sometimes frustrating man-child responding to stimuli occurring only in the mind of the rock of my soul. This was my father.

Finally, time ran out. He'd not only battled hard against his own mind, but he'd beaten up his body pretty well over the years. He'd had the triple bypass, the strokes, been defibrillated back from the dead, and still hung on. Now there was only so much modern medicine could do. His heart gave out and the medication that made one thing better made something else worse; the law of diminishing returns had come to stay. I sat with him in hospice during the last days of April as they brought into his bedroom the machines that would try to keep him alive a little longer. He looked at them, looked at me and said, "Bruce, am I gonna make it?" I answered, "You usually do." But this time my dad didn't make it. He would leave in his style, the old immutable presence, his body white and raw, final thoughts known only to my mother.

Before he passed, I stood over my father and studied his body. It was the body of his generation. It was not shined or shaped into a suit of armor. It was just the body of a man. As I looked at my dad on what would be his deathbed, I saw the thinning black curly hair and the high forehead I see reflected back at me when I look in the mirror. There's the blotchy roughhouse of a face, the bull neck, the still-muscly shoulders and arms, and the swale between his chest and beer belly, half-covered by a wrinkled white sheet. Protruding from the bottom of that sheet are elephant stumps for calves and clubs for feet. The feet are red and yellow, scarred by psoriasis. Shaped in stone, they have no more miles left in them. They are the feet of my foe, and of my hero. They are crumbling now at their base. I scan back up to see boxer shorts in twisted disarray, then puffed armored slits holding reddened brown eyes. I stand there for a long moment and I lean over and lift a weighted, scaly hand between my palms. I feel warm breath as my lips kiss a sandpaper cheek and I whisper my good-bye.

On the evening of April 26, 1998, wrapped in my mother's arms, my dad quietly let out his last breath and died in his sleep.

With those extra years that were gifted to us, I got to see my children love my father and I got to watch his patience and kindness toward them. I got to see them mourn my father's death. My dad loved the sea, spending hours at the shore, staring at the water, admiring the boats. When my parents lived in San Francisco, he had a small boat he bobbed around the bay on. At his wake, my children approached his coffin and laid on his hands his "captain's" hat. It was one like the guy in the Captain and Tennille used to wear, a child's costume, a totem of an unlived life, of desire unattained. It served as a shield to cover my dad's beautiful, rocky-shaped, now nearly bald head and as a symbol of an imaginary commanding manhood and masculinity my pop always felt was just out of reach and under siege.

I understood that hunger. For me there'd be no captain's hat! Just "THE BOSS!" Bulging muscles, judo and the lifting of thousands and thousands of pounds' worth of meaningless objects every . . . single . . . day, until I finally brought my father the physical presence he'd been looking for.

Months later, in the evening twilight, returning from our local video store with my children, out of the blue I mentioned my father's death. The car went silent. I peered into the rearview mirror and saw my young son and daughter, mouths wide open, crying, but no sound had come out yet. Then, like thunder delayed after lightning, "Whaaaaaaaa . . . you mean the guy in the captain's hat?" It felt so good watching my children cry for my dad. As we pulled up to the house, they ran inside, still bawling. Patti saw me follow in behind with a smile. "What happened?" "It's Pop, they're crying over Pop."

He was returned to Freehold, the town he said he hated, and that other limousine, the one that brings the tears, brought them. We drove him straight out Throckmorton Street to St. Rose of Lima Cemetery to lie with his mother, his father, his sister and all the troubled souls who'd come before. Whirrrrr . . . Whirrrrr . . . the machinery of Freeman Funeral Home, a crowd I already had a long relationship with going back to the Irish and Italian wakes of my youth, lowered his casket six feet down. Then I, my brother-in-law, my nephews and my close friends the Delia brothers buried him ourselves. We shoveled the earth that landed with a hollow thunk upon his casket, patted the dirt down, then stood there in silence, the traffic shushing along the highway far down the hill below.

My father was not a modern man. He wore no mask. Maybe it was his illness, but as he aged he had a face without veils. It was ancient, tired, often puzzled. It was primitive and extinct, powerful, clueless as to its fate, noble in its struggle and purposeless in what he had suffered. At my father's funeral, my long-reformed greaser brother-in-law, Mickey Shave, gave a moving and funny eulogy. He described the day we pushed my father in his wheelchair, with flat tires, onto a bluff overlooking a windy California beach as his children and grandchildren played in the sand and wintry surf below. He described my father sitting there with a smile, as close to peace as he ever got, "gazing down upon all he created," his "art," his love, his family.

One morning in the days before I was about to become a father, my dad showed up at my bungalow doorstep in LA. He'd driven down from San Mateo and "just wanted to say hi." I invited him in, and at eleven o'clock in a small sun-drenched dining area, we sat at the table nursing beers. My father, in his normal state, had little talent for small talk so I did the best I could.

Suddenly, he said, "Bruce, you've been very good to us." I acknowledged that I had. Pause. His eyes drifted out over the Los Angeles haze. He continued, ". . . And I wasn't very good to you." A small silence caught us.

"You did the best you could," I said.

That was it. It was all I needed, all that was necessary. I was blessed on that day and given something by my father I thought I'd never live to see . . . a brief recognition of the truth. It was why he'd come five hundred miles that morning. He'd come to tell me, on the eve of my fatherhood, that he loved me, and to warn me to be careful, to do better, to not make the same painful mistakes he'd made. I try to honor it.

Immediately after he died, I felt suffocatingly claustrophobic. It rained solidly for two weeks. I slept outdoors for that time on the porch, in the cold, in the rain; I still don't know exactly why. I suppose it was just "death closing in . . . the next man in line" and all that. I just couldn't find my way back into the house. During the days I visited all his old haunts: the Blue Moon Tavern; the Belmar Marina; the Manasquan Inlet, a place where my father parked alone for hours, cigarette dangling from his left hand out the driver's-side window, as the fishing boats left and came in from the sea. Then finally, one night, with Patti's help, I came inside and gave in to the tears.

We honor our parents by carrying their best forward and laying the rest down. By fighting and taming the demons that laid them low and now reside in us. It's all we can do if we're lucky. I'm lucky. I have a wife I love, a beautiful daughter and two handsome sons. We are close. We do not suffer the alienation and confusion I experienced in my family. Still, the seeds of my father's troubles lie buried deep in our bloodline . . . so we have to watch.

I learned many a rough lesson from my father. The rigidity and the blue-collar narcissism of "manhood" 1950s-style. An inner yearning for isolation, for the world on your terms or not at all. A deep attraction to silence, secrets and secretiveness. You always withhold something, you do not lower your mask. The distorted idea that the beautiful things in your life, the love itself you struggled to win, to create, will turn and possess you, robbing you of your imagined long-fought-for freedoms. The hard blues of constant disaffection. The rituals of the barroom. A misogyny grown from the fear of all the dangerous, beautiful, strong women in our lives crossed with the carrying of an underlying physical threat, a psychological bullying that is meant to frighten and communicate that the dark thing in you is barely restrained. You use it to intimidate those you love. And of course . . . the disappearing act: you're there but not there, not really present; inaccessibility, its pleasures and its discontents. All leading ultimately to the black seductive fantasy of a wreck of a life, the maddening boil lanced, the masks dropped and the long endless free fall into the chasm that at certain moments can smell so sweet from a distance. Of course, once you stop romanticizing it, more likely you're just another chaos-sowing schmuck on the block, sacrificing your treasured family's trust to your "issues." You're a dime a dozen in every burb across America. I can't lay it all at my pop's feet; plenty of it is my own weakness and inability at this late date to put it all away, my favorite harpies, the ones I count on to return to flit and nibble around the edges of my beautiful reward. Through hard work and Patti's great love I have overcome much of this, though not all of it. I have days when my boundaries wobble, my darkness and the blues seem to beckon and I seek to medicate myself in whatever way I can. But on my best days, I can freely enjoy the slow passing of time, the tenderness that is in my life; I can feel the love I'm a part of surrounding me and flowing through me; I am near home and I am standing hand in hand with those I love, past and present, in the sun, on the outskirts of something that feels, almost . . . like being free.

Those whose love we wanted but could not get, we emulate. It is dangerous but it makes us feel closer, gives us an illusion of the intimacy we never had. It stakes our claim upon that which was rightfully ours but denied. In my twenties, as my song and my story began to take shape, I searched for the voice I would blend with mine to do the telling. It is a moment when through creativity and will you can rework, repossess and rebirth the conflicting voices of your childhood, to turn them into something alive, powerful and seeking light. I'm a repairman. That's part of my job. So I, who'd never done a week's worth of manual labor in my life (hail, hail rock 'n' roll!), put on a factory worker's clothes, my father's clothes, and went to work.

One night I had a dream. I'm onstage in full flight, the night is burning and my dad, long dead, sits quietly in an aisle seat in the audience. Then . . . I'm kneeling next to him in the aisle, and for a moment, we both watch the man on fire onstage. I touch his forearm and say to my dad, who for so many years sat paralyzed by depression, "Look, Dad, look . . . that guy onstage . . . that's you . . . that's how I see you."

# SIXTY-TWO

# EASTERN WOMAN

When my mom went to California, she didn't return to New Jersey until thirty years later, after my father's death. A lot of water had gone under the bridge, but for my sister Virginia and me, our father's primacy was a bitter pill. He came first . . . always. My mother has great and profound love for her children but she will tell you to this day, those were her choices; they were all she knew how to do.

My mother had married my father by the age of twenty-three. By her generation's standards, this was when people began families, went to war, went out on their own. When she left, my sister and I were eighteen and nineteen respectively and living under rather harsh circumstances. We had our lives handed to us. We took charge of them. My mother was married. Maybe she figured my father just needed her more than we did. Without her my dad's illness could've killed him or left him living out on the street.

More likely, he just would've come back home or would never have left. My dad was ill but wily. He held us all hostage for many years—in my mom's case, right up until he died. And she never called him on it.

The other life my mom seemed built for and could've had, the life of dining, dancing, laughter, adult partnership, the equal sharing of life's burdens, she was not compelled to pursue. We don't always want what seems best suited for us; we want what we "need." You make your choices and you pay the piper. She chose and she paid. We all did.

My mother stood behind my wildest dreams, accepted me at face value for who I truly was and nurtured the unlikely scenario I held deepest in my heart, that I was going to make music and that someone, somewhere, was going to want to hear it. She shone her light on me at a time when it was all the light there was.

When I hit it big, my mom believed the saints had come marching in and blessed us for the hard times we'd endured. I suppose they had.

Amongst many things, my mother taught me the dangerous but timely lesson that there is a love seemingly beyond love, beyond our control, and it will take us through our lives bestowing blessings and curses as they fall. It will set you on fire, confuse you, drive you to passion and extreme deeds, and may smite the reasonable, modestly loving parts of who you are. Love has a great deal to do with humility. In my parents' love, there was kindness, a beyond-human compassion, an anger, a compulsive fidelity, a generosity and an unconditionality that scorched everything in its path. It was exclusive. It was not humble. It was their love.

My mom remains magic; people love her when they meet her, as they should. At ninety-one and battling Alzheimer's, she delivers a warmth and exuberance the world as it is may not merit. She continues to be filled with an indomitable spirit of optimism, a heartbreaking toughness, no cynicism, laughter and great humor (for Christmas one year she gave me the complete third season of Columbo—"You know, that guy in the raincoat!"). To this day she can give me a true, deeply hopeful feeling about life over the course of an otherwise-ordinary one-hour lunch at a local diner. My mom is very, very funny, always bringing laughs. She is a natural show woman, a dancer and stylishly put together to a T for even the most casual outing. She is democratic, egalitarian, without a clue as to how those words might pertain to her. She is heart, heart, heart. Since her return to New Jersey, she has learned (not easily) how to place herself amongst my family. We had our small showdowns, even an afternoon of some yelling (very rare in Springsteen households). Then I watched her work, contain herself, use her intelligence and love to give herself to us. My mother and father had outlaw in them, and despite my mother's great warmth, such things don't necessarily come easy to outlaws. Her resilience, good soul and desire to do right still guide her. She settled in as Mother and Grandma. If you met her, you would know her in an instant . . . and you would love her. Like I do. She is a raw, rough wonder.

Shortly after my pop passed away, I met "Queenie" (my mom's childhood alias) for the first time. It was payback time, and my mom enjoys the good life as much as anyone. She's occasionally traveled around the world with us. She takes pride in the accomplishments of her children, her grandchildren—my youngest sister's motherhood and photography career; Virginia's motherhood, grandmotherhood and work life; and the exploits of her guitar-playing son. We share the laughter, memories and pain of the Freehold days and we take pride in the survival of our love.

My youngest sister, Pam, still lives in California, where my mother visits often. My sister Virginia and I see my mom quite regularly at our Sunday evening family dinners, just after she's returned from the headstones at St. Rose of Lima Cemetery, visiting my dad.

# SIXTY-THREE

# KING OF NEW JERSEY (HOLLYWOOD DAYS)

There's a tap on my shoulder. I turn around and get lost in a sea of blue. A Jersey-accented voice says, "It's about time, kid," and Frank Sinatra rattles the ice in his glass of Jack Daniel's. Looking at the swirling deep-brown liquid, he whispers, "Ain't it beautiful?" This is my introduction to the Chairman of the Board. We spend the next half hour talking Jersey, Hoboken, swimming in the Hudson River and the Shore. We then sit down for dinner at a table with Robert De Niro, Angie Dickinson and Frank and his wife, Barbara. This is all occurring at the Hollywood "Guinea Party" Patti and I have been invited to, courtesy of Tita Cahn. Patti had met Tita a few weeks previous at the nail parlor. She's the wife of Sammy Cahn, famous for such songs as "All The Way," "Teach Me Tonight" and "Only the Lonely." She called one afternoon and told us she was hosting a private event. She said it would be very quiet and couldn't tell us who would be there, but assured us we'd be very comfortable. So off into the LA night we went.

During the evening, we befriend the Sinatras and are quietly invited into the circle of the last of the old Hollywood stars. Over the next several years we attend a few very private events where Frank and the remaining clan hold forth. The only other musician in the room is often Quincy Jones, and besides Patti and I there is rarely a rocker in sight. The Sinatras are gracious hosts and our acquaintance culminates in our being invited to Frank's eightieth birthday party dinner. It's a sedate event at the Sinatras' Los Angeles home. Sometime after dinner, we find ourselves around the living room piano with Steve and Eydie Gorme and Bob Dylan. Steve is playing the piano and up close he and Eydie can really sing the great standards. Patti has been thoroughly schooled in jazz by Jerry Coker, one of the great jazz educators at the Frost School of Music at the University of Miami. She was there at the same time as Bruce Hornsby, Jaco Pastorius and Pat Metheny, and she learned her stuff. At Frank's, as the music drifts on, she slips gently in on "My One and Only Love." Patti is a secret weapon. She can sing torch like a cross between Peggy Lee and Julie London (I'm not kidding). Eydie Gorme hears Patti, stops the music and says, "Frank, come over here. We've got a singer!" Frank moves to the piano and I then get to watch my wife beautifully serenade Frank Sinatra and Bob Dylan, to be met by a torrent of applause when she's finished. The next day we play Frank's eightieth birthday celebration for ABC TV and I get to escort him to the stage along with Tony Bennett. It's a beautiful evening and a fitting celebration for the greatest pop singer of all time.

Two years later Frank passed away and we were generously invited to his funeral. A classic bright sunny day dawned in Los Angeles. But upon approaching the church, the scene outside looked like something out of Nathanael West's *The Day of the Locust*. Television trucks and cameras were set up everywhere, with reporters stationed on the rooftops of nearby homes.

There was a horde of protestors being kept on the far side of the street with signs blaming Frank for everything from God's indifference to the decline of brown shoelaces. Inside the church, however, all was serene. There, along with Kirk Douglas, Don Rickles, Frank Jr. and the last of the old Hollywood stars, we said our goodbyes as Frank's voice filled the church. At the end of the ceremony I stood for a moment with Jack Nicholson on the church's front steps. He turned to me and said, "King of New Jersey."

## SIXTY-FOUR
# BRINGING IT ALL
# BACK HOME

There were two catalysts that got me thinking about reactivating the E Street Band. One late summer evening as I stepped out of Federici's Pizza Parlor in Freehold, two young kids came up to me, introduced themselves and said they were big fans of the E Street Band but unfortunately were too young to have ever seen us live. They may have been in their early twenties. That meant at the last E Street Band show, perhaps they were ten years old. I started realizing there was a sea of young people out there who never saw the greatest thing I did: PLAY LIVE . . . with the E Street Band. Then, visiting my parents in San Francisco, I opened the newspaper to see Bob Dylan, Van Morrison and Joni Mitchell were performing at the San Jose Arena, an hour south of my folks' house. That's quite a bill. I asked my mom if she was game, and we drove down and took our seats stage right as the house lights lowered.

Joni came on and did a beautiful set, followed by Van, swinging and lifting the house. Van Morrison has always been one of my great, great heroes and an enormous source of inspiration for everything I've done. Van put the white soul into our early E Street records. Without Van, there is no "New York City Serenade" or jazz soul of "Kitty's Back." Then out came Dylan in great form. Playing with a band he'd been working with for quite a while, he'd tightened his music into roadhouse poetry. They felt like they'd be at home in an arena this size or in the little bar down the road a ways. The band grooved joyous blues that even got their front man dancing a little! This music, his happiness, these artists, made me happy as I stood alongside my mom and we danced in our seats. Watching the crowd was funny and a little disorienting. I felt like I'd fallen asleep, a sixteen-year-old with *Highway 61 Revisited* spinning endlessly in the dark night of my bedroom, and woken up fifty years hence in a rock 'n' roll, Rip Van Winkle–like dream. We'd all gotten . . . OLD! The seats were filled with middle-aged, wrinkled, out-of-shape, balding, gray-bearded rock fans straight out of the Beatles' "When I'm Sixty-Four." We all looked kind of . . . ridiculous! But something else was happening. Young hipsters and teenagers were scattered through the crowd. Little kids were there, brought by their parents to see and hear the great man. Some were bored, some sleeping and many dancing alongside Mom and Pop. People were filled with heart, good cheer and emotion. I thought about my gray hairs and the wrinkles on my face. I looked over at my mother, seventy-two, her face a loving map of all our pain and resilience. She was beaming ear to ear, her arm tucked in mine. The floor was a mass of smiles and swaying bodies, and as I watched, I thought, "I can do this. I can bring this, this happiness, these smiles." I went home and called the E Street Band.

# SIXTY-FIVE

# REVIVAL

. . . First, of course, I fretted, worried, questioned, discussed, debated, dismissed, rethought, reconsidered and thought some more. I wanted my reasoning to be sound and I did not want to reconstitute a nostalgia act to run the new oldies circuit. (Though I've actually gotten plenty of pleasure out of some of those oldies shows when the performers are laying down their hearts. If your heart is in it, it ain't old.) Still, I was coming off a deeply satisfying solo tour that had felt very *present*, hadn't played with the band in ten years, still held a few mild grudges and was worried about whether the whole thing would actually work.

It came down to this: I'd studied, honed, worked and sweated to acquire a set of skills that when put into action made me one of the best in the world at what I did. Those skills were at their apex with a hard-driving band, and, I'd come to realize, not just any band. Time, history, memory, collective experience had made this so. Working with my band of the early nineties, I'd learned that as much as I enjoyed playing with a new set of musicians and as good as I thought we were, there would be, in my lifetime, no other group of musicians with whom I would step onto the stage with a quarter century of blood, sweat and tears under our belt but the E Street Band. There were only these eight men and women. Their style and playing abilities had long been hand stitched to fit me perfectly. More important, when the fans looked at those faces onstage, they saw themselves, their lives, their friends looking back at them. In the new digital world of three-second attention spans, where the cold, hard hand of impermanence and numbered anonymity holds sway, this was irreplaceable. It was real, and we'd built it the way real things are built, moment upon moment, hour upon hour, day after day, year after year. I came to the conclusion I'd need a pretty good reason to *not* exercise my skills at the still-very-young age of forty-eight with this group of musicians sitting at home. I didn't have one. Everyone had found their own way but no one had found—and they wouldn't, not now or ever—another E Street Band.

There was residual tension in the band but a lot more love than in most, or any, I knew of. And . . . it had been ten years. I wasn't hearing myself so regularly on the radio anymore. What we'd done was getting farther away, receding into rock's glorious but embalmed past. I didn't like that. We were far too formidable a unit to go gently into that good night. I remained too filled with ambition, ego, hunger, desire and a righteous sense of musical power to let a life's work slip into the respectful annals of rock history. As surely as death, taxes and the hunger for new heroes, that day would come . . . but not . . . right . . . now! Not if I had anything to do with it. Not while I was a mighty, strapping, psychosis-filled rock 'n' soul shouter. Not yet.

## It's On!

Rock 'n' roll bands that *last* have to come to one basic human realization. It is: the guy standing next to you is more important than you think he is.

And that man or woman must come to the same realization about the man or woman standing next to him or her, about *you*. Or: everyone must be broke, living far beyond their means and in need of hard currency. Or: both.

A decade of seat-warming the ex–rock 'n' roll gods' bench sharpens the mind and softens everyone's perspective on any mild mistreatments from the past. That is a good thing. We all must wake up one morning, or different mornings, and think, "You know, that thing, that thing I had, was one of the best things that ever happened to me. It was good for my life, it was good in my life and if the opportunity should ever again arise . . ." It arose, for all of us, and we were about to make the most of it, whatever each individual's motivations may have been.

In our last incarnation there had been no Steve Van Zandt. I had to think about that. If we were going, I wanted all of us to go. First I needed to make a courtesy call to Nils. Nils had done much more than step in and replace my old friend Steve over the years. He became a very responsible second lieutenant, fully committed to his position in the band and giving everything he had. On top of that, Nils was just a beautiful guy to be around. He was an assured, calming, inspiring presence and one of the world's great guitarists. Within the band, he was ego-free. If an entire night passed without a solo, no problem. He was a total team player who arrived at the hall hours before everyone else to ready himself for the work. He carried an archive of music for every possible song choice I might pull out of the hat, prepared himself and tutored others in chord structure and arrangements for the night's specialty items. Between Nils and Max, another deep student of our work, I always had somewhere to go if *I* had any questions about something I'd written. I called Nils, told him what I wanted to do, assured him I appreciated and understood the great work and commitment he'd shown our band, explained his position would not change and asked his blessing. Nils, ever the gentleman and loyal soldier, told me if that's what I thought was best, he was behind me. Then I called Steve.

Despite our great friendship, or because of it, Steve can be a powerful force, and with his great energy he can be unintentionally destabilizing. Steve's word on something will often tip the scales for me one way or another. His often hilarious point of view constantly loosens things up, keeps me grounded, and his mere presence makes me feel all will be well. He's also a serious thinker about rock 'n' roll, what it means and can do. The friction and the rub in Steve's opinions is often where he is most valuable to me, but in the past, he could unintentionally cross the line, entering into band politics in a way that sometimes made my job tougher. We'd need to talk about that. We did, one afternoon at my home. We had a friendly but tough conversation. I got to air my remaining grievances and hear Steve's point of view, and we put it away. We proceeded to have the best eighteen years of our work life and friendship.

When I called Clarence, he told me he'd been waiting for ten years and asked where I had been. As I've said, plenty of the guys had found their own second acts and been very successful, but there is something about walking onstage in front of seventy-five thousand screaming fans with the oldest friends of your life, playing music that is ingrained in you, that's hard to replace. If you had it for one—just *one*—evening, you'd never forget it. To go there night after night, over a lifetime, is an unimaginable, immeasurable pleasure and privilege. After ten years apart, *this* was something we all understood and had come to appreciate in a new way. We were nine of a handful of people on the planet who had earned that privilege. Now, firmly and finally, in our middle age, we understood its significance. But if we were going to do this, if *I* was going to do it, I wanted to be sure it would be "easy," that it would be fun. The work would be hard enough. The past had to be over and done with; all grudges, money issues, slights—real or imagined—would need to be put away.

An example: One day I had one of my musicians come to me and explain he would need more money if he were to continue doing his work. I told him if he could find a more highly paid musician at his job in the world, I would gladly up his percentage. I also told him I could spare him the time to search. All he had to do was walk into the bathroom, close the door and walk over and take a look in the mirror. There he'd find the highest-paid musician in the world at his post. I told him, "That's how it works in the real world." He then looked straight at me and, without a trace of irony, asked, "What do we have to do with the real world?" At that moment I knew I had sheltered some of my colleagues perhaps a bit too much.

Right now, I just wanted to enjoy myself with my great friends doing the thing we do best together. If we couldn't do that, I'd prefer simply to leave it. We were still young but too old to recomplicate our lives by engaging in any venture that wasn't going to be rewarding and a pleasure to all.

Along with (when necessary) supreme confidence, doubt and all of its many manifestations is in my wheelhouse. You work that right and it's a blessing. You work it wrong and you're paralyzed. Doubt can be the starting point for deeper critical thought. It can keep you from selling yourself and your audience short and it can bring you hard down to Earth if needed. Before our ten-years-coming Asbury Park opening night, I'd experience plenty of it.

## Rock and Roll Hall of Fame

I'd attended several early ceremonies of the new Rock and Roll Hall of Fame. In its second year, I'd gone to induct Roy Orbison, then had the honor of inducting Bob Dylan. These were two of my most telling influences. To be chosen to present them with their induction meant a great deal to me. After the ceremonies, during the all-star jam, which in those days featured every musician in the house, I'd stood onstage between Mick Jagger and George Harrison, all of us together on one mike, singing "I Saw Her Standing There." I was thinking, "What's wrong with this picture?" How did a kid from New Jersey end up, on this evening, between these two men whose work had driven so deeply into his soul that he had to follow the road they laid out before him, follow it with everything he had?

Look at it like this: In 1964, millions of kids saw the Stones and the Beatles and decided, "That looks like fun." *Some* of them went out and bought instruments. *Some* of them learned to play a little. *Some* got good enough to maybe join a local band. *Some* might have even made a demo tape. *Some* might have lucked out and gotten a record deal of some sort. A *few* of those might have sold some records and done some touring. A *few* of those might have had a small hit, a short career in music, and managed to eke out a modest living. A *very few* of those might have managed to make a life as a musician, and a *very, very few* might have had some continuing success that brought them fame, fortune and deep gratification, and tonight, *one* of those ended up standing between Mick Jagger and George Harrison, a Stone and a Beatle. I did not fool myself about what the odds were back in 1964 that that *one* would've been the acne-faced fifteen-year-old kid with the cheap Kent guitar from Freehold, New Jersey. My parents were RIGHT! My chances *were* ONE, ONE in a MILLION, in MANY MILLIONS. But still . . . here I was. I knew my talents and I knew I worked hard, but THESE, THESE WERE THE GODS, and I was, well . . . one hardworking guitar man. I carried the journeyman in me for better or for worse, a commonness, and I always would.

These were the days at the Hall of Fame when the ceremonies were NOT televised. People got up and were glorious, hateful, hilarious, spiteful, smashed, insane and often deeply moving. If you were still enmeshed in intergroup grudges and fighting, the podium at the Rock and Roll Hall of Fame was your one last shot at sticking it in a little deeper to that guy or those guys. The Hall of Fame induction—by its nature, a moment of reflection—brought out the best and worst in folks and was never less than wildly entertaining. These were the days when rock's true giants were still being inducted. You'd find yourself onstage at night, not just between Mick and George, but alongside of Keith Richards, with Bob Dylan to your left, B. B. King on your right, Smokey Robinson to his left, Jeff Beck stage-side with Les Paul. It was a living pageant of Guy Peellaert's early illustrations of the gatherings of rock's Olympus, *Rock Dreams*. What resulted musically was often a train wreck but there was something to just being there. There amid your dreams, your gods, your heroes, like a misplaced stowaway on the ride of his life. It was a rock da Vinci's *Last Supper*, and Steve and I often ruminated on how we felt we'd been born at exactly the right moment. We were teenagers in the sixties, when rock and radio had their golden age, when the best pop music was also the most popular, when a new language was being formed and spoken to young people all across the world, when it remained an alien dialect to most parents, when it defined a community of souls wrapped in the ecstasy and confusions of their time but connected in blood brotherhood by the disciple's voice of their local deejay.

We were rock's early third generation. Born in time to get the best of rock's reinventors of blues, pop and soul, the British wave, yet young enough to experience its originators, Muddy Waters, Howlin' Wolf, Chuck Berry, Fats Domino, Roy Orbison, Jerry Lee Lewis, Elvis . . . all still alive and active at the crest of the wave of the sixties. It was rock's most vibrant and turbulent era. I saw the Doors, Janis Joplin and the Who in Asbury Park's Convention Hall. The Who opened for Herman's Hermits! And were preceded by a New York City band, the Blues Magoos, who wore electric suits that glowed in the dark. Janis had in her band one of my great guitar heroes, Danny Weis from the band Rhinoceros, whom Steve and I followed slavishly whenever they came into the Jersey area. I received all these hands like a supplicant directly upon my trembling forehead and fell stunned by their power. With the radio and country exploding, there was enough rough fuel to last a poor boy a lifetime . . . and it has.

Much great and inspirational music has come since, particularly the punk explosion of the late seventies and hip-hop in the eighties, but all in all, we had the luck of the draw. It's part of what's made our band unique: the cross-tensions of the fifties blue-collar world and sixties social experience clashing and melding in our music. We are pre- and post-hippie sixties soul survivors. It's a blend that won't exactly exist firsthand anymore when we're done. The world and society changes too quickly and too much. The birthing conditions of today's musicians will be different—just as valid, but different. And as the social conditions that gave rise to Motown, Stax, the blues and rockabilly slip out of existence, the elements that form the basis of what was created, the golden age of radio, the industrial age, pre-Internet localism, post-industrialism, will shift into an entirely different set of influences and create the next generation's rock heroes. It's already happened quite a few times and is happening as we speak. Long live rock! (Whatever that may be.)

## Induction

Come '98 I got the word I was to be inducted into the Rock and Roll Hall of Fame. It'd been twenty-five years since the release of *Greetings from Asbury Park* and that was the criterion for inclusion. Our old paradox would be revisited. I'd long ago signed as a solo artist and recorded as "Bruce Springsteen" for twenty-five years. The Hall of Fame induction rules stated you were inducted under the name of your earliest recording. We'd toured since 1975 as Bruce Springsteen and the E Street Band and what I'd accomplished was inseparable from my work with my friends. A few weeks before my induction, Steve visited me in my Rumson home and made his case that I should push for the Hall of Fame to induct us as Bruce Springsteen and the E Street Band because, in his words, "that was the legend."

He had a point but it'd been ten years since we'd played live together. I still had a good deal of ambivalence, and the closeness we'd rekindle over the next decade had not yet taken hold. And . . . I had a lot of pride about walking into John Hammond's office on my own that day in 1972. I'd set the band aside in the early seventies and determined to be a solo artist. I put together the greatest band in the world to further that purpose and in doing so we created something that was not quite fish nor fowl. My primary heroes were solo artists—Frank, Elvis, Dylan—and I went in on my own with the determination to forge a solo voice. My model was the individual traveler, the frontiersman, the man in the wilderness, the highwayman, the existential American adventurer, connected but not beholden to society: John Wayne in *The Searchers*, James Dean in *Rebel Without a Cause*, Bob Dylan in *Highway 61 Revisited*. These would later be joined by Woody Guthrie, James M. Cain, Jim Thompson, Flannery O'Connor—*individuals* who worked on the edges of society to shift impressions, create worlds, imagine possibilities that would then be assimilated and become a part of the culture at large. I needed a grand instrument and more, the feeling of heart-and-soul commitment that gave me the room, the time to make the music I felt within me. That was the E Street Band.

The Hall of Fame did not have an apparatus to consider the gray area my work and my collaboration with the band fell into. There wasn't a structure specific enough to take the important subtleties of our kind of musical entity into account. Steve was probably right; I could've petitioned the Hall of Fame to make an exception as to how I'd be inducted. Though it had never been done with any other group or individual, I'm sure they would've in this case. But to do so I would've had to have felt with absolute clarity that that was what I wanted to do. In 1970, when I walked out of Steel Mill as a twenty-year-old kid and decided that was the last of small-unit democracy and "bands" for me, I'd chosen a different path.

On March 15, 1999, I was inducted into the Rock and Roll Hall of Fame with the guys at my side. Some had hurt feelings and some were simply happy for me, but at the end of the day, they all came through. We'd soon commence the tour that would signal a decade of some of our most productive years and bring us to several new generations of E Street fans.

# Rehearsal

On March 11, 1999, we went back to our roots and set up band rehearsals in Asbury Park's Convention Hall. In '99, Asbury was still blighted and struggling mightily from decades of neglect and corruption, but down on the fringes of Cookman Avenue, there was movement. A small group of artists/frontiersmen and gays drifting in from New York had found the town's low rents and laissez-faire social attitudes attractive. Asbury was now the borderlands, a canvas driven blank by poverty and abandonment, leaving room for something new to be created. There was a faint light at the end of the city's long, dark tunnel. Here we set about finding who we were *now*.

On the first day, as I kicked the band into "Prove It All Night," I could feel it was all there. I was startled by some things I'd forgotten. My ears had lost their insensitivity to how loud we were. That, along with deafness, would soon return. The big rolling sound of the band, the weight it carried, felt both welcoming and unsettling. If I was going to release this big machine again, I'd better know what I wanted to do with it. Midway through "Prove It" it felt like we could've played this song just two weeks ago. Ten years vanished into faint remembrance. It was an enjoyable day but still I went home unconvinced. I held long conversations with Jon about my ambivalence. Ambivalence, of course, being one of my specialties, I couldn't have honestly expected to make my way to where we were heading without a full-on wrestling match with my own dissonance. So be it. I was drawing a lot of our set from *Tracks*, a sixty-six-song set of outtakes, which would be released simultaneously with our tour. I was resisting going to the classics for fear of relying too heavily upon yesterday.

One evening I sat with Jon in the Film Center Café on Ninth Avenue in Hell's Kitchen and I wrote out my proposed set list. He looked it over and said, "We're a little short on the songs that after ten years, people might want to hear." "Really?" I made my protestations: I can't . . . I won't . . . blah, blah, blah. Then I confided in him that I was unsure if the whole thing was going to work. If I could make it "real." Jon calmly responded, "If you come out with your band and play your best music, people are going to like it." Oh.

The next afternoon at Convention Hall, I went through a stressful rehearsal, running through music we'd long known that was feeling somehow leaden and lifeless to me. I was quietly seething with anxiety but I didn't want to disturb or draw the confidence out of the band. There had been about fifty or so fans milling around outside of the hall for the past few weeks and around midafternoon, with a few songs left to rehearse, I told one of the crew to let them in. A rush of shining, excited faces rushed stage front as I counted into "Promised Land" and suddenly, there it was . . . liftoff. The band felt light as a feather and deep as the sea. I'd looked into those faces and found what I was missing. It was all there inside of me. A great relief washed over me and it all made sense. As we'd slogged away for weeks on the Convention Hall stage in isolation, trying to pump life into our much-vaunted songbook, there'd been only one thing missing: you.

With these few souls in front of me, I could feel not only our shared history but the *presentness* of what we were doing. It'd be all right.

The day before our opening-night concert I brought in a song called "Land of Hope and Dreams." I wanted something new to start this new stage of the band's life with. "Land of Hope" summed up a lot of what I wanted our band to be about and renewed our pledge to our audience, to point the way forward and, once again, become a living presence in our listeners' lives. That evening we closed the show with it and we were off.

We started on April 9, 1999, in Barcelona, one of the cities that had become an epicenter of our European popularity, and were met with a blind hysteria that would continue to bring us back to this beautiful city for the next decade. It was not a reunion but a revival, and the band played hard and well for 133 shows, winding down to a last stand in New York City that would crystallize our return in a way we hadn't expected.

## "American Skin"

As our first tour in a decade drew to its close, I wanted to write something new for our New York engagement at Madison Square Garden as a signpost to where we were heading. The shooting of Amadou Diallo, an African immigrant, by plainclothes police officers as he was reaching for his wallet seemed to underscore the danger and deadly confusion of roaming the inner-city streets in black skin that still existed in late-twentieth-century America. I wrote as thoughtfully as I could, trying to take in the perspective of not just the Diallo family but the officers as well. I tried the song out in Atlanta, our last show before New York City. I just thought it was another piece of music I had written that followed my long career path of dealing with topical subjects and I was mildly shocked when Steve came running into our Fort Monmouth rehearsal on the day before our Garden gig saying, "Have you seen this?" There on the cover of the venerable *New York Post* was the head of the New York State Fraternal Order of Police calling me a "dirtbag" and a "floating fag." I understood "dirtbag" but I had to retreat to my pre-*Wikipedia Webster*'s for a definition of "floating fag." It wasn't there. I received letters, one from the police commissioner asking me NOT to play the song! . . . Huh? It's a SONG! No one, except the folks in Atlanta, had even heard it yet! But the storm continued on CNN and in newspaper editorials.

Come opening night at the Garden, needless to say, some tension filled the air. You could feel the restlessness of the audience, perhaps smelling a little blood. The police backstage, usually a great part of my audience, were unsmiling and uncommunicative. Mr. and Mrs. Diallo had requested to be in attendance. I met them both briefly backstage, two elegant and beautiful Africans who in gentle voices spoke a little of Amadou and thanked me for writing about their son. Despite the press ruckus, I had no big presentation to make. I simply inserted the song in the part of the set where it would naturally come and went out to do my job. I gathered the band in a circle backstage, explained that something unusual might occur but that this was what we did at our best. We held hands, the house lights dropped and we took the stage.

The opening of the set was stiff with apprehension, both our own and the audience's. You could feel it was not going to be a normal evening. I've never stood onstage and felt people waiting, waiting, waiting for just *one* song. Finally, six songs in, I cued Roy and Max to go into the dark, drawing riff and clocklike rhythm that introduced "American Skin." Some in the crowd began to incongruously clap along and I asked for some quiet, then each band member, beginning with Clarence, chanted the opening lyric, "Forty-one shots." At that point I could hear some scattered booing (regardless of what they say, it is quite distinctive to the ear from "Bruuuuuuce"-ing!). Well, that was to be expected. Then several angry young men, one flashing a badge and saluting me with the New Jersey state bird, rushed to the front of the stage. They stood for a moment shouting at my feet; what, I couldn't quite tell, but it wasn't greetings and salutations. They were shortly hustled away by Garden security. We played on to a mixture of supportive applause and boos with the Diallos in view in their seats and that was it. I followed "American Skin" with "Promised Land," two songs about the demand for and refusal to give human recognition and the cost of that refusal.

Though "American Skin" was critical, it was not anti-police, as some thought. The first lines you hear after the intro are from the policeman's point of view: "Kneeling over his body in the vestibule, praying for his life." In the second verse, a mother tries to impress on her young son the importance of his simplest actions in a neighborhood where the most innocent of motions (your hand reaching for your wallet or moving out of sight) can be misinterpreted with deadly consequences.

In the bridge, the lyrics "Is it in your heart, is it in your eyes" ask the singer and his audience to look inside themselves for their collaboration in events. The third verse, "We're baptized in these waters and in each other's blood . . . it ain't no secret, no secret my friend. You can get killed just for living in your American skin," spoke of life in the land of brotherly fear.

The sheer number of shots, forty-one, seemed to gauge the size of our betrayal of one another. "Forty-one shots . . . forty-one shots": that was the mantra I wanted to repeat over and over throughout my song, the daily compounding of crimes, large and small, against one another. I worked hard for a balanced voice. I knew a diatribe would do no good. I just wanted to help people see the other guy's point of view. The idea was: here is what systematic racial injustice, fear and paranoia do to our children, our loved ones, ourselves. Here's the price in blood.

At the end of "American Skin" you could feel the audience in the Garden breathe a sigh of relief. The world had not ended. Many of those who booed us cheered the rest of the show, but the cleaving scar of this one song, more than any other I'd written, stayed with us for a long time. On one of my motorcycle forays through western New York, I stopped at a little roadhouse and ran into a few local officers with a few beers under their belt who were thoroughly displeased with my editorializing. I wisely left. Years later, when I played the song at the closing night of our *Rising* tour at Shea Stadium, the police contingent refused to assist us out of the hall (poor us) and we made our way through the crowded streets on our own. No problem, but I was saddened that the song was still so misunderstood by some good men toeing the blue line. On the other hand, I also encountered men and women who showed me their badge, thanked me and said they understood what I was saying.

My sweetest memory of the whole fiasco is that as I sauntered down Monmouth Avenue in Red Bank one afternoon, an elderly black woman approached me and said, "They just don't want to hear the truth." I received a small plaque that year from our local NAACP and I was always glad that the song brought me just a little closer to the black community I always wished I'd served better.

No other song I'd written, including "Born in the USA," ever received as confused and controversial a reaction as "American Skin." It truly pissed people off. It was the first song where I stepped directly into the divide of race, and in America, to this day, race cuts deep.

The first E Street revival was over. I'd regained my confidence in the band, and with "Land of Hope and Dreams" and "American Skin" I found I was able to write material that stood with the songs of our past. Now we needed to make a great modern record.

SIXTY-SIX

# THE RISING

After the '99 tour I took the band into the studio to do some preliminary recording. We headed into our old stomping grounds in New York City, the Hit Factory. I had "Land of Hope and Dreams," "American Skin" and some material I'd cowritten with blue-collar Pittsburgh rocker Joe Grushecky to get us started. I gathered our old production squad, including Chuck Plotkin, and we spent a few days cutting what we had. I'd made some pretty good demos of my new songs for the band to crib from and we headed home with eight things or so basically recorded.

Upon second listening in the weeks that followed, it all just didn't add up. The band was playing well, the music had been recorded fine, but there was no freshness, no spark, no center, no *record* there. It all lay flat on the tape like nothing was happening. All great rock 'n' roll records convince you of one essential thing: that SOMETHING is HAPPENING! Something you

NEED to hear! There are many very listenable bad records that hold your attention because they are not dull. They have been written, constructed, arranged and produced in a way that holds the ear. It may not be art, but it's admirable craft. We didn't have that. When I listened back to what we'd recorded, my final judgment was: WE WERE DULL! I knew some of the songs I had written weren't dull—they'd raised a shitstorm—but the records we were making of those songs were.

After a quarter century of success, Jon and I had to acknowledge that *we* no longer knew how to make our records. The art of production had simply moved its center, and our ideas and techniques were no longer current, ear-friendly, exciting or competent. We were now much better singers, songwriters, performers, managers than we were record producers. So be it. Who's next? We were both still hungry to make great records. We'd now have to open our very closed little universe and find out how to do that.

Several years previous Donnie Ienner, then president of Columbia Records, had told me Brendan O'Brien, producer of Pearl Jam and Rage Against the Machine, was interested in working with me. His name, among a few others, now came up again. Jon and I scheduled a meeting between Brendan and myself at my home studio in New Jersey. We'd talk, I'd play him a little of what I had and we'd see where it was going to go. The day came. I met Mr. O'Brien, a youngish-looking man in his thirties. He was sane, easy to talk to and be with, without pretension and confident. I ran by him some things I had, recent recordings, old demos, new demos. He focused on a few songs, said he'd come up just to make sure "I was still me" and informed me that I was, and we went on to plan another meeting and a recording date in his home base of Atlanta. There we'd give each other a full audition, but before that date arrived, a beautiful, sunlit fall day would blossom over the tristate area.

·   ·   ·

On September 11, 2001, I came down from bed and walked into the kitchen, and one of the women who worked in our home told me a plane had flown into the World Trade Center. Remembering a small plane had once flown into the Empire State Building in a heavy fog, my first thought was, "Poor bastard." I figured a misguided, inexperienced pilot had flown his Cessna or whatever way off the mark. There was just one thing. As I sat at our sunny breakfast table, the skies outside could not have been clearer. There couldn't have been a visibility problem. Curious, I went into the living room and turned on the television. Smoke was billowing from one of the Trade Center towers, and as I watched, another plane flew into the second tower. This was not a Cessna but a full-size passenger plane. I learned that so was the first, and shortly thereafter came the report that one had also flown into the Pentagon. We were under attack. I sat, like the rest of the country, transfixed by a television screen, where the unimaginable was occurring, feeling like anything, truly anything, could or might happen next. We were untethered and skimming across deadly and absolutely unpredictable waters as I saw the towers fall, such an impossible and confounding event that the newsman on the scene could not conceive of what he was witnessing and did not report that that was what was happening.

In the late afternoon, I drove to the Rumson–Sea Bright Bridge. There, usually, on a clear day the Twin Towers struck two tiny vertical lines on the horizon at the bridge's apex. Today, torrents of smoke lifted from the end of Manhattan Island, a mere fifteen miles away by boat. I stopped in at my local beach and walked to the water's edge, looking north; a thin gray line of smoke, dust and ash spread out due east over the water line. It appeared like the smudged edge of a hard blue sheet folding and resting upon the autumn Atlantic.

I sat for a while, alone, the September beach empty beneath the eerie quiet of silent skies. We live along a very busy air corridor. Planes are constantly flying just off the Eastern Seaboard on their way to Kennedy and Newark airports, and the low buzz of airplane engines is as much a part of the sound tapestry at the Shore as are the gently crashing waves. Not today. All air traffic grounded. A deadly *On the Beach*, science fiction–like quiet unfolded over the sand.

After a short while, I headed home to join Patti and pick up our children from school. As I drove over the gravel of the beach club parking lot, I hesitated before pulling into traffic on Ocean Boulevard. Just then a car careening off Rumson–Sea Bright Bridge shot past, its window down, and its driver, recognizing me, shouted, "Bruce, we need you." I sort of knew what he meant, but . . .

On the way home, trying to put the morning in context proved almost impossible. All I was brought back to was myself in gym clothes on our high school soccer pitch as someone came running, shouting across the parking lot from the school cafeteria. I remember my face pressed up against a chain-link fence as I heard, "The president's been assassinated, Kennedy's been shot." I pulled in front of Rumson Country Day School, where a crowd of parents with that same jittery silence running through them were picking up their children. I met Evan, Jessie and Sam and took them home.

Monmouth County had lost one hundred fifty husbands, brothers, sons, wives, daughters. For weeks, the long black limousines pulled up to churches, and candlelit vigils were held in the neighborhood park. In Rumson, a town full of Wall Street commuters, almost everyone knew someone who lost somebody. A benefit was held at the Count Basie Theatre, where local musicians met and played to raise funds for many of the surviving families. Here I was introduced to the Jersey Girls, who would soon do so much to push the government to be openly accountable for the events of that day; their efforts would lead to the formation of the 9/11 Commission. The nation owes them a debt of gratitude.

*The Rising* had its origins in the national telethon we were invited to be a part of the week after September 11. I wrote "Into the Fire" for that show (it remained incomplete, so I performed "My City of Ruins," the song I'd written a year earlier for Asbury Park). Of the many tragic images of that day, the picture I couldn't let go of was of the emergency workers going *up* the stairs as others rushed down to safety. The sense of duty, the courage, ascending into . . . what? The religious image of ascension, the crossing of the line between this world, the world of blood, work, family, your children, the breath in your lungs, the ground beneath your feet, all that is life, and . . . the next, flooded my imagination. If you love life or any part of it, the depth of their sacrifice is unthinkable and incomprehensible. Yet what they left behind was tangible. Death, along with all its anger, pain and loss, opens a window of possibility for the living. It removes the veil that the "ordinary" gently drapes over our eyes. Renewed sight is the hero's last loving gift to those left behind.

The telethon seemed a small way to give thanks for community protected and preserved to the people and their families who take that burden on as part of their everyday lives.

I didn't sit around wondering about whether I should or should not write about this day. I just did. I went down to Atlanta with "Into the Fire" and "You're Missing."

Brendan brought a fresh power and focus to the band's sound and playing. He didn't comment on the subject matter; he just said, "These are good. Now go home and write some more." I knew from the beginning if I was going to continue to write thematically, my songs could not depend on simply being tied to the event. They needed an independent life, a life where their internal coherency would be completely understood even if there'd been no 9/11. So I wrote rock music, love songs, breakup songs, spirituals, blues, hit songs, and I allowed my theme and the events of the day to breathe and find their place within the framework I created. I went home, searched my book for unfinished songs and continued to write.

"Waitin' on a Sunny Day" I'd had for a year or so, and it found its place within this new material. We recut "Nothing Man," a song I'd had since '94 that, along with "Secret Garden," had been a part of my "Streets of Philly" album. It captured the awkwardness and isolation of survival. "I don't remember how I felt . . . I'd never thought I'd live . . ." "Empty Sky" was the last song I wrote. My art director had sent me a photo of clouds in an empty sky and in a few days, sitting on the edge of my hotel bed in Atlanta, I had the song. For "Worlds Apart" I wanted other voices, other situations than just American ones. The Eleventh was an international tragedy. I wanted Eastern voices, the presence of Allah. I wanted to find a place where worlds collide and meet. My old friend Chuck Plotkin assisted me in getting the voices of Pakistani Qawwali singers, Asif Ali Khan and his group, onto "Worlds Apart." "Let's Be Friends" . . . beach music! "Further On" . . . the band tearing down the house. "The Fuse" . . . images of life at home during wartime immediately following the Eleventh.

The record rises to the house party of "Mary's Place," party music with the blues hidden inside. I wanted some of the warmth and familiarity of *The Wild, the Innocent and the E Street Shuffle*, a home place, the comfort music and friendship may bring in a crisis. "The Rising" was written late in the record as a bookend to "Into the Fire." Secular stations of the cross, steps of duty irretraceable, the hard realization of all the life and love left behind . . . the opening sky. "Paradise," written late, was a study of different impressions of an afterlife. In the first verse, a young Palestinian suicide bomber contemplates his last moments on Earth. In the second, a navy wife longs for her husband lost at the Pentagon, the absence of the physical, the smells, the human longing for a return to wholeness. In the last verse, my character swims deep into the water between worlds, where he confronts his lost love, whose eyes are "as empty as paradise." The dead have their own business to do, as do the living. Finally we circle back around to "My City of Ruins," the soul gospel of my favorite sixties records, speaking not just of Asbury but hopefully of other places and other lands. That was my record.

Our band was built well, over many years, for difficult times. When people wanted a dialogue, a conversation about events, internal and external, we developed a language that suited those moments. We were there. It was a language that I hoped would entertain, inspire, comfort and reveal. The professionalism, the showmanship, the hours of hard work are all very important, but I always believed that it was this dialogue, this language, that was at the heart of our resiliency with our audience. *The Rising* was a renewal of that conversation and the ideas that forged our band.

For the next year, the E Street Band crisscrossed the nation trying to contextualize the uncontextualizable. Perhaps the physical and psychic horrors were beyond music and art's ability to communicate, explain, heal or even comment upon. I don't know. Coming from a place that had been hit so hard, speaking to firemen who served at Ground Zero, ships' captains whose ferries crossed Sandy Hook Bay bringing back survivors, their decks inch-deep in ash, and my own desire to use the language I learned as a musician to sort through what was in my own head turned me to writing those songs. First, you write for yourself . . . always, to make sense of experience and the world around you. It's one of the ways I stay sane. Our stories, our books, our films are how we cope with the random trauma-inducing chaos of life as it plays. When that guy yelled out, "Bruce, we need you," that was a tall order, but I knew what he meant; I needed something, someone, too. As I drove home on that lonely day to find my children, my wife, my people and you again, I turned to the only language I've ever known to fight off the night terrors, real and imagined, time and time again. It was all I could do.

# SIXTY-SEVEN

# WILD EAST

After two consecutive tours with the reconstituted E Street Band, I wanted to return to the music I had written during the *Tom Joad* tour. I went back; chose the best of it; wrote a new song, "Devils and Dust"; and Brendan O'Brien helped me finish the record I'd started in my farmhouse at *Joad*'s end. Brendan wanted to cut the songs from scratch, but I'd grown very fond of my home-recorded versions and decided to stick with those. We added some small embellishments, some subtle strings and horns; Brendan mixed; and there we were. I followed it with a solo tour of acoustic shows and came back home.

I'd always wanted some land near my home town. A piece came up that I'd biked past since my thirties. I'd looked down its beautiful lane and often thought . . . some day. The woman who owned it was an artist and she lived there until she died. It came up for sale. Patti and I looked at it for a long time and then we bought it.

Since we'd gotten together, Patti always told me she loved horses. The last time I'd been on a horse, I'd had on a Cub Scout uniform, but something's got to roam these pastures. A few weeks after we'd closed, a trailer arrived at our newly acquired ponderosa with horses from the Saratoga race track. We were told by the kindly gentleman doing the selling they were all of fine stock and could be ridden by an inebriated chimpanzee. Okay. With no riding experience, I climbed on. I'd seen a million Westerns, how hard could it be?

I was then pulled all over our farm by one son of Secretariat after another until I found one who "sort of" listened to my unskilled commands. Over the next several months we put together a stable of animals ranging from the very rideable to some only for the suicide prone.

**LESSON 1:** Never get on a horse named "Lightning," "Thunder," "Widow Maker," "Undertaker," "Acid Trip," "Hurricane" or "Sudden Death."

**LESSON 2:** Take a few lessons.

We hired an instructor who put me through my paces on one of our nags, but no good came of it. My back was killing me, and I had no idea of where the half ton under me might go next. Then a miracle occurred. Patti found a dusty old palomino. As I sat astride him, I felt at home. He had a beautiful light gait, smooth as a Cadillac, and was extremely quiet, old and confident. He was unruffled by the clumsy reining of the neophyte on his back. "I dub thee 'Cadillac Jack.'"

This horse taught me how to ride until I had him full gallop, belly flat to the ground, breezing him at speeds they make over at Monmouth Park. In the woods, the deer and small creatures did not startle him, the wind did not unnerve him nor the dark cause him to quicken his pace home. Once I sat in the saddle as he sank up to his haunches in the mud of a shallow creek after a hard rain. I ended up astride him, still in the saddle but with both feet planted firmly on the ground. I calmly stepped off, he slowly worked his way out and we carried on.

During our early years at the farm I was thrown from horseback many times. I'd brush myself off and hop back on, but still I'm glad this occurred during my forties, when my durability remained at an all-time high. I was thrown from all sides and then would gaily reunite with my steed, if lucky, a few feet away. If not, back at the barn. Many of our equine companions earned their names. A beautiful Black Beauty–like gelding unfortunately became known as "He Who Is Afraid of Small Things." If any rabbit, gopher, fox or squirrel darted into his path, it was Hi-Yo Silver, Away! as I ate pods of dust, dirt and grass from flat on my back. In my late thirties, I had a short tenure in a local judo dojo where I became rather adept at being thrown. During those two years I spent a reasonable amount of time weightless and shoulder-high, tracking through space until I came to a thudding halt upon the mat. Oh how this came in handy when I cowboy'd up. We had another horse, a great, well-trained, parade horse and show animal named "Cal." He also was named "He Who Does Not Like Things Upside His Head." He was the greatest horse I've ever owned and the equestrian love of my life but . . . he had one tick. As a colt, someone must have struck him hard on the side of his face because any object in the area of his eyes would send him to the hills. I learned after a few forgetful occasions to honor his request.

One afternoon, at one of our fall fiestas attended by about a hundred of our relatives and friends, we'd hired a twenty-piece mariachi band from New York City. The singer requested to have his picture taken on "a fiery steed," so we brought out Cal, my best. The singer climbed aboard but had left his sombrero on the ground. He called for a bandmate to hand it to him just as I was about to warn that it wasn't a good idea. Too late. Just as he grabbed his sombrero near Cal's face, my finest started to spin in the opposite direction of the hat. This caused our singer to windmill wildly in search of balance, bringing the sombrero again and again to Cal's eye level. This of course caused him to spin and spin. Cal, with his rear hooves remaining steady, did a hard series of 360-degree pirouettes while my amigo, his eyes rolled back in his head, was launched, NASA-like, into the dirt. The great man landed in a cloud of dust at the feet of his *compañeros*, who exploded in uproarious laughter. He calmly got up, dusted himself off and moved toward the dining tables, where the whole group burst into "Guadalajara! Guadalajara!" followed by an all-hands-on-deck "Macarena."

We'd often hold small rodeos with pro bronc riders, barrel races and team penning that we all joined in on. Team penning is pretty basic. The tequila gets lined up in shot glasses along the fence. The cows are numbered. You draw a number and you and a partner cut that cow out of the herd and drive him toward a small pen. The team that performs this task the fastest wins. The others drink up. In short time, hilarity rules.

## El Charro

Most of our rodeo events were hosted by Juan Marrufo Sanchez. Juan hailed from Mexico, where he'd been awarded All-Around Mexican Cowboy in 1994. He ended up marrying a Jersey girl on vacation in Mexico and now incongruously resided in an apartment in Brick, New Jersey. As a new Hispanic immigrant whose heavily accented English left him at a disadvantage, he'd ended up working at local farms, mucking stalls and taking care of horses—his great skill as a horseman undiscovered. One day I asked my assistant Terry Magovern to do some research on a section of Mexico I was writing about for my song "Reno." Terry answered, "Hey, there's a Mexican cowboy living upstairs in an apartment in Brick. Maybe you should speak to him." A few weeks later, Juan showed up at our farm and stayed. He gave me a few books on the topics I was interested in and we talked a while. But most of that first afternoon was taken up in a display of horsemanship Charro-style. Juan was also a master of the lariat, and beneath his tutoring my cousin Ricky and I became pretty good at some basic rope tricks.

One evening as we herded the cows back into the trailer, one cut loose. My bull-riding brother-in-law, Mickey, literally grabbed the bull by the horns, though it became quickly apparent that that's not as easy as it sounds. Small cows are strong and will easily lift you up off your feet with one good swipe of their heads. Our cow broke loose, heading at speed toward the western edge of our property and Route 34. It was a summer weekend. Route 34 was packed with Mom, Pop, little Billy, Sally, Sue and Grandma, heading home from the beach in their SUVs. Juan in the meantime had disappeared into the barn and came galloping out, with lariat in hand, on "Ranger," his trick horse.

We were off. I hopped on an ATV. Along with Juan's father and Max Weinberg's eight-year-old son, Jay, we pursued our fleeing bovine as he headed for a stand of trees. This was the last obstacle separating our property from an open field and two packed weekend lanes of unsuspecting suburban drivers. I had visions of a full-on disaster and headlines reading: "Bennie's Bronco Bashed By Boss's Bull!" Fifty feet from the tree line I watched Juan and Ranger make their move. Juan's right arm raised, lariat at the ready, Ranger suddenly shifted gears and a thin line of rope arced through the air and . . . wham! Right on the money. The rope landed perfectly, unimaginably, right over the cow's horns as Juan wrapped the opposite end around his saddle horn and our prey was stopped in his tracks. Juan's dad slid off the rear of our ATV and lightly tossed another rope around the horns and then I triangulated with another. It took the three of us, soaked in sun and sweat, to move this strong little cow back to its trailer. Jay Weinberg had the last word as he looked at Juan and said, "Wow. A real cowboy."

SIXTY-EIGHT

# THE SEEGER SESSIONS

In 1997 I recorded "We Shall Overcome" for *Where Have All the Flowers Gone: The Songs of Pete Seeger*. Growing up a rock 'n' roll kid, I didn't know a lot about Pete's music or the depth of his influence. But once I started listening, I was overwhelmed by the wealth of songs, their richness and their power. It changed what I thought I knew about "folk music." Through Soozie Tyrell, I met a group of musicians out of New York City who occasionally came down and played at our farm. Accordion, fiddle, banjo, upright bass, washboard—this is the sound I was envisioning for the Pete Seeger project. We set up next to one another in the living room of our farmhouse (horns in the hall), counted off the opening chords to "Jesse James" and away we went.

We made a half-dozen recordings. I sat on them for almost a decade but from time to time I kept being drawn back to them. They weren't quite like anything else I'd cut before and their freshness kept commanding my ear. I set up another session in 2005 and then one more in 2006. Everything on the record was cut in those three one-day sessions ('97, '05 and '06), mostly first or second takes, all live and all with a band I'd never played a note with before they showed up at our farm barn dance. The Sessions Band was born.

There was one show in America that stood out as not only one of the finest of but one of the most meaningful of my work life: New Orleans.

I'd been invited to play the first post-Katrina New Orleans Jazz and Heritage Festival as a headliner. I finally had a band that I felt would contextually fit Jazz Fest and might be able to pull the weight of that position.

I understood the great symbolism the festival would have to New Orleans that year and I wanted to make sure we honored it. They'd been through hell, with half the population lost, their city destroyed; people would be attending for deep, deep reasons and that would need to be taken into consideration.

Shortly before we were to leave for Louisiana, I thought of the city's unofficial theme song, "When the Saints Go Marching In." I was compelled to seek out *all* the lyrics. I saw most of them had never been heard and that this was a much deeper piece of music than what had been popularly known over the years. I slowed the song down to a meditation on resilience, survival and commitment to a dream that lives on through storm, wreckage and ruin. It was a quiet hymn, the way we presented it, but it was our thanks and our prayer for the city that had birthed blues, jazz, rock 'n' roll and so much of the most epic American culture.

In order to sound check at the festival grounds, we would need to be onstage at eight thirty a.m. on the day of our show. That's gut-level brutal for musicians but we *needed* to sound check. This was a new band's first gig in front of people. I had to make sure my musicians were comfortable and left the stage knowing we could be great. The Edge of U2 was there at the crack of dawn with us, checking it out. I'd been longtime compadres with the guys in U2, going back to that 1981 club appearance in London. I feel a great bond with their band. Bono had emceed my induction into the Rock and Roll Hall of Fame, and besides being one of the last of the rock bands always willing to play for *all* the marbles, they also happen to be some of the nicest people I've met in the music business. Years later they continue to support me and show up at our gigs regularly, so it was great to see the Edge's goatee smiling by the side of the stage.

It'd been pouring rain all morning; the field was soaked and looked like the land of a thousand lakes. It was bone-chilly and damp. We kicked into Blind Alfred Reed's "How Can a Poor Man Stand Such Times and Live" and the first thing I noticed was the stage was acoustically dead; there was very little ambient sound. This can make things sound flat and unexciting, even too quiet, to the group. The house sound was too far away to add that little extra buzz and fullness that lets you know you're hearing some of what the crowd is responding to. All of this often happens in outside venues. For the audience, the sound will be clear and unfiltered by arena echo, but for the band, it can make you feel cut off from the crowd, and that's always deadly to me. So, you adapt. You concentrate and *will* that bridge between yourself and the audience. Then let your showtime adrenaline fix do the rest.

We came off the stage after sound check smiling. It'd do. I stood in the wings, greeted the band stage-side and told them we'd have a great afternoon.

## Showtime in New Orleans

Allen Toussaint, New Orleans's spiritual godfather (who passed away in November of 2015), went on right before us. That's a hell of an opening act and tough to follow. After his set, Allen came down and met the band. He was the gracious, elegant mayor of New Orleans and welcomed us to his city. Now it was time for the "kids." We walked on to a nice round of applause—not tumultuous, but welcoming—and kicked into "Mary Don't You Weep." I immediately sensed the crowd was not going to be easy. They were seeing something even our fans who were there to support us hadn't seen before, and much of the audience had come to see many of the great other acts of the day. So we went to work. Sometimes two pieces have to move around a little bit, squirm and find some wiggle room until they lock into place. I could feel that was what was happening and I knew when that arises, you just put your head down and play your music. You have to be confident in all of the thought and rehearsal that brought you to that stage. Still, it's always unnerving.

It turned into a beautiful evening. We were in the last hour before sundown and the weather was glorious. Gradually, things moved, loosened up; people started dancing, swaying, taking in the noise we were making and going with it. We had the balls to blow "Jersey Dixieland" in Dixieland! The crowd was judging but generous too. Then we hit "How Can a Poor Man" and I made sure I annunciated every line as clearly as I could to be understood. We were an hour and fifteen minutes in and I was pushing our rhythm as far toward rock while still letting the band swing. Slowly I could feel those two pieces sliding together. Then "My City of Ruins"; that's what it took. A mutual acknowledgment of pain and hard times.

We closed at exactly sunset. I walked to the front of the stage, where to my left, over the field's rim, the sun sat, a red ball on the horizon. I let its golden light wash over me like no spotlight could and I felt the band and the crowd fall into each other's arms. We finished with the prayerful arrangement of "Saints" we'd worked out just for this moment. I watched white handkerchiefs flutter from a thousand hands in the last rays of the sun. There were some tears both on and off the stage as the cool evening rose up and the crowd dispersed back onto the streets of the Crescent City.

I've played many, many, many shows, but few like this one. I had to work very hard and lead the band with a conviction I wasn't sure I felt myself. But maybe that's what the evening was all about: trying to rise above the uncertainty of the day and find something to stand on. You cannot book, manufacture or contrive these dates. It's a matter of moment, place, need, and a desire to serve in your own small way the events of the day. There, in New Orleans, there was a *real* job to do. One the lovely but fleeting notes that poured out of that day's participants and off the stage onto the streets of New Orleans could only scratch the surface of. Still, something as seemingly inconsequential as music does certain things very well. There's a coming together and a lifting, a fortifying, that occurs when people gather and move *in time* with one another. It's a beautiful thing.

This was one of the shows that went to the very top of the list for me. I don't know if *we* were great but I know it was a great evening. Sometimes, that covers a lot of ground and is all the day calls for.

In the 1970s I went to a Grateful Dead show at a community college. I watched the crowd swaying and doing its trance-dance thing and I stood very outside of it. To me—sober, nonmystical, only half hippie, if that, me—they sounded like a not-very-talented bar band. I went home gently mystified. I don't know if the Grateful Dead were great but I know they *did* something great. Years later, when I came to appreciate their subtle musicality, Jerry Garcia's beautifully lyrical guitar playing and the folk purity of their voices, I understood that I'd missed it. They had a unique ability to build community and sometimes, it ain't what you're doing but what happens while you're doing it that counts. In New Orleans that year, we were a left-field but good fit and filled our important slot well. Then New Orleans did the rest.

A lot of what the E Street Band does is hand-me-down shtick transformed by will, power and an intense communication with our audience into something transcendent. Sometimes that's all you need. I once read a review of a very competent hit-making group where the reviewer stated, "They do all the unimportant things very well." I knew exactly what he meant. Rock 'n' roll music, in the end, *is* a source of religious and mystical power. Your playing can suck, your singing can be barely viable, but if when you get together with your pals in front of *your* audience and make *the noise*, the one that is drawn from the center of your being, from your godhead, from your gutter, from the universe's infinitesimal genesis point . . . you're rockin' and you're a rock 'n' roll *star* in every sense of the word. The punks instinctively knew this and created a third revolution out of it, but it is an essential element in the equation of every great musical unit and rock 'n' roll band, no matter how down-to-earth their presentation.

## SIXTY-NINE
# *MAGIC*

At the end of the *Rising* tour, I had a few songs from my road writing. Brendan O'Brien once again paid me a visit. I played him what I had and we took it from there. I remember working on a decent amount of *Magic* at my worktable in Rumson, but by this time I tended to write anywhere and everywhere. I no longer separated touring and writing as I had in my early years. I wrote in my dressing room often before the show or after in my hotel room. It became a way I meditated before or after a raucous night. Quiet, lost in my own thoughts, traveling to places I'd never been, looking through the eyes of those I'd never met, I dreamt the dreams of refugees and strangers. Those dreams were somehow also mine. I felt their fears, their hopes, their desires, and when it was good, I'd lift off from my hotel digs and find myself back on some metaphysical highway searching for life and rock 'n' roll. *Magic* was my state-of-the-nation dissent over the Iraq War and the Bush years.

Still, I aimed everywhere on *Magic* for the political and the personal to meld together. You can listen to the whole thing without ever thinking of the politics of the day or you can hear them ticking deadly through the internal thread of the music.

Like many before, our *Magic* tour started in Asbury Park's Convention Hall. There, as a young aspiring musician, I'd seen the Doors with Jim Morrison, whose live presence and command of the stage completely engulfed you, and in 1966 I somehow managed to miss the Rolling Stones as they passed through. I'd seen the Who demolish their equipment in a cloud of smoke in front of wide-eyed teenyboppers with Mom and Dad in tow, who were waiting to see the headlining act, Herman's Hermits. The Who's show sent me running in a fever out to pick up a strobe light and smoke bomb for my upcoming CYO gig with the Castiles. There, at the end of our last set, in the basement of St. Rose of Lima on a Saturday night, I switched on the strobe, set off the smoke bomb, climbed on a chair and smashed a vase of flowers I'd lifted from a first-grade classroom onto the floor. This didn't quite pack the nihilistic punch of Pete Townshend bashing his guitar to bits against his smoky Vox amplifier, but limited funds and one good guitar could only take you so far.

Convention Hall was the first mansion of my rock 'n' roll dreams. There under its roof a wider world awaited, real magicians appeared and anything could happen. Midget wrestling, boat shows with yachts the size of your backyard, hot-rod exhibitions, roller derby and rock 'n' roll baptisms all coursed through the veins of this modest concert hall that seemed to me the size of Madison Square Garden. Its front doors opened onto the interior of the Convention Hall promenade. There stands of cotton candy, cheap T-shirts, seashells, pinball arcades and an endless amount of shore tchotchkes lined your walk to the hall's brass doors, which promised absurdity and transcendence. It's still pretty much the same.

For me now, it's just a home. A home of my own, the Asbury

boardwalk, where I bring my band to reconnect with where we come from and to tighten up and get ready for battle on our newest adventure. Here on the boardwalk I now play the role of the ghost of Christmas past as the city and its exciting new development passes me by. There is even a ridiculous bust of me somewhere in town primed and ready for seagull shit. Still, on any summer night, I feel comfortably at home walking the boards wearing my ninja cloak of invisibility, a baseball hat, all while going almost as unrecognized as I did in 1969. I still feel amongst friends and my people. It's still my place and I still feed off and love it. So on a fresh September morning, we packed our gear and left Asbury for Hartford, Connecticut. We were off.

This was the first tour where an illness would sideline a band member into missing shows. Danny Federici had contracted melanoma and now needed serious medical treatment. Danny had been misdiagnosed early on and the cancer was now moving through his system. He had been quietly receiving care for a while but could no longer keep it from the band, and so began a long and difficult journey. Charlie Giordano from the Sessions Band was tutored for a few shows by Dan, then quietly stepped in to take over the organ duties while Danny was treated.

One evening on one of Danny's short returns to the band, he stepped into my dressing room before the show and sat in the chair opposite me. He basically explained things weren't looking so good. At one point he seemed to run out of words and, gesturing silently, moved one palm over the other, trying to tell me what I already knew. His eyes filled and finally we sat there looking at each other . . . it'd been thirty-five years. I gave him what assurances I could that might ease his mind. We stood up, held each other for a long moment and went out and played. Not long thereafter, Danny appeared with us for the last time, at Conseco Fieldhouse in Indianapolis on March 20, 2008. In the band we all knew this was it. We wouldn't see Danny onstage again.

Danny was a believer in the world as it stands. We never spoke a single word about a single lyric or idea that was in the many hundreds of songs I wrote. The same songs that his fingers and heart magically and instinctively knew how to color perfectly. Danny and I were closest on evenings when he found me in my lowest self. He never judged. He just observed and breathed a sigh. I always felt it was a bad way to bridge the gap between the two of us. It was. But when I tried it the other way, to bring Danny to personal accountability, I felt like his taskmaster or his old man with a pole so far up my ass it embarrassed me.

As a leader, even of a rock 'n' roll band, there is always a little of the *padrone* in your job description, but it's a fine line. And the members for whom I played that role too fully usually fared the worst.

But Danny tried hard. He beat alcoholism, stayed pretty true to his AA program and worked to put a life together. But in the end, for Dan Federici it would never be easy.

One spring afternoon a few of us gathered in a Manhattan hospital around Danny's bed. We circled the bed holding hands and said our individual prayers and farewells.

Danny died on April 17, 2008. He left behind a son, Jason; two daughters, Harley and Madison; and his wife, Maya. There was a lovely, light-filled service held for Danny at the United Methodist Church in Red Bank on April 21. To an overflow crowd, music was played, remembrances given, good-byes said.

I had watched Danny fight and conquer some tough addictions. I watched him struggle to put his life together and, in the last decade, when the band reunited, thrive on sitting in his seat behind that big B3. I watched him fight his cancer without complaint and with great courage and spirit. He was a sunny-side-up fatalist. He never gave up, right to the end.

Before we went on for that last night in Indiana, I asked him what he wanted to play and he said "Sandy." He wanted to strap on the accordion and revisit the boardwalk of our youth during the summer nights when we'd walk along the boards with all the time in the world.

He wanted to play once more the song that is of course about the end of something wonderful and the beginning of something unknown and new.

Pete Townshend once said, "A rock 'n' roll band is a crazy thing. You meet some people when you're a kid, and unlike any occupation in the whole world, you're stuck with them for the rest of your life no matter who they are or what crazy things they do."

If we didn't play together, the E Street Band would probably not know one another. We wouldn't be in a room together. But we do . . . we do play together and every night at eight we walk out onstage together, and that, my friends, is a place where miracles occur . . . old and new miracles. And those you are with in the presence of miracles, you never forget. Life does not separate you. Death does not separate you. Those you are with who create miracles for you, like Danny did for me every night, you are honored to be amongst.

Of course, we all grow up, and we know "it's only rock 'n' roll" . . . but it's not. After a lifetime of watching a man perform his miracle for you, night after night, it feels an awful lot like love.

# SEVENTY

# SUPER BOWL SUNDAY

Six air force Thunderbirds have just roared overhead at what felt like inches above our backstage area, giving myself and the entire E Street Band a brush cut. With twenty minutes to go, I'm sitting in my trailer trying to decide which boots to wear. I've got a nice pair of cowboy boots my feet look really good in, but I'm concerned about their stability. There is no canopy overhead at the Super Bowl and two days ago we rehearsed in full rain on the field. We all got soaked and the stage became as slick as a frozen pond. It was so slippery I crashed into Mike Colucci, our cameraman, coming off my knee slide, his camera the only thing that kept me from launching out onto the soggy turf. Then our "referee" for "Glory Days" came running out, couldn't stop himself and executed one of the most painfully perfect "man slips on a banana peel" falls I've ever seen. This sent Steve, myself and the entire band into one of the biggest stress-induced laughs of our lives that lasted all the way back to our trailers.

I better go with the combat boots I always carry. The round toes will give me better braking power than the pointy-toed cowboy boots when I hit the deck. I stuff my boots with two innersoles to make them as fitted as possible, zip them up snugly around my ankles, stomp around in my trailer a bit and feel pretty grounded. Fifteen minutes . . . I'm nervous. It's not the usual preshow jitters or "butterflies" I've had before. I'm talking about a "five minutes to beach landing," *Right Stuff*, "Lord, don't let me screw the pooch in front of a hundred million people" kind of semiterror. It only lasts for a minute . . . I check my hair, spray it with something that turns it into concrete, and I'm out the door.

I catch sight of Patti smiling. She's been my rock all week. I put my arm around her and away we go. They take us by golf cart to a holding tunnel right off the field. The problem is there are a thousand people there: TV cameras, media of all kinds and general chaos. Suddenly, hundreds of people rush by us in a column shouting, cheering . . . our fans! And tonight also our stage builders. These are "the volunteers." They've been here for two weeks on their own dime in a field day after day, putting together and pulling apart pieces of our stage over and over again, theoretically achieving military precision. Now it's for real. I hope they've got it down because as we're escorted onto the field, lights in the stadium fully up, the banshee wail of seventy thousand screaming football fanatics rising in our ears, there's nothing there. Nothing . . . no sound, no lights, no instruments, no stage, nothing but brightly lit unwelcoming green turf. Suddenly an army of ants comes from all sides of what seems like nowhere, each rolling a piece of our lifeline, our Earth, onto the field. The cavalry has arrived. What takes us on a concert day eight hours to do is done in five minutes. Unbelievable. Everything in our world is there . . . we hope. We gather a few feet off the stage, form a circle of hands; I say a few words drowned out by the crowd and it's smiles all around. I've been in a lot of high-stakes situations like this—though not *exactly* like this—with these people before. It's stressful, but our band is made for it . . . and it's about to begin . . . so, happy warriors, we bound up onto the stage.

The NFL stage manager gives me the three-minutes sign . . . two minutes . . . one . . . there's a guy jumping up and down on sections of the stage to get them to sit evenly on the grass field . . . thirty seconds . . . white noise screams from our monitors . . . they're still testing all the speakers and equipment . . . that's cutting it close! The lights in the stadium go down. The crowd erupts and Max's drumbeat opens "Tenth Avenue." I feel a white light silhouette . . . Clarence and I share a moment. I hear Roy's piano. I give C's hand a pat. I'm on the move, tossing my guitar in a high arc for Kevin, my guitar tech, to catch, and it's . . . "Ladies and gentlemen, for the next twelve minutes we will be bringing the righteous and mighty power of the E Street Band into your beautiful home. I want you to step back from the guacamole dip. I want you to put the chicken fingers down! And turn the television ALL THE WAY UP!" Because, of course, there is just ONE thing I've got to know: "IS THERE ANYBODY ALIVE OUT THERE?!" I feel like I've just taken a syringe of adrenaline straight to the heart. Then I'm on top of the piano (good old boots). I'm down. One . . . two . . . three, knee drop in front of the microphone and I'm bending back almost flat on the stage. I close my eyes for a moment and when I open them, I see nothing but blue night sky. No band, no crowd, no stadium. I hear and feel all of it in the form of a great sirenlike din surrounding me, but with my back nearly flat against the stage I see nothing but beautiful night sky with a halo of a thousand stadium suns at its edges.

I take several deep breaths and a calm comes over me. Since the inception of our band it's been our ambition to play for everyone. We've achieved a lot but we haven't achieved that. Our audience remains tribal . . . that is, predominantly white. On occasion—the Obama inaugural concert; touring through Africa in '88; during a political campaign, particularly in Cleveland with President Obama—I looked out and sang "Promised Land" to the audience I intended it for, young people, old people, black, white, brown, cutting across religious and class lines. That's who I'm singing to today. Today we play for everyone. For free! I pull myself upright with the mike stand, back into the world, this world, my world, the one with everybody in it, and the stadium, the crowd, my band, my best friends, my wife, come rushing into view and it's "Teardrops on the city . . ."

During "Tenth Avenue" I tell the story of my band—and other things—"when the change was made uptown" . . . It goes rushing by, then the knee slide. Too much adrenaline, a late drop, too much speed, here I come, Mike . . . BOOM! And I'm onto his camera, the lens implanted into my crotch with one leg off the stage. I use his camera to push myself back up and . . . say it, say it, say it, say it . . . BLAM! "BORN TO RUN" . . . my story . . . Something bright and hot blows up behind me. Later I'll hear there were fireworks. I never see any. Just the ones going off in my head. I'm out of breath. I try to slow it down. That ain't gonna happen. I already hear the crowd singing the last eight bars of "Born to Run," oh, oh, oh, oh . . . then it's straight into "Working on a Dream" . . . your story . . . and mine I hope. Steve is on my right, Patti on my left. I catch a smile and the wonderful choir, the Joyce Garrett Singers, that backed me in Washington during the inaugural concert is behind us. I turn to see their faces and listen to the sound of their voices . . . "working on a dream." Done. Moments later, we're ripping straight into "Glory Days" . . . the end of the story. A last party steeped in happy fatalism and some laughs with my old pal Steve. The Ump doesn't fall on his ass tonight. He just throws the yellow penalty flag for the precious forty-five seconds we've gone overtime . . . home stretch. Everyone is out front now, forming that great line. Out of the corner of my eye, I catch the horns raising their instruments high; my guitar is wheeling around my neck and on the seventh beat, I'm going to Disneyland. I'm already someplace a lot farther away and more fun than that. I look around: we're alive, it's over, we link arms and take a bow as the stage comes apart beneath our feet. It's chaos again all the way back to the trailer.

The theory of relativity holds. Onstage your exhilaration is in direct proportion to the void you're dancing over. A gig I always looked a little askance at and was a little wary of turned out to have surprising emotional power and resonance for me and my band. It was a high point, a marker of some sort, and went up with the biggest shows of our work life. The NFL threw us an anniversary party the likes of which we'd never have thrown for ourselves, with fireworks and everything! In the middle of their football game, they let us hammer out a little part of our story. I love playing long and hard but it was the thirty-five years in twelve minutes . . . that was the trick. You start here, you end there, that's it. That's the time you've got to give it everything you have . . . twelve minutes . . . give or take a few seconds.

The Super Bowl helped me sell a few new records and probably put a few extra fannies in the seats that tour. But what it was really about was this: I felt my band remained one of the mightiest in the land and I wanted you to know it. We wanted to show you . . . just because we could.

By three a.m., I was back home, everyone in the house fast asleep. I was sitting in the yard in front of an open fire, watching the sparks light, fly and vanish into the black evening sky, my ears ringing good and hard . . . "Oh yeah, it's all right."

# SEVENTY-ONE

# MOVING ON

The rest of 2009 was taken up with the release of our *Working on a Dream* album and tour. Max's son, Jay, stepped in for his dad, who was taking care of business with Conan O'Brien, and at age eighteen Jay became only the second man to sit on that drum stool in thirty-five years. After a few ragged starts, it was obvious Jay had the power, the precision, the ears, the discipline, his father's work ethic and willingness to learn. Plus he brought his own brand of young punk energy that kicked the shit out of our playbook. Still, something didn't feel quite right. When Jay initially started playing with us, my skin wasn't moving right. Then, I realized, with all his technique and power, he was playing "on top" of the band, riding over the surface of our arrangements. We took a break. I walked over to him and quietly explained that the drums are not part of the exoskeleton of these arrangements. The drums are the soul engine, buried down and breathing inside the band. You play not on top but immersed in the band. You power every-thing from within. I said, "Take a breath, take it back down and dig deep. When you hit that right position, when the beat is placed correctly, you'll drop inside the band naturally."

That could be a pretty sophisticated idea for anyone to wrap their head around, much less an eighteen-year-old who up to this point had mostly played in front of approximately thirty people at a local club. But like father, like son.

That afternoon, Jay Weinberg took out his shovel and dug himself a hole so deep inside the rhythm section that the question of who was going to do the job became moot. Jay brought fire, youth, intensity and his own brand of showmanship to the band. When we stepped on stage in front of 50,000 screaming fans, he blew the place apart.

Later that year we played the twenty-fifth anniversary of the Rock and Roll Hall of Fame. We had a blast backing Darlene Love, Sam Moore and Billy Joel. I sang "I Still Haven't Found What I'm Looking For" with U2 and "Because the Night" with my second-favorite Jersey girl, Patti Smith.

We had three weeks of touring left. My great concern was Clarence's physical condition. This is something I had watched deteriorate for a long time. First, the knees, then the hips, then the back, then it got worse. C trav-eled with a trainer and someone who monitored his medical condition but he still had to sit through much of the *Working on a Dream* tour. Getting him on and off the stage became a small production. An elevator was built. We walked on together so he had some support. But his inner strength, heart and commitment to playing never wavered. He had mellowed greatly with age until he often felt like this half-sleeping lion. He was not the danger he once was but you still did not want to disturb him.

C's presence remained large and his will ironclad. That's why he was still there. He willed it, and if it'd been up to him, he would've died there. That always worried me. We found doctors before each tour to provide him with a full checkup. Somehow he was always ready to play. I told him, "I

need to know exactly what you can do and what you can't do," but he grew
furious if I poked my nose too deeply into his medical business. During the
*Dream* tour he brought along a young mixed-race man as his assistant. For
months I never really knew who he was. I just figured he was one of C's people, who fluctuated regularly and brought some service or comfort to him.
It was Jake Clemons, Clarence's nephew, a saxophonist himself, though he
never played, with the exception of joining C one night on "Tenth Avenue
Freeze Out."

Clarence was always the last band member off the stage. As I held up
that big body night after night and we slowly made it down the stairs, he
often whispered, "Thanks for letting me be here." I was thankful he was
there. Even in his diminished state Clarence's presence remained rocklike
and essential to me. We flew up to Buffalo, New York, where we played
the *Greetings from Asbury Park* album start to finish for the first time. It was
the last show of the tour, and the night was filled with high anticipation,
camaraderie and the excitement of an adventure completed. The place was
in an uproar and the party was on. Old ghosts were there. Mike Appel had
accompanied us to the concert, stood in the circle of hands before the show
and was deeply welcome. We were alive and farther down the road. The
place filled with Mike's old cackling laugh and carny energy; music played,
people drank. Back on the plane, as we drew closer to Newark, from his seat,
Clarence lifted his glass and said, "I've just got something I want to say . . .
this could be the start of something big." Everyone laughed.

But that's how it felt. The band was playing great and we were navigating this part of our work life with grace and energy. Half of our set was
drawn from new material of the past ten years and we were still thrilled to be
amongst one another. We remained in love with the music, with our band
and with our audience. With the lights of the Eastern Seaboard sparkling
beneath us, carrying us home, we knew we'd worked hard and been lucky.

SEVENTY-TWO
# *WRECKING BALL*

One afternoon, driving back from a séance at my local watering hole, I started singing at the wheel, "You put on your coat, I'll put on my hat, you put out the dog, I'll put out the cat . . ." "Easy Money." Bing . . . the light went on. The muse had materialized along the roadside. "Easy Money" was the key to a record I needed to make.

After the crash of 2008, I was furious at what had been done by a handful of trading companies on Wall Street. *Wrecking Ball* was a shot of anger at the injustice that continues on and has widened with deregulation, dysfunctional regulatory agencies and capitalism gone wild at the expense of hardworking Americans. The middle class? Stomped on. Income disparity climbed as we lived through a new Gilded Age. This was what I wanted to write about.

I'd been following and writing about America's post-industrial trauma, the killing of our manufacturing presence and working class, for thirty-five years. So I went to work. I had some music in my notebooks waiting. "Jack of All Trades," written in a fury. "We Take Care of Our Own" and "Wrecking Ball." Then I wrote "Easy Money," "Death to My Hometown" and "This Depression." I had "Shackled and Drawn" and "Rocky Ground" from a gospel film project I'd been working on and they fit perfectly. Finally, I knew I needed a closer. I had "Land of Hope and Dreams," with which we struggled to beat our own live version until Bob Clearmountain came in with a transcendent mix. But still, I needed the song that would address the new voices of immigration, the civil rights movement and anyone who'd ever stuck their neck out for some righteous justice and was knocked down or killed for their effort. Where were they? I decided they were all here now and speaking to those who would listen. Those spirits don't go away. They haunt, they rabble-rouse, from beyond the grave. They have not been and can never be silenced. Death has given them an eternal voice. All we have to do is listen. That would be the message of my last song, "We Are Alive." Listen and learn from the souls and spirits who've come before.

I knew this was the music I should make now. It was my job. I felt the country was at a critical juncture. If this much damage can be done to average citizens with basically no accountability, then the game is off and the thin veil of democracy is revealed for what it is, a shallow disguise for a growing plutocracy that is here now and permanent.

*Wrecking Ball* was received with a lot less fanfare than I thought it would be. I was sure I had it. I still think I do and did. Maybe my voice had been too compromised by my own success, but I don't think so. I've worked hard and long to write about these subjects and I know them well. I knew *Wrecking Ball* was one of my best, most contemporary and accessible albums since *Born in the USA*. I'm no conspiracy theorist, so basically I realized that the presentation of these ideas in this form had a powerful but limited interest to a reasonably large but still select group of people, especially in the United States. For the next several years we toured, crisscrossing the globe, to a wild reception, where Europe, as usual, was a whole other story. There there was a deep and abiding interest in American affairs and anyone singing about them. Their interview questions were political and filled with the stakes I knew I was writing about when I wrote the record. I came to terms with the fact that in the States, the power of rock music as a vehicle for these ideas had diminished. A new kind of super-pop, hip-hop and a variety of other exciting genres had become the hotline of the day, more suited to the current zeitgeist. Don't get me wrong. I can't complain. *Wrecking Ball* went to number one and had a fine success of its own in the United States. Appreciative and understanding audiences met us everywhere. But I thought this was one of my most powerful records and I went out looking for it all.

SEVENTY-THREE

# LOSING
# THE RAIN

I was in the studio at my farm on a rainy, wind-soaked day between tours
when I received a phone call from Clarence. I'd been trying to get hold of
him for a sax session on the new version of "Land of Hope and Dreams"
we'd cut for the upcoming *Wrecking Ball*. He was calling from Los Angeles,
where he'd just performed with Lady Gaga on *American Idol*. He'd played a
great solo on her "Edge of Glory" single as well as appearing in the video. I
asked how he was and he said he had some numbness in his hand that was
inhibiting his sax playing and was making him very nervous. I asked him
what he wanted to do and for the first time in our history he begged off a
session and asked if he could return home to Florida to see a neurologist and
have his hand checked out. I assured him he could catch the session later
and told him I'd call him in a week or so and see how he was doing.

Patti's and my anniversary came up and we left to spend five or so days in Paris. About three days in, Gil Gamboa, our security person, knocked on our hotel door in the afternoon. When I opened the door, all I saw was his eyes glazed with tears. He choked out that Clarence had had a very serious stroke and was in the hospital. I left for Florida.

Clarence's stroke was massive, shutting the lights out on an entire side of his brain. It had happened in moments as he fell out of bed onto the floor. I visited St. Mary's Medical Center in West Palm Beach, where I was greeted by Clarence's brother, Bill; Jake, his nephew; and Victoria, his wife, and I was ushered in to see the Big Man. He lay in bed breathing heavily in a dimly lit room with tubes and cords emanating from underneath his gown. Clarence's eyelids, which were always like soft steel doors, languorously opening and closing, were heavily shut. Victoria spoke to him and told him I was there. I took his hand, spoke gently to him and could feel a light grip form around my fingers. Some part of him somewhere was responding. Clarence's hands were always like heavy stones but when he placed them upon your shoulders, the most comforting, secure feeling swept through your body and heart. Very, very strong and exceedingly gentle—that was C with me.

The folks at St. Mary's were kind enough to provide us with a small room where Clarence's brother, nephews, children and friends could gather, play some music and talk about C. It was far enough away not to disturb the other patients and before long, we had the saxophone, guitars and our voices singing during the days and nights we waited to see how Clarence would respond to the efforts of his doctors. There were procedures, medical decisions to be made by the family, doctor's consultations, but one afternoon, I was taken aside by Clarence's main physician and was told it would be near miraculous if he ever regained consciousness. If he did, he would most certainly be wheelchair bound, an entire half of his body paralyzed. His speech, his face, his hands dysfunctional. He would certainly never play the saxophone again. I don't know how Clarence would've handled this. He was a strong man with a staggering life force but I know not playing, and not playing in the band, would've hurt big. It really wasn't meant to be. Clarence had been a natural creature of excess, lived hard, never really taken great care of himself and never looked back.

A week passed; C's condition continued to worsen and all that could be done had been done.

The morning sun laid a pinkish veil over the St. Mary's parking lot as we entered through the rear door and gathered bedside in Clarence's small room. His wife, his sons, his brother, his nephews, myself, Max and Garry prepared to say our good-byes. I strummed my guitar gently to "Land of Hope and Dreams" and then something inexplicable happened. Something great and timeless and beautiful and confounding just disappeared. Something was gone . . . gone for good.

There is no evidence of the soul except in its sudden absence. A nothingness enters, taking the place where something was before. A night without stars falls and for a moment covers everything in the room. Clarence's great body became still. His name was called. A lot of tears fell. We took some time, said our prayers and were ushered gently out by the nun who'd been C's nurse. Clarence's brother, Bill, took it very hard for the rest of us. The stillness was broken. In the hallway we comforted one another, talked for a while, kissed and hugged one another, then just went home.

Back in the world, it had turned into a beautiful sunny Florida day, just the kind C loved for his fishing expeditions. I went back to my hotel and took a swim deep into the sea until the noise of the shore drifted from my ears. I tried to imagine my world without Clarence. Then, turning over on my back, I felt the sun take my face and I swam back to land, went inside and fell asleep soaking on my bed.

The thick Florida air filled my lungs with cotton as we entered the Royal Poinciana Chapel. All of E Street, Jackson Browne, and Clarence's wives and children, along with Eric Meola, who took the iconic picture of Clarence and me on the cover of *Born to Run*, were there. Victoria spoke lovingly of Clarence and read his last wishes, which were basically that C wanted his ashes scattered in Hawaii in the presence of his wife and all of the other "special" women in his life. Only Clarence, alive or dead, could pull this one off.

The first time I'd seen C's massive form striding out of the shadows of a half-empty bar in Asbury Park, I'd thought, "Here comes my brother." Yet as solid as the Big Man was, he was also very fragile. And in some funny way we became each other's protectors; I think perhaps I protected C from a world where it still wasn't so easy to be big and black. Racism was still there and over our years together, occasionally we saw it. Clarence's celebrity and size did not always make him immune. I think perhaps C protected me from a world where it wasn't always so easy to be an insecure, weird and skinny white boy either. Standing together, we were badass, on any given night, some of the baddest asses on the planet. And we were coming to your town to shake you and to wake you up.

Together, we told a story that transcended those I'd written in my songs and in my music. It was a story about the possibilities of friendship, a story that Clarence carried in his heart. We both did. It was a story where the Scooter and the Big Man busted the city in half. A story where we kicked ass and *remade* the city, reshaping it into the kind of place where our friendship would not be such an anomaly. I knew that that was what I was going to miss: the chance to stand alongside Clarence and renew that vow on a nightly basis. That was *the* thing that we did together.

Clarence was one of the most authentic people I'd ever come across. He had no postmodern bullshit about him. Other than my old man, a true Bukowski character come to ass-on-a-bar-stool life, I never met anyone else as real as Clarence Clemons. His life was often a mess. He could spout the most inane bullshit you've ever heard and believe it, but there was something inside of his skin that screamed life was ON and he was the master of ceremonies! He made himself extremely happy and horribly miserable, he dogged me and blessed me, was side-splittingly hilarious and always tread-ing near pathos. He collected a cast of characters around him that often had to be seen to be believed. He was sexually mysterious and voracious but he was also incredibly lovely and my friend. We didn't hang out. We couldn't. It would've ruined my life. There was always too much. But the time I spent with him was filled with thrills and big laughs. We were physically comfort-able with each other, often hugging and embracing. Clarence's body was a vast world in and of itself. He was a mountainous, moving, kind citadel of flesh in a storm.

I miss my friend. But I still have the story that he gave me, that he whispered in my ear, that we told together, the one we whispered into your ear, and that is going to carry on. If I were a mystic, Clarence's and my friendship would lead me to believe that we must have stood together in other, older times, along other rivers, in other cities, in other fields, doing our modest version of God's work.

Clarence was elemental in my life and losing him was like losing the rain. In his last days, he moved slowly to the stage but when he got there, there was a big man in the house.

On returning to New Jersey and work, I reentered the studio. My producer Ron Aniello was there working on *Wrecking Ball*. He gave me his condolences and said after he heard about Clarence's death, he didn't know what to do. So while he was in LA, he had carefully pieced together Clar-ence's solo from a live take to fit our new version of "Land of Hope and Dreams." I sat there as C's sax filled the room.

# SEVENTY-FOUR

# THE WRECKING BALL TOUR

Clarence once mentioned to me during a negotiation that he should be paid not only for playing but for being Clarence. I said no and it was funny, but he had a point. Was there another one? Nope. There was only that one. In truth he *was* paid for being Clarence, as he'd been the most highly remunerated member of the E Street Band since close to its inception. So what did we do now? That was all that was on my mind as our tour approached.

Ed Manion, our longtime Jukes/E Street/Seeger saxophonist, was a great player and an all-around good guy and would get the job done. But "the job" was tricky. It was less of a "job" than a position of faith that had some distinctly shamanistic requirements. There was a fellow out in Freehold whom I'd played successfully with, who had C's tone down, was great on-stage, but . . .

I received a small collection of DVDs from guys who could play rings around the moon, but we didn't need John Coltrane. We needed a to-the-bone rock 'n' roll saxophonist. I sat in bed going through them one morning as Patti sat at my side going, "Nope, nope, nope, nope." Out of curiosity I even went on the Internet and checked out the top "tribute" bands to see how they were handling it . . . No.

## Jake

Though he traveled with the band for the better part of the *Magic/Dream* tour, I'd never really heard Jake play 'til Clarence's funeral. There, he did a lovely version of "Amazing Grace." He was physically big like C. He and his brothers, to the unknowing eye, could appear to be a misplaced tribe of Maori warriors. Jake was bespectacled, sweet and soft too. Somewhere along the way, a mama had been good to him, and he carried with him the limit-less sunshine that was C's specialty on a good day. He was talented, a good songwriter and singer. He loved music, was young and hungry, and I could perceive inside of him the beginning of a star.

After C's death, many months went by. Jake and I stayed casually in touch and though we both knew what we were thinking, it was appropri-ately never mentioned. On the street I was confronted regularly with the same question from friends and fans. "Whaddyagonnado?" That's how it always came out. One thought, one word, one critical, life-defining, all-important, existential "I gotta know NOW 'cause it's driving me CRAZY that this thing I loved might no longer be there!!!" question. "Whaddyagon-nado?" My answer was always "We're gonna think of something."

Steve on Jake: "He's black. He plays the saxophone. His name is Clemons. He's the guy! He's the only guy!" Steve dismissed my other can-didates as . . . white.

I knew what he meant. He was saying that "thing," that world, that possibility that Clarence symbolized going back to the early days of race-divided Asbury Park was tied to his overwhelming blackness. It was. And that "thing" *was* a critical piece of the living philosophy of the E Street Band.

I agreed that Steve was right but by definition, there being only one true Big Man, one true Big Man whom neither chops, nor size, nor the blackness of night could replicate, it didn't really matter . . . maybe. I knew the band had changed the minute C breathed his last. That version of the E Street Band would be Never No More! There would be no *replacing* Clarence Clemons. So the real question was, "So what's next?" Next . . . now.

Jake's very existence gave him the first shot. Besides, I had already played with the other guys I was thinking about and Jake was the only real question mark. I needed to find out who he was. So, many months after we'd sat in that little room at St. Mary's passing the guitar around, I made the call he must've been expecting. I laid out the situation. It was an audition. It'd be just him and me. We'd meet and see if there was reason to take it further.

On tour, some had expressed reservations about Jake's maturity. In my experience with him I could feel some swagger but after speaking with him during Clarence's illness, I felt there was a lot more there. It was time to see.

Jake came to his first professional meeting with me an inauspicious hour late. I was ready and steaming. When he walked in I said, "Did you have something more important to do?" He said, no he did not, but he had gotten lost. I said, "Let's go to work."

Over the phone I'd given Jake four or five songs to familiarize himself with: "Promised Land," "Badlands" and a few other ringers. I wanted to hear his tone, his phrasing, and find out his learning ability. When he arrived, he "sort of" knew them. Lesson number one: in the E Street Band we don't "sort of" do . . . ANYTHING. James Brown was my father, god and hero as bandleader. Sam Moore was also a great inspiration. At their best, these were men whose lives forbade them to fuck around with the thing that was lifting them up. On the bandstand, with their bands, they gave NO QUARTER!

People always asked me how the band played like it did night after night, almost murderously consistent, NEVER stagnant and always full balls to the wall. There are two answers. One is they loved and respected their jobs, one another, their leader and the audience. The other is . . . because I MADE them! Do not underestimate the second answer. I needed Jake to deeply understand them both, so I said, "Let me get this straight. You are coming in to audition for Clarence 'Big Man' Clemons's seat in the E Street Band, which is not a job, by the way, but a sacred fucking position, and you are going to play Clarence's most famous solos for Bruce Springsteen [referring to myself in the third person], the man who stood beside him for forty years, who created those solos with him, and you're gonna 'sort of' know them? Where . . . do . . . you . . . think . . . you . . . are? If you don't know, let me tell you. You are in a CITADEL OF ROCK 'N' ROLL. You don't DARE come in here and play this music for Bruce Springsteen without having your SHIT DOWN COLD! You embarrass yourself and waste my precious time."

I don't usually talk like this and I was exaggerating for his and my benefit, but not much. I needed to know who Jake *was*. Because even if he could play in the E Street Band, who you ARE, what you've got inside, your degree of emotional understanding of the stakes we're playing for, FUCK-ING MATTERS! It's not intellectual. Dan Federici was all instinct but he understood the brotherhood. Did Jake?

After a few times around, I instructed him to go to the hotel room from whence he came and not to return until he had these solos down. I said before I'd take him to sit in with the band, he'd have to play this material perfectly with just him and me. Then we would play and record to a live tape of the band in full flight. Then, and only then, would I bring him before the group. He called me a day or two later and said he was ready. When he came in this time, he was.

Over the next few days I found Jake to be a soulful, hardworking young sax player whom I had a deep feeling for. I was rooting for him, for us. C was in the room, big-time. He drew us closer. He'd been Jake's uncle, had mentioned Jake to me when he wasn't well, and I knew he'd have smiled over Jake's being here. This felt like it had his blessing. That would've meant nothing if Jake hadn't had "it." There could have been an army of sax players with C's looks, his playing ability and the Clemons name, but if they didn't have that deep connection to *why* we were in all this, we would've come up zero. Jake had E Street soul in his blood and bones. He was a big, good-looking, talented kid. That's cool. You want stars, and Jake had that kind of confidence. Before the day was over, he'd need it. I also knew that Jake was ready to put his talents, body and soul, at the service of my band and our ideas, and we, in turn . . . would change his life.

Some of the band members who'd played with Jake before found him undisciplined and were skeptical. Jake and I had to be ready to wash that away in one fell swoop. We drove to the abandoned military base of Fort Monmouth, where the band had a rented theater in which we rehearsed. Jake and I walked in and greeted the band, and I called the tunes as Jake killed them, one by one. For Steve and several others it was a done deal. A guy or two wanted to hear possible other options. Jon Landau was initially made anxious by Jake's physical similarity to C. "He looks like a young Clarence," he said, face wrinkled in consternation. I looked but that's not what I saw. I saw that somebody up there liked me and had sent us this very lovely kid with all the right ingredients to take what was potentially the most damaging injury to our family and help us move past it and down the road. This was not a job for a hired gun or mercenary, no matter how well intended, at least not on this tour or at this moment.

•  •  •

The Apollo Theater . . . holy house of soul. The most sacred stage in a rock 'n' souler's world. This is where the next-generation E Street Band will fittingly, frighteningly, have its debut. As we arrive for sound check, the stagehands greet us, thank us for coming and show us the tree stump sitting stage right that every Apollo wannabe rubs for good luck before their moment of truth. I suggested Jake give it a rub. This is the stage where James Brown "took it to the bridge," where Smokey didn't leave a dry seat in the house, where Joe Tex dug the women, "skinny legs and all," then sagely counseled his followers, "Hold on to what you've got." Tonight, after forty years of road work, we're wannabes like the rest. You just want to live up to the place and deserve your short moment onstage in one of the great shrines of music.

From this stage, Sam and Dave schooled the crowd on what it took to be a "soul man." Soul man, soul man, soul man . . . that's the term. As an R & B singer, I will never be more than "pretty close," but "soul man" is a much broader term. It encompasses your life, your work and the way you approach both. Joe Strummer, Neil Young, Bob Dylan, Mick and Keith, Joey Ramone, John and Paul—all white boys who could rest comfortably with that sobriquet. It's all-inclusive, and I'd be perfectly happy with just those two words on my gravestone.

At sound check I walk back to Jake's station within the horn section. I don't want to do anything obvious that would place Jake in the position of having to stand in Clarence's stead. C's spot won't be reinhabited by another sax player and the Big Man will be something our band and audience will have to get used to missing. That's why Jake plays out of the horn section or out of his own position. It's his. It's open ground waiting to be claimed. But he *will* play those solos. I've instructed Jake that those solos are compositions, collaborations between Clarence and me that are engraved on our fans' hearts. You don't need to do anything fancy, just play them. Reach back for your best sound, breathe where C breathed and play them as they were written and recorded. The work Jake has to do comes from the inside. Knowing the notes is easy. Any reasonable sax player can blow those notes, but *understanding* them—knowing what they *mean*, their power within the song—is what's transformative.

As time passed and our music bored its way into our fans' souls, Clarence's entrance within one of our classic songs was almost always greeted with thunderous applause. Why? He wasn't playing something hard, but he was doing something hard and singular. He was *meaning* it. As Branford Marsalis said in a beautiful essay he wrote upon Clarence's death, C was blessed with "the power of musical intent."

The solos themselves are beautiful. They're simple, elegant I suppose, but they're not going to win us any blue ribbons at Berklee College of Music unless you understand how difficult it is to create within a framework of limits something slightly new under the sun. Clarence reinvented and reinvigorated the rock 'n' roll saxophone for the seventies and eighties. Yes, there were King Curtis, Junior Walker, Lee Allen and many other of Clarence's mentors, but for me, Clarence goes right up there with the greatest (and he is a big part of what carries me up there in whatever slot I may fill).

Jake's job, his service, is to understand those notes, to *mean* them. Then he will become a part of that collaboration, and that's something you can't fake. You either do it or you don't.

Technically, Jake is a fine saxophonist, and when he does his work he restores those solos to their shining brightness. C himself struggled to play them in the later years due to his physical degeneration, so Jake gets to fill them with the power of youth one more time. It's good to hear.


I walk up to Jake at the end of sound check and stand alongside him. I can't resist. Smiling, I take six paces forward to a small landing. This is where Jake will perform his pieces. I look at him and say, "Two hours from now, these are the steps that are going to change your life for better or for worse," and I slap him on the shoulder. He smiles that thousand-watt smile that is one of Jake's most potent weapons and nods.

Showtime. Jake appears backstage moments before we go on without his glasses. I say, "Where are your glasses?" He says, "I'm wearing contacts." I say, "Put your glasses back on. You're the student." "We Take Care of Our Own," no solo. "Badlands." The air sucks out of the room, a beat, then the two dozen notes or so of the "Badlands" solo roar out of Jake's sax and roll across the interior of the Apollo. The briefest of moments, then an explosion of applause and screams storms back from the audience and we're on the other side. He's never late again.

Before the Apollo I explained to Jake that at this moment we were in a great dance with our audience. They would tell us what we, as a duo, could and could not do. All we had to do was watch and listen. At first I never put Jake in any staged position Clarence and I had been known for. That meant no opposite risers, no shoulder to shoulder or any of the variety of other iconic poses C and I casually knocked off. We were careful to tread respectfully, but Jake proved to be himself right from the start. He performed the difficult task of allowing C's spirit to inhabit him without giving up his own identity. Slowly, most of our rules fell away and we began, with our audience's approval, to simply do whatever felt right. The tour was going to be not only the hello to this new version of the band but an international good-bye and a sad and joyous wake for the Big Man. That's the way it was at every stop. Clarence's presence hovered over us without ever stopping our forward march toward our new direction. That was Clarence's parting gift to us.

# SEVENTY-FIVE

# ZERO TO SIXTY IN NOTHING FLAT

The blues don't jump right on you. They come creeping. Shortly after my sixtieth I slipped into a depression like I hadn't experienced since that dusty night in Texas thirty years earlier. It lasted for a year and a half and devastated me. When these moods hit me, usually few will notice— not Mr. Landau, no one I work with in the studio, not the band, never the audience, hopefully not the children—but Patti will observe a freight train bearing down, loaded with nitroglycerin and running quickly out of track. During these periods I can be cruel: I run, I dissemble, I dodge, I weave, I disappear, I return, I rarely apologize, and all the while Patti holds down the fort as I'm trying to burn it down. She stops me. She gets me to the doctors and says, "This man needs a pill." I do. I've been on anti-depressants for the last twelve to fifteen years of my life, and to a lesser degree but with the same effect they had for my father, they have given me a life I would not have been able to maintain without them. They work. I return to Earth, home and my family. The worst of my destructive behavior curtails itself and my humanity returns. I was crushed between sixty and sixty-two, good for a year and out again from sixty-three to sixty-four. Not a good record.

During this time I lost quite a few friends and family. Clarence; Danny; my aunt Eda and aunt Dora; Tony Strollo, my friend and trainer of a decade, to his own depression; and Terry Magovern. Terry was my aide for twenty-three years and the man who'd fired Steve and me from our last-chance bar gig at the Captain's Garter forty years earlier. Some people take whole worlds with them when they die. That was Terry Magovern. A navy SEAL, Terry was the last great symbol of the raging honky-tonk Jersey Shore scene of the sixties and seventies. Bar manager, feared bouncer, lifeguard, father, grandfather, loyal friend and working companion—Terry covered it all, and I wrote "Terry's Song" for him on *Magic*.

At first I thought it might have been all this death around me. But as deeply as I loved all of these people, death I can handle; it's this other . . . *thing*. This thing I have studied and fought against for the better part of sixty-five years. It comes in darkness or in broad daylight, each time wearing a subtly different mask, so subtle that some like myself who have fought it and named it multiple times welcome it in like an old friend. Then once again it takes up deep residence in my mind, heart and soul until it is finally routed out after doing its wreckage.

Antidepression medication is temperamental. Somewhere around fifty-nine or sixty I noticed the drug I'd been taking seemed to have stopped working. This is not unusual. The drugs interact with your body chemistry in different ways over time and often need to be tweaked. After the death of Dr. Myers, my therapist of twenty-five years, I'd been seeing a new doctor whom I'd been having great success with. Together we decided to stop the medication I'd been on for five years and see what would happen . . . DEATH TO MY HOMETOWN!! I nose-dived like the diving horse at the old Atlantic City steel pier into a sloshing tub of grief and tears the likes of which I'd never experienced before. Even when this happens to me, not wanting to look too needy, I can be pretty good at hiding the severity of my feelings from most of the folks around me, even my doctor. I was succeeding well with this for a while except for one strange thing: TEARS! Buckets of 'em, oceans of 'em, cold, black tears pouring down my face like tidewater rushing over Niagara during any and all hours of the day. What was this about? It was like somebody opened the floodgates and ran off with the key. There was NO stopping it. *Bambi* tears . . . *Old Yeller* tears . . . *Fried Green Tomatoes* tears . . . rain . . . tears . . . sun . . . tears . . . I can't find my keys . . . tears. Every mundane daily event, any bump in the sentimental road, became a cause to let it all hang out. It would've been funny except it wasn't.

Every meaningless thing became the subject of a world-shattering existential crisis filling me with an awful profound foreboding and sadness. All was lost. All . . . everything . . . the future was grim . . . and the only thing that would lift the burden was one-hundred-plus on two wheels or other distressing things. I would be reckless with myself. Extreme physical exertion was the order of the day and one of the few things that helped. I hit the weights harder than ever and paddleboarded the equivalent of the Atlantic, all for a few moments of respite. I would do anything to get Churchill's black dog's teeth out of my ass.

Through much of this I wasn't touring. I'd taken off the last year and a half of my youngest son's high school years to stay close to family and home. It worked and we became closer than ever. But that meant my trustiest form of self-medication, touring, was not at hand. I remember one September day paddleboarding from Sea Bright to Long Branch and back in choppy Atlantic seas. I called Jon and said, "Mr. Landau, book me anywhere, please." I then of course broke down in tears. Whaaaaaaaaaa. I'm surprised they didn't hear me in lower Manhattan. A kindly elderly woman walking her dog along the beach on this beautiful fall day saw my distress and came up to see if there was anything she could do. Whaaaaaaaaaa. How kind. I offered her tickets to the show. I'd seen this symptom before in my father after he had a stroke. He'd often mist up. The old man was usually as cool as Robert Mitchum his whole life, so his crying was something I loved and welcomed. He'd cry when I'd arrive. He'd cry when I left. He'd cry when I mentioned our old dog. I thought, "Now it's me."

I told my doc I could not live like this. I earned my living doing shows, giving interviews and being closely observed. And as soon as someone said "Clarence," it was going to be all over. So, wisely, off to the psychopharma-cologist he sent me. Patti and I walked in and met a vibrant, white-haired, welcoming but professional gentleman in his sixties or so. I sat down and of course, I broke into tears. I motioned to him with my hand; this is it. This is why I'm here. I can't stop crying! He looked at me and said, "We can fix this." Three days and a pill later the waterworks stopped, on a dime. Unbe-lievable. I returned to myself. I no longer needed to paddle, pump, play or challenge fate. I didn't *need* to tour. I felt normal.

# SEVENTY-SIX

# GARAGE LAND

The phone rings. Mick Jagger is on the line. I had a teenage daydream about receiving a call like this many years ago, but, no, the Stones do not need an ex–pimply faced front man for the next evening's show. But it's THE NEXT BEST THING! They're playing in Newark, New Jersey, and have decided one extra New Jersey guitar man and voice for "Tumbling Dice" might get some of the local fannies wagging.

By the time I was fifty, I'd met many of my heroes (Sinatra, Dylan, Morrison, McCartney, Orbison) and I'd enjoyed it, though I still gave them a wide berth. They still meant too much to me to surrender my star-struck feelings. And that's the way I liked it. But the following evening I find my-self walking into a brightly lit, busy reception area of a New York rehearsal studio. The girl behind the desk gives me a nod and points to a door. I open the door to a modestly sized room where there's a band in a tight-knit garage setup against one wall. There are two guitars, bass and drums, and a B3 organ in a corner. The lead singer comes up, giving me a smile that still lights up the entire room. Mick welcomes me to rehearsal. Keith, Ronnie and Charlie (from back behind his drums) follow with warm greetings.

They have their small Fender amps, set side by side, in the exact positions in which any band at the Fort Monmouth Teen Club would've set up on any empty sixties Saturday night. There are no fancy pedals, no mountain of speakers, just the barebones equipment for making rock music, pure and unchanged. There are few handlers, no entourage, and I am suddenly transported back to the little dining room I rehearsed in daily with the Castiles, except . . . these are the guys who INVENTED my job! They have been stamped on my heart since the chunking chords of "Not Fade Away" came ripping off the little 45 I bought at Britt's Department Store in the first strip mall in our area.

After some pleasantries, there are two mike stands alongside one another, a few feet in front of the band. Mick, still all sharp edges and pragmatism, moves to the mike on the left. I take the right as he counts off and Keith, the man whose recorded playing taught me my first guitar solo, slithers into the opening riff of "Tumbling Dice." I've come across many spirit-filled folk in my travels but no one as spectrally beautiful as Keith Richards. Some years ago Patti sang backup for the Stones and on Keith's first solo record. One night we visited him in the studio. He took Patti's hand, looked me in the eye and, with great regard for her, said, "Oh . . . oh . . . this one."

From my left, in the voice that's wet millions of knickers comes "Women think I'm tasty, but they're always trying to waste me" . . . I'm pretending to be a peer but it's not easy. Inside I'm reeling as Mick motions to me to take the second verse. It feels good. It's within the meat of my voice, and if I can't swing "Tumbling Dice" I should go back to my broom handle and my mirror.

A great group is always about chemistry. Up close the chemistry amongst these players is unique. Keith's guitar plays off of Charlie's drums, creating a swing that puts the roll back into the rock. This is the last of the rock 'n' roll bands. Combine that with the most underrated songbook in rock history and the Stones have always stood heads above their competition. Still do.

I'm having so much fun and I can't let anyone know! "You got to roll me . . . You got to roll me . . ." Mick and I are trading lines in the coda back and forth like a couple of white Sam and Daves, then it's over. Mick says, "That was great."

We played it exactly one time.

I went home. On the way home I kept thinking, "I GOTTA CALL STEVE! He will completely, one hundred percent, full-tilt, rock 'n' roll crazy understand." He did.

The next night we did it for twenty thousand thunderstruck New Jerseyans in Newark. It was a thrill but it didn't have the mystic kick of the night before, when I got to sit in, in that little room with just those four guys, the GREATEST GARAGE BAND IN THE WORLD, in my small piece of rock 'n' roll heaven.

SEVENTY-SEVEN

# *HIGH HOPES*

When I'm on tour, I'll often carry with me a collection of my unfinished music. I'll bring a few unfinished projects along that I'll pop on in the wee wee hours after the show and listen to. I'm looking to see if there's something there whispering in my ear. I still had a nice set of songs from my production work with Brendan and night after night, they'd call to me, looking for a home. This coincided with Tom Morello's joining the band and suggesting we dust off "High Hopes," a song by LA group the Havalinas that we'd covered in the nineties. "I could really jam on that," he said. As we gathered in Australia at our first rehearsal for the *Wrecking Ball* tour's resumption, I had an arrangement that I thought might work. This was going to be Tom's first stint subbing for Steve, who was busy with his acting commitments, so I wanted him to be able to put his imprint on the show. He did that. The arrangement caught fire live and we decided to cut it in a

Sydney studio along with a favorite song of mine by the Australian group the Saints, "Just Like Fire Would." With the inclusion of these songs and studio recordings we made of "American Skin" and "The Ghost of Tom Joad," a real album began to take shape. I then recorded Tom onto some of our Brendan O'Brien tracks and things really began to spark. Tom proved to be a fabulous and fascinating substitute for Steve, melding into the band seamlessly while greatly increasing our sonic palette.

Before resuming the tour, however, I had some business to take care of. For at least the past five years I had noticed the fingers in my left hand growing successively weaker with each tour. On a long solo my hand and fingers could fatigue almost to failure. I'd found a variety of ways to get around this so the audience wouldn't notice and my playing didn't suffer, but by the start of our *Wrecking Ball* tour it was becoming a problem I could no longer ignore.

Probably since my forties, some physical problem had come along with every tour. One tour it's your knee, then it's your back, then it's tendinitis in your elbows from all the hard strumming. These maladies appear and disappear quite frequently over the latter part of your work life and are rarely critical. I'd just find a way to manage them and continue on. However, the paralysis of my guitar-playing hand was something else. That was accompanied by a numbness and tingling down my left arm, and I noticed in the weight room that I was now significantly weaker on the left side of my body.

I consulted a variety of physicians, had the MRIs done and found out I had some cervical disc problems on the left side of my neck, pinching and numbing the nerves that controlled my left side from the shoulder down. I found a great surgeon at the Hospital for Special Surgery in New York and we set a date. The surgery went like this: they knock you out; cut an incision into your throat; tie your vocal cords off to one side; get in there with a wrench, screwdriver and some titanium; they take a chunk of bone out of your hip and go about building you a few new disks. It worked! Because all of this takes place around the vocal cords your voice is gone for a couple of nerve-racking months. Also you get to wear one of those whiplash collars for about two months. But sure enough, right on the doc's timeline, three months in I was ready to work again. With my new discs and rehabilitated voice, we headed Down Under with just one instruction: no crowd surfing! But there is no fool like an old fool, so the first night I dove right on in. Everything was fine.

About my voice. First of all, I don't have much of one. I have a bar-man's power, range and durability, but I don't have a lot of tonal beauty or finesse. Five sets a night, no problem. Three and a half full-on hours, can do. Need for warm-up, light to none. My voice gets the job done. But it's a journeyman's instrument and on its own, it's never going to take you to higher ground. I need all my skills to get by and to communicate deeply. For me to sell you what you're buying, I've got to write, arrange, play, perform and, yes, sing to the best of my ability. I am a sum of all my parts. I learned early this is not something to fret about. Every performer has his or her weak link. Part of getting there is knowing what to do with what you have and knowing what to do with what you DON'T have. As Clint Eastwood said, "A man's got to know his limitations." Then forget about them and walk on.

I was teased endlessly in the Castiles and dismissed as a vocalist. For a long time that was fine with me. George Theiss was a great singer and I was perfectly content to work on my guitar skills. I always saw myself primarily as a lead guitarist anyway.

Then I got to where I could carry a melody and, to my ear, sound half decent. At some point in the Castiles, George and I began to share more of the vocal duties. Once that band folded and I moved onto my next band,

Earth, I became a full-fledged playing-and-singing front man. I was still earning my keep as one of the few guitarists in the area who could half-ass Clapton and Hendrix, but I was singing everything too. Then I began to write acoustically and I would spend my off nights singing solo, accompanied by just my twelve-string Ovation guitar, in the local coffee houses. I wrote a lot and got used to depending on my voice, along with the quality of my songs and playing, to carry the show. I thought I was getting pretty good. Then when George, my short-lived New York producer, invited me to his apartment, he had that two-track tape recorder. One afternoon he said, "Let's record some of your songs." As I was performing for the tape, I was thinking, "Damn, I'm good!" Then I heard it back. It sounded like a cat with its tail on fire. It was out of tune, amateurish, dumb and unknowing. The sound that came back off that tape killed what little confidence I had in myself and my vocals. It was truly demoralizing.

But what could I do? It was the only voice I had. And I decided after the Castiles I would never depend on another lead singer again. It was not independent enough for me. So I learned as I've mentioned that the sound in your head has little to do with how you actually sound. Just the way you think you look better than you do, until the iPhone photo your Auntie Jane takes cold-slaps you in the face. Tape performs this same function for your voice. It's a dead-on bullshit detector. You can't kid yourself once you've heard yourself on tape. That, my friend, IS the way you sound. You can only live with it.

So I figured if I didn't have a voice, I was going to really need to learn to write, perform and use what voice I had to its fullest ability. I was going to have to learn all the tricks, singing from your chest, singing from your abdomen, singing from your throat, great phrasing, timing and dynamics. I noted a lot of singers had a very limited instrument but could sound convincing. I studied everyone I loved who sounded real to me, whose voices excited me and touched my heart. Soul, blues, Motown, rock, folk; I listened and I learned. I learned the most important thing was how believable you could sound. How deeply you could inhabit your song. If it came from your heart, then there was some ineffable element "X" that made the way you technically sounded secondary. There are many good, even great, voices out there tied to people who will never sound convincing or exciting. They are all over TV talent shows and in lounges in Holiday Inns all across America. They can carry a tune, sound tonally impeccable, they can hit all the high notes, but they cannot capture the full emotional content of a song. They cannot sing deeply.

If you were lucky enough to be born with an instrument and the instinctive knowledge to know what to do with it, you are blessed indeed. Even after all my success I sit here in envy of Rod Stewart, Bob Seger, Sam Moore and many other greats who can sing magnificently and know what to do with it. My vocal imperfections made me work harder on my writing, my band leading, my performing and my singing. I learned to excel at those elements of my craft in a way I might otherwise never had if I had a more perfect instrument. My ability to power through three-hour-plus shows for forty years (itself a display of my manic insecurity that I'd never be enough) with a thoroughbred's endurance came from realizing I had to bring it all to take you where I wanted us to go. Your blessings and your curses often come in the same package. Think of all the eccentric voices in rock who've made historic records and keep singing. Then build up your supportive skills because you never know what's going to come out of your heart and find its way out of your mouth.

With the reconstituted E Street Band playing at its peak, we decided to take it to a few places we hadn't toured. We did a ten-day run in South America, where we hadn't visited since the Amnesty tour, then South Africa, where we had never played. We ended up with a return trip to Australia, building on the success we'd had the previous year Down Under. This time we had Steve *and* Tom along, kicking off each night's show with our Aussie favorites, "Highway to Hell," "Friday on My Mind," and "Stayin' Alive" complete with an all-female string section. Finally one last stop in New Zealand and we headed back home for a short US leg, then took down the tent on the most successful, well-attended and popular tour the E Street Band had ever done.

SEVENTY-EIGHT

# HOME
# FRONT

At the end of the tour, rather than returning immediately home, I joined Patti and my daughter, Jessica, in Europe, where she was touring internationally as a professional show jumper. All my children had left school, were on their own, doing well and mostly out of the house. Twenty years of parenting had gone by and we now served them in an advisory capacity.

Evan graduated from Boston College. He had gone into the music business, living in the West Village only blocks away from my old Café' Wha? stomping grounds. He works in radio as a program director and festival producer. He has become quite a good singer and songwriter in his own right. Independent, creative and bright, with a hard moral compass, he proudly makes his own way. Sam went to Bard College and studied to become a writer. He left after a year, feeling that he needed to do something with more immediate impact on people's lives. He became a firefighter, reentering the blue-collar world I'd known so well. His graduation from the fire academy near my hometown of Freehold amid all my old friends and neighbors brought tears and made Dad and Mom very proud. He also set up a project to bring returning veterans to our shows on a nightly basis. There he hosts vets in a friendly environment where they can enjoy the show and a night on the town. Jessica graduated from Duke University and had gone on to some fame of her own, becoming a world-class athlete, winning the American Gold Cup in Old Salem, New York, in 2014 and riding for the US team as they won the Nations Cup in Dublin, Ireland, at RDS Arena, my and the E Street Band's old stomping grounds. Patti manages our lives, plays in the band, makes her music and holds it all together. The success of our children is largely due to her strength, great compassion and deep interest in who they really are.

Mild post-tour depression can usually be expected. Sometime in June I noticed I wasn't feeling all that well. The shows are an insane high. The adulation, the touring company, the fact that it's all about you. When you come off the road, that stops on a dime and you're a father and husband, but now the kids are driving, so you're an out-of-work chauffeur. The bump is natural but the crash that I experienced this time was something else altogether. It was hard to explain, bearing symptoms I'd never encountered before in my life. I had an attack of what was called an "agitated depression." During this period, I was so profoundly uncomfortable in my own skin that I just wanted OUT. It feels dangerous and brings plenty of unwanted thoughts. I was uncomfortable doing anything. Standing . . . walking . . . sitting down . . . everything brought waves of an agitated anxiety that I'd spend every waking minute trying to dispel. Demise and foreboding were all that awaited and sleep was the only respite. During waking hours, I'd spend the day trying to find a position I would feel all right in for the next few minutes. I was not hyper. In fact, I was too depressed to concentrate on anything of substance.

I'd pace the room looking for the twelve square inches of carpet where I might find release. If I could get myself to work out, that might produce a short relief, but really all I wanted was the bed, the bed, the bed and unconsciousness. I spent good portions of the day with the covers up to my nose waiting for it to stop. Reading, or even watching television, felt beyond my ability. All my favorite things—listening to music, watching some film noir—caused such an unbearable anxiety in me because they were undoable. Once I was cut off from all my favorite things, the things that tell me who I am, I felt myself dangerously slipping away. I became a stranger in a borrowed and disagreeable body and mind.

This lasted for six weeks. All the while we were overseas. It affected me physically, sexually, emotionally, spiritually, you name it. It all went out the door. I was truly unsure if I could ever perform in this condition. The fire in me felt like it had gone out and I felt dark and hollow inside. Bad thoughts had a heyday. If I can't work, how will I provide for my family? Will I be bedridden? Who the fuck am I? You feel the thinness of the veil of your identity and an accompanying panic that seems to be just around the corner.

I couldn't live like this, not forever. For the first time, I felt I understood what drives people toward the abyss. The fact that I understood this, that I *could* feel this, emptied my heart out and left me in a cold fright. There was no life here, just an endless irritating existential angst embedded in my bones. It was demanding answers I did not have. And there was no respite. If I was awake, it was happening. So . . . I'd try to sleep; twelve, fourteen hours weren't enough. I hated the gray light of morning. It would mean the day was coming. The day, when people would be waking up, going to work, eating, drinking, laughing, fucking. The day when you're supposed to rise and shine, be filled with purpose, with life. I couldn't get out of bed. Hell, I couldn't even get a hard-on. It was like all my notorious energy, something that had been mine to command for most of my life, had been cruelly stolen away. I was a walking husk.

Patti coaxed me out of bed and tried to get me moving. She steadied me, gave me the confidence to feel I'd be all right and that this was something that was just passing. Without her strength and calm, I don't know what I would have done.

One night in Ireland Patti and I went out to dinner with a group of people. I was doing my best to fake that I was a sane citizen. Under these conditions that can be hard to do. I had to leave the table somewhat regularly to let my mind off its leash (or to keep it on). Finally, on the street, I phoned my pharmacologist. I explained to him things were condition red.

He asked, "Does anything make you feel better?"

"If I take a Klonopin," I said.

"Take one," he said.

I did and it stopped. Graciously, mercifully, thankfully, yes there is a God, it stopped. After a short period on Klonopin I was able to stop the medication and the agitation did not return. But it was a terrifying window into mental debilitation and I don't think I could've gone on like that indefinitely. All of this brought back the ghost of my father's mental illness and my family's history, and taunted me with the possibility that even after all I'd done, all I'd accomplished, I could fall to the same path. The only thing that kept me right side up during this was Patti. Her love, compassion and assurance that I'd be all right were, during many dark hours, all I had to go on.

Mentally, just when I thought I was in the part of my life where I'm supposed to be cruising, my sixties were a rough, rough ride. I came back to the States slightly changed and still wrestling with myself day by day. But things became a little more normal as time passed. I've long ago stopped struggling to get out of bed and I've got my work energy back. That feels good. Two years have passed and it can feel like it never really happened. I can't specifically recall the state. The best I can do is think, "What the fuck was that? That's not me." But it's in me, chemically, genetically, whatever you want to call it, and as I've said before, I've got to watch. The only real bulwark against it was love.

•   •   •

Writing about yourself is a funny business. At the end of the day it's just another story, the story you've chosen from the events of your life. I haven't told you "all" about myself. Discretion and the feelings of others don't allow it. But in a project like this, the writer has made one promise: to show the reader his mind. In these pages I've tried to do that.

# SEVENTY-NINE

# LONG TIME COMIN'

My father's house shines hard and bright.
It stands like a beacon calling me in the night
Calling and calling so cold and alone
Shining cross this dark highway
Where our sins lie unatoned . . .

"My Father's House"

If I had one wish in this godforsaken world, kids
It'd be that your mistakes will be your own
Your sins will be your own . . .

"Long Time Comin'"

"My Father's House" is probably the best song I've written about my dad, but its conclusion wasn't going to be enough for me. In "Long Time Comin'" I lay out the wish I've had for my children. We honor our parents by not accepting as the final equation the most troubling characteristics of our relationship. I decided between my father and me that the sum of our troubles would not be the summation of our lives together. In analysis you work to turn the ghosts that haunt you into ancestors who accompany you. That takes hard work and a lot of love, but it's the way we lessen the burdens our children have to carry. Insisting on our own experience, our own final calculus of love, trouble, hard times and, if we're lucky, a little transcendence. This is how we claim our own lives as sons and daughters, independent souls on our piece of ground. It's not always an option. There are irretrievable lives and unredeemable sins, but the chance to rise above is one I wish for yours and mine.

I work to be an ancestor. I hope my summation will be written by my sons and daughter, with our family's help, and their sons and daughters with their guidance. The morning of my dad's visit to Los Angeles before my fatherhood stands out now as a pivotal moment between us. He had come to petition me, to settle a new sum from the dark and confusing elements that had been our lives. He had some faith that it could be done, came searching for a miracle whose embers he felt stirring in his own heart and that he hoped was burning and buried somewhere in the heart of his son.

He was asking me to write a new ending to our story and I've worked to do that, but this kind of story has no end. It is simply told in your own blood until it is passed along to be told in the blood of those you love, who inherit it. As it's told, it is altered, as all stories are in the telling, by time, will, perception, faith, love, work, by hope, deceit, imagination, fear, history and the thousand other variable powers that play upon our personal narratives. It continues to be told because along with the seed of its own immolation, the story carries with it the rebirthing seed of renewal, a different destiny for those who hear it than the painful one my father and I struggled through. Slowly, a new story emerges from the old, of differently realized lives, building upon the rough experience of those who've come before and stepping over the battle-worn carcasses of the past. On a good day this is how we live. This is love. This is what life is. The possibility of finding root, safety and nurturing in a new season.

The tree sprouts, its branches thicken, mature, bloom. It is scarred by lightning, shaken by thunder, sickness, human events and God's hand. Drawn black, it grows itself back toward light, rising higher toward heaven while thrusting itself deeper, more firmly, into the earth. Its history and memory retained, its presence felt.

On a November evening during the writing of this book, I drove once again back to my hometown, back to my neighborhood. The streets were quiet. My corner church was silent and unchanged. Tonight there were no weddings and no funerals. I rolled slowly another fifty yards up my block to find my great towering copper beech tree gone, cut to the street. My heart went blank . . . then settled. I looked again. It was gone but still there. The very air and space above it was still filled with the form, soul and lifting presence of my old friend, its leaves and branches now outlined and shot through by evening stars and sky. A square of musty earth, carved into the parking lot blacktop at pavement's edge, was all that remained. It still held small snakes of root slightly submerged by dust and dirt, and there the arc of my tree, my life, lay plainly visible. My great tree's life by county dictum or blade could not be ended or erased. Its history, its *magic*, was too old and too strong. Like my father, my grandmothers, my aunt Virginia, my two grand-fathers, my father-in-law Joe, my aunt Dora and aunt Eda, Ray and Walter Cichon, Bart Haynes, Terry, Danny, Clarence and Tony, my own family gone from these houses now filled by strangers—we remain. We remain in the air, the empty space, in the dusty roots and deep earth, in the echo and stories, the songs of the time and place we have inhabited. My clan, my blood, my place, my people.

Once again in the shadow of the steeple, as I stood feeling the old soul of my tree, of my town, weighing upon me, the words and a benediction came back to me. I'd chanted them singsong, unthinkingly, endlessly in the green blazer, ivory shirt and green tie of all of St. Rose's unwilling disciples. Tonight they came to me and flowed differently. Our father, who art in heaven, hallowed be thy name. Thy kingdom come, thy will be done, on earth as it is in heaven. Give us this day our daily bread and forgive us our trespasses as we forgive those who trespass against us, and lead us not into temptation, but deliver us from evil . . . all of us, forever and ever, amen.

I fought my whole life, studied, played, worked, because I wanted to hear and know the whole story, my story, our story, and understand as much of it as I could. I wanted to understand in order to free myself of its most damaging influences, its malevolent forces, to celebrate and honor its beauty, its power, and to be able to tell it well to my friends, my family and to you. I don't know if I've done that, and the devil is always just a day away, but I know this was my young promise to myself, to you. This, I pursued as my service. This, I presented as my long and noisy prayer, my magic trick. Hoping it would rock your very soul and then pass on, its spirit rendered, to be read, heard, sung and altered by you and your blood, that it might strengthen and help make sense of your story. Go tell it.

# EPILOGUE

A few weeks before Thanksgiving, a sunny late fall day springs upon Central Jersey. Sixty-degree temperatures send me out to the garage to fire up my motorcycle and catch the last good riding weather of the season. I head south to Manasquan Inlet. A two-day nor'easter has just subsided, blowing through, driving the ocean up to the dune grass at the boardwalk's edge and washing away a significant amount of my old beach back into the white-capped, still-churning sea. The jetty my sister and I so gingerly tiptoed out upon in the late-summer dark is topped with a good three or four inches of damp sand over black rock that makes navigating its shifting surface in engineer boots a minor adventure.

Here in November the sun sets over the southwest—Point Pleasant—side of the inlet, unsheathing and casting a shimmering sword north across the gray inlet waters to the Manasquan side. There I sit on the jetty at sword's point. As the waves lap upon the rocks at my boot heels the tip of that sword shatters into shards of golden light on the waters below, breaking into mini suns, microcosms of the God source that brings life to our planet. Here I am amongst and greeted by friends known and unknown. It comes with the turf. A well-meaning menagerie of schoolkids, old folks with their metal detectors, dogs, surfers, fishermen, folks from Freehold who've always used Manasquan as their Shore getaway, the kids behind the counter at Carlson's Corner, the endless strangers who wait in cars, sitting in line facing the inlet. There behind those driver's-side windows could sit the merry, puzzled ghost of my old man dreaming of another life somewhere, someplace, far away from all the goodness he has wrought and his beautiful treasures. It's my place now, another small and bittersweet inheritance.

As the sun sets into a range of gray-blue clouds I fire the engine on my bike back to life, tighten my helmet, throw my scarf around my face, toss a wave good-bye and slip from the small town of Manasquan out into the five o'clock traffic along Route 34. The sun is down now and a cool evening falls. At a light, I zip my leather jacket to the neck, notice my boot heel resting upon the hot, wrapped exhaust pipe of my V-twin, leaving a swatch of rubber and lifting a thin swirling slipstream of blue smoke into the crisp autumn air. The light goes green and the road stirs and rumbles beneath me as I pop over small sections of highway that have expanded in the summer heat, then cooled, leaving irregular ridges, sequential speed bumps where sections of asphalt meet. Rumble, rumble, rumble . . . pop . . . rumble, rumble, rumble . . . pop. With every "pop," I'm bouncing up off my sprung seat and suddenly I'm back going round and round, rolling over the blue slate driveway outside the convent house of St. Rose and waiting, wanting, once again, to hear my grandmother's voice calling to me at dusk. I listen . . . but tonight the past fades and there's only the present voice of sparks, firing pistons . . . sweet cold mechanics.

I travel into a stream of headlights as commuter cars holding their day travelers flash by inches from my left handle grip. I move north up the highway until the traffic recedes, leaving only my headlight illuminating blank road and dashes of white line . . . white line . . . white line . . .

white line . . . My "ape hanger," high-rise handlebars thrust my arms out and skyward to shoulder height, opening me up to the winds full force—a rough embrace—as my gloved hands tighten their grip on that new evening sky. The cosmos begins to flicker to life in the twilight above me. With no fairing, a sixty-mile-per-hour gale steadily pounds into my chest, nudging me to the back of my seat, subtly threatening to blow me off six hundred pounds of speeding steel, reminding me of how the next moment holds no guarantees . . . and of how good things are, this day, this life, how lucky I've been, how lucky I am. I turn the corner off the highway onto a dark country road. I hit my high beams, scan the flat farm fields looking for deer. All clear, I twist the throttle as rushing into my arms comes home.

# ACKNOWLEDGMENTS

This book was written over a period of seven years. I'd write longhand into my notebook, then put it away at intervals, sometimes for a year or more while we toured or recorded. I was in no hurry and had no time pressures. This allowed me to come back to the book with fresh eyes to judge what I'd written. My story slowly unfolded into a long session of writing toward the end. Then, with the help of those below, it reached completion.

All my love and thanks to Patti for giving me the room and understanding to tell the story I needed to tell.

Thanks to Jon Landau, one of my earliest readers, for his enthusiasm, advice and encouragement.

Many thanks to Jonathan Karp, who first worked with us on *Outlaw Pete,* for giving us a home. His eye and advice guided me to the best of my writing and brought this book to its final fruition.

Special thanks to Mary Mac, my companion through the endless hours of rewrites as we transcribed my scribble into our home computer.

Thanks to Michelle Holme for curating our photo section, and to Frank Stefanko for our cover photo.

Thanks to my friend and old bandmate George Theiss for jogging my memory on some of our Castiles adventures.

I would like to thank Jon Landau, Allen Grubman, Jonathan Ehrlich and Don Friedman, who took care of the practical arrangements with Simon & Schuster, and a special thanks to Les Moonves for his helpfulness in this area, as well.

Thanks to Barbara Carr, who has handled the entire project with utmost dedication and effectiveness.

And thanks to Marilyn Laverty, who has been doing my public relations for thirty-seven years, and Tracy Nurse, who has worked on our presentation internationally for thirty years.

Thanks to all at Simon & Schuster who have contributed to this effort, especially Marie Florio, Cary Goldstein, Richard Rhorer, Stephen Bedford, Jonathan Evans, John Paul Jones, Aja Pollock, Erica Ferguson, Lisa Erwin, Ruth Lee-Mui, Meryll Preposi, Miah Saunders, Samantha Cohen, Kristen Lemire, Allison Har-zvi, Megan Hogan, Jackie Seow, Elisa Rivlin, Chris Lynch, Michael Selleck, Gary Urda, Paula Amendolara, Colin Shields, Sumya Ojakli, Dennis Eulau, Craig Mandeville, Jeff Wilson, John Felice, Liz Perl, Wendy Sheanin, Sue Fleming, Jofie Ferrari-Adler, Adam Rothberg, Irene Kheradi, Dave Schaeffer, Ian Chapman, Kevin Hanson, Iain MacGregor, Rahul Srivastava, Dan Ruffino and Carolyn Reidy.

Thanks to Greg Linn and Betsy Whitney at Sony Music for their ongoing efforts. And finally, thanks to everyone in the management office who lent a hand: Jan Stabile, Alison Oscar and Laura Kraus.

# PHOTO CREDITS

(Arranged by insert page number.)

Bruce 9/23/49

Born In The U.S.A.

*my Grandfather's Electrical shop*

*my parents' wedding day*

Easter Sunday, Atlantic Highlands, N.J.

Outlaw pete

Summer In Manasquan

Me and my sis Virginia

Mom and Pop at the diner

glory days, Freehold, N.J.

# THE CASTILES

(Left to Right) George Theiss, Bruce Springsteen Curt Fluhr, Paul Popkin, Vince Manniello.

*playing at the Surf'N Sea beach club*

*George theiss and myself (show opener perched on a lifeguard stand)*

steel mill

me And my hair playing At
Tinker's surfboard factory

my little sis Pam California bound 1969

At my mom and dad's Apartment
in SAn MAteo, California

*checking out my record for the first time*

*early E Street*

breakin' out AT the Bottoms Line

Double Whammy!

me and the Big MAN at the Eric Meola photo shoot for Born to Run

Frank Stefanko photos from Darkness On the Edge of Town

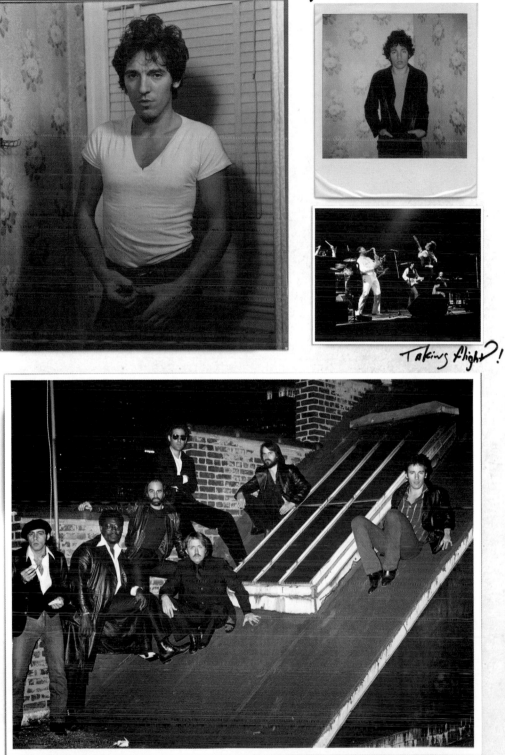

Taking flight?!

AT the Record plant

N.Y.C. the River

Mr. Landau and the Artist

Nebraska

my muscles got muscles...

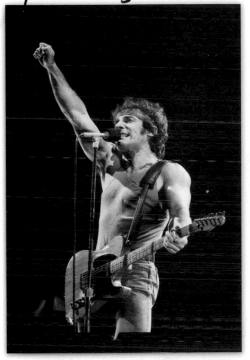

me and my redhead

the Big big Time

driving cross country in '88

the Delia brothers

In Las Vegas

At Sun Studios

in the Arizona sun

ms. parth and Cody

On Route 66

in Monument Valley

Honeymoon log cabin

Evan, playing football with Dad

Sam, the Mayor of Sea Bright Beach

Jessie's first pony

Farm fiesta and rodeo